Lecture Notes
in Economics and
Mathematical Systems

Managing Editors: M. Beckmann and W. Krelle

332

T. R. Gulledge, Jr. L. A. Litteral (Eds.)

Cost Analysis Applications
of Economics
and Operations Research

Proceedings of the Institute of Cost Analysis
National Conference, Washington, D.C., July 5–7, 1989

Springer-Verlag

New York Berlin Heidelberg London Paris Tokyo Hong Kong

934020

Managing Editors

Prof. Dr. M. Beckmann
Brown University
Providence, RI 02912, USA

Prof. Dr. W. Krelle
Institut für Gesellschafts- und Wirtschaftswissenschaften
der Universität Bonn
Adenauerallee 24–42, D-5300 Bonn, FRG

Editors

Thomas R. Gulledge, Jr.
Decision Sciences Department, George Mason University
Fairfax, VA 22030, USA

Lewis A. Litteral
E. Claiborne Robins School of Business
University of Richmond
Richmond, VA 23173, USA

In cooperation with:

Stephen J. Balut
Thomas P. Frazier
Cost Analysis and Research Division
Institute for Defense Analyses
1801 North Beauregard Street
Alexandria, VA 22311, USA

ISBN 3-540-97048-7 Springer-Verlag Berlin Heidelberg New York
ISBN 0-387-97048-7 Springer-Verlag New York Berlin Heidelberg

Printing and binding: Druckhaus Beltz, Hemsbach/Bergstr.
2847/3140-543210

FOREWORD

Cost analysis, long the stepchild of engineering, economics, and operations research, is emerging as a discipline it its own right. Universities are expanding their offerings of courses and degree-granting programs, and researchers in government and industry, as well as at universities, are refining and extending current methods.

The Institute of Cost Analysis (ICA) is dedicated to improving the effectiveness of cost and price analysis and enhancing the professional competence of its members. We encourage and promote exchange of research findings and applications between the academic community and cost professionals in industry and government. The 1989 National Meeting in Washington, D.C., jointly sponsored by ICA and the National Estimating Society (NES), provides such a forum. Presentations will address timely, important cost analysis applications of economics and operations research.

The 23 articles in this volume were refereed and selected from over 100 submitted for presentation at the Washington meeting. The quality of research and clarity of reporting is exceptional and the breadth of subject matter is illustrative of the significance of cost analysis as practiced today.

This volume is the most important contribution to cost analysis in decades. On behalf of all of us who will benefit from using it, I want to thank those who brought it to us. Thomas R. Gulledge conceived the idea, gained the support of the ICA Board, inspired his colleagues to participate, and worked continually to ensure it happened. Tom joins us in thanking our contributors for sharing their research findings, and also in giving special thanks to Lewis A. Litteral and Thomas P. Frazier for their editorial and administrative efforts.

Stephen J. Balut
President
Institute of Cost Analysis

REFEREES

The following persons served as referees for this book. ICA and NES appreciate the time and energy each of them devoted to the advancement of cost analysis.

Bruce N. Angier
Gordon W. Arbogast
Stephen J. Balut
Avijit Banerjee
Ronald S. Barden
Michael N. Beltramo
Tim Burwell
Patricia Byrnes
Jeffrey D. Camm
David S. Christensen
Joseph W. Coleman
Sidartha Das
Gary Fellers
Janet F. Fowler
Thomas P. Frazier
Irwin Greenberg
Robert T. Greenberg
Thomas R. Gulledge, Jr.
Stanley A. Horowitz
William P. Hutzler
Carl R. Jones
Phil Jones
Edward M. Kaitz

Roland Kankey
Paul Kantor
Behrokh Khosnevis
Edward P. Laughlin
Daniel B. Levine
Lewis A. Litteral
Rodney D. McConnell
Gerald Nadler
Richard Y. Pei
Michael H. Peters
Judy Powell
Amitabh Raturi
William Rogerson
Edward J. Schmitz
James Schweikart
Michael J. Seibel
Richard M. Soland
Charles J. Teplitz
Jack R. Truitt
Karen W. Tyson
K. T. Wallenius
Norman K. Womer
Chin-Wei Yang

TABLE OF CONTENTS

I. Procurement and Contracting

THE PROTOTYPE MODEL OF DEFENSE PROCUREMENT

Katsuaki L. Terasawa and Stanley M. Besen

U.S. Naval Postgraduate School and Columbia University

I. INTRODUCTION

The modern economic theory of procurement[1] has added significantly to our understanding of the forces that affect the efficiency with which large-scale acquisitions are made. Nonetheless, this theory, which is intended generally to describe the acquisition of items such as major weapons systems, electricity generation plants, and manufacturing facilities, contains little detail about any specific acquisition environment. Consequently, the theory must be modified in order to apply its lessons in any particular context. This paper is an attempt to show how the theory might be applied to the acquisition of major weapons systems by the Department of Defense by developing a simple prototype model of defense acquisition. The prototype model, which is intended to capture some of the specific features of the defense acquisition process,[2] illustrates the questions that any analysis of defense acquisition must answer. Although the analysis provides some tentative answers to these questions, a more elaborate model is clearly needed to address them more definitively.

In its most general terms, the economic theory of procurement addresses two questions. The first concerns the selection of the contractor who can be expected to produce the item being procured at the lowest cost.[3] The second involves the incentives of the chosen contractor to produce at the lowest cost.[4] Significantly, the nature of the item

---

[1] See Besen and Terasawa (1987) for a summary.

[2] See Rich and Dews (1986) for a useful description of many of these features.

[3] In some models, the contractor selection stage is not present, presumably on the assumption either that there is only one potential contractor or that past procurement actions have eliminated other contractors from future consideration.

[4] It is generally assumed that employing more than one contractor is inefficient due to economies of scale in production. Issues of split-buys and dual sourcing are addressed briefly below.

to be procured is known in advance. The objective is then to procure the item at the lowest possible cost or, if the number of units to be acquired is a variable, the objective is to maximize the surplus, i.e., the combined value of the units acquired less their cost, obtained by the buyer. In short, these models address contracts for the *production* of specific pieces of hardware.

It is our view that this perspective reduces the applicability of these models for the analysis of the acquisition of major weapons systems because a central feature of such acquisitions is that they generate information about the technical possibilities available to the buyer. As a result, in the prototype model we have separated the acquisitions process into two stages. In the first stage, the winning contractor engages in the production of "knowledge."[5] Formally, we treat this activity as enabling the contractor to lower the cost of producing hardware with a given level of technical performance, or increasing the technical performance of hardware with a given production cost, or both.[6]

In the second stage, DOD or the Service determines, on the basis of information provided to it by the contractor, the number of units of output of hardware that it desires as well as, possibly, the technical performance of that hardware.[7] To distinguish sharply between the two stages, we assume that learning is completed before the production stage begins.[8]

In the next section, we develop an extremely simple model of research and development and production that captures many of the features of defense acquisition.

---

[5] Actually, this stage is frequently divided into research and full scale development. We combine these here for the sake of simplicity. It may be argued that a realistic acquisition model should include the operation and maintenance stages of the system that is acquired. We have also omitted these stages from the prototype model.

[6] In many of the models in the literature, there is uncertainty about the costs of producing the desired output. This uncertainty is represented by assuming that a contractor knows only the expected value of production costs at the time he bids for, or negotiates, a contract. Significantly, the contractor is unable to reduce production costs by investing in research and development but, instead, learns what his costs are by engaging in production. Here, we assume that the expected production costs may be reduced before production begins and that these costs are subject to some control by the contractor.

[7] In the prototype model, there is no possibility of transferring knowledge from the contractor who carries out the first stage to other contractors who might bid for the right to produce the output. A more general model might allow one set of firms to specialize in the production of knowledge and another to specialize in the production of output. The assumption made here seems consistent with the characteristics of the defense acquisition process.

[8] This is clearly a caricature. It is well known that unit production costs tend to decline as cumulative production increases through the operation of the "learning curve." However, if the firm knows the amount of expected "learning," it can anticipate this decline in cost although it may not know precisely what form learning will take.

The assumptions underlying this basic model can be divided into two types. The first type—the standard assumptions—are maintained throughout the paper. Alternatives to assumptions of the second type—the optional assumptions—are examined in subsequent sections. We explore the *entire* workings of the basic model under a set of assumptions that includes both types, focusing especially on the interactions among these assumptions. In sections III-VI, we examine how various *components* of the model are affected by changing, one at time, the optional assumptions. However, we do not attempt to explore the full ramifications of these changes. Since the behavior of the entire model depends on the full set of assumptions that is employed, there are "n to the m" types of behavior to be analyzed if the model contains m assumptions and there are n forms of each assumption. With 3 optional assumptions and 2 variants of each there would be 8 such types to be examined. In subsequent analyses, it would, however, be appropriate to carry out comprehensive examinations of the behavior of the model for a larger number of sets of assumptions.[9]

In the final section, we briefly explore a number of issues that a more comprehensive model than that contained in this paper might address.

II. THE BASIC MODEL

The standard assumptions about defense acquisition that are made throughout this paper are:

(S1) Defense acquisition is made in two stages. In the first stage, research and development is conducted, but no hardware is acquired. The output of this stage is knowledge about the cost of producing hardware and the performance characteristics of that hardware. In the second stage, hardware is produced but no additional knowledge is acquired.

(S2) There is a minimum level of technical performance that is acceptable for a new system. Systems that meet, or exceed, this level of performance are candidates to proceed to production while those that fail to do so are not. The level of technical performance of a system is known after research and development is completed and before production is authorized.

(S3) There is a maximum acceptable level of target research and development costs for a new defense system. The government will not initiate a new research

---

[9] One way to reduce the number of sets to be examined is to conduct further analysis that would result in shifting some assumptions from the optional to the standard category.

and development effort unless the target development cost is below that level. Contracts for research and development are awarded on a cost plus incentive fee basis.[10] Under such a contract, the government agrees to reimburse the contractor's cost and to pay a portion of any cost overrun and guarantees both maximum and minimum fee levels. However, since the government may terminate cost-plus contracts at virtually any time, the government limits its maximum payment to a prescribed level. The contractor may spend significant non-reimbursable private resources on research and development when exceeding the government's maximum payment would otherwise threaten the entire project.

(S4) There is a maximum level of target production costs that is acceptable for a new system. Only systems that have cost targets at or below this level will proceed to production. However, actual production costs are known only after production is completed, so that actual costs may be higher than the target production costs.

(S5) The research and development contract for a new system will be awarded to a single firm and, if a production contract is awarded, it will be carried out by by the same firm.[11] Contracts for production are negotiated on a price-incentive basis. These contracts also require the government to pay a portion of any cost overrun up to a ceiling price.[12]

(S6) The amount of "effort" expended by a contractor to limit costs or improve technical performance are unobservable by the government. Thus, the government is unable to determine whether the contractor has taken all activities that reduce costs or increase performance benefits by more than they cost in terms of effort.

The optional assumptions made in the basic model are:

---

[10] In addition to cost plus incentive fee contracts (CPIF), cost plus fixed fee (CPFF) and cost plus award fee contracts (CPAF) are often used in the research and development stage. CPFF may be viewed as a special case of CPIF where the government cost share is 100 percent.

[11] The assumption that only a single contract is awarded for research and production, respectively, follows from the implicit assumption that economies of scale and/or learning curve effects are so great that it is inefficient to split these contracts between vendors. The assumption that the developer also obtains the production contract follows from the implicit assumption that the costs of technology transfer are too great for other firms to compete effectively for the production contract. Below, we briefly discuss how the model might be generalized to permit split-awards and dual sourcing.

[12] In the models presented below, all costs are combined into a single category. In fact, the allowable profit margin differs among cost categories and may influence the contractor's choice among inputs. This issue is not considered in this paper.

(01) The quantity of hardware the government will acquire, if it decides to proceed with production, is fixed and does not depend on actual production costs or on the level of technical performance achieved.[13]

(02) The actual costs incurred in carrying out research and development and production are observable by the government. Note that this does not include the amount of "effort" expended by the contractor. (See Standard Assumption (S6).)

(03) A number of contractors bid for the research and development contract.

In this model, the contractor that is selected to conduct research and development will work to improve the performance of the system (P) and to limit the production costs of the system (C). For these efforts, he is partially reimbursed by the government according to

$$G(1) = Ao + TD + A1(D - TD),\qquad(1)$$

which states that the government payment in the first period, $G(1)$, is a linear function of both target and actual development costs, TD and D, respectively. Ao denotes the target fee and $A1$ denotes the government's share of any cost overrun, $0 < A1 < 1$.[14] If target development costs, TD, equal actual development costs, the payment by the government to the developer is $Ao + TD$. If there is a cost overrun (underrun), the government's payment increases (decreases) by $A1$ times the overrun (underrun). Implicit in this formulation is the assumption that actual development costs can be observed by the government.

The research and development stage is considered a success if (i) the firm can demonstrate that the performance of the system equals or exceeds some prescribed minimum, i.e., $P > Pmin$, (ii) the development cost does not exceed some maximum threshold, i.e., $D < Dmax$, and (iii) the firm accepts a production contract with a target production cost that is acceptable to the government, i.e., $TC < TCmax$.

In this simple model, the main focus is on cost-reducing activities, since the contractor does not receive extra "credit" for achieving a performance level that exceeds $Pmin$. Therefore, $Pmin$ is the performance level that is achieved. Thus, our interest is on how, in the first period, the contractor incurs private (non-reimbursible) costs, m,

---

[13] Obviously, for contracts that involve the acquisition of a single unit of output, e.g., a space station or construction projects, this condition will necessarily be fulfilled.

[14] If $A1 = 0$, then we have a firm fixed price contract, and if $A1 = 1$ we have a cost plus fixed fee contract.

and partially reimbursible costs, D, to reduce future production cost, C, by accumulating knowledge, K. In particular, we assume:

$$K = Ko + k(D) + h(m) + (rvK), \tag{2}$$

where Ko denotes the contractor's initial knowledge, k and h are concave production function for knowledge, and (rvK) denotes a random variable for knowledge production in the first period.

Second period production cost is related to knowledge through the following relationship:

$$C = a(P) - g(K, e) + (rvC), \tag{3}$$

where $a(P)$ is a positive convex function in performance, indicating that production cost rises more than proportionately with increased performance, $g(K, e)$ is a positive concave function in K and the contractor's private "effort," e, in the second period, and (rvC) denotes a random variable for production costs in the second period.

If development is successful, as defined above, the contractor will bid target production cost, TC, at the beginning of the second period, will spend $(C + e)$ for production, and will be paid $G(2)$ for his effort, where

$$G(2) = Bo + TC + B1(C - TC). \tag{4}$$

In this reimbursement schedule, Bo denotes target profit and $B1$ denotes the government share of any cost overrun, $0 < B1 < 1$. Then the second period expected profit is given by:

$$E\{\text{profit}(2)\} = Bo + (1 - B1)(TC - E\{C\}) - e. \tag{5}$$

The characterization of this two-stage expected profit maximization can proceed in the usual dynamic programming approach, that is, starting from the last period in the time sequence and proceeding backward in time. Thus, at the start of the second period, the contractor determines the expected profit maximizing level of his private effort e, and target production cost TC. Since $(1 - B1)$ is positive, the contractor will set target production cost as high as possible. In the absence of competition, TC will be set at the allowed maximum, $TCmax$.[15] The random variable is assumed to appear

---

[15]If DOD wants the contractor to set TC at its expected cost, then DOD can make both Bo and $B1$ as a function of TC such that $(B1 - 1) = dBo/dTC < 0$, and $d(dBo/dTC)/dTC > 0$. For example, let $Bo = \exp[-aTC]$, and $(1 - B1) = (-a)\exp[-aTC]$, then the target production cost TC is always set equal to expected cost. To see this, consider the expected profit in the second period, $E\{\text{profit}(2)\} = \exp[-aTC] + (a)\exp[-aTC]\{TC - E(C)\} - e = \exp[-aTC]\{1 + a(TC - E(C))\}$. The profit maximizing TC is given by differentiating this with respect to TC and setting it equal to zero: $0 = (-a)\exp[-aTC]\{1 + a(TC - E(C))\} + \exp[-aTC]a = (-a)\exp[-aTC]\{a(TC - E(C))\}$. We now have $TC = E(C)$, and this eliminates ex-ante buy-in and cost overrun phenomena.

in additive form in the cost function, so that the timing of choosing e can either be before or after the realization of (rvC). Formally, the contractor chooses e for given K and $Pmin$ such that:

$$(1 - B1)g2(K, e) - 1 = 0, \tag{6}$$

where $g2$ denotes the first partial derivative of g with respect to e. Solving for e in terms of K yields,

$$e = e(K). \tag{7}$$

Note that the sign of de/dK can be either negative or positive depending on whether e and K are substitutes or complements, i.e., $de/dK = -g12/g22$.

Figure 1 shows graphically the profit-maximizing choice of effort level, e^*, by the contractor.[16]

Now we move back in time to the start of the first period. First, let $E\{\text{profit}(2:K)\}$ denote the maximum expected profit in the second period given that the contractor enters the second period with knowledge level K. Then we have:

$$E\{\text{profit}(2:K)\} = Bo + (1 - B1)[TC - E\{C(K)\}] - e(K) \tag{5'}$$

Also, for the expected total profits, the sum of the first and the second period profit, we have:[17]

$$E\{\text{profit}\} = E\{[Ao + (1 - A1)(TD - \{D\}) - m] + E\{\text{profit}(2:K)\}\}. \tag{8}$$

Maximize this with respect to D, m and TD, subject to

$$E\{\text{profit}(2:K)\} = Bo + (1 - B1)[TC - E\{C(K)\}] - e(K),$$
$$C(K) = a - g[K, e(K)] + (rvC),$$

and

$$K = Ko + k(D) + h(m) + (rvK).$$

Since $(1 - A1)$ is positive, the contractor will set the target development cost as high as he can in the absence of competition. However, because there is competition

---

[16]One may wonder whether the profit maximizing level of effort by the contractor also represents the socially efficient level. In general, this is not the case. Let $W(C) - e$ be the social objective function. Then we have, $W'(-g2) - 1 = 0$ as the first order condition. Thus, unless the risk-sharing parameter $(1 - B1)$ happens to be the marginal welfare gain represented by an incremental reduction in the production cost $(-W')$, we will not achieve societal efficiency.

[17]For simplicity, a zero discount rate is assumed.

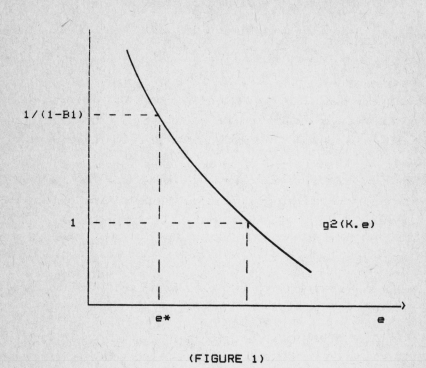

(FIGURE 1)

for the development contract, each contractor is forced to outbid others by bidding ever lower TD. In fact, if the expected profit in the second stage is large, then the contractor is likely to bid TD so low that he actually loses money in the first period. So called "buy-in", and "cost overrun" phenomena are partly due to this initial competition to capture second period profits.[18]

In this model, we will not explicitly solve for the choice of target development cost but simply note that it will be set between the government reservation level, $TDmax$, and the target development cost associated with zero expected profit, TDo.[19]

The first order conditions are both necessary and sufficient for an interior maximum since the concavity of the production function guarantees that the second order conditions will be met. These conditions are:

$$m : -1 + (1 - B1)[\{g1(h') + g2(e'h'\} - e'h'] = 0$$
$$\implies h'(m) = 1/\{(1 - B1)(g1 + g2e') - e'\} \tag{9a}$$

and

$$D : -(1 - A1) + (1 - B1)[\{g1(k') + g2(e'k')\} - e'k'] = 0$$
$$\implies k'(D) = (1 - A1)/\{(1 - B1)(g1 + g2e') - e'\}. \tag{9b}$$

Figure 2 below illustrates the maximization condition involved. It is drawn under the assumption that the functional forms of k and h are identical.

_____

[18] If DOD wants the contractor to set its target development cost equal to its expected development cost thereby eliminating ex-ante buy-in, DOD can achieve this by making Ao and $A1$ functions of target development cost. This can be accomplished just the same way as in the case of target production cost as long as development costs are observable ex-post.

[19] Let $E\{\text{profit}^*\} = E\{[Ao + (1 - A1)(TD - \{D^*\}) - m^*] + E\{\text{profit}(2 : K^*)\}\}$ be the maximum expected total profit. Then TDo is given by: $0 = E\{[Ao + (1 - A1)(TDo - D^*) - m^*] + E\{\text{profit}(2 : K^*)\}\}$. McAfee and McMillan (1986) provide an explicit solution for TD in a model in which contractors employ symmetric Nash equilibrium bidding strategies.

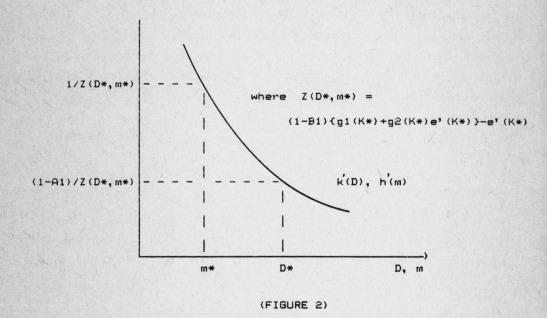

(FIGURE 2)

Examination of the first order condition reveals the following comparative static results:

(i) As the government cost share $A1$ increases, D^* and $E\{\text{profit}\pi2(K)\}$ increase and this, in turn, decreases TDo. Thus, an increase in $A1$ increases the possibilities of "buy-in", and "cost overrun" phenomena by reducing TDo.

(ii) In general, the effect of a change in $A1$ on optimal private effort, m^*, is unknown. This effect depends on, among other things, how the knowledge accumulated in the first period, K, interacts with the private effort, e, in the second period in reducing production cost. If, for example, they are independent, i.e., $g12 = 0$, then an increase in the government's cost share, $A1$, which leads to an increase of D^*, will decrease private effort, m^*.

Several results can be obtained directly from this model. First, there will be a tendency for the contractor to "shirk," i.e., to fail to expend effort in all cases where the cost to him of this effort is less than the resulting reduction in costs. This follows from the fact that the incentive contracts give the contractor only a fraction of any cost saving while he incurs all of the costs of effort.[20]

Second, in this model, the contractor will report as his expected production costs the maximum level that will be acceptable to the government. If the contractor reports that his production costs are *higher* than this amount, the production contract will not be awarded and the potential profits from production will be lost. At the same time, the contractor will have no incentive to claim that his costs are *lower* than the maximum acceptable level, even if he expects that this is the case, since he receives his cost claim minus a fraction of the amount by which his actual costs fall short of his claim. This assumes, of course, that he faces no competition from other contractors and that he knows DOD's "reservation price."[21] If the government's target production cost is overoptimistic, cost overruns will be commonplace.

---

[20]This does not mean that the government will pay the contractor for all costs that he incurs. One approach is for the government to estimate what the item should cost and to refuse to negotiate a contract that would pay the contractor more than that amount. The success of such a policy is, of course, dependent on how well the government can perform such estimates. If it sets the "should cost" level too high, it may still leave the contractor with a substantial opportunity to shirk. If it sets the level too low, the contractor may find production unprofitable. It must be the case that the government is not as good as the contractor in determining what an item should cost because, otherwise, the government could itself direct production. However, there may be instances in which the government is able to make reasonably accurate estimates.

[21]DOD may be able to obtain a lower price by misrepresenting or reducing "the maximum acceptable cost." However, this runs the risk that contractors who could expect to meet the "true" cost target will be discouraged from entering the bidding. The use of such distortions or "guideline" is considered below.

Third, the combined effect of the two contracts on the incentive to expend resources on research and development is ambiguous. One the one hand, because the R&D contract contains an incentive feature, if the contractor spends an additional \$1 on R&D, his additional private costs are less than \$1, which encourages him to undertake more research. On the other, if, by undertaking additional R&D, the contractor can reduce expected production costs by \$1, but his private benefit from this cost reduction is less than \$1, this discourages him from undertaking more R&D. The net effect depends on the relative importance of these two factors.[22]

Fourth, the winning contractor will generally expect to lose money on the R&D contract and to (at least) make up the loss on the production contract. The maximum expected loss that a contractor will accept on the R&D contract is his expected profit on the production contract. This establishes the minimum bid, TDo, for the R&D contract.[23] Although the winning contractor is engaged in "buying in," he does not necessarily expect to offset his losses by renegotiating a contract. Instead, he expects to be able to take advantage of his monopoly position during the initial negotiation of the production contract.[24]

In this scenario, the amount that the contractor loses during the R&D stage depends on his target development cost and on the size of any cost overrun. The contractor's bid, and thus his loss on R&D, is based on his expected profit from production. The payment he actually receives for R&D is limited by the fact that he receives only a portion of any cost overrun. Typical incentive contracts limit contractor cost exposure by guaranteeing a minimum fee. However, there may be an additional constraint that is actually the binding one. The government may establish a ceiling on the largest payment it will make to the contractor. Beyond that point, the only way for the project to proceed to the production stage is for the supplier to pay all additional costs. Since

---

[22]Note that if the production contract is firm fixed price, then only the first effect is present. Moreover, if the research contract is cost plus fixed fee, then the first effect will dominate the second. If the societal objective is to maximize a function such as $W(C)-(D+m+e(K))$, where $W(C)$ denotes the public's demand for the hardware, then the optimum R&D level m and D are given by, $h'(m) = 1/\{-W'[g1+g2e']-e'\}$, $k'(D) = 1/\{-W'(g1 + g2e') - e'\}$. Therefore, unless the R&D contract is a firm-fixed-price contract $(A1 = 0)$, and the production contract is such that the cost share $(1 - B1)$ equals to the marginal welfare gain associated with cost reduction $(-W')$, we will not have the "optimal" R&D level.

[23]Recall that the R&D contract has an incentive feature.

[24]Note that this analysis does not explicitly consider the possibility that the production stage may be cancelled, or the number of units to be procured reduced, for reasons unrelated to the contractor's performance during the research and development stage. However, these factors do affect the level of expected profit in the second period, which in turn affects first period research and development resource allocation.

his maximum expected profit from production is known at this point, the contractor's target development cost will be affected by the existence of a ceiling on the payment for R&D as well. The lower is the ceiling, the higher will be the target development cost.[25]

Finally, it is also instructive to examine the effects of changes in the sharing ratios, the proportion of any cost overruns that are covered by the government. The larger is the proportion of the cost overrun that is covered, the smaller is the incentive of the contractor to control costs.[26] What is less obvious is how changes in a sharing rate affect behavior not only in the particular contract directly affected, e.g., the research and development contract, but also the other contract, e.g., the one for production.

Consider a reduction in the proportion of any cost overrun in R&D that is covered by the government, A1 in the previous notation. Assuming that the ceiling on production costs is not binding and that previously the contractor earned zero expected profits, the contractor must raise target development cost to restore profits. Moreover, since the incentive to undertake R&D is reduced by the change in the sharing rate, other things equal, profits from production are also reduced so that target production costs must also be increased. Thus, a reduction in the sharing rate for the R&D contracts can be expected to have effects not only on R&D but on production as well. A similar argument can be made to show the effect of a change in the sharing rate on the production contract on R&D.

III. VARIABLE QUALITY

In the basic model, we assumed that the contractor received no additional payment for exceeding the minimum acceptable technical level for a new system, nor did exceeding this minimum affect the probability that the contract would proceed to the production stage. Here, we consider, in a simple way, the effect of modifying this assumption. To examine this question, even in a fairly simple fashion, we must modify the previous model in a number of ways.

We assume that expenditures on research and development can be divided into two mutually exclusive and exhaustive categories, those that lower production costs,

---

[25]There is also an indirect way in which the ceiling affects target costs. If the ceiling is effective, the contractor will spend less on R&D than would otherwise be the case. As a result, his production costs will be higher and his profits from production will be lower. This, in turn, will reduce the maximum loss he will accept on his R&D contract and, thus, will likely increase his target cost on that R&D contract.

[26]The limiting cases are firm fixed price contracts, where the proportion is zero, and cost plus fixed fee contracts, where the proportion is one.

and those that improve system performance. Higher expenditures on R&D to improve system performance will improve the technical capabilities of the system, a fact that is known at the time the production contract is negotiated. We also assume that, other things equal, production costs increase with improved technical performance. The lower production costs result from knowledge gained during R&D. However, by our previous assumption, actual production costs are known only *after* production is completed. We continue to assume that there is a floor to performance and a ceiling to target production costs that cannot be violated if production is to occur. We also assume that there are incentive contracts both for R&D and production. Finally, we assume that the target profit the government is willing to offer in the production contract is greater, the higher is the level of system performance.

The assumption that the contractor can earn higher profits by improving performance above the minimum acceptable level is what distinguishes this model from the basic model.[27] As a result of this assumption, the contractor may attempt to exceed the minimum performance level, unlike the situation in the basic model. However, as higher performance is sought, there will be a penalty in terms of higher production costs. This, in turn, will lead to even higher R&D expenditures to lower production costs, although equilibrium production costs will be higher, the higher the level of technical performance that is achieved. The desire to improve technical performance will eventually be limited by (i) the higher production costs, which limit the profits to be earned from production, and (ii) the higher R&D costs, resulting both from improved performance and the associated need to limit production costs, which limit the profit to be earned from production. The contractor can be thought of as trading off higher production and R&D costs against the additional profits he will be allowed if he exceeds the minimum performance level.[28]

In taking "quality" into account explicitly, the optimization in the second period must be changed to allow for the possibility that the performance level may not be

---

[27] In view of the well-known difficulties of contractors in achieving required levels of technical performance, it may seem odd to be discussing the achievement of performance levels in excess of the minimum level required. However, our notion of the minimum acceptable performance level is different from performance specifications that may appear in research and development contracts. We view the latter as desires on the part of DOD and the Services, but ones that they realize will be difficult to meet. For this reason, the contractor believes that the contract will not necessarily be cancelled if these specifications are not met. However, the contractor may have to accept a lower price, other things equal, if he falls short of the specifications in the R&D contract or, to say the same thing, he will be rewarded if performance exceeds the minimum.

[28] The result may not be an interior solution if the production cost ceiling is reached before the additional cost equals the additional revenue. It is also possible for the solution to occur at the minimum performance level if marginal cost exceeds marginal revenue for any performance improvement beyond that point.

Pmin, as in the previous model. The reimbursement schedule in the second period reflects the new situation:

$$G(2) = Bo(P) + TC + B1(C - TC). \tag{4'}$$

where target profit Bo now is an increasing function of performance.

However, the main difference between the models lies in the first period. Now, R&D effort in the first period can be expended both on performance enhancement, Dp, and on production cost reduction, Dc. For simplicity, we assume that the firm's managerial effort in the first period m, is spent only to improve performance.

Let $P = Po + s(Dp) + f(m) + (rvP)$ be the performance level achieved at the end of the research and development stage. Po denotes the contractor's initial capability and (rvP) denotes the random variable, indicating the stochastic nature of research. Let $K = Ko + k(Dc) + (rvK)$ be the level of knowledge pertaining to production. Again Ko denotes the contractor's initial knowledge and (rvK) denotes the random variable involved in this process. Production cost is affected both by the performance level, P, and the level of production knowledge, K as in the previous section. Recall equation (3) of the production cost:

$$C = a(P) - g(K, e) + (rvC). \tag{3}$$

The first period maximization involves finding Dp, Dc, and m that would maximize the expected total profit:

$$E\{\text{profit}\} = E\{[Ao + (1 - A1)(TD - \{D\}) - m] + E\{\text{profit}(2 : K, P)\}\},$$

where

$$E\{\text{profit}(2 : K, P)\} = Bo(P) + (1 - B1)[TC - E\{C(K)\}] - e(K),$$

$$C(K) = a(P) - g[K, e(K)] + (rvC),$$

$$K = Ko + k(Dc) + (rvK)$$

$$P = Po + s(Dp) + f(m) + (rvP) \qquad \text{with} \qquad P > Pmin.$$

The first order conditions for an interior maximum are given by:

$$m : -1 + [Bo' - (1 - B1)a']f' = 0$$

$$\implies f'(m) = 1/[Bo' - (1 - B1)a'] \tag{10a}$$

$$Dp : -(1 - A1) + s'[Bo' - (1 - B1)a'] = 0$$

$$\implies s'(Dp) = (1 - A1)/[Bo' - (1 - B1)a'] \tag{10b}$$

$$Dc : -(1 - A1) + (1 - B1)g1(k') + g2(e'k') - e'k' = 0$$

$$\implies k'(Dc) = (1 - A1)/\{(1 - B1)(g1 + g2e') - e'\} \tag{10c}$$

As in the previous model, one can see the effect of changes in $A1$ on the profit maximizing levels of Dp, Dc, P and TDo. An increase in $A1$ leads to an increase in Dp^*, Dc^*, P^*, and $E\{\text{profit}(2 : K^*)\}$, which in turn leads to a decrease in TDo. Thus an increase in $A1$ again increases the possibility of "buy-in", and "cost over-run" phenomena, as well as higher performance specifications. In this particular formulation, an increase in Dp^* will lead to a decrease in m^*, indicating a substitute relationship between government funded research, Dp, and privately funded research, m. Figure 3 illustrates the maximization condition involved. It is drawn under the assumption that the functional forms of f and s are identical.

We should note that the outcome of this model, in which firms exceed performance minima but cost overruns are commonplace, is broadly consistent with the folklore about defense procurement that DOD values performance improvements highly but places relatively little weight on cost overruns. However, this folklore is based in part on the observation that performance targets tend to be met while cost targets are not, but the minimum performance levels in the theory are not the same as the performance targets.

IV. VARIABLE QUANTITY

To this point, we have treated the number of units of hardware to be purchased by DOD, assuming that production goes forward, as fixed. In this section, we consider the impact of changing this assumption. In particular, we assume that DOD informs the contractor that the number of units of hardware that will be purchased depends on the cost of production. That is, we assume that, prior to the start of research and development, DOD provides to all potential contractors a schedule that indicates how the number of units purchased will depend on the production cost. To simplify the analysis, we return to our earlier assumption that the contractor must meet the minimum performance level for production to proceed, but that the contractor receives no reward for exceeding that level. On this assumption, we can treat the performance level as fixed at the minimum, if production is to take place.

There are two distinct reasons why DOD would wish to present a contractor with a demand schedule rather than with an order for a fixed quantity of output if the contractor can produce at less than target cost. The first is the familiar reason that additional units of hardware will have declining marginal utility, so that the number of units that DOD will wish to purchase will depend on the price that it is charged. By presenting the contractor with a downward sloping demand schedule, DOD will purchase

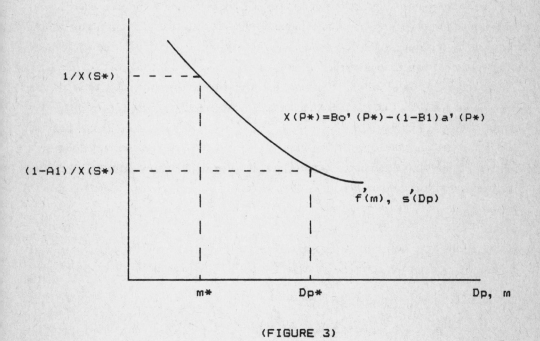

(FIGURE 3)

(This figure is drawn under the assumption f and s have identical functional form.)

fewer units the higher the price that the contractor offers.[29] Moreover, by informing the contractor of how marginal utility declines, DOD can create some incentive for the contractor to limit its costs since the lower is its price, the larger the number of units that will be purchased.[30]

The second reason for offering the contractor a downward sloping demand schedule results from the fact that, contrary to the assumption made in the basic model, the true cost of the contractor may not be observable by DOD. In such circumstances, it may be desirable to offer the contractor a demand schedule that is even flatter than DOD's true demand schedule. Indeed, we can show that it would be useful for the government to claim that it had a downward sloping demand curve even if that was not the case. The reason for doing so is to create more an incentive for the contractor to reveal the truth about his costs and, as a result, for the buyer, DOD, to retain some consumer surplus.

In this section, we consider the impact of assuming that the number of units of hardware that will be purchased depends on the price DOD expects to pay for a unit and that actual production costs are observable.[31] The actual price depends on both the target and the actual cost, as in the previous models. We also assume that the marginal cost of production is constant.

Formally, let p be the unit price that DOD pays for the product, $p = Bo + TC + B1(C - TC)$. Then the contractor's expected profit in the second period is given by:

$$E\{\text{profit}(2)\} = E\{(p - C)Q(p) - e\}$$
$$= E\{[Bo + (1 - B1)(TC - C)]Q(p) - e\}, \tag{12}$$

where

$$C = a - g[K, e] + (rvC).$$

In contrast to earlier models, the contractor no longer negotiates for the highest target cost allowed but chooses a somewhat lower target. This is because, other things equal, the lower is the target cost, the larger is the quantity purchased. By selling a

---

[29] For an analysis in which a contract to serve a market with a downward sloping demand curve is awarded using an auction, see Hansen (forthcoming).

[30] For reasons discussed above, even if the contractor is presented with DOD's "true" demand schedule, it will not have the appropriate incentives to expend effort. However, there may still be advantages for DOD to offer the contractor a demand schedule rather than a single level of output that is demanded.

[31] In the next section, we examine the effect of assuming that DOD cannot observe the contractor's actual cost.

larger number of units, the contractor may be able to increase his profits. As before, the contractor expends his own effort, e, and incurs unit cost, C, and produces $Q(p)$. In particular, the profit maximizing contractor effort for a given level of production knowledge, K, and performance level $Pmin$ is:

$$e : (1 - B1)g2Q(p) + (p - C)Q'B1(-g2) - 1 = 0$$

or,

$$g2(K, e) = 1/\{(1 - B1)Q(p) - (p - C)Q'B1\}.$$

The contractor's private effort tends to be larger at low cost levels and smaller at high ones than where the quantity to be purchased is fixed. This is due to the smaller adverse effect of increased cost on profit when the quantity purchased is more sensitive to a cost change. We can solve for e as a function of K and demand $Q(p)$.

The maximization in the first period is essentially the same as in the basic model except that the TC is no longer set at $TCmax$, and the effort function in the second period is more complex in that it takes into account DOD's demand schedule for hardware.

V. PRODUCTION COSTS NOT OBSERVABLE

To this point, we have assumed that actual production cost is observable by DOD after production. Indeed, DOD spends considerable resources to monitor and identify contractor's costs and has built up a significant institutional apparatus to do so. However, it is not clear that total observability of cost is the most appropriate assumption in describing DOD acquisition. Moreover, it is important to understand how the analysis of acquisition is affected if costs cannot be observed perfectly. In this section, we make the extreme assumption that DOD cannot observe production costs even after production has been completed.

We know from Loeb-Magat (1979) that the contractor can be induced to reveal his true cost if he is paid an amount equal to his total cost plus the entire consumer surplus of DOD. However, this would leave no surplus for the DOD. Although there are some auctioning methods that can be combined with Loeb-Magat approach to recover much of consumer surplus from the contractor back to DOD, it may be difficult politically and administratively to implement such schemes.[32] Thus, we consider here the more likely situation where DOD's interest is to maximize its surplus directly through its contract without the need to conduct an auction to do so. To accomplish this, DOD would announce a payment schedule that modifies, or distorts, its original demand schedule. The result is that DOD must accept a lower level of social efficiency to obtain a larger surplus.

Before proceeding to a general treatment of this issue, it is useful to provide an illustrative example.[33] Suppose that, prior to the beginning of production, DOD knows that the contractor's marginal cost of production is either 50 or 80, but that it does not know which. The contractor knows his true cost. DOD's "true" demand curve for the hardware is $Q = 100 - p$. We know that the contractor can be induced to reveal his true cost by paying the contractor an amount equal to his total cost plus the entire consumer surplus of DOD. However, this would leave no surplus for the DOD. An alternative is for the buyer to announce to the contractor that if he reports cost of 80, the government will not purchase any hardware,[34] and if the contractor reports 50, the government will purchase 50 units, pay the contractor his costs, 2500, plus a profit of, say, 1.[35] Now, if the contractor's true cost is 50 and he reports that it is 50, he receive a surplus of 1. If, in these circumstances, he reports 80, he obtains no surplus. Thus, telling the truth is the best he can do if his costs are 50. Suppose, instead, that the contractor's true cost is 80. If he reports that his cost is 80 he obtains no sales and his profit is zero. However, if he reports that his cost is 50, he sells 50 units, has total cost of 4000 = (50 × 80) and receives a payment of only 2501, for a loss of 1499. Once again, truthful reporting is the best he can do. On the assumption that the two possible cost levels are equally likely, this strategy leaves DOD with an expected surplus of 624.5 or (3750 − 2501)/2, instead of zero as in the Loeb-Magat scheme.

Consider the alternative of having DOD announce that it will purchase according to its true demand curve. The contractor will obtain zero surplus if he tells the truth about his costs since the payment from DOD will just equal these costs. He can improve his situation by always reporting that his costs are 80. If his costs are actually 80, he receives a surplus of zero, but if they are only 50 his surplus is 600 = 20(80 − 50) since 20 units are purchased at a price that substantially exceeds his cost. Significantly, by purchasing according to its true demand curve, DOD always receives a surplus of only

---

[32]See Besen and Terasawa (1987) for a discussion of some of these difficulties.

[33]For a very general treatment see Baron and Myerson (1982), and Riordan and Sappington (1987).

[34]Under DOD's true demand curve, it would wish to purchase 20 units at a price of 80.

[35]Under DOD's true demand curve, it would wish to purchase 50 units at a price of 50.

200, which is less than its expected surplus when it "distorted" its demand curve in the above example. By committing itself to buying less than it "really" wants when costs are reported to be high, DOD is able to induce the contractor to truthfully report his costs when they are low, thus producing a larger expected surplus for DOD.[36] Thus, DOD should be willing to bargain hard, and should even be willing to forego what otherwise would be attractive purchases, to induce truthful revelation of the part of the contractor about his costs. Even apparently "unreasonable" demands may, therefore, be justified.

It may even be desirable for DOD to claim that its demand curve is downward sloping when it is not. Suppose that the true demand curve for a new system is perfectly inelastic at a quantity of 50 up to a price of 80 and perfectly elastic thereafter. In short, DOD is willing to pay *any* price up to 80 for 50 units of the system rather than go without it, but it is unwilling to pay more than 80, which is the price ceiling discussed previously. Moreover, we continue to assume that there are only two possible levels of marginal cost, 50 and 80, that the contractor knows which cost level obtains prior to beginning production, and that production costs are completely unobservable by DOD.[37] Despite the fact that DOD would "really" want to purchase 50 units of the system if the cost was really 80, it is better off committing itself to never pay more than 50 per unit plus, say, 1, in this example. If the price is 80, the surplus obtained by DOD is zero. If the price is 50 per unit plus 1, the surplus is 1499. If DOD does not distort its demand curve, the contractor will always report that his cost is 80, and DOD will never obtain a surplus. If, however, the demand curve is distorted as indicated, the contractor will report that his costs are 50 when they are 50, and DOD will obtain a large surplus.[38] Here, this scheme strictly dominates truthful reporting by DOD of its demand curve.

We were able to identify a relatively simple scheme that DOD could employ to increase its expected surplus in the previous case because there were only two possible outcomes for marginal costs and they were equally likely. In general, where marginal cost can take on a large number of values, determining the distortion is far more complex. Here, we sketch how the optimal distortion is accomplished.

---

[36]Note that there will be occasions when, *ex post*, the buyer is worse off than if he did not distort his demand curve. However, if he has an accurate estimate of the probability distribution of contractor costs, he can increase his *expected* surplus by the appropriate distortion.

[37]Obviously, the last assumption, that costs are completely unobservable, is a caricature.

[38]The contractor will, of course, report that his costs are 80 when that is the case, but the DOD would have obtained no surplus at a price of 80 in any event.

If C is the (constant) marginal production cost, then the surplus maximizing price for DOD, p, depends only on the contractor's reported marginal cost $R(C)$,[39] where the relationship is given by,

$$p(R) = R + [F(R)/f(R)].\tag{13}$$

$F(R)$ and $f(R)$ denote the DOD's subjective cumulative and density functions of marginal cost, respectively.

In order to implement this policy, it is necessary to provide the contractor with enough profit that it is worthwhile for it to produce. It is shown by Dupuit (1952) and Hotelling (1938) that, under complete information with a constant marginal cost and a fixed cost, a transfer equal to the fixed cost can be used to induce the contractor to produce. In the incomplete information case considered here, a transfer is used both to reward the contractor sufficiently so that it will produce and to induce the contractor to reveal its costs. Thus the transfer, $T(R)$ is:

$$T(R) = \int_R^\infty Q(r)dr + [Co - \{p(R) - R\}Q(R)],\tag{14}$$

where the square bracketed term guarantees that production is profitable to the contractor in that the fixed cost, Co, is covered. The first term in the transfer encourages the contractor to report his costs truthfully since the value of this term increases as the reported cost R decreases. In fact, the profit of a contractor who experiences marginal cost of C and reports it as $R(C)$ is given by:

$$\{\text{profit}(2)\} = \{p(R) - C\}Q(R) + T(R) - Co$$
$$= \{R - C\}Q(R) + \int_R^\infty Q(r)dr.\tag{15}$$

Thus, the profit maximizing contractor's report on his marginal cost is given by differentiating the above with respect to R:

$$0 = R'Q(R) + \{R - C\}Q'(R) - Q(R)R'\tag{16}$$

which states that the contractor's profit is maximized when he reports truthfully, i.e., $R = C$. With this, we can replace $R(C)$ by C in the analysis below. Moreover, unlike under the Loeb-Magat scheme, DOD's gain from the procurement is maximized. DOD's gain, $GS(C)$ is shown below.

$$GS(C) = \int_{p(C)}^\infty Q(p)dp - \int_C^\infty Q(c)dc,\tag{17}$$

To illustrate the above approach, consider the following numerical example. Figure 4 provides a graphical presentation of this example.

---

[39] See Baron and Myerson (1982), pp. 925-927 for detail.

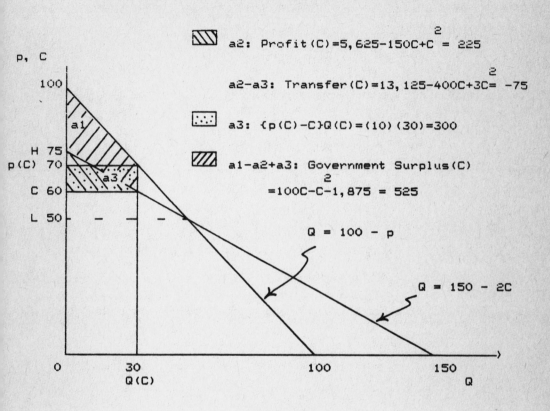

(FIGURE 4)

Let $Q = 100 - p$ be the original demand function, and let marginal cost be uniformly distributed on $[L = 50, H = 75]$, i.e., it is equally likely that marginal cost will take on any value from 50 to 75. The density function of C is $f(C) = 1/(H - L) = 1/25$. To simplify further, we assume that the fixed cost, Co, is zero. The surplus maximizing price is then given by:

$$p(C) = C + (C - 50) = 2C - 50 \qquad \text{for} \qquad C \in [50, 75] \tag{18}$$

which is increasing in C and has a range $[50, 100]$. Then the quantity $Q(C)$ that the DOD will buy is given by:

$$Q(C) = 100 - (2C - 50) = 150 - 2C \qquad \text{for} \qquad C \in [50, 75] \tag{19}$$

The transfer for this case is given by:

$$\begin{aligned}
T(C) &= \int_C^{75} \{150 - 2C^*\} dC^* - (C - 50)(150 - 2C) \\
&= \{150(75 - C) - (75)^2 + (C)^2\} - (C - 50)(150 - 2C) \\
&= 24,375 - 400C - C^2
\end{aligned} \tag{20}$$

The profit to the contractor experiencing marginal cost C and reporting R to DOD is given by:

$$\text{Profit}(C; R) = 5,625 - 150C + R(2C - R) \qquad \text{for} \qquad C \in [50, 75] \tag{21}$$

While, the profit associated with truth-telling is:

$$\text{Profit}(C; C) = 5,625 - 150C + C^2 \qquad \text{for} \qquad C \in [50, 75] \tag{22}$$

Thus, it pays the contractor be truthful in this environment, even if the DOD cannot observe the cost at all. Moreover, DOD's surplus is maximized and ranges from zero to 625 depending on marginal cost:

$$\begin{aligned}
GS(C) &= \int_{2C-50}^{100} (100 - p) dp - \int_C^{75} (150 - 2C^*) dC^* + (C - 50)(150 - 2C) \\
&= 100(100 - 2C + 50) - (1/2)\{(100)^2 - (2C - 50)^2\} \\
&\quad - [150(75 - C) - (75)^2 + (C)^2] + (250C - 2C^2 - 7,500) \\
&= 100C - C^2 - 1,875 \qquad \text{for} \qquad C \in [50, 75].
\end{aligned} \tag{23}$$

In this section, we examined how DOD's gain from the procurement may be maximized even under complete asymmetry of information. DOD's gain is achieved through the choice of a less than optimal (first-best) production level, and allocative efficiency is traded off to obtain a gain for DOD. Of course, if complete information is costlessly available then we can achieve the first-best solution, where DOD's gain is maximized without sacrificing the allocative efficiency. To the extent that DOD can improve its information on contractor's cost, it can reduce the damage resulting from purchasing less than its optimal production quantity. However, it should also be recognized that obtaining improved information on contractor costs is not costless and the cost of improved monitoring must be taken into account in a complete analysis.

The reduction of expected contractor's profit in the second period through this approach will likely to produce a more realistic development cost target in the first period, and diminished "buy-in" and "cost-overrun" phenomena in general. The maximization in the first period associated with this approach is fundamentally the same as in the basic model, and is thus omitted here.

VI. WHAT THE PROTOTYPE MODEL DOES NOT CONSIDER

The prototype model presented in this paper contains several features that must be present in all models of defense procurement. These models must: (a) allow for the fact that the procurement of major weapons systems involves the production both of knowledge and hardware; (b) allow for constraints, in terms of floors and ceilings, on the performance and cost of these systems; (c) take account of the importance of economies of scale and learning that limit the number of contractors that can be employed on a single system; (d) recognize the asymmetry of information between DOD and contractors, with the latter having superior information about technological opportunities and costs and the former having superior information about the value of the system; and (e) consider the fact that contractor profits are generally limited through regulation. Moreover, that models that purport to analyze defense procurement should: (f) allow for the central role of "quality" in determining the demand for weapons systems and (g) recognize that varying the number of units that are purchased is an important strategy that can be used by DOD. The various analyses presented in this Draft represent an initial attempt to incorporate these features in a unified framework. However, the reader should note that not only have we treated most of these issues in a preliminary way, but that we have omitted a number of factors that should be present in a full-scale model.

Competition in the Second Stage

Clearly, one of the "stylized facts" about defense procurement is that the developer of a weapons system is almost certain to obtain the initial production contract and that "fact" is assumed in the model presented above. However, it is also a fact that production contracts are sometimes divided between two or more contractors, usually after the developer has produced some units himself.[40] More rarely, the developer is replaced as the sole producer, usually in cases in which there is significant dissatisfaction on the part of the buyer about either cost or performance. In addition, the production contract obtained by the developer will generally be somewhat constrained by potential competition.[41] Even where we observe the developer undertaking all production, the terms of the contract can be affected by the fact that, at some additional cost, production can be shifted to another firm.

Issues of supplier switching have been addressed recently in Anton and Yao (1987a) and Demski, Sappington, and Spiller (1987). In both models, there are significant economies of scale or learning effects. These economies are so great that, if the buyer knew the sellers' costs, only one firm, almost certainly the developer, would undertake all required production. However, because of asymmetric information, the buyer's cost may be reduced if, under certain circumstances, he awards all or part of the contract to the less efficient firm. The willingness of the buyer to act in this manner has some of the same properties as the distortions in demand described above. There, by being willing to reduce the quantity demanded in response to a higher price by more than is justified by his "true" demand curve, the buyer may be able to obtain a larger surplus. Here, although there are costs to the buyer when purchases are made from less efficient firms, there may be countervailing benefits when the most efficient firm is forced to report its costs more truthfully.[42]

---

[40] Anton and Yao (1987b) survey the available empirical studies of the effect of split buys.

[41] There are, of course, a few situations in which there are no credible alternative suppliers.

[42] Another way to think about this behavior is to imagine the buyer threatening to switch his patronage to another firm unless he obtains a lower price from the developer. Even where both the buyer and the developer know that the other firm is less efficient, the buyer may, on occasion, find it desirable to carry out such a threat. The reason is that the threat of losing business may induce the developer to offer a lower price. Again, the effect of this reduction in second period profit will reduce the level of R&D and moderate the "buy-in" phenomena.

We can extend our previous example of demand distortions to show how supplier switching might be used to increase the buyer's surplus. Suppose, as in the previous example, that the developer's production costs are either 50 or 80, with equal probability, and that the buyer is not able to observe these costs even after production is completed. We also assume that there is an alternative supplier with a known production cost of 81. Thus, the buyer is certain that the developer is the lowest cost supplier. We also assume that the value of the hardware to the buyer is 82. To permit us to focus on the role of supplier switching, we assume that the buyer wants to purchase a single unit and must only decide from whom to make the purchase. Under these circumstances, the buyer can increase his surplus by adopting the following scheme. If the developer reports a cost of 50 he obtains the production contract and receives a payment of 51. If the developer reports a cost of 80, the contract is awarded to the alternative supplier for a price of 81.

Clearly, if the developer's cost is 50, he will report that is the case and receive a surplus of $1 = (51 - 50)$, since otherwise he will not receive the production contract. If his costs are 80, he will report that is the case and the production contract will be awarded to the other firm. He will not report that his costs are 50 even though that will obtain the contract for him, because that will result in a loss of $29 = (51 - 80)$. If the contractor's costs are 50, the buyer receives a surplus of $31 = (82 - 51)$. If the contractor's costs are 80, the buyer receives a surplus of $1 = (82 - 81)$. His expected surplus is, therefore, $16 = .5(31) + .5(1)$.

Without the buyer's announced willingness to switch to the other supplier, the developer would always announce that his costs are 80, he would always receive the production contract, and the buyer would always receive a surplus of 2. By distorting his choice, the buyer is better off than if he always purchased from the developer.[43]

Note that the buyer cannot obtain the same surplus by conducting an auction in which contractors compete by offering to supply the good at successively lower prices until only one contractor remains. In such an auction, the alternative supplier will drop out at a price below 81, so that the developer can win the contract at a bid of 80. He will thus obtain a surplus of either 30 or zero, depending on whether his costs are 50 or 80. As a result, the buyer will always receive a surplus of 2. Only by being willing to switch to the alternative supplier when the developer reports that his cost is 80 can the

---

[43] Obviously, the value of this simple scheme to the buyer depends on the costs of the alternative supplier and on the value of the good. In this example, if the other supplier's costs exceed 82, a better alternative would be to refuse to buy if the developer quoted a price of 80, the scheme discussed above. Issue then becomes the credibility of such threats. If the value of the good was, say, 120, it would pay for the buyer to threaten to switch to the other supplier only if the latter's costs were less than 109.

buyer expect to obtain some of the surplus that would otherwise accrue to the developer because of the informational asymmetry.[44]

Clearly, a full-blown model of defense procurement will have to allow for the possibility that actual or potential competition can limit the payment that DOD must make for a weapons system. Moreover, such a model will have to allow not only for standard forms of competition but also for the fact that DOD may be able to use the existence of alternative suppliers strategically to limit its payments to developers.[45]

Dual Sourcing

The previous section discussed the possibility that DOD might wish to retain the option of awarding the entire production contract to a firm other than the developer. Still another possibility is to split the production contract between the developer and another firm. By carefully specifying the terms on which such a split will be made, DOD may be able to obtain a larger surplus than if it awarded the entire contract to either the developer or an alternative supplier.

The following split award scheme is presented to show that it is better than always awarding the entire contract to the firm that is known to have the lowest cost. We have not verified that it is better than distorting the demand curve or switching all of production to an alternative supplier under certain circumstances. However, since it gives the buyer an additional strategy, there may be circumstances in which it is the preferred alternative.

Assume that DOD has the same demand curve for a weapons system as presented above, i.e., $Q = 100 - p$. Assume also that the marginal cost of the developer is, with equal probability, 20, 50, and 80. An alternative supplier has known marginal cost of 81. If DOD reports its true demand curve, the developer will report that its marginal

---

[44] Another way to put this is that the differential rent that the developer will obtain through competition can be extracted only through a willingness on the part of the buyer to accept an occasional inefficient outcome.

[45] The possibility that DOD can behave in this manner means that it is very difficult to interpret the results of studies that purport to measure the effect of competition on costs. If DOD can credibly threaten to employ an alternative supplier should the developer's costs exceed a certain level, many of the benefits of competition may be observed even if no actual competition is observed. In addition, the value of competition will depend on the availability of other means to discipline the developer. In the previous example in this section, DOD would do almost as well by threatening not to issue a production contract if the developer's cost is 80 as it would by threatening to switch to the other contractor. The benefit of competition is only the *differential* surplus obtained by DOD as a result of the having an alternative supplier.

cost is 50 when it is 20, receiving a profit of 1500; that its marginal cost is 80 when it is 50, receiving a profit of 600; and that its marginal cost is 80 when it is 80, receiving no profit. In these circumstances, DOD receives a surplus of 1250 when marginal cost of 50 is reported and a surplus of 200, otherwise, for an expected surplus of 550.

DOD can improve on this situation by offering the developer 2900 for 50 units, his costs plus a profit of 400, when he reports that his marginal cost is 50, and 800 for 10 units, his costs, when reported marginal cost is 80, purchasing 10 additional units from the alternative supplier for a price of 81.[46] Under these circumstances, the developer will report that his marginal cost is 50 when it is 50.[47] This occurs because he earns 400 if he reports that his marginal cost is 50 and satisfies the entire demand, but only 300 if he reports that his marginal cost is 80 and 10 units are purchased from the alternative supplier. Here, DOD's surplus is only 850 when marginal cost is reported as 50, but this report occurs more often because the developer reports truthfully when his marginal cost is 50. At the same time, when the developer reports that his marginal cost is 80, DOD's surplus declines to 190. The net effect is to raise the expected surplus to 630.[48] It is easier for DOD to threaten to withdraw some purchases from the developer when there is an alternative supplier because the cost of exercising the threat is smaller.[49]

CONCLUSION

As the title of this paper makes clear, the model presented here is intended to be the forerunner of future analyses of defense procurement. We believe that future work should focus on four sets of questions:

(1) What is the link between the research and development and production stages? How does the fact that winning a DOD development contract virtually guarantees obtaining the production contract affect bidding for R&D contracts and the behavior of the contractor during the development stage?

(2) How does the fact that DOD is concerned about technical performance as well as cost manifest itself? How are the contracts that DOD offers affected and, in turn, how is contractor behavior changed?

---

[46]Note that these quantities are chosen from DOD's true demand curve with the exception that DOD purchases 20 units even when 10 are purchased at a price of 81.

[47]He will also report that his marginal cost is 50 when it is 20.

[48]Recall that we have not demonstrated the optimality of this scheme but only that it is better for DOD behaving this manner than behaving according to its true demand curve.

[49]Of course, the significance of this alternative depends on the costs of the other supplier.

(3) How is the size of a DOD procurement order affected by target cost and how, in turn, is contractor behavior changed?

(4) How can and does DOD adapt to information asymmetries? How does DOD distort the demand curve faced by the contractor because it cannot otherwise obtain truthful information about contractor costs? What alternatives are available to DOD to obtain improved cost information?

Each of these sets of questions poses challenges both for future theoretical analyses and empirical studies. Nonetheless, we believe that providing better answers to them is central to improving our ability to manage the defense acquisition process. The present paper is an attempt to contribute to such an improvement.

ACKNOWLEDGMENTS

This research was supported in part by the Office of the Secretary of Defense, which is not responsible for the opinions or findings of the authors.

The authors would like to thank James Quirk, Bill Gates and an anonymous referee for their comments and suggestions. Remaining errors of commission and omission are entirely the authors'.

REFERENCES

Anton, J.J. and D.A. Yao, "Second Sourcing and the Experience Curve: Price Competition in Defense Procurement," 18 *The RAND Journal of Economics*, 57-76 (1987a).

Anton, J.J. and D.A. Yao, "Measuring the Effectiveness of Competition in Defense Procurement: A Survey," in "Proceedings of the Second RAND Economics of Defense Procurement Research Conference," WD-3521-PA&E, July 1987.

Baron, D.P., and R.B. Myerson, "Regulating a Monopolist with Unknown Costs," 50 *Econometrica*, 911-930 (1982).

Besen, S.M., and K.L. Terasawa, "An Introduction to the Economics of Procurement," The RAND Corporation, WD-3555-PA&E, August 1987.

Demski, J.S., D. Sappington, and P.T. Spiller, "Managing Supplier Switching," 18 *The RAND Journal of Economics*, 77-97 (1987).

Dupuit, J., "On the Measurement of the Utility of Public Works," *International Economics Papers*, 2 (1952), 83-110 (translated by R.H. Barback from "de la Mesure de l'Utilite des Travaux Publics," *Annales des Ponts et Chaussees*, 2nd Series, Vol. 8, 1844).

Hansen, R.G., "Auctions with Endogenous Quantity," *The RAND Journal of Economics*, forthcoming.

Hotelling, H., "The General Welfare in Relation to Problems of Taxation and of Railway and Utility Rates," *Econometrica*, 6 (1938), 242-269.

Loeb, M., and W.A. Magat, "A Decentralized Method for Utility Regulation," 22 *Journal of Law and Economics*, 399-404 (1979).

McAfee, R.P. and J. McMillan, "Bidding for Contracts: A Principal-Agent Approach," 17 *Rand Journal of Economics*, 326-338 (1986).

Rich, M. and E. Dews, with C.L. Batten, Jr., *Improving the Military Acquisition Process*, The RAND Corporation, R-3373-AF/RC, February 1986.

Riordan, M.H. and D.E.M. Sappington, "Awarding Monopoly Franchises," 77 *American Economic Review*, 375-387 (1987).

A CONTRACT TERMINATION PROCESSING MODEL AND SYSTEM
FOR NAVAL SUPPLY DEMAND REVIEW (SDR) ACTIONS

Christopher K. Carlson, Stephen R. Ruth, Merrill E. Warkentin
Department of Decision Sciences, George Mason University
4400 University Drive, Fairfax, Virginia 22030
Jerry Zamer, Naval Supply Systems Command, Washington, D. C.

SUMMARY

This paper presents a microcomputer-based contract termination
processing model developed for the U.S. Naval Supply Systems Command
(NAVSUP). The model, implemented as a microcomputer program, serves
as an Expert Advisory/advanced Decision Support System for processing
contracts recommended as termination candidates by the Supply Demand
Review (SDR) component. The system employs a benefit-cost model
approach to evaluate potential supply contract termination actions.
It replicates expert decision behavior typical of competent contract
administrators in this focused area of performance. Additional features are provided for documentation of the evaluation, processing,
collection of data for subsequent analysis, and merging and reporting
collective statistics from operational use. The computer model and
program, known as TERMINATOR, were developed and implemented in a
relatively short period of time and currently have wide operational
use.

1. NEED/BACKGROUND

The Naval Supply Systems Command (NAVSUP) is responsible for the
US Navy's logistics management. Among many other activities, NAVSUP
provides for the provisioning of all US Navy commands and ships.
Supplies and supporting supply contract arrangements need to be
arranged well in advance of materials requirement determination to
support fleet and ship operations and activities. This involves
creating and maintaining in advance a supply contract process, or
"pipeline", of hundreds of thousands of distinct items needed to
support and replenish ships and supporting facilities. In FY 1988,

with significant reductions in funding, the Navy was faced with a major resystemization effort in its Stock Requisition/Termination/ Disposal Functions. Because of these cutbacks it was necessary to consider many supply contracts already awarded for early termination. But the decision to terminate involves many expert judgments and a careful review of a number of variables -- in order to make the most economical decision.

NAVSUP began considering termination processing procedures in late FY 1987 in anticipation of the potential for FY 1988 budgetary reductions and, by mid FY1988, had developed the necessary approaches for processing potential termination actions (NAVSUP letter 1988). Since NAVSUP had concurrently outfitted many of its major and head-quarters commands with personal computers (PCs), a way was sought to use these resources extensively in day-to-day work activities. The termination processing procedure, beyond being a resystemization issue, represented a modernization effort applicable to the PC re-source base. Thus, a rapid turn-around effort to develop a Personal Computer (PC)-based termination processing model was needed. This effort led to the TERMINATOR system described in this paper.

2. MODEL APPROACH AND SYSTEM USE

This section reviews the policy and procedures employed for the execution of potential termination actions. PC termination model candidates are contracts recommended from Supply Demand Review (SDR) for termination consideration. A contract value threshold was de-rived by NAVSUP cost analysts from a sensitivity analysis by simu-lating a range of values in the termination benefit-cost equation. The threshold represents the point at which potential savings from early termination of contracts are greater than the costs of person-nel resources required to execute the terminations. NAVSUP directed that all contracts with dollar values greater than $10,000 should be pursued for termination. Contracts with termination values less than $10,000 are not processed through the PC termination model.

The termination processing procedures also require that contrac-tor termination fees must be obtained for all contracts with termina-tion values greater than $10,000. These dollar values, together with probability distributions related to their recovery, must be consid-ered to determine whether a contract is feasible to terminate. The

dollar value of usable completed products, piece parts and raw material anticipated to be returned to the Navy are subtracted from the
dollar value of the contract withheld by a manufacturer to determine
termination fees. Termination fees are requested for the total termination quantity as well as the manufacturer's suggested optimal
termination quantity. (The manufacturer may have completed or nearly
completed a portion of the contract quantity.)

Details of the input data to the model are described in the next
section of this paper.

Multiple Termination Quantities

The model processes more than one termination quantity (total
and manufacturer's suggested) for a single contract and recommends
the more feasible solution. The model requests whether more than one
termination quantity is to be evaluated. The item manager enters the
multiple termination quantities, dollar values and contractor fees.
Other standard information is entered only once.

Multiple Contracts

The model determines the feasibility of terminating two contracts for the same item and compares the results to terminating only
the most recently awarded contract. The model requests whether more
than one contract is to be evaluated. The item manager enters termination quantities, dollar values and contractor fees and contract
award dates separately for both contracts. When more than two contracts are in long supply for the same item, the assumption is made
that any contract awarded before the two most recent is not feasible
to terminate.

Multiple Contracts and Multiple Termination Quantities for the Same Contract

To process multiple termination quantities for one or two of the
contracts, the item manager enters the termination quantity, dollar

value and contractor fees and processes the model again. The item
manager can determine the most feasible solution by choosing the
termination quantity producing the largest net savings from the
various runs.

Partial Termination Estimation

The model evaluates a partial termination when just one termination quantity is entered for a single contract and no termination is
recommended. The model processes the contract using 50 percent of
the original input termination quantity, dollar value and contractor
fees.

Model Processing Data Collection

Percentage of termination fees and percentage of elapsed production lead time provided by the PC model are saved on an item-by-item
basis, whether the contract is recommended for termination or not.
The X-Y scatterplot of the two statistics shown below allows NAVSUP
cost analysts to predict termination fees for future termination
candidates at the time SDR recommends termination.

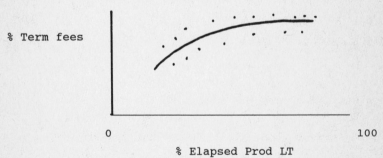

% Term fees

0   100

% Elapsed Prod LT

The following statistics are saved for analysis:
(1) The total number, dollar value and quantities (and average
     dollar value and quantity per contract) for contracts which
     are processed by the model:
     (a) those identified for termination
     (b) those terminated (net savings provided by the termina-
         tion model are also presented for this category)

    (c)   estimated contractor termination fees

    (d)   contractor provided termination fee estimates

    (e)   actual contractor termination fees obtained

(2)   The average percentage of termination fees and percentage elapsed production lead time for all items processed through the PC model. This data is provided by the PC model on an item basis to the supply cost analysis component of the overall system.

(3)   The statistics described above are also segmented into the following dollar value categories:

$0 - $5,000

$5,000 - $10,000

$10,000 - $25,000

$25,000 - $50,000

$50,000 - $100,000

$100,000 - $500,000

$500,000 - $1,000,000

greater than $1,000,000

(4)   The PC model provides the projected date of next procurement for items recommended for termination. This information is saved on an item basis and will be used to help identify items which had contracts terminated and were reprocured sooner than anticipated.

3. TERMINATION PROCESSING MODEL

This section presents the detailed benefit-cost equation model to determine whether a contract qualifies for termination. The model is based on the standard benefit-cost analysis practice of comparing projected cost savings (benefits) against the dollar costs associated with early termination of contracts. Expert judgment of NAVSUP Headquarters cost analysts in carrying out this comparison and determining net savings from an early termination is represented in the model approach and encoded in the implementing computer program. The format of the termination equation (and as contained in the program) allows for precise intermediate results for the purpose of analysis after the model executes. The termination equation is presented below:

BENEFITS (SAVINGS)   VS   COSTS

$$(I)(DR)(HP_I) + (S)(DQ_T)(HP_S) + (O)(DQ_T)(HP_O)$$

$$vs \quad DCTF + DADM + (F) \; MIN \begin{Bmatrix} DQ_T \\ DQ \end{Bmatrix} (HP_F)$$

Where

I = interest rate (.10); this default value implies a cost of money to the Navy of 10 %

S = storage rate (.01); this value assumes a storage and storage loss cost rate of 1 %

O = Obsolescence rate (.10); this default value implies the life expectancy of the item is 10 years from the time of processing (1/.10 = 10)

F = inflation rate (.04)

DQ_T = total dollar value of termination quantity

$DCTF$ = contractor termination fees

DR = dollars and dollar value of material returned to Navy after termination

$DADM$ = administrative cost to award and terminate a contract ($2,000)

DQ = dollar value economic order quantity

HP = holding period for the horizon identified by subscript

HP_I = T_{RL} + ALT/4

HP_S = T_{RL} + (PDLT$_E$ + ALT)/4

HP_F = T_{RL} + (PDLT$_E$ + ALT)/4

    Where

        T_{rl} = time to reach reorder level after termination

        ALT = administrative lead time

      $PDLT_e$ = elapsed production lead time (difference between current and contract award julian dates in quarters)

$$T_{RL} = \cfrac{[OH_A + (OH_F)SR + DI] - [RL + PPR_S + BO + DO] - Q_T}{\cfrac{4(D - R) + 4(PPR_S)}{PCLT}}$$

    Where

        OH_A = on hand ready for issue (RFI) assets

        OH_F = on hand non RFI assets

        SR = survival rate

$$DI = \text{due in assets}$$
$$RL = \text{reorder level}$$
$$PPR_S = \text{planned program requirements}$$
$$D = \text{quarterly demand forecast}$$
$$R = \text{quarterly regenerations forecast}$$
$$BO = \text{backorders}$$
$$DO = \text{due out}$$
$$O_T = \text{termination quantity}$$
$$PCLT = \text{procurement lead time}$$
$$\frac{DCTF}{DQ_T} = \%\text{ termination fees}$$
$$\frac{PDLT_E}{PDLT} = \%\text{ elapsed production lead time}$$

In the detailed termination equation, obsolescence rate is set at .10 to be more uniform with other cost analysis equations and inflation costs are included as a cost to terminate. Since it is anticipated that material that is terminated today will be reprocured in the future, inflation costs are computed over the time to reach the reorder level. When the time to reach the reorder level exceeds 20 years, inflation costs are excluded from the equation because the item will become obsolete before it is reprocured.

When HP_F is greater than 20, the inflation rate factor (F) in the termination equation is set to zero. When determining the feasibility of terminating both contracts, the termination quantities, dollar values and fees are summed individually and used as input when processing both contracts. When determining the feasibility of terminating the most recent contract, only the termination quantity, dollar value, contractor fee and contract award date corresponding to the more recent contract are entered as input to the model. The contract with the greater contract award date is considered the more recent of the two contracts.

The partial termination quantity computed as 50 percent of the original termination quantity is rounded down to the nearest whole number, and must be greater than zero to process for termination. When the denominator of the T_{RL} equation calculates to zero, T_{RL} is set equal to 99. Otherwise division by zero would result and the T_{RL} value would be infinite, implying an infinite amount of time to reach the item reorder level. The assumption is made in the model that 99 years is a reasonable maximum value for time to reach reorder level. Hence, the T_{RL} value is constrained to a maximum of 99.

Net savings are calculated in the system by subtracting the right side of the termination equation from the left side. When the model calculates a negative or zero net savings, the model recommendation is to not terminate the contract. When the model calculates a positive net savings, the model recommendation is to terminate the contract. When evaluating multiple contracts or termination quantities, the termination producing the greater net savings is the final recommendation of the model. The corresponding quantity resulting in the greater net savings is then provided as output. The final net savings result is further constrained to be less than or equal to the dollar value of the termination quantity.

The TERMINATOR model can be installed onto any IBM PC-compatible microcomputer (such as the Navy's Zenith PCs) with a fixed (hard) disk and at least one floppy disk drive. RAM requirements are a full 640K configuration. The cost analysis display feature requires a minimal color graphics display adapter (CGA) capability. In short, the system is designed to be easily used at Navy sites all over the world with little or no hardware changes.

4. DEVELOPING AND TESTING THE SYSTEM

The TERMINATOR system was developed under a rapid turnaround effort beginning in April 1988. The termination processing policy and procedures had previously been developed and reviewed by all appropriate elements with NAVSUP and other relevant Navy offices. Thus, following formal establishment in February, it was desired to move ahead very rapidly with an operational computer system for early implementation.

A rapid prototype development process was utilized, with a first working version of TERMINATOR available in early May 1988. Following limited trial testing, several enhancements, modifications, and a few corrections, were made and an operational system version was completed by early June. This version was then provided to a number of Navy contract item managers in Philadelphia and Mechanicsburg, PA for full field testing. The fielded version was found to be acceptable and of considerable assistance in supporting contract termination processing actions. Field user comments and suggestions for further improvement, primarily in the form of ease-of-use conveniences, were received in July and incorporated into the system during August. A final operational version of the TERMINATOR system was released to contract item managers in October 1988.

5. FURTHER DETAILS OF SYSTEM OPERATION

At the beginning of system processing, the model provides a menu requesting the item manager to select which type of termination is to be processed: (1) single contract single termination quantity, (2) single contract multiple termination quantities, and (3) two contracts for a single item. The holding cost rates and DADM are not available to the item managers to change, but the values are provided from an external system parameter file. A processing options switch is provided to allow $HP_O = T_{RL}$ and $HP_O = T_{RL} + (PDLT_e + ALT)/4$. The default value as shown in the detailed equation is $HP_O = T_{RL} + PDLT_e/4$. This switch is also hidden from the item manager.

Once the system completes processing, the program requests whether the user wants to selectively change a few input parameters, process a different termination candidate or end program processing. This allows the user to correct a few input parameters without entering all data elements again. This also provides the user with the capability to evaluate multiple termination quantities for multiple contracts. When a new termination candidate is entered, all previous input values are removed from the input screen.

Finally, the model provides the following data on the display screen and as a hard copy output listing:

    (1) user input parameter values
    (2) parameter constants
    (3) model recommendation
    (4) termination quantity
    (5) termination quantity dollar value
    (6) contractor termination fees
    (7) net savings
    (8) % termination fees
    (9) % elapsed production lead time
    (10) projected julian date of next buy after termination;
         current julian date + T_{RL} (years)
    (11) interim results for the termination and T_{RL} equations

The input data elements entered by the item manager users are as follows:

a. total dollar value of termination quantity

b. termination quantity

c. termination fees

d. administrative lead time

e. production lead time

f. procurement lead time

g. contract award date (julian)

h. current julian date

i. on hand RFI assets

j. on hand NRFI assets

k. due in assets (including long supply material)

l. survival rate

m. reorder level

n. total PPRs over procurement lead time

o. dollar value economic order quantity

p. backorders

q. due out

r. quarterly demand forecast quantity

s. quarterly regenerations forecast quantity

t. contract number

6. THE PAYOFF

As described above, NAVSUP developed and implemented the TERMINATOR system in order to support the evaluation of decisions in supply contract termination actions. The system, which cost about $15,000, may have paid for itself during the first month of use. The leverage and high payoff in this application arises from the large number of users who operate this system in their daily work activities. Over four hundred contract item managers across the United States are currently employing this decision support system tool in considering recommendations for termination. Each potential termination action may be evaluated in minutes (20-30) using the system compared to hours (3-4) with the previous manual procedure, providing a five fold increase in personal productivity. Annual cost avoidance is 13-15 staff years, based on a level of 10,000 actions per year. (Time savings and volume level estimates were provided by NAVSUP

Headquarters Cost Analysts based on field experience at Navy East Coast installations through January 1989.) The system further serves to enhance consistency and standardization of procedural practices across the large and diverse body of users.

7. THE FUTURE

The main point of this paper has been to show one example of how microcomputers can be used to provide useful, and valuable, support for decision-making purposes in organizations. We have described a system that embodies several characteristics that will be typical of applications in large volume sensitive organizations. First, as a successful Decision Support System, TERMINATOR shows promise of allowing key managerial issues to be considered more efficiently and at lower unit cost. Second, TERMINATOR has many of the characteristics of Expert System design, permitting major modules of expertise to be integrated as required. But the major benefit of TERMINATOR would seem to be the incorporation of contemporary management support capability in the most common work station now found in large organizations -- the multifunction Personal Computer.

Benefit-cost analytic models are but one managerial tool which may be readily fielded with today's PC hardware. Today's microcomputers are quite capable of delivering advanced decision support systems in many areas of organization activity. The TERMINATOR system is providing high personal productivity to its users. The contract item managers employ the system in considering recommendations for termination. The system also enhances consistency and standardization of procedural practices for a large number of users. Finally, the TERMINATOR system provides requisite documentation of processing results in both hard copy and electronic form. The documentation supports subsequent processing actions and provides data for later studies by Navy cost analysts.

HELLFIRE MISSILE COMPETITION CASE STUDY

Bruce M. Miller
Institute for Defense Analyses
1801 N. Beauregard Street
Alexandria, Virginia 22311

This case study is part of a larger effort by the Institute for Defense Analyses to document procurement histories of 19 new and modified tactical munition programs. The case studies do not advocate competition or any other acquisition initiative, but rather they highlight the successes and failures of various systems in order to document lessons learned.

A recent article in the *Washington Post* business section [1] stated that the days of compeititon at the Pentagon seemed numbered in the face of tight budgets. Establishing a second source usually requires the government to make a substantial investment before the start of competition. The Hellfire missile provides an example where a second source of production was established at no apparent cost to the government.

The "shift and rotate" theory, wherein the introduction of a second source produces a shift downward and a steepening of the cost improvement curve, has had numerous proponents. The recurring hardware price curve of the Hellfire missile, however, does not exhibit this behavior. The net effect of the dual-source capitalization strategy and pressures of competition appear to have cancelled each other out. The result to the government has been a smooth price-reduction curve and no large initial investment by the government at the start of competition.

PROGRAM DESCRIPTION

Hellfire is an air-to-ground missile system designed to defeat individual hardpoint targets and to minimize exposure of the delivery vehicle to enemy fire. The missile is being produced by Rockwell International Corporation and Martin Marietta Corporation for both the Army and the Marine Corps. Hellfire uses semiactive laser terminal homing guidance and is designed to accept various other guidance packages. Hellfire can be employed in a wide variety of modes, including autonomous, ground remote, airborne remote, direct or indirect fire, and rapid or ripple fire.

Mission

The AGM-114A version of the missile is employed as the primary antiarmor weapon system of the Army's AH-64 Apache attack helicopter. The AH-64 will normally carry four launchers with a total payload of 16 missiles. The AGM-114B version of the missile is employed by the Marines on modified AH-1 helicopters. Targets are acquired by a target acquisition/detection system on the helicopter or through designation provided by the Ground Laser Locator Designator. In addition, Hellfire is a candidate for a surface-to-surface role in the close combat antiarmor mission.

History

The Hellfire program began advanced development in 1972. Rockwell International and Hughes Aircraft competed to develop a modular missile, launcher, and control and display systems. In 1974, Rockwell won a development contract for a tri-service laser seeker and was selected in 1976 to enter into Hellfire full scale development (FSD). Martin Marietta, in 1977, submitted an unsolicited proposal for a low-cost alternative seeker that had been developed privately. The Army then initiated a seeker competition between Rockwell and Martin Marietta, which was Martin Marietta won in 1977.

An ASARC III review was held in November 1981 and Hellfire was approved for production in March 1982 after OSD decided that a DSARC review was not needed. The Army was delegated authority for full-rate production.

Table 1 presents a summary of the Hellfire development costs and schedule. Approximately 10 years elapsed between milestone II and the initial operational capability (IOC). The program schedule slipped by about two years during FSD. Schedule changes resulted from reductions in RDT&E funding, delays in procurement funding, and delays in testing caused by late delivery of hardware and correction of deficiencies revealed in earlier tests. The completion of production validation testing was delayed six months because of problems that occurred in production start-up. The current estimate for IOC was changed to July 1986 to reflect the actual date the missile achieved IOC on the AH-64.

FSD cost measured in constant FY 1975 dollars increased from the milestone II estimate of $210.3 million to $230.2 million, an increase of only 9.5 percent. However, the number of test articles was also reduced from 241 to 229 during FSD.

The total production quantity for the Army increased from 24,600 missiles to 48,696. Total program cost increased in constant FY 1975 dollars from $508.2 million to $1,017.1 million. Figure 1 shows the estimated program size and the estimated program average unit cost (PAUC) by year since 1976. A revised cost estimate provided the basis for the 1980 increase in the PAUC. The revision in the baseline cost was due to higher estimates for production hardware, an allowance for schedule slippage, and a revision in the estimating methodology applied to the missile flyaway cost estimate.

At the time of the development estimate (6/76), a first-unit cost of $215,300 with a cost improvement curve slope of 82.1 percent were anticipated. Experience from the first six years of production indicates an estimated first-unit cost of $1,310,500 with a slope of 75.0 percent.

If the original quantity of 24,600 missiles was produced at the costs being experienced, total program cost would be $708.8 million, as indicated in column 3 of Table 1, representing a 38.9 percent increase over the development estimate.

Table 1. Hellfire Program Data Summary

Program: Hellfire	Service: Army
Equipment: Missile, Launcher	New/Modification: New
Year Dollars: 1975	

Milestone	Development Estimate (6/76)	Current Estimate (12/87)	Current Estimate for Development Estimate Quantity
Milestone II[a]	2/76	2/76	2/76
Development Start Date	12/72	12/72	12/72
Development End Date (IOC)	5/83	7/86	7/86
Development Quantity	241	229	229
Development Cost	$210.3M	$230.2M	$230.2M
Milestone III	11/81	3/82	3/82
Production Start Date	4/80	3/82	3/82
Production Quantity	24,600	48.696	24,600
Unit One Cost	$215.3K	$1,310.5K	$1,310.5K
Slope of Cost-Quantity Curve	82.1	75.0	75.0
Production Cost	$297.9M	$786.9M	$478.6M
Total Program Cost	$508.2M	$1,017.1M	$708.8M

Years of Actual Data
Development   Completed
Production   6

[a]Milestone 0 occurred during 12/72. There was no milesone I, and the program completed milestone II during 1/76.

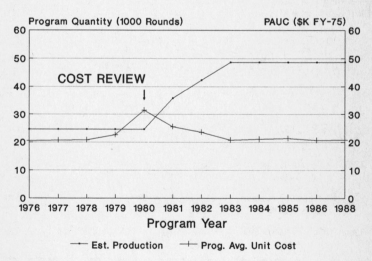

Figure 1. Hellfire Program Quantity and Average Unit Cost

Initial production contracts were awarded in FY 1982 to Rockwell for missile buses and to Martin Marietta for seekers. A revised acquisition plan approved in December 1982 called for an alternative dual-source competitive strategy. Each contractor would produce a limited number of all-up rounds for certification in 1983. Head-to-head competition began in 1984. Each of the two contractors was guaranteed a minimum of 40 percent in FY 1984 and 25 percent thereafter through the FY 1988 acquisition.

Tables 2 and 3 show Hellfire missile production data and contract prices, respectively. Figure 2 graphically displays the total annual production rates and the rate by individual contractor. Martin Marietta and Rockwell International have alternated in obtaining the larger contract award since the start of head-to-head competition. The weighted average unit cost in then-year dollars decreased through the FY 1986 buy, but increased with the latest procurement. The cost in constant dollars decreased each year.

Table 2. Hellfire Missile Production

	1982	1983	1984[a]	1985	1986	1988
Rockwell International						
Missiles	680	2,077				
All-Up Rounds		947	2,771	1,803	5,478	1,598
Martin Marietta						
Seekers	762	2,137				
All-Up Rounds		947	2,095	4,415	1,826	4,680

Note:Quantities reflect totals for Army and Navy procurement. Data provided by the Department of the Army, SARD-KAS.
[a]First year of head-to-head competition.

Table 3. Hellfire Unit Prices

Fiscal Year	Contractor	Units	Unit Price	Weighted Average	1975 Dollars
1984	Rockwell International	2,771	$40.9K	42.9	$17.6K
	Martin Marietta	2,095	$45.5K		
1985	Rockwell International	1,803	$38.7K	33.1	$13.1K
	Martin Marietta	4,415	$30.8K		
1986	Rockwell International	5,478	$23.8K	26.5	$10.2K
	Martin Marietta	1,826	$34.7K		
1988[a]	Rockwell International	1,598	$34.0K	28.0	$10.1K
	Martin Marietta	4,680	$26.0K		

[a]No contracts were awarded in 1987. Both contractors were behind in deliveries, and plant loading did not decline due to elimination of a year's procurement.

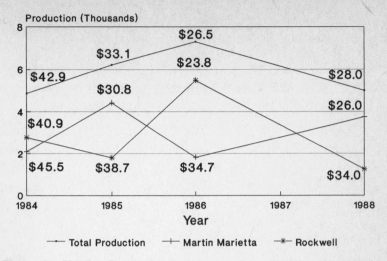

Figure 2. Hellfire Production and Lot Average Cost by Contractor

Acquisition Strategy

In establishing dual-source competition for all-up rounds (AURs), the Hellfire Project Office (HPO) executed memoranda of agreement (MOAs) with each of the contractors. An MOA was also reached between the contractors to confirm their mutual undertaking to transfer technology. The reasons for pursuing dual-source production given by the HPO were:

1. To be able to contract for support by two separate contractors for various activities, including verification of flight missions and investigation of flight accidents.

2. To obtain competition throughout the Hellfire laser missile program.

3. To obtain the ability to expand production facilities rapidly to meet industrial mobilization needs.

4. To have geographical dispersion of the manufacturing sources to ensure redundancy and survivability in the event of natural disasters.

Program Initiatives

Table 4 lists the acquisition initiatives showing those that have been applied to the Hellfire program.

Competition Process

A technology transfer plan was established that delineated the data and knowledge that would be delivered by each contractor to the other. During the technology transfer phase, the contractors were required to deliver a minimum of seven AURs plus six missile buses from Martin Marietta and six seekers from Rockwell at various subassembly levels specified in the technology transfer plan.

Table 4. Hellfire Acquisition Initiatives

Initiative	Yes	No	Date Applied	Reference
Competition in Advanced Devel.	X			
System	X		1972	12/79 SAR
Subsystem				
Prototype	X		1972	12/79 SAR
Competitive Prototype	X		1972	12/79 SAR
Design-to-Cost	X			12/79 SAR
Should-Cost Analysis		X		
Competition in FSD	X			
System		X		
Subsystem	X		1977	Seeker competition
Foreign Production		X		
Foreign Military Sales		X		
Independent Cost Estimate	X		1980	12/80 SAR
Multiyear Procurement		X		
Total Package Procurement		X		
DSARCs or DABs	X		1976	DSARC II
Delegated DSARCs or DABs	X		1981	DSARC III
Independent Testing		X		
Streamlining		X		
Modification to Existing System		X		
Competition in Production	X		1982	12/82 SAR
System	X			
Subsystem	X			Rocket motors
Other Competition		X		
Warranty		X		
System				
Subsystem				
Contract Type–Development				
CPFF		X		
CPAF		X		
CPIF	X		1976	12/79 SAR
FFP		X		
FPI		X		
Other		X		
Contract Type–Production				
CPFF		X		
CPAF		X		
CPIF		X	1980	
FFP	X		1984	12/86 SAR
FPI	X		1982	12/84 SAR
Other		X		
Cancelled Program		X		

Note:Blanks in both the "Yes" and "No" columns indicate that information was unavailable.

The contractors established special collection accounts for the following costs:

1. Purchase of required data/assistance from the other contractor and training of personnel.

2. Costs to review specifications, purposes, manufacturing methods, inspection and test procedures, and peculiar requirements by engineering, manufacturing, tooling, and quality assurance to confirm and develop procedures.

3. Costs of computer effort, travel, and other direct costs related to technology transfer.

4. Any costs described in numbers 1-3 above assocated with providing the seven AURs and six sets of subassemblies described in the technology transfer plan.

The contractors were allowed to recover up to $5,000,000 of these costs over the first 6,000 missiles purchased from the contractor. If these costs were included in the proposal, they would also be included in the competitive evaluation.

Costs for AUR production facilities in excess of costs for facilities required to achieve Hellfire production rates of 190 per month (on the basis of a 40-hour, 5-day work week) were segregated into the following categories:

1. Special tooling and test equipment.

2. Programming, proofing, and certification of numerical control and special test equipment.

3. Planning, including descriptive planning and setup sheets.

4. Manufacturing engineering, tool administration, manufacturing research and technology, measurements and controls, industrial engineering, and production control.

5. Manufacturing aids and process plans/sheets.

6. Plant/facilities rearrangement and other costs required to achieve the production capacity specified in the MOA.

The costs were to be collected in an assets account plus full overhead and general administrative (G&A) expenses. For the period FY 1984 through FY 1988, these costs could be liquidated on a five-year, straight-line basis. Should the contractor elect to exclude these costs from its proposal in any applicable year, the government liability would be liquidated to the extent it would have been had the contractor included such costs in the proposal. If the costs were included in the proposal, they would also be included in the competitive evaluation.

Split Award Criteria[1]

The contractors' proposals were to contain per unit prices for a range of quantities from 1,125 through 4,500 missiles. Prices were to be presented so that unit prices for any given quantity fell on a single continuous logarithmic price line from 1,125 to 4500 units. Unit prices were to include recovery

---

[1] The material in this section is based upon the FY 1988 Request for Proposals.

cost of production facilitization, technology transfer cost, and special cost of money. To measure the degree of competition among the contractors, the proposals were evaluated in the following manner:

(1) The proposed total prices were calculated from the unit price at 25, 50, and 75 percent of the contemplated award quantity.

(2) The proposed total prices were adjusted for evaluation purposes by the appropriate charges for use of government-furnished property and transportation to obtain an adjusted contractor price (ACP).

(3) To the adjusted price, a formula was applied for comparison of the offeror's proposal. This formula provided an average adjusted contractor proposal (AACP). The formula encompassed the price calculations at three percentage points:

$$AACP = ACP_{25} + ACP_{50} + ACP_{75}$$

(4) A second formula incorporating the AACP was applied to determine the delta between the two offers. Using the lowest AACP as a base, a percentage difference ($\Delta\%$) between the two offers was calculated as follows:

$$\Delta \% = \frac{(\text{Highest ACCP} - \text{Lowest AACP})}{\text{Lowest AACP}} \times 100$$

The $\Delta\%$ was then used to determine the award split from the following matrix:

Percentage Difference	Percentage of Award	
	Lowest AACP	Highest AACP
0–.5%	50	50
>.5–1.0%	55	45
>1.–2.0%	60	40
>2.–4.0%	70	30
>4.–6.0%	71	29
>6.–10.0%	72	28
>8.–10.0%	73	27
Greater than 10%	75	25

The matrix was used to determine the respective award percentage and the resulting award quantities for each offeror. If the matrix determined a 75/25 split, the government reserved the right to award the 75-percent quantity and further negotiate for the 25-percent quantity. If the methodology did not result in reasonable prices, the government would negotiate with one or both contractors.

SYSTEM TECHNICAL DESCRIPTION

The Hellfire semiactive laser guidance system offers both remote and autonomous modes of employment. In the remote mode, the target is illuminated by a Ground (or airborne) Laser Locator Designator (GLLD), allowing the attack helicopter to remain behind cover, and the missile locks onto the target after following a pre-selected trajectory. The target acquisition and designation sight (TADS), also built by Martin Marietta, provides the AH-64 helicopter with an autonomous mode of employment.

The missile also has two launch modes, rapid fire and ripple fire. The rapid-fire mode employs a single laser designator, which illuminates the targets in succession as the missiles are launched at intervals of several seconds. The ripple-fire mode uses two or more laser designators and is faster – up to 16 missiles launched per minute. The designators are coded to different missiles. The laser-guided Hellfire employs two designation modes: LOAL (lock on after launch) and LOBL (lock on before launch).

Elements/Subsystems

Hellfire is approximately five and one-half feet long, weights 99 pounds, and has a 20-pound warhead. It employs a semiactive laser seeker and has a range of about 4 miles. The major sections with the relative proportions of their costs include the seeker (46%), guidance and control (37%), warhead (7%), and rocket motor (10%).

The seeker comprises a two-axis gyro-stabilized platform, a detector/pre-amplifier assembly, dome processing electronics, and an impact sensor. The optical lens provides protection for the internal components and allows transmission of target-reflected laser energy to the detector/pre-amplifier subassembly, which generates error signals to indicate the angular error between the target and detector line-of-sight relative to the detector plane. An electronics assembly processes the sensor information and generates control signals.

Other modular seekers considered for Hellfire have included a defense suppression missile seeker and an imaging infrared and millimeter wave seeker. None of the alternative seekers have entered into production.

The guidance section of the missile consists of a pneumatic accumulator, yaw/roll gyro, pitch gyro, battery, and auto-pilot electronics. Also, development work on a minimum smoke motor has been completed. This will significantly reduce the detectability of the missile after launch.

Performance/Technical Characteristics

Hellfire satisfies all its mission requirements except missile weight. Weight reduction from the current nominal weight of 99.8 pounds to the required 95 pounds is not considered feasible without degrading system performance.

Testing

The 229 missile quantity includes 14 modified Hornet missiles procured and tested in the advanced development phase plus 215 missiles for engineering development. A total of 169 missiles were flight tested during the Hellfire and AH-64 engineering development programs. The remaining 46 missiles are spares for development testing/operational testing (DT/OT), environmental storage tests, Advanced Attack Helicopter (AAH) Battlefield observation tests, minimum smoke motor tests, and Marine Corps testing.

PROGRAM COST/SCHEDULE ASSESSMENT

Cost/Schedule Estimates

Table 5 summarizes information from the initial program SAR and subsequent December SARs. Comparison of the estimates indicates the magnitude and timing of changes in the program.

Table 5. Hellfire Program Estimates

	6/76 SAR	12/76 SAR	12/77 SAR	12/78 SAR	12/79 SAR
Schedule Estimates					
Program Initiated (Milestone 0)	12/72	12/72			
Milestone I	N/A	N/A			
Milestone II	2/76	2/76			
Award FSD Contracts	10/76	10/76			
Milestone III	2/80	2/80	4/80	4/80	10/80
Milestone IIIA	10/81	10/81	1/82	1/82	N/A[a]
Award Pilot Production Contracts	4/80	4/80	10/80	10/80	11/81
Award Full-Scale Prod. Contracts	1/82	1/82	3/82	3/82	N/A
IOC	5/83	5/83	11/83	11/83	10/84
Cost Estimates (Thousands of Dollars)					
Development	$210.3	$221.5	$219.3	$220.6	$230.0
Procurement	297.9	297.9	296.3	296.3	332.9
Construction					
Total Base-Year Dollars (1975)	508.2	519.4	515.5	516.9	562.9
Escalation					
Development	$55.9	$61.2	$62.6	$66.3	$80.0
Procurement	171.0	190.2	225.1	231.1	343.9
Construction					
Total Then-Year Dollars	735.1	770.8	803.2	814.3	986.8
Quantity Estimates					
Development	241	241	241	229	229
Procurement	24,600	24,600	24,600	24,600	24,600
PAUC (Thousands of 1975 Dollars)	$20.46	$20.91	$20.74	$20.82	$22.67

[a] Deleted because of changes in acquisition strategy.

Table 5. Hellfire Program Estimates (Continued)

	12/80 SAR	12/81 SAR	12/82 SAR	12/83 SAR	12/84 SAR
Schedule Estimates					
Program Initiated (Milestone 0)					
Milestone I					
Milestone II					
Award FSD Contracts					
Milestone III	12/81	3/82	3/82	3/82	3/82
Milestone IIIA	N/A	N/A	N/A	N/A	N/A
Award Pilot Production Contracts	12/81	3/82	3/82	3/82	3/82
Award Full-Scale Prod. Contracts	N/A	3/82	3/82	3/82	3/82
IOC	1/85	1/85	FY 85	FY 85	4/86
Cost Estimates (Thousands of Dollars)					
Development	$231.0	$238.2	$234.2	$240.1	$244.8
Procurement	551.7	684.2	766.5	775.5	786.9
Construction			3.4	2.0	9.0
Total Base-Year Dollars (1975)	782.7	922.4	1,004.1	1,017.6	1,032.8
Escalation					
Development	$89.3	$99.5	$94.9	$95.7	$105.0
Procurement	781.4	1,025.7	1,128.7	1,341.4	1,417.1
Construction			3.8	2.3	1.1
Total Then-Year Dollars	1,653.4	2,047.6	2,231.5	2,457.0	2,555.8
Quantity Estimates					
Development	229	229	229	229	229
Procurement	24,600	35,756	42,332	48,698	48,698
PAUC (Thousands of 1975 Dollars)	$31.52	$25.63	$23.59	$20.80	$21.11

Table 5. Hellfire Program Estimates (Continued)

	12/85 SAR	12/86 SAR	12/87 SAR
Schedule Estimates			
Program Initiated (Milestone 0)			
Milestone I			
Milestone II			
Award FSD Contracts			
Milestone III	3/82	3/82	
Milestone IIIA	N/A	N/A	
Award Pilot Production Contracts	3/82	3/82	
Award Full-Scale Prod. Contracts	3/82	3/82	
IOC	8/86	7/86	7/86
Cost Estimates (Thousands of Dollars)			
Development	$230.3	$230.2	$230.2
Procurement	815.6	783.5	786.9
Construction	0.9	0.0	0.0
Total Base-Year Dollars (1975)	1,046.8	1,013.7	1,017.1
Escalation			
Development	$87.3	$87.0	$87.0
Procurement	1,419.1	1,306.9	1,316.6
Construction	1.1	0.0	0.0
Total Then-Year Dollars	2,554.3	2,407.6	2.420.7
Quantity Estimates			
Development	229	229	229
Procurement	48,696	48,696	48,696
PAUC (Thousands of 1975 Dollars)	$21.40	$20.72	$20.79

Program Funding

Table 6 shows the program funding for procurement as contained in the Presidential Budget for the years indicated. Comparison of the data across columns indicates the stability of the program as the planning years become the budget year estimate. Since the program reached its current size, first indicated in the December 1983 SAR, there has been only one stretchout of three years. The impact of the stretchout on the PAUC listed in Table 5 appears to be minimal.

Cost-Quantity Relationships

Figure 3 presents three price improvement curves from the Hellfire program. (The curves illustrate changes in unit price as paid by the government.) The prices included in the plots are total procurement prices (recurring and nonrecurring) taken from SARs and DCPs.

The development estimate curve represents the estimate of the program as of the milestone II review in 1976 with a first-unit price of $215,000 and a slope of 82 percent. The production estimate is from the milestone III review and the "actuals" curve represents data taken from the December 1987 SAR.

The actuals show a lower T_1 than the production estimate ($1.150 million vs. $1.311 million), and the slopes are almost parallel. The slope of the actuals is 75 percent, somewhat steeper than the development estimate slope of 82 percent.

Figure 4 is a unit price improvement curve for recurring hardware costs contained in the December 1987 SAR. Price improvement through the first six production lots is characterized by a 79.5-percent slope. The R^2 of .998 for the curve indicates extremely small variance of the plot points around the fitted regression line. There is no evidence of a significant shift or rotation of the price improvement curve starting with the introduction of competition in FY1984.

LESSONS LEARNED

Threat/Requirements/Technology

The technology to build the semiactive-laser-seeking Hellfire was available at the time of development. There were numerous other laser programs, such as Copperhead and IIR Maverick, being developed at approximately the same time.

One of the original objectives of Hellfire was to build a variety of seekers that would use a common missile bus. The technology to produce a fire-and-forget Hellfire has not yet come to fruition. Until that capability is developed, Hellfire will be limited operationally in that a helicopter that employs its organic laser designator is at considerable risk while the missile is tracking towards its target.

Table 6. Hellfire Procurement Funding

Funding (Millions of FYDP Dollars) and Quantities

Fiscal Year	6/76 $	6/76 #	12/77 $	12/77 #	12/78 $	12/78 #	12/79 $	12/79 #	12/80 $	12/80 #	12/81 $	12/81 #	12/82 $	12/82 #	12/83 $	12/83 #	12/84 $	12/84 #	12/85 $	12/85 #	12/86 $	12/86 #	12/87 $	12/87 #
80	27.0	375	14.7	-*		-*																		
81	28.6	1,050	16.3	-*	27.7	-*	20.8	-	21.0	-	27.7	-	25.7						23.1	-	22.6	-		
82	108.3	5,225	83.5	-*	85.0	-*	126.0	2,760	96.5	502	114.4	2,760	119.7	680					109.3	680	113.1	-		
83	117.2	6,000	125.4	-*	128.0	-*	160.7	6,074	120.7	1,213	267.5	6,074	247.4	3,971	218.6	4,651			241.7	3,971	247.1	-		
84	106.4	6,000	126.3	-*	128.0	-*	159.1	6,242	135.3	1,785	275.5	6,242	240.7	5,351	237.5	-	216.7		218.6	-	218.5	-		
85	107.8	5,950	119.5	-*	121.5	-*	136.0	6,414	239.5	5,183	246.6	6,414	238.0	6,026	241.9	-	225.0	5,342	225.3	5,780	224.5	-		
86			35.7	-*	36.4	-*	74.2	3,110	263.5	6,227	270.9	3,110	245.6	6,576	238.0	-	250.7	-	225.9	5,750	215.0	6,000	204.4	-
87	.5								253.5		255.9		243.1	6,576	239.4	-	249.7	-	0	0	.1	0	-	0
88									203.1		246.6		254.3	6,576	251.5	6,758	254.0	-	192.9	4,800	168.9	5,000	168.4	5,000
89													263.5	6,576	280.0	6,882	268.5	-	192.4	4,800	146.9	4,000	180.5	5,000
90																	223.5	5,000	189.7	4,800	180.4	5,000	180.6	5,000
91																			286.9	5,000	209.7	5,000	210.8	5,000
92																			191.0	5,000	297.3	5,000	207.6	5,000
93																			134.9	3,464	136.3	3,614	118.5	2,614

*No data available.

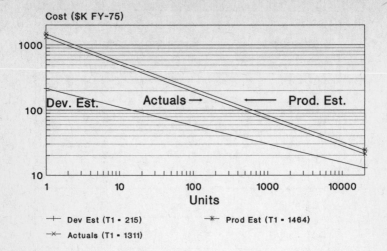

Figure 3. Hellfire Cumulative Average Price Curves

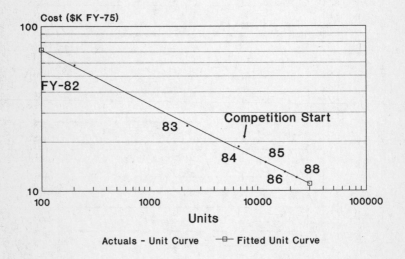

Figure 4. Hellfire Recurring Hardware Price Curve

Acquisition Policy

The acquisition policy employed by the Hellfire program office appears to have been highly successful. Two prime contractors have been developed that are capable of providing fully assembled missiles. The cost to establish these capabilities through the second source development process was initially borne by the contractors. Although the technology transfer and initial production facilitization costs have been repaid, they appear to have been offset by the pressures of competition. The net result is that dual-source competition was established with no apparent cost to the government. With both manufacturers now able to produce individually the Army's near-term annual requirements, the government is now in a position to adopt a new acquisition strategy of a winner-take-all, multiyear-buyout competition between the two prime contractors.

SUMMARY

The prominent characteristic of the Hellfire missile acquisition program has been competition. Competitive prototyping was employed during advanced development and additional seeker competition was introduced during full-scale development. Head-to-head, dual-source competition was initiated after the first two years of production. When formulating its acquisition strategy, the Army stated that its objectives included obtaining competition, expanding the production base for mobilization, and providing for geographical dispersion to ensure redundancy in the event of natural disasters.

Research conducted in support of this case study indicates that the Army's objectives were not fully met. While there has been some degree of geographical dispersion achieved for the prime contractors, there are several major components that are still made by a single second-tier vendor. This may change to some degree in the future if a second source is used for procurement of the rocket motor. Regarding competition, the price performance does not exhibit a shift or rotation in the price improvement curve. Cost experience during competition did not deviate from forecasts of cost progress for a program without competition. In this regard, DoD did develop a second source at no increase in cost.

How does the performance of Hellfire compare with other ordnance systems being developed during the same timeframe? How successful was the Hellfire program in meeting the original objective stated in the competition Memorandum of Agreement (MOA)? Two contractors are now producing all-up rounds, but to what degree is there true redundancy? The MOA did not state a savings goal for competition. What has been the financial impact of competition? The answers to these questions are addressed in the sections that follow.

Program Performance

The Hellfire case study is part of a larger study involving analyses of tactical munitions procurement. Table 7 displays several summary parameters for Hellfire and compares them to the averages for 10 new development tactical munitions that comprise the study population. The Hellfire parameters are computed from the schedule and cost data presented in Table 1.

Table 7. Hellfire Summary Parameters

	Hellfire	Population Average
Development Cost Growth	1.09	1.27
Production Cost Growth[a]	1.61	1.72
Development Schedule Growth	1.44	1.38
Production Schedule Growth	3.38	1.70
Production Quantity Change[b]	1.98	.97
Development Quantity Change	.95	.84
Total Program Cost Growth[a]	1.39	1.44

[a]Based upon current estimate of the cost of the program quantity contained in the development estimate.
[b]Based upon the increase from the development estimate quantity to the current quantity estimate.

Industrial Base Expansion

After five years of head-to-head competition, several major components (warhead, body, gyros, and rocket motor) are still supplied by a single vendor. Martin Marietta attempted to qualify a second source, Hercules, to compete with Morton Thiokol, the original rocket motor producer. Threatened by the competition, Morton Thiokol reduced its prices to the point where anticipated future savings from competition were not sufficient to offset the development and qualification expense associated with certifying Hercules as a second producer. There are some indications that Hercules may be awarded some portion of the FY 1989 procurement of rocket motors. Martin Marietta has been successful in qualifying a second source for production of the missile control section.

The objectives of expanding the industrial base for mobilization and establishing geographical redundancy in location of the manufacturers of Hellfire have been only partially achieved. A more detailed study is required to determine the degree to which the common second-tier vendors could expand production to meet the needs of the two prime contractors producing at capacity.

Effects of Competition

It is obvious that the unit price of Hellfire has been reduced over the years. However, it is very difficult to isolate the effects of competition from the expected price reduction associated with cost improvement curve theory. The slope of the unit recurring price curve is approximately 80 percent. This is not either unusually high or low. There is no evidence of a shift or rotation at the initiation of competition.

The manner in which the government formulated the acquisition strategy wherein the contractors financed the costs of developing the dual-source capability may have counterbalanced any shift in the price curve. The contractors were almost "dared" by the government to recapture their expenses over the first several procurements under the head-to-head competition. If the contractors added these expenses to their bids, then the lower price due to competition would be masked to some degree.

In any event, the competition in the Hellfire program has demonstrated that a second source can be added to the program with no apparent additional cost to the government.

During the second year of competition, Martin Marietta won the larger portion of the split award. (See Tables 3 and 4 for quantities and prices.) Martin Marietta had reduced its price by over 30 percent from the previous year. In the third year of competition, Rockwell made a 39-percent reduction and regained the larger award. Such reductions cannot be attributed to the effect of the price improvement curve by itself. Apparently, management decisions were made to obtain the larger portions of the award by dramatically reducing prices. It is interesting to note that in each year following such a large price reduction, the contractor raised its price for the next year. This see-saw effect appears to cancel out over time, so, from the government's perspective, the price improvement in the program has held very closely to a smooth price reduction curve.

REFERENCE

[1] Sugawara, Sandra. "A Winning Strategy In Defense-Cost War," *The Washington Post*, February 12, 1989, p. H-1.

STRATEGIES FOR RELIABILITY INCENTIVE CONTRACTING

Irwin Greenberg
Department of Operations Research and Applied Statistics
George Mason University, Fairfax, VA 22030-4444, USA

INTRODUCTION

An _incentive_ is a payment or set of payments offered by one party to a contract to the other party in exchange for receiving better performance than has been contracted for. For example, consider a customer who has negotiated a contract to obtain a product of some specified reliability to be delivered at a stated time. An incentive payment might be offered to the producer if a more reliable product is provided and/or if delivery is made early. The improved reliability would have to be demonstrated by subjecting the delivered product to a more rigorous inspection than might be called for in the original contract. The decision problem for the customer is the determination of what constitutes the optimum incentive. The decision problem for the producer is whether or not to improve the performance and if so, to what level?

Flehinger and Miller [1] treated the reliability incentive problem postulating that each party " ... seeks that agreement that will maximize his own expected profit. However, each is willing to accept an agreement which maximizes the profit of the other, for any given profit to himself." Their methodology generates a set of "admissible strategies" such that the sum of the benefits to both sides is maximized subject to the constraints that both sides have positive benefits. A more realistic approach would be to assume that once the customer specifies the incentive plan, the producer will take that course of action that maximizes his or her expected gain. The customer prepares for this by choosing the incentive plan that maximizes his or her gain in light of the producer's anticipated actions.

These two philosophies mirror the differences in approach that have been suggested to treat the problem of what quantity discounts a contractor should offer to a purchaser to encourage the latter to place larger orders. A discount for large purchases can be considered to be an incentive payment to the purchaser to provide better performance (from the contractor's point of view), that is, to allow longer, and hence, fewer production runs to reduce the set-up costs. Goyal

[2] treated this problem by maximizing the sum of the benefits, an approach that is nearly identical to the "admissible strategies" method. It was pointed out that this approach would have particular pertinence if the purchaser and contractor were both units of the same organization. Monahan [3] adopted the point of view that each side will attempt to maximize its own benefit while recognizing that the other side will do the same.

FORMULATION

The general incentive problem can be formulated as follows: one of the two parties to a fixed price contract (in the reliability problem it will be the customer) will offer or suggest the incentive to the other party (the producer) who will consider his or her response. The offer will involve some number n of the specifications in the contract which the customer would like to see improved; they will be denoted by the vector $S = |S(1),S(2),...,S(n)|$. If the values in the delivered product are improved to $s = |s(1),s(2),...,s(n)|$ the customer would benefit by an amount $V(s)$, representing the dollar value of the increased utility due to the improvements. The cost to the producer of achieving this improvement is $K(s)$ and this is known to the customer. One or more of the improvements might be observable without error such as a delivery earlier than had been contracted for. Other improvements (such as increased reliability) may have to be inferred from a test. As will be explained in the next paragraph, the latter situation is more general than the the former and includes the former as a special case. Thus, the general formulation will be in terms of demonstrating the achievement of a particular value of s(i) by means of a random variable which takes on the value x(i). Let x be the multivariate random vector $x = |x(1),x(2),...,x(n)|$.

The tests are specified by a set of m test parameters $R = \{r(1), r(2),...,r(m)\}$. For example, if the first of the specifications is "mean time to failure," the test could involve placing $r(1)$ units on test for time $r(2)$. If the number of failures, $x(1)$, is less than or equal to some specified value $r(3)$, the improved reliability will be considered to have been demonstrated. Define the multivariate cumulative distribution function (CDF) $F(x|s,R)$, the probability that the n test variables take on values less than or equal to $x = |x(1),x(2),...,x(n)|$ given the set R of test parameters and that the specifications of the delivered product is s. $F_i(x(i)|s,R)$ is the marginal CDF, the probability that the ith test result is less than or equal to x(i), and $f_i(x(i)|\underline{s},\underline{R})$ is the associated probability density or probability frequency function. For those specifications which are observable without error rather than being inferred from tests, the subset of $\underline{R}$ associated with each of their values is empty and $f_i(x(i)|\underline{s},\underline{R})$ is the delta function: $\text{Prob}\{x(i) = s(i)\} = 1$.

The incentive schedule $\underline{I}$ provides an incentive payment $A_i(x(i))$ if the realization of the test for the ith specification is $x(i)$. More precisely, the test outcomes are subdivided into mutually exclusive and exhaustive sets $X_j(i)$ and

$$A_i(x(i)) = a_j(i) \text{ if } x(i) \in X_j(i) \tag{1}$$

where $a_j(i)$ is the amount of the incentive payment if $x(i)$ is in the set $X_j(i)$. In the reliability life test mentioned in the preceding paragraph equation (1) becomes

$$\begin{aligned} A_1(x(1)) &= D \text{ if } x(1) = 0, 1, \ldots, r(3) \\ &= 0 \text{ if } x(1) = r(3)+1, r(3)+2, \ldots, r(1) \end{aligned}$$

and provides an incentive payment of $a_1(1) = D$ if $r(3)$ or fewer failures occur during the test (that is, if $X_1(1) = \{x(1)\leq r(3)\}$). It provides no payment $(a_2(1) = 0)$ if $r(3)+1$ or more failures occur (that is, if $X_2(1) = \{x(1)>r(3)\}$). In general,

$$\underline{I} = \{a_j(i), X_j(i)\} \text{ for } i=1,2,\ldots,n$$

and j running through the number of sets into which the $x(i)$ could fall.

The total incentive payment for the outcomes $\underline{x}$ is

$$A(\underline{x}) = \Sigma_i A_i(x(i))$$

and the expected total incentive payment can be expressed in Stieltjes notation

$$E\{A(\underline{x})|\underline{s},\underline{I},\underline{R}\} = \Sigma_i \Sigma_j \int_{X_j(i)} a_j(i) \, dF_i(x(i)|\underline{s},\underline{R})$$

which implies that $f_i(x(i)|\underline{s},\underline{R})dx(i)$ is integrated over continuous portions of $X_j(i)$ and $f_i(x(i)|\underline{s},\underline{R})$ is summed over discrete portions of $X_j(i)$. Note that if specification i does not require testing its contribution to $E\{A(\underline{x})|\underline{s},\underline{I},\underline{R}\}$ is $a_j(i)$ where $X_j(i) = s(i)$, the incentive payment for the accomplishment of $s(i)$.

The cost of the test for specification i is $T(i)$ (zero for those specifications not requiring tests) of which some fraction $h(i)$ is borne by the customer. Thus, the producer pays $[1-h(i)]T(i)$ and assumes a producer's risk of achieving a specification value $s(i)$ but receiving less than the earned incentive because of the probabilistic nature of the test outcomes. The customer pays $h(i)T(i)$ and faces a consumer's risk of making a higher incentive payment although $s(i)$ has not been achieved.

The expected gain realized by the customer if the final specification vector is $\underline{s}$ is

$$C(\underline{s}|\underline{I},\underline{R}) = V(\underline{s}) - E\{A(\underline{x})|\underline{s},\underline{I},\underline{R}\} - \Sigma_i \, h(i)T(i) \qquad (2)$$

and the expected gain to the producer is

$$P(\underline{s}|\underline{I},\underline{R}) = E\{A(\underline{x})|\underline{s},\underline{I},\underline{R}\} - K(\underline{s}) - \Sigma_i \, [1-h(i)]T(i). \qquad (3)$$

The mathematical problem can be stated as follows:

maximize$_{\underline{s}}$ $P(\underline{s}|\underline{I},\underline{R})$

subject to $P(\underline{s}|\underline{I},\underline{R}) \geq \max[0, \, P(\underline{S}|\underline{I},\underline{R})]$. $\qquad (4)$

Solution is $\underline{s}*$, a function of $\underline{I}$ and $\underline{R}$.

maximize$_{\underline{I},\underline{R}}$ $C(\underline{s}*|\underline{I},\underline{R})$

subject to $C(\underline{s}*|\underline{I},\underline{R}) \geq 0$.

Solution is $\underline{I}*,\underline{R}*$.

In this formulation the customer specifies the incentive schedule $\underline{I}$ and the test parameters $\underline{R}$. The producer would determine the values of $s(i)$ that maximize $P(\underline{s}|\underline{I},\underline{R})$ subject to $P(\underline{s}|\underline{I},\underline{R})>0$. That is, he or she would solve for

$\underline{s} = \underline{s}*$ such that $P(\underline{s}*|\underline{I},\underline{R}) = \max P(\underline{s}|\underline{I},\underline{R})$

provided that the resulting $P(\underline{s}|\underline{I},\underline{R})$ is neither less than zero nor the expected gain if no change is made: $P(\underline{S}|\underline{I},\underline{R})$. If no such $\underline{s}*$ exists, the original contract specification vector $\underline{S}$ is delivered and no incentive payment is made.

This optimum $\underline{s}*$ is a function of $\underline{I}$ and $\underline{R}$. The customer chooses optimum $\underline{I}*$ and $\underline{R}*$ to obtain the maximum gain in anticipation of the producer's action; that is, he or she chooses

$\underline{I} = \underline{I}*, \; \underline{R} = \underline{R}*$ such that $C(\underline{s}*|\underline{I}*,\underline{R}*) = \max C(\underline{s}*|\underline{I},\underline{R})$

provided that the resulting $C(\underline{s}*|\underline{I}*,\underline{R}*)$ is non-negative. If only negative gains are possible, no incentive should be offered.

The methods used to obtain the maxima will depend upon the structure of the problem. The general procedure is to obtain the mathematical expression for the $\underline{s}$ that maximizes $P(\underline{s}|\underline{I},\underline{R})$, equation (3), subject to the constraint (4) in terms of $\underline{I}$ and $\underline{R}$. This maximizing $\underline{s}$ vector is denoted by $\underline{s}*$. If explicit solutions for the components $s*(i)$ of $\underline{s}*$ are available, these are substituted for the $s(i)$ in equation (2). The vectors $\underline{I}$ and $\underline{R}$ that maximize equation (2) are $\underline{I}*$ and $\underline{R}*$; when substituted into the explicit expressions for the $s*(i)$, the numerical values of the $\underline{s}*$ vector are obtained. If the maximizing vector is obtained implicitly, equation (2) is maximized subject to this implicit solution as a constraint.

For some incentive situations this approach yields a solution for which $C(\underline{s}*|\underline{I}*,\underline{R}*)>0$, $P(\underline{s}*|\underline{I}*,\underline{R}*)=0$, that is, while there is no cost to the producer, there is no expected gain either in bettering the specification to the advantage of the customer. Here, the Flehinger-Miller "admissible strategies" approach might be desirable:

$\qquad$ maximize$_\underline{s}$ $\quad$ $P(\underline{s}|\underline{I},\underline{R}) + C(\underline{s}|\underline{I},\underline{R})$.

$\quad$ Solution is $\underline{s}^o$.

$\qquad$ maximize$_\underline{s}$ $\quad$ $P(\underline{s}|\underline{I},\underline{R})$

$\qquad$ subject to $\quad$ $P(\underline{s}|\underline{I},\underline{R}) \geq \max[0, P(\underline{S}|\underline{I},\underline{R})]$.

$\quad$ Solution is $\underline{s}^*$, a function of $\underline{I}$ and $\underline{R}$.

Any $\underline{I}$ and $\underline{R}$ that satisfy this expression for $\underline{s}^*$ with the numerical values of $\underline{s}^*$ set equal to $\underline{s}^o$ and the constraint $C(\underline{s}^o|\underline{I},\underline{R}) \geq 0$ are admissible.

$\quad$ Here, the sum of the gains,

$$P(\underline{s}|\underline{I},\underline{R}) + C(\underline{s}|\underline{I},\underline{R}) = V(\underline{s}) - K(\underline{s}) - \Sigma_i\, T(i)$$

is maximized. The maximizing vector, $\underline{s}^o$, involves neither $\underline{I}$ nor $\underline{R}$ but consists only of the numerical values of the specifications that maximizes the joint gain. The incentive offer will be accepted if it results in a positive gain for the producer. The producer will maximize equation (3), determining the maximizing vector $\underline{s}^*$ in terms of $\underline{I}$ and $\underline{R}$. Following this maximization, any $\underline{I}$ and $\underline{R}$ that result in non-negative gains to both parties are admissible. The customer chooses one that will give him or herself a satisfactory gain while giving the producer a large enough expected gain to encourage cooperation. This last choice is subjective and cannot be dealt with objectively - a major weakness of this method.

OPTIMUM RELIABILITY INCENTIVES FOR 'REPAIRABLE' SYSTEMS

$\quad$ The repairable system considered by Flehinger and Miller has a single specification, failure rate, that the customer would like to see changed from its specified value $S(1)$ to a new value $s(1) < S(1)$. The customer knows that the producer can do this by spending an amount $K(\underline{s}) = k_1 \log [S(1)/s(1)]$. The value to the customer is proportional to the decrease in the expected number of failures during the total of the times, L, that the systems will be in use: $V(\underline{s}) = k_2 L[S(1)-s(1)]$. The customer proposes that $r(1)$ systems be tested for time $r(2)$ and if the number of failures, $x(1)$, is less than or equal to $r(3)$, an incentive payment of D will be made. The cost of the test is k_3 dollars per system per hour. In terms of the notation introduced earlier,

$\qquad$ $\underline{R} = \{r(1),r(2),r(3)\}$

$\qquad$ $\underline{I} = \{a_1(1)=D,\ X_1(1)=\{x(1)\leq r(3)\};$

$\qquad\qquad$ $a_2(1)=0,\ X_2(1)=\{x(1)>r(3)\}\}$

$\qquad$ $T(1) = k_3 r(1) r(2)$.

The number of failures in this test plan will have a binomial probability frequency function

$$f_1(x(1)|\underline{s},\underline{R}) = c[r(1),x(1)] \{1-\exp[-s(1)r(2)]\}^{x(1)}$$
$$\cdot \exp\{[-s(1)r(2)][r(1)-x(1)]\}$$

where $c[a,b]$ represents the combinatorial $a!/[b!(a-b)!]$. Also,

$$E\{A(\underline{x})|\underline{s},\underline{I},\underline{R}\} = D[F_1(r(3)|\underline{s},\underline{R})]$$

so that equations (2) and (3) become, respectively,

$$C(\underline{s}|\underline{I},\underline{R}) = k_2L[S(1)-s(1)]-D[F_1(r(3)|\underline{s},\underline{R})]-h(1)k_3r(1)r(2)$$
$$P(\underline{s}|\underline{I},\underline{R}) = D[F_1(r(3)|\underline{s},\underline{R})]-k_1\log[S(1)/s(1)]$$
$$- [1-h(1)]k_3r(1)r(2).$$

Flehinger and Miller have shown that the optimum test program is that $r(1) = 1$ system will be tested for time $r(2)$ and the incentive payment will be made if there are $r(3) = 0$ failures. Hence,

$$C(\underline{s}|\underline{I},\underline{R}) = k_2L[S(1)-s(1)]-D\{\exp[-s(1)r(2)]\}-h(1)k_3r(2)$$
$$P(\underline{s}|\underline{I},\underline{R}) = D\{\exp[-s(1)r(2)]\}-k_1\log[S(1)/s(1)]-[1-h(1)]k_3r(2).$$

For example, if the systems are to be used for a total $L = 10,000$ hours and the specification calls for a failure rate of $S(1) = 0.05$ per hour; assume the proportionality constants take on the values $k_1 = 2500$ and $k_2 = 50$, the test cost is $k_3 = 100$ and the customer pays it all. The expected gains are

$$C(\underline{s}|\underline{I},\underline{R}) = 500,000[0.05-s(1)]-D\{\exp[-s(1)r(2)]\}-100r(2)$$
$$P(\underline{s}|\underline{I},\underline{R}) = D\{\exp[-s(1)r(2)]\}-2500\{\log(0.05)-\log[s(1)]\}.$$

Once the customer specifies the remaining $\underline{R}$ component [the test time $r(2)$] and the remaining $\underline{I}$ component [the incentive payment D], the producer can maximize his or her expected gain by setting the partial derivative of $P(\underline{s}|\underline{I},\underline{R})$ with respect to $s(1)$ equal to zero. This leads to the functional equation that defines the $s*(1)$, the failure rate that maximizes the producer's expected gain:

$$s*(1) = \{2500/[r(2)D]\}\exp[s*(1)r(2)].$$

The values $D*$ and $r*(2)$ of D and $r(2)$ that maximizes $C(\underline{s}|\underline{I},\underline{R})$ subject to this constraint on $s*(1)$ can be obtained: $D* = 8244$, $r*(2) = 50$ so that $s*(1) = 0.01$. The producer should build the system with failure rate 0.01 per hour (MTTF = 100 hours) instead of the 0.05 per hour (MTTF = 20 hours) contracted for. The system test will be for 50 hours and if the test system survives, the customer will pay the producer an incentive payment of \$8244. The expected net gain to the customer is \$10,000 and the expected net gain to the producer is \$976. The producer runs a risk $1-\exp[-r*(2)s*(1)] = 1-\exp(-0.5) = 0.39$ of achieving a failure rate of 0.01 but not passing the test. The customer runs a risk of having an unimproved product with failure rate 0.05 pass the test; the size of this risk is $\exp[-r*(2)S(1)] = \exp(-2.5) = 0.08$.

Because of the positive gains to both, the admissible strategies method is not required here. However, if the method of Flehinger and

Miller is used, the maximum gain that the customer could receive is $8357 with optimum $s^o(1) = 0.005$ failures per hour (MTTF = 200 hours), test duration $r(2) = 70.7$ hours and incentive payment D = $10,070. The resulting expected gain for the producer is $1315. Another admissible strategy, this time with $s^o(1) = 0.005$ per hour, is $r(2) = 25$ hours and D = $22,663. This yields the maximum sum of the expected gains all of which accrues to the producer: $14,244. The admissible strategy that yields equal benefits to each party is to test for $r(2) = 41.5$ hours with an incentive payment of D = $14,832 for surviving. The benefit to each side is $6298.

Assume now that in addition to the reliability incentive a premium payment is offered for early delivery. Call the reliability incentive payment D(1) rather than D. If delivery is made at time $s(2) < S(2)$, where $S(2)$ is the value specified in the contract, an incentive payment of $D(2)[S(2)-s(2)]$ is made. The $\underline{I}$ set is now

$$\underline{I} = \{a_1(1)=D(1), X_1(1)=\{x(1)=0\}; a_2(1)=0, X_2(1)=\{x(1)=1\}$$
$$a_1(2)=D(2)[S(2)-s(2)], X_1(2)=\{s(2)\leq S(2)\}\}.$$

The value to the customer of the early delivery is that the new systems will be on line earlier replacing less reliable systems currently in use. Assume that the current systems are used an average of H hours per day and the failure rate of each system is y. The lower failure rate will be available for an additional $H[S(2)-s(2)]$ hours and thus, the value of early delivery is $k_2H[y-s(1)][S(2)-s(2)]$; hence

$$V(\underline{s}) = k_2L[S(1)-s(1)] + k_2H[y-s(1)][S(2)-s(2)].$$

The cost of achieving failure rate $s(1)$ delivered in $s(2)$ days is assumed to be $\{M+k_1\log[S(1)/s(1)]\}\exp\{b[S(2)-s(2)]/[S(2)-t]\}$ where M is the cost of achieving the specification values of failure rate $S(1)$ delivered in $S(2)$ days, t is the earliest possible delivery time and b is a positive parameter. For a given failure rate $s(1)$ this cost function is increasing at an exponential rate as the delivery date is "crashed" as is often assumed in PERT/CPM calculations. For fixed delivery time $s(2)$ the rate of change of the cost is inversely proportional to the failure rate; the lower the failure rate desired within a given time the greater the rate of increase in the cost. While these properties are intuitively appealing, no claim is made that they will hold in an actual situation - the cost function has been chosen for illustrative purposes only.

The added cost to the producer of making this early delivery at the lower failure rate is

$$K(\underline{s}) = \{M+k_1\log[S(1)/s(1)]\}\exp\{b[S(2)-s(2)]/[S(2)-t]\}-M$$

which corresponds to the $K(\underline{s})$ obtained earlier when $s(2) = S(2)$. This leads to

$$C(\underline{s}|\underline{I},\underline{R}) = k_2L[S(1)-s(1)]+k_2H[y-s(1)][S(2)-s(2)]$$
$$-D(1)\{\exp[-s(1)r(2)]\}-D(2)[S(2)-s(2)]-k_3r(2)$$
$$P(\underline{s}|\underline{I},\underline{R}) = D(1)\{\exp[-s(1)r(2)]\}+D(2)[S(2)-s(2)]$$
$$-\{M+k_1\log[S(1)/s(1)]\}\exp\{b[S(2)-s(2)]/[S(2)-t]\}+M.$$

The components of $\underline{s}*$ can be obtained by equating the partial derivatives of $P(\underline{s}|\underline{I},\underline{R})$ to zero. The derivative with respect to s(1) yields

$$s*(2) = \max\{t, \; S(2)-[S(2)-t][\log(D(1)s*(1)r(2)/k_1)$$
$$-s*(1)r(2)]/b\} \qquad (5)$$

as the optimum delivery time for a specified reliability incentive payment D(1) and test time r(2) once the optimum failure rate s*(1) has been determined.

Equating the derivative with respect to s(2) to zero yields the second condition that would have to be met:

$$b\{M+k_1\log[S(1)/s*(1)]\}\exp\{b[S(2)-s*(2)]/[S(2)-t]\}$$
$$-D(2)[S(2)-t] = 0. \qquad (6)$$

The optima D*(1), D*(2) and r*(2) that maximize $C(\underline{s}*|\underline{I},\underline{R})$ subject to equations (5) and (6) and the condition that the resulting $P(\underline{s}*|\underline{I}*,\underline{R}*)$ and $C(\underline{s}*|\underline{I}*,\underline{R}*)$ are both positive can then be obtained.

To illustrate, suppose that the repairable systems described earlier are being purchased to replace systems that are in use an average of H = 10 hours per day and whose failure rates are y = S(1) = 0.05 failures per hour. The contract calls for delivery in S(2) = 400 days. The producer could complete the work and make delivery in as little as t = 150 days. The cost of building and delivering the systems called for in the specifications, failure rate of 0.05 per hour and delivery in 400 days, is M = $25,000. The coefficient b in the cost function is estimated to be 0.25. The customer must choose the values of D(1), D(2) and r(2) to maximize

$$C(\underline{s}*|\underline{I},\underline{R}) = 500s*(1)s*(2)-700000s*(1)-25s*(2)-D(1)\exp[-s*(1)r(2)]$$
$$-400D(2)-100r(2)+D(2)s*(2)+35000$$

subject to

$$s*(2) = \max\{150, \; 400-1000[\log(D(1)s*(1)r(2)/2500)-r(2)s*(1)]\}$$

and

$$\{17511-2500\log[s*(1)]\}\exp[0.4-0.001s*(2)]-1000D(2) = 0.$$

The maximizing values are r*(2) = 58.5 hours of test, incentive payment D*(1) = $10,130 if the system tested does not fail, and incentive payment of D*(2) = $36.47 per day for early delivery. The producer should deliver systems with mean failure rate s*(1) = 0.0094 per hour in s*(2) = 150 days. Note that the optimum failure rate is virtually the same as in the example without the early delivery incentive and the test time is 17% longer. Note also that the daily savings due to early delivery, a failure rate reduction of 0.0406 per hour multiplied by 10 hours of usage per day multiplied by $100 per failure, is $40.60 which is more than the daily incentive payment. This difference is caused by the lower bound of 150 days on delivery time; with this constraint the optimum value of D(2) is equal to the marginal increase in the cost of reducing the delivery from day 151 to 150.

DISCUSSION

One of the key assumptions in this methodology is that both sides will act to maximize their respective gains. Clearly, if the producer does not choose the value for mean time to failure that yields the largest $P(\underline{s}|\underline{I},\underline{R})$ then the customer's gain will not be maximum. The producer might be risk averse and decide not to invest the extra money in light of the not insignificant chance of failing the life test. In the example with the single parameter s(1) = mean time to failure in which the optimum value is s*(1) = 0.01 per hour, the customer's gain is positive as long as s(1) < 0.0375; even this mild improvement in the reliability will bring some expected benefit to the customer in spite of the possibility of paying a $10,000 bonus that was not truly earned by the producer.

A second major assumption is that $K(\underline{s})$, the cost to the producer of achieving the improved specification vector $\underline{s}$ is known to the customer. This does not appear to be a likely occurrence and it may be that this precludes using this model as an optimization tool. The model would still have value in a normative way - even with fairly gross estimates of the cost function some ball park estimates of the sizes of reasonable test parameters and incentive payments should be forthcoming. At the very least, the philosophy of setting an incentive schedule that addresses both the desire of the customer for a better product and the cost to the producer of making the better product could go a long way in satisfying the desires of both parties.

REFERENCES

[1] Flehinger, B.J. and J. Miller, "Incentive Contracts and Price Differential Acceptance Tests," _Journal of the American Statistical Association_, Vol. 59, pp. 149-159, 1964.
[2] Goyal, S.K., "An Integrated Inventory Model for a Single Supplier - Single Customer Problem," _International Journal of Production Research_, Vol. 15, pp. 107-111, 1977.

[3] Monahan, J.P., "A Quantity Discount Pricing Model to Increase Vendor Profits," <u>Management Science</u>, Vol. 30, pp. 720-726, 1984.

II. Cost and Economics

A Stochastic Theory of the Generalized Cobb-Douglas Production Function

John F. Muth[*]

Indiana University

Abstract

Factor substitution relations and returns to scale found in empirical studies of production functions are modeled in a way that is fully integrated with technological change and process innovation. The model is based on the Pareto boundary of random n-tuples, which is a rectangular hyperbola, asymptotic to the axes, whose parameter depends on the amount of sampling (search) activity. Conversion from probability fractiles to natural units of measurement of the factors give the Cobb-Douglas factor substitution relations. The influence of inputs on outputs is somewhat different because an upper bound on output cannot be assumed.

[*]The author is indebted to Robert A. Becker, Abraham Charnes, William W. Cooper, Thomas R. Gulledge Jr., Kenneth Laitinen, Steven A. Lippman, Clarence C. Morrison, Charles Plosser, Marc L. Nerlove, Robert M. Solow, Lester G. Telser, N. Keith Womer, and Louis E. Yelle for their suggestions and comments. However, none necessarily subscribes to any views expressed in this paper. An earlier version was presented at the Winter Meetings of the Econometric Society, San Francisco, December 28-30, 1983.

1. Introduction

Cost phenomena are explained jointly by market and technical transformations. Although various structures leading to the market transformations have been studied, production functions characterizing the technical transformations have seldom been explained in terms of more fundamental concepts. Engineering production functions (Chenery, 1949; Ferguson, 1951; Kurtz & Manne, 1963; and Smith, 1957) might be regarded as exceptions. However, these are not very satisfactory as explanations, because they are based on empirical laws, such as Boyle's Law, rather than theories, such as the Kinetic Theory of Gases.

The costs of contract production are affected by economies of scale, of planned total volume, and of experience (Alchian, 1959). Only the output rate is incorporated in the generally accepted theory of the firm. When the last two are considered at all, they are often confused with one another. Economies of total volume usually arise from investment in tooling and other equipment, the degree of which depends on the size of the contract. Such economies are realized as fully by the first item produced as the last. Economies of experience, on the other hand, result from improved methods and skill as knowledge is acquired during production activity. Economies of experience for the last item exceed those of the first.

Economies of experience recently have had a role in explaining certain phenomena in contract production. Womer (1984) and Womer & Terasawa (forthcoming) used a generalization of the Cobb-Douglas production function:

$$y = K \ Y^\gamma \ L^\alpha \ C^\beta \tag{1}$$

where y is the output rate, Y the amount of cumulative output, L the rate of use of labor services, C is the rate of use of capital services, and K, α, ß, and γ are constants.

The object of this paper is to show how Equation 1 may be derived from more fundamental considerations, namely search activity under uncertainty within a space of technological possibilities. The theory is based upon hypotheses about decisions that are made about potential technologies and relies on unrestricted random search in a space having a very simple structure, utilizing certain ideas from the statistical theory of extreme values. The resulting Pareto boundary of random n-tuples is a rectangular hyperbola, asymptotic to the axes, whose parameter depends on the amount of sampling (search) activity.

Conversion from probability fractiles to natural units of measurement of the factors gives the Cobb-Douglas factor substitution relations. The influence of inputs on outputs is somewhat different because an upper bound on output is rather unlikely. When such a bound does not exist, two cases are identified: the Cauchy (*i. e.*, Pareto) and the exponential limits. The former, with independence, leads to the Cobb-Douglas production function.

The remainder of the paper consists of four parts. Section 2 reviews certain aspects of the statistical theory of extreme values and its application to the manufacturing progress function. Section 3 examines factor substitution in terms of a generalization of the expected extreme of a univariate distribution function. Section 4 discusses returns to scale in terms of a minimaximization problem, one case leading to the Cobb-Douglas production function. Section 5 finally presents some conclusions of the paper.

2. Search and Experience

The problem of finding efficient combinations of the factors of production for a specified rate of output is discussed first. This is a vector minimization problem whose solution gives the isoquants of the production function. Random sampling from a space having a very simple structure leads to isoquants of the production function proposed by Cobb and Douglas (1928).

This section utilizes the statistical theory of sample extremes, which originated in the work of Tippett (1925), Fréchet (1927), Fisher and Tippett (1928), and von Mises (1936). It has long been applied to models of certain physical phenomena. An early use explained the size effect in the strength of materials (Weibull, 1939). Other areas include the analysis of data involving floods, droughts, extreme duration of human life, and radioactivity (see Gumbel, 1958). The theory of extremes plays only a minor role in economic models. However, Telser (1982) incorporated certain extreme-value relations for innovation and its effects. It was used by Muth (1986b) to explain the manufacturing progress function (also called the learning, or experience, curve).

A fundamental hypothesis of this paper is:

H1. *Factor combinations for a given output are determined by independent random sampling in a sample space of technological alternatives.*

Unrestricted random sampling is probably an extreme assumption: other search strategies may be adopted as well and have been compared by Muth (1986a). It is as hard to justify as the usual assumptions about the production possibility set, such as closure, convexity, free disposal and boundedness.

> H2. *The best factor combinations (in a vector minimization sense) are immediately retained when they are found.*

The options in general may be evaluated according to a number of criteria, namely the amounts of each of the factors of production. Immediate adoption rules out any consideration of investment effects and performance uncertainty, which generally confront real innovations. (Work under way by Dongwook Shin and the author is concerned with the effects of investment outlays on time lags in adoption of new techniques.)

Let U_n be the minimum observation in a sample of size n from an infinite population uniformly distributed in the unit interval. Its expected value is

$$EU_n = n \int_0^1 u(1-u)^{n-1} du = nB(2,n) = 1/(n+1) \tag{2}$$

where $B(m,n)$ is the complete Beta function. The quantity above is sometimes called the expected extreme despite the fact that it is the expected extreme fractile. The expected mean-square is

$$EU_n^2 = n \int_0^1 u^2(1-u)^{n-1} du = nB(3,n) = 2/(n+1)(n+2) \tag{3}$$

Hence the variance of the extreme is

$$Var \ U_n = n/(n+1)^2(n+2) \tag{4}$$

Tchebysheff's inequality gives:

$$\text{Plim } |U_n - 1/(n+1)| = 0 \tag{5}$$
$$n \to 0$$

Convergence is quite rapid because the variance, from Equation 4, is $O(n^{-2})$.

Simulated sample minima drawn from the uniform distribution over the unit interval are plotted in Figure 1 together with their

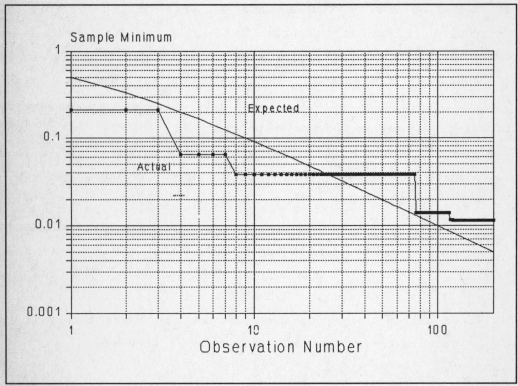

Figure 1. Successive Sample Minima Drawn from the Uniform Distribution.

expected values, which are given by Equation 2. The sample minima are plotted on a logarithmic scale, together with the log of the expected value

Let $v = n\,F(x)$. Then the distribution of v converges in the mean (and hence in probability) to the exponential form:

$$H(v) = 1 - exp(-v) \tag{6}$$

(See Gnedenko, 1948, or Galambos, 1978.) The result can be written, somewhat inaccurately, as:

$$G(x) = 1 - exp[-nF(x)] \tag{7}$$

H3. *The joint distribution function of the factors of production required to achieve a given output rate has a lower bound of zero, which is approached according to some power of $x\text{-}x^{o}$. That is*

$$\lim_{x \to x^{o}} F(x)/(x\text{-}x^{o})^{k} = c, \tag{8}$$

a constant. The lower bound is assumed to be zero $(x^{o}=0)$.

This hyothesis come very close to assuming the answer. Muth (1988) has shown how information guiding search activity can lead to the same effect even when $k = 1$. The assumption of derivatives at the origin also rules out certain distributions, such as the lognormal.

H4. *The factors of production required for a given rate of output are distributed independently of one another.*

This would seem to rule out substitution among the factors, but it does not because the boundary of the set of efficient combinations is the object of interest, not a regression line through the center.

The exponent k indicates the degree of tangency of the distribution function as its argument approaches its lower limit. The curve for certain values of k is drawn in Figure 2. From Equations 7 and 8 such distributions possess the limit:

$$G(x) = 1 - exp\{-[(cn)^{1/k}(x-x^o)]^k\} \qquad (9)$$

Thus the variable $t = (cn)^{1/k}(x-x^o)$ has the Weibull distribution. Its mean value is

$$\mu_x = x^o + \Gamma(1+1/k)(cn)^{-1/k} \qquad (10)$$

The expected fractile of the Weibull distribution approximates the mean value. Let ξ be the expected extreme, defined by the relation:

$$F(\xi) = EF(x) \qquad (11)$$

Then, from Equation 2,

$$F(\xi) = 1/(n+1) \qquad (12)$$

For x close to x^o, $F(x)$ may be approximated, according to Equation 8, by $c(x-x^o)^k$. For the uniform distribution the expected probability point of the minimum is $1/(n+1)$, an expression which may be replaced by $1/n$ for large n. Hence the expected extreme is

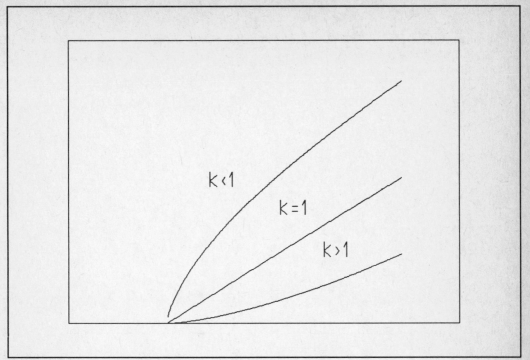

Figure 2. Approaches toward Lower Limit.

given by $c(\xi-x^o)^k = 1/n$. Solving for ξ gives:

$$\xi = x^o + (cn)^{-1/k} \tag{13}$$

3. Factor Substitution

Figure 3 shows pairs of independent, uniformly distributed variables over the unit interval. Such a scatter diagram does not look very interesting, but a plot of the logarithms of the variables suggests that something more can be said about the expected boundary of the points. (See Figure 4.) The Pareto boundaries of point for samples of size 10, 100, and 1000 are given in Figure 5. Let the allowable factor combinations be described by a r-dimensional vector $x = (x_1, x_2, \ldots, x_r)$, whose cumulative distribution function is $F(x)$.

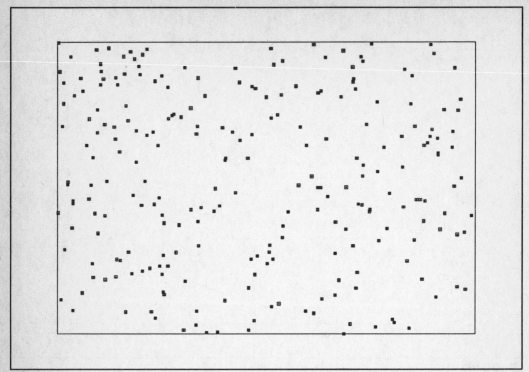

Figure 3. Pairs of Independent, Uniformly Distributed Variates over the Unit Interval.

Equation 2 still applies when the argument of $F(x)$ is an r-dimensional vector. Consequently, the relation $F(\xi) = 1/(n+1)$ (Equation 13) still applies if $\xi = \{\xi_1, \xi_2, \ldots, \xi_r\}$ is defined by $F(\xi) = EF(x)$ (as in Equation 12).

The four hypotheses, including that of independence, are shown below to imply a constant elasticity of substitution of unity. The independence hypothesis, H4, implies:

$$F(\xi) = \prod_{i=1}^{r} H_i(\xi_i) \tag{14}$$

The power function approach to the lower bound $x^o = 0$ according to H3 gives:

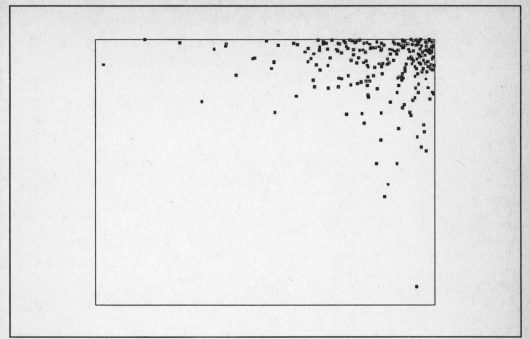

Figure 4.   Logarithms of Pairs of Independent, Uniformly Distributed Variates over the Unit Interval.

$$H_i(\xi_i) = K(\xi_i - \xi_i^o)^{k_i} = K\xi_i^{k_i} \qquad (15)$$

Substituting Equations 15 and 14 into 2 leads to the main conclusion of this section:

C1. *The factor combinations required to produce a given*
(mix of) output after sampling n possibilities is
characterized by:

$$\prod_{i=1}^{r} \xi_i^{k_i} = K/(n+1) \qquad (16)$$

where n is an integer and K is some constant.

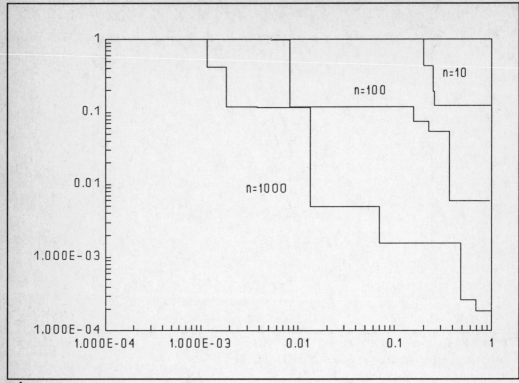

Figure 5. Pareto Boundaries for Samples of Various Sizes.

This evidently gives, after a specified amount of search, the trade-offs allowed by the Cobb-Douglas production function.

When the variates are not independent, analogous results maybe expected even though they can not be described so simply. Figure 6 gives the Pareto boundary for 1000 pairs of normally distributed variates with correlation ratios of 0.5, 0, and -0.5.

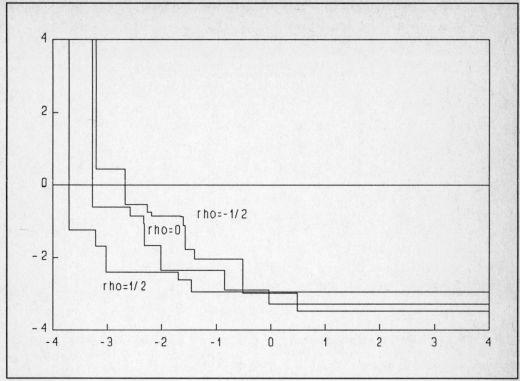

Figure 6. Pareto Boundary of Normally Distributed Variates.

4. Returns to Scale

Output possibilities can now be integrated with those of the factors of production. The joint distribution of inputs, x, and output, y, is F(x,y), which refers to the left-hand tail for x and the right-hand tail for y. There is no maximum output rate.

The tradeoffs after a given amount of search is the solution of:

$$F(\xi, \eta) = 1/(n+1) \tag{17}$$

for ξ. The joint distribution of inputs and output is the product of the conditional and marginal distributions:

$$F(\xi,\eta) = G(\xi|\eta)[1 - H(\eta)] \qquad (18)$$

Its expected value, according to Equation 17, is $1/(n+1)$, so that:

$$G(\xi,\eta) = 1/(n+1)[1 - H(\eta)] \qquad (19)$$

It is now assumed that:

H5. *The distribution of output given the quantities of the factors is independent of the inputs.*

The assumption of independence contained in H5 is, as is the distribution of factor inputs, very strong. Nevertheless it leads to commonly observed production relations and might serve as a basis for further generalizations of production functions. Under this assumption, the conditional distribution $G(\xi|\eta)$ is equal to the marginal, $G(\xi)$. Consequently, we draw the following conclusion:

C3. *The production function has the form:*

$$\eta = H^{-1}[1-1/(n+1)G(\xi)]$$

$$= H^{-1}[1-K/(n+1) \prod_{i=1}^{r} \xi_i^{k_i}] \qquad (20)$$

provided the inverse function exists.

Note that H^{-1} is monotonically increasing wherever it exists.

It is not reasonable to assume that the outputs are bounded, so somewhat different limiting distributions may be involved. This hypothesis is suggested:

H6. *The distribution of output given the quantities of the factors is unbounded.*

Distributions without a finite bound on the values of the variates have either the Cauchy limit or the exponential limit. We consider the case of the Cauchy limit:

H7. *The distribution of output given the quantities of the factors has the limiting form:*

$$1 - H(\eta) = K\eta^{-k}, \qquad \eta > 0 \tag{21}$$

Substitution into Equation 20 gives:

C4. *With the Cauchy-Pareto distribution of outputs, the production function is:*

$$\eta = K[(n+1)G(\xi)]^{1/k} = K(n+1)^{1/k} \prod_{i=1}^{r} \xi_i^{k_i/k} \tag{22}$$

where n is an integer.

This, of course, is the Cobb-Douglas production function, except for the factor involving the number of observations. Related functions have been used by Lele and O'Leary (1972) and Mansfield (1965) when incorporating R and D expenditures in a production function. Their versions are not quite legitimate production functions because the expenditure is not necessarily an index of real R and D activity. It was also used by Womer (1979).

An additional hypothesis is needed to relate search activity to the remaining variables in the system. Consider

H8. *Search (i. e. sampling) activity is associated with output of the good or service:*

$$n = K\,Y \tag{23}$$

where Y is the cumulative output.

This is reasonable for individual learning of a manufacturing task and other activity, but is not necessarily so for organizational learning, *i. e.* improved methods and technologies. For the latter, improvements may be associated with batches of production (Hirsch, 1952) or with investment in new capital goods (Arrow, 1962).

Substituting into the Cobb-Douglas production function, Equation 22, gives the differential equation for large *n*:

$$y = dY/dt = KY^{1/k}X \tag{24}$$

where

$$X = \prod_{i=1}^{r} \xi_i^{k_i/k} \tag{25}$$

is also a function of t. Taking $Y(0) = 0$, Equation 24 may be solved to yield:

$$y = K \left(\int_0^t X \, d\tau\right)^{1/(k-1)} X, \qquad k > 1 \qquad (26)$$

Interactions of this sort have been further studied by Rosen (1972), who particularly emphasized growth, and by Womer (1979).

5. Conclusions

This paper describes a theory explaining some factor substitution relations and returns to scale found in empirical studies of production functions in such a way that technological change and process innovation are fully integrated with it. The theory rests on hypotheses about decisions that are made about potential technologies and relies on unrestricted random search in a space having a very simple structure, utilizing certain ideas from the statistical theory of extreme values. The resulting Pareto boundary of random n-tuples is a rectangular hyperbola, asymptotic to the axes, whose parameter depends on the amount of sampling (search) activity.

Conversion from probability fractiles to natural units of measurement of the factors gives the Cobb-Douglas factor substitution relations. The influence of inputs on outputs is somewhat different because an upper bound on output is rather unlikely. When such a bound does not exist, the Cauchy (i. e. Pareto) limit, with independence, leads to the generalized Cobb-Douglas production function.

The characteristics of the production function do not seem to be very sensitive to the properties of the technology space. A large class of distributions leads to the same parametric family of production functions (the Cobb-Douglas). The results are apparently not as sensitive to the technology space as to the search strategy. (A comparison of the effectiveness of several kinds of search strategies may be found in Muth, 1986a.)

Related theories also explain the manufacturing progress function and the distribution of lags in the adoption of new technology (Muth, 1986, 1982). It is not the only one, however. Other that have been proposed for the progress function include those of Crossman (1959), Levy (1965), Sahal (1979), Roberts (1983), and Venezia (1985). Numerous models have also been used for lags in the adoption of new technology. Most of these emphasize information transfer and influence processes, but others are based on profitability differences, competitive structure, uncertainty resolution, and search. (See Evenson & Kislev, 1975, and Kamien & Schwartz, 1982.) The search model outlined here constitutes a unified theory of production functions, manufacturing progress functions and lags in the adoption of new technology.

An additional feature of the theory is its stochastic nature. Hence it may be possible to derive theories of estimation and hypothesis testing from it. Deterministic models, of course, require *ad hoc* stochastic assumptions.

References

Alchian, A. A. (1959), "Costs and Outputs," M. Abramovitz *et al.* (Eds.), *The Allocation of Economic Resources*, Stanford University Press, pp. 23-40.

Arrow, K. J. (1962) "The Economic Implications of Learning by Doing," *Review of Economic Studies 29*, pp. 155-173.

Chenery, H. B. (1949), "Engineering Production Functions," *Quarterly Journal of Economics 63*, pp. 507-531.

Cobb, C. W., and P. H. Douglas (1928), "A Theory of Production," *American Economic Review 18 (Supplement)*, pp.139-165.

Crossman, E. R. F. W. (1959), "A Theory of the Acquisition of Speed Skill," *Ergonomics 2*, pp. 153-166.

Evenson, R. E., and Y. Kislev (1975), "A Stochastic Model of Applied Research," *Journal of Political Economy 84*, pp. 265-281.

Ferguson, A. R. (1951), "An Airline Production Function" (Abstract), *Econometrica 19*, pp. 57-58.

Fisher, R. A., and L. H. C. Tippett (1928), "Limiting Forms of the Frequency Distribution of the Largest or Smallest Member of a Sample," *Proceedings of the Cambridge Philosophical Society 24*, pp. 180-190.

Fréchet, M. (1927), "Sur la Loi de Probabilité de l'Écart Maximum," *Annales de la Societe Polonaise de Mathematiques 6*, pp. 93-116.

Galambos, J. (1978), *The Asymptotic Theory of Extreme Order Statistics*, Wiley.

Gnedenko, B. (1943), "Sur la Distribution Limite du Terme Maximum d'une Serie Aleatoire," *Annals of Mathematics 44*, pp.423-453.

Gumbel, E. J. (1958), *Statistics of Extremes*, Columbia University Press.

Hirsch, Werner Z. (1952), "Manufacturing Progress Functions," *Review of Economics and Statistics 34*, pp. 143-155.

Kamien, Morton I., and Nancy L. Schwartz (1982), *Market Structure and Innovation*, Cambridge University Press.

Kurz, M., and A. S. Manne (1963), "Engineering Estimates of Capital-Labor Substitution in Metal Machinery," *American Economic Review 53*, pp. 662-681.

Lele, P. T., and J. W. O'Leary (1972), "Applications of Production Functions in Management Decisions," *American Institute of Industrial Engineers Transactions 4*, pp. 36-42.

Levy, F. K. (1965), "Adaptation in the Production Process," *Management Science 11(B)*, pp. 136-154.

Mansfield, Edwin (1965), "Rates of Return from Industrial Research and Development," *American Economic Review 55 (Supplement)*, pp. 310-322.

Misès, R. de (1936), "La Distribution de la Plus Grande de *n* Valeurs," *Revue Mathematique de l'Union Interbalkanique 1*, pp.141-160.

Muth, John F. (1982), "Process Life Cycles and ExperienceCurves," ORSA/TIMS National Meeting, San Diego, October 25-27.(Indiana University, School of Business, Discussion Paper #199, October 25, 1982.)

_____ (1986a), "Search Strategies for Invention and Productivity Improvement," ORSA/TIMS National Meeting, Atlanta, November 4-6, 1985. (Indiana University, School of Business, Discussion Paper #306, April 8, 1986.)

_____ (1986b), "Search Theory and the Manufacturing Progress Function," *Management Science 32*, pp. 948-962.

_____ (1988), "A Model of Learning Curves with Restricted Random Sampling." (Indiana University, School of Business, Discussion Paper #391, July 5, 1988.)

Roberts, Peter C. (1983), "A Theory of the Learning Process," *Journal of the Operational Research Society 34*, pp. 71-79.

Rosen, Sherwin (1972): "Learning by Experience as Joint Production," *Quarterly Journal of Economics 86*, pp. 579-594.

Sahal, D. (1979), "A Theory of Progress Functions," *American Institute of Industrial Engineers Transactions 11*, pp. 23-29.

Smith, V. L. (1957), "Engineering Data and Statistical Techniques in Analysis of Production and Technological Change: Fuel Requirements in the Trucking Industry," *Econometrica 25*, pp. 281-301.

Telser, Lester G. (1982), "A Theory of Innovation and Its Effects," *Bell Journal of Economics 13*, pp. 69-92.

Tippett, L. H. C. (1925), "On the Extreme Individuals and the Range of Samples Taken from a Normal Population," *Biometrica 17*, pp. 364-387.

Venezia, Itzhak (1985), "On the Statistical Origins of the Learning Curve," *European Journal of Operational Research 19*, pp. 191-200.

Weibull, E. H. Waloddi (1939), "A Statistical Theory of the Strength of Materials," *Ingeniors Vetenskaps Akademiens Handlingar Nr. 151*.

Womer, N. Keith (1979), "Learning Curves, Production Rate, and Program Costs," *Management Science 25*, pp. 312-319.

_____ (1984), "Estimating Learning Curves from Aggregate Monthly Data," *Management Science 30*, pp. 982-992.

_____ & Katsuaki Terasawa (forthcoming), "The Effect of Defense Program Uncertainty on Cost, Schedule, and Capital Investment," *Journal of Productivity Analysis*.

TURBULENCE, COST ESCALATION AND CAPITAL INTENSITY BIAS IN DEFENSE CONTRACTING

Katsuaki Terasawa, James Quirk, and Keith Womer

U.S. Naval Postgraduate School, California Institute of Technology (Retired), and the University of Mississippi

I. INTRODUCTION

The recent growth of defense expenditures has once more raised public concern about cost overruns on defense contractors. Economists have pointed out that cost overruns are not necessarily bad per se; instead, attention should be directed to the question as to whether the procurement policies of the Department of Defense (DoD) satisfy the criterion of economic efficiency (see Peck and Sherer (1962)). In connection with this, applications of the principal-agent model to defense contracting show that not only do cost plus fixed fee (CPFF) contracts create moral hazard problems, but that in fact so long as contractors are risk averse and perfect monitoring of their activities is not possible, inefficiencies will arise whatever the form of the contract employed in DoD procurement (see Ross (1973), Harris and Raviv (1979), and Weitzman (1980)). It has been suggested that improvements in efficiency might be achieved if contracts more closely resembling Arrow-Debreu contingent claims were employed (see Cummins (1977)), but this raises problems of manipulation of the probabilities of occurrence of the relevant states of the world. Looking at the problem of cost escalation from a completely different point of view, biases might be introduced into cost comparisons and into decision making with respect to risky projects simply because of the methodology by cost estimators (see Quirk and Terasawa (1983)).

In this paper, we examine effects of cost escalation and inefficiency in defense contracting. By turbulence we mean fluctuations over time in product specifications, in delivery schedules, in order quantities, and in other aspects of procurement. In the present paper, we restrict our attention to turbulence with respect to order quantities, but the approach we use can be extended to other forms of turbulence as well. Turbulence in order quantities is introduced into defense contracting because most DoD contracts (the so called "annual" contracts) provide only for tentative time paths of purchase by DoD, time paths that can be changed unilaterally by DoD. Turbulence in order quantities occurs as a result of the Congressional budgeting process, DoD decision making, the cost history of a weapon system, and a myriad of other factors, both random and nonrandom. A portion at least of the turbulence that is observed represents simply a rational response on the part of DoD to new information as it becomes available–a change in the nature of external threats as perceived by DoD, or developments or lack of developments in competing and complementary weapon systems, for example. Uncertainties introduced into the procurement process by the availability of new information may be an inherent part of the acquisition process. If so, this kind of uncertainty is the price for flexibility and there is no ground for arguing that is should be removed from the procurement process by means of guarantees or legislative action. On the other hand, if the turbulence observed in order quantities is due to poor planning or the lack of coordination between DoD and the contractor, reduction of such uncertainties would be a desirable endeavor in a move toward an efficient allocation of resources.

In any case, it is generally believed in DoD that turbulence is a major source of cost escalation in weapon systems, and that reforms in the budgeting process that would permit long term commitments by DoD to definite time paths of procurement levels, could substantially decrease the cost of defense procurement. One way in which reducing turbulence might produce savings is through the adoption of more capital intensive production processes by defense contractors, who are known to be characterized by low capital intensity coefficients, presumably in part because of the uncertainty as to the time path of orders under defense contracts.

Documentation as to the effect of turbulence on procurement costs is difficult to obtain, becuase the accounting system used by DoD to identify the causes of cost growth in a weapon system provides little in the way of useful information on this score. In the next section, we illustrate the kinds of changes that occur in DoD procurement schedules by looking at the case of one recently developed weapon system. In addition, we summarize some empirical evidence for the low capital/output ration of defense contractors.

We then examine the effect of turbulence on the behavior of defense contractors in the setting of a simplified two period model. If a contractor is risk neutral, then under any of the usual DoD contracting approaches except CPFF, an increase in turbulence results in an increase in expected cost of production for the contractor, assuming a convex cost function. Increases in turbulence have a less predictable effect on the amount of capital used in production. In the case of a CES production function, less capital is employed if capital and labor are close substitutes for one another, under constant or increasing returns to scale. But this conclusion is reversed when capital and labor are poor substitutes for one another, under constant or decreasing returns.

The appropriate measure of "cost" in the risk averse case is the lump sum payment required by the contractor to restore him to the level of expected utility enjoyed before turbulence was increased. This sum is always positive for the risk neutral or risk averse contractors, given a convex cost function, under any of the usual DoD contracting arrangements other than CPFF. Moreover, considering the terms arrived at in the contract to be the result of a bargaining game between DoD and the contractor, DoD will share some of the increased costs due to turbulence except in the case where all the gains from trade are captured by the contractor. While a high degree of substitutability between capital and labor provides an explanation for a capital intensity bias in the risk neutral case, more complicated conditions wold be required to extend this result in the risk averse cases. Consequently an alternative explanation is explored. What is argued here is that the renegotiation process employed by DoD might offer an explanation for a capital intensity bias. If it is assumed that contracts get renegotiated when the contractor would suffer out of pocket losses (revenue does not cover variable costs), then this form of renegotiation induces a capital intensity bias–defense contractors use less capital than they would under the same circumstances (but without renegotiation) in nondefense work. Renegotiation might also result in a preference by contractors for more rather than less turbulence, depending upon whether they are over or under compensated for turbulence through renegotiation.

II. TURBULENCE: AN EXAMPLE

Turbulence in the time path of order quantities is present in most defense contracting. Here we present data on a major weapon system, the UH-60A (Black Hawk) helicopter, based on an excellent recent study by Gates [1983]. The UH-60A is the first new helicopter to be developed by the Army since the 1960s. Its operational mission is that of expanding on the role of the UH-1 Huey helicopter, with added lifting capacity, speed, maneuverabiltiy and range.

The Black Hawk is currently in production and has been a technical success, meeting or exceeding all of the operational requirements set forth in the initial performance specifications. Moreover, development of the Black Hawk came within four months of meeting schedule deadlines set six and one half years earlier. The original schedule provided for initial operational capability to occur in July, 1977. (Initial operational capability was defined as one company equipped with 15 Black Hawk helicopters, complete with training and all support equipment on line). Actual initial operational capability was achieved in November, 1977.

However, the procurement schedule for the Black Hawk has been revised several times over the course of its development history. The total number of units to be produced has remained constant in all of these revisions, but the schedule has been stretched out and the time path of order quantities varied. Table 1 provides a summary of these changes.

During the course of development of the Black Hawk, cost estimates have been prepared on a more or less regular basis, reflecting both supply side factors such as delays, inflation and the like, and the effect or turbulence and ohter demand side factors. The cost history of the Black Hawk has shown a pronounced escalation over time. Table 2 summarizeds cost estimates for the projected 1,107 helicopters over the period 1971-1982.

Gates' study does not attempt to estimate the qunatitative impact of turbulence on cost or cost estimates. The Gates study simply identifies turbulence as one of several factors contributing to cost growth for the Black Hawk, while recognizing the "chicken and egg" nature of the links between turbulence and costs. Thus an increase in cost can lead to a stretch out of orders (turbulence) because of budgetary constraints on DoD, just as a change in order quantities can induce growth in cost due to the need to cancel or accelerate input orders, revise delivery dates for components, provide for overtime or for layoffs, increase overhead rates, and the like.

III. CAPITAL INTENSITY BIAS IN DEFENSE CONTRACTING

The empirical evidence for a capital intensity bias in defense contracting comes from several studies, beginning with one by Weidenbaum (1967). Weidenbaum selected a small sample of firms engaged in defense contracting, and compared data on these firms with data from a small sample of non-defense firms, using the periods 1952-55 and 1962-65. The defense firms showed a lower profit margin on sales (roughly 2.8% vs. 4.5% for the non- defense firms), and a higher rate of return on net worth (18% vs. 12% for the non-defense firms). The reason for this discrepancy between return on sales and return on net worth is that the "capital turnover" ratio of defense firms was

TABLE 1

BLACK HAWK PROCUREMENT SCHEDULE

Fiscal Year	Initial Schedule	Fiscal Year 1976	Fiscal Year 1980	Fiscal Year 1981	Sept. 1981	Oct. 1982
1977	15	15	15	15	15	15
1978	24	56	56	56	56	56
1979	46	129	129	92	92	92
1980	121	168	145	94	94	94
1981	168	168	145	80	80	80
1982	168	168	145	96	96	96
1983	168	180	145	75	96	96
1984	180	180	145	29	84	84
1985	180	43	145	31	63	78
1986	37		37	65	54	78
1987				96	70	78
1988				96	54	85
1989				96	96	96
1990				96	96	96
1991				90	61	79
Totals	1,107	1,107	1,107	1,107	1,107	1,107

(The original (1971) procurement schedule provided for a delivery of 276 aircraft over the initial three year period. This was revised down to 85 before the 1976 Baseline Cost Estimate was prepared).

Source: Gates [1983].

TABLE 2

BLACK HAWK COST ESTIMATES, 1971-1982

| | Cost Estimate | |
Date	Millions of Current $	Millions of 1971 $
December 31, 1971	$1,897.4	$1,584.4
December 31, 1973	2,249.6	1,575.7
June 30, 1974	2,955.8	1,574.0
September 30, 1974	3,520.2	1,574.0
March 31, 1975	3,157.5	1,479.4
June 30, 1975	2,864.0	1,343.5
December 31, 1979	5,242.7	1,687.0
December 31, 1980	6,099.6	1,789.3
March 31, 1981	6,812.6	2,096.5
September 30, 1981	7,262.7	2,218.4
September 30, 1982	7,230.8	2,036.5

(Current year dollars costs estimates include anticipated future inflation.)

Source: Gates [1983].

significantly higher than that for non-defense firms (6.5 vs. 2.6). Capital turnover is the ratio of sales to net worth. Weidenbaum argues that the higher capital turnover ratio of defense firms reflects the large amounts of government supplied capital that defense firms use, this capital not being accounted for in net worth. Weidenbaum deos not explain why it is that defense firms rely on government supplied capital rather than investing in capital on their own.

Belden (1969) divided the Fortune 500 into three groups, based on the fraction of total sales represented by DoD and NASA sales for each firm over the period 1957-1967. Belden finds that the average capital turnover ratios for firms with zero or low DoD and NASA sales was low (around 2.75) as compared to the capital turnover ratios for firms for which DoD and NASA sales represent more than 50% of total sales (average capital turnover ratio of 5.80).

A GAO (1969) study involved a survey of 74 large defense contractors to determine financial data broken down by type of business. The GAO study found that the average capital turnover ratio on DoD business was 4.9 as compared to a turnover ratio of 2.3 on commercial business.

Pegram (1963) looks instead at the value of property, plant and equipment (PP& E) per employee. Using a sample of four large defense contractors and a sample of 6 non-defense firms, data over the 1977-1982 period show that PP& E per employee for the defense contractors is \$11,716 while the figure for non-defnese contractors is \$16,157.[1] Thus all of these studies show a capital intensity bias for defense contractors as compared to non-defense firms.

IV. THE THEORY—THE RISK NEUTRAL CASE

Turning next to the theory, consider the following simplified model. A defense contractor is engaged in the production of a weapon system, under a DoD contract. This is a two-period model. At time 1, the quantity ordered for the first period, q_1 is known with certainty, but q_2, the second period order quantity, is a random variable with probability density function $f(q_2)$. The production function for the contractor is time independent, being given by

$$q_t = g(K, L_t) \quad t = 1, 2 \tag{1}$$

Capital K is a fixed input; K is chosen at time 1 and is fixed thereafter. Labor L_t is a variable input. In particular, L_2 is chosen only after the order quantity q_2 is known. Production must meet order qunatities.

We are interested in determining the effects of turbulence on cost and on the capital intensity of the procution process chosen by the contractor. In this section we examine the case of a risk neutral contractor; in the succeeding sections we look at the case of a risk averse contractor.

Let $C(q_1, q_2, K)$ denote the discounted cost of production to the contractor for order quantities q_1, q_2, and a choice of capital K. Then $C(\cdot)$ is given by

$$C(q_1, q_2, K) = PK + wL_1(q_1, K) + \delta wL_2(q_2, K) \tag{2}$$

where P is the price per unit of capital, w is the wage rate, δ is a discount factor, and L_1, L_2 satisfy

$$g(L_1(q_1, K), K) = q_1; g(L_2(q_2, K), K) = q_2 \tag{3}$$

---

[1] These figures include government owned PP& E in the calculation. When the government owned PP& E are excluded from the calculation, the PP& E per employee becomes even lower for the defense contractors in comparison to non-defense contractors. In 1982, for example, the difference is enlarged by an additional seven percentage points.

We assume that $g_L > 0$, $g_K > 0$, $g_{LL} < 0$, $g_{LK} > 0$. Under these assumptions, it follows that C is monotome increasing and strictly convex in q_2 for any given K, since $C_{q_2} = \delta w/g_L > 0$, $C_{q_2 q_2} = (-\delta w g_{LL})/g_L^3 > 0$.

Consider next the expected value of cost under the pdf f, $E_f C$:

$$E_f C = PK + wL_1(q_1, K) + \delta w \int_0^\infty L_2(q_2, K) f(q_2) dq_2 \qquad (4)$$

Suppose that f is replaced by the pdf $h(q_2)$ where h represents a mean preseving increase in the spread of f. We will interpret the change from f to h to be an increase in "turbulence."[2] Then Proposition 1 follows:

Proposition 1. An increase in turbulence results in an increase in $\min_K EC$; that is if h is a mean preserving increase in the spread of f, then $\min_K E_h C > \min_K E_f C$.

Proof: Following Rothschild and Stiglitz (1970), if h is a mena preserving increase in the spread of f, then f stochastically dominates h in the sense of second degree stochastic dominance (see Hadar and Russell (1968)). That is

$$\int_0^{q_2} F(t) dt \le \int_0^{q_2} H(t) dt$$

for all $q_2 \ge 0$, with strict inequality for some q_2. When f stochastically dominates h in the sense of second degree stochastic dominance, then $E_f \emptyset(q_2) < E_h \emptyset(q_2)$ for all strictly convex functions $\emptyset(q_2)$.

Since $C(\cdot)$ is strictly convex in q_2 for any given K, it follows that $\min_K E_f C < \min_K E_h C$.[3]

Proposition 1 asserts that if K is chosen to minimize expected cost, then an increase in turbulence increases expected cost. Does an increase in turbulence also have a predictable effect on the capital intensity of production, under a cost minimizing strategy? Proposition 2 indicates that this depends on the third derivative of the production function:

Proposition 2. If K is chosen to minimize expected cost, then an increase in turbulence results in a decrease (increase) in K if C_K is strictly ocnvex (strictly concave) in q_2, for every K.

---

[2] "Turbulence" may be interpreted other than how it is used in this paper, where probability density function is spread symmetrically around its mean. So called "stretch out" and "cancellation," where the probability of future production has shifted asymmetrically around the mean are analyzed in Womer/Terasawa (1989).

[3] See the appendix for an alternative proof of this proposition.

Proof: This is another application of Rothschild and Stiglitz' result. If f stochastically dominates h in the sense of second degree stochastic dominance, then

$$E_f\big(C_K(q_2, K)\big) < E_h\big(C_K(q_2, K)\big)$$

if C_K is strictly convex in q_2 for any K. Let K_f be the cost minimizing choice of K under f, and let K_h be the cost minimizing choice of K under h, so that $E_f\big(C_K(q_2, K_f)\big) = E_h\big(C_K(q_2, K_h)\big) = 0$. It follows that $E_h\big(C_K(q_2, K_f)\big) > 0$, so that $K_h < K_f$. If C_K is strictly concave in q_2 for any given K, then $K_h > K_f$.

The condition that C_K be convex in q_2 is clearly highly restrictive. For example, if the production function g is of the CES variety, then C_K is convex in q_2 if the elasticity of substitution coefficient is greater than 2, and if there are constant or increasing returns to scale. If the elasticity of substitution coefficient is less than 1, then under constant or decreasing returns to scale, C_K is concave. (See the appendix for details).

In the case of the CES function, an increase in turbulence leads to less capital being used when capital and labor are relatively good substitutes for one another (and the scale parameter is sufficiently large), and to more capital being used when the inputs are poor substitutes (and the scale parameter is sufficiently small). Just what the interpretation is in the general case is somewhat problematic.

Thus far, we have looked at the way in which expected cost and capital intensity respond to turbulence under an expected cost minimizing strategy. Consider next the choices of defense contractors acting to maximize expected profits. Contractors are employed by DoD under one of four kinds of contracts: fixed price (FP), cost plus a fixed fee (CPFF), incentive contract (IF), or a modified fixed price contract (MFP). In this grouping, cost-plus-incentive (IF) and fixed-price-incentive (FPIF) are grouped together under incentive fee contract (IF) for their formal similarity and to allow consideration of more distinct contract type such as MFP. It must be noted, however, that IF and FPIF are quite distinct and different in their application. Whereas the IF contracts provide for the application formula, the FPIF contracts provide for costs to be negotiated and applied to the incentive formula to determine the amount of earned profit.[4] We examine the effects of turbulence on expected cost and capital intensity treating the contractual arrrangement as given. Later we look at the role of contract renegotiation in the decision making of contractors.

---

[4]The grouping of IF and FPIF together is not uncommon in the literature. Although this paper follows that tradition, it should not be ignored that the two contract types are different in their applicability of ceiling price, performance guarantees, and maximum and minimum fee levels.

Let $R(q_1, q_2, K)$ denote the discounted revenue function for the contractor. Then $R(\cdot)$ varies by contract type as follows:

Fixed Price contract:

$R(\cdot) = pq_1 + \delta pq_2$, for some constant p;[5]

Cost Plus Fixed Fee contract:

$R(\cdot) = C(q_1, q_2, K) + A$, for some constant A;

Incentive contract:

$R(\cdot) = aC(q_1, q_2, K) + p'q_1 + \delta p'q_2$, for some constants $p', a, 0 < a < 1$;

Modified Fixed Price contract:

$R(\cdot) = p''q_1 + \delta p''q_2 + bPK$ for some constants $p'', b, 0 < b < 1$.

Given a risk neutral contractor, and given one of the above types of contracts, the contractor chooses K to maximize expected profits $E\pi$, where

$$\pi = R(q_1, q_2, K) - C(q_1, q_2, K) \qquad (5)$$

Then the following proposition holds:

Proposition 3. Given a risk neutral contractor, the effects of an increase in turbulence are the following:

(1) Fixed Price: Expected cost of production increases, capital intensity decreases (increases) if C_K is convex (concave) in q_2;

(2) Cost Plus a Fixed Fee: Effects on EC and K are indeterminate;

(3) Incentive Fee: Effects are as with fixed price;

(4) Modified Fixed Price: Effects are as with fixed price.

Proof:

(1) Under a fixed price contract, K is chosen to maximize $E\pi = ER - EC$. Since $ER = pq_1 + pq_2$ is independent of K, this means K is chosen to minimize EC. Hence the conclusions of Propositions 1 and 2 apply.

(2) Under a CPFF contract, $E\pi = A$, where A is a constant independent of K. Thus the choice of K and the resulting EC are indeterminate for any pdf.

---

[5]Strictly speaking, fixed price contracts can be divided into fixed price with redetermination (of the price) at some future date, and firm fixed price contracts. See Morse (1962).

(3) Under an IF contract, $E\pi = p'q_1 + \delta p'Eq_2 - (1-a)EC$, $0 < a < 1$. Clearly the argument of (1) applies.

(4) Under an MFP contract, $E\pi = p''q_1 + \delta p''Eq_2 - EC + bPK$, where $-EC + bPK = -(1-b)PK - wL_1 - \delta wEL_2$. Because $(1-b)P$ is the implicit price of K, EC is not minimized. However, changes in EC and in K because of turbulence are those predicted in Propositions 1 and 2, since the $EC - bPK$ function is an EC function with $(1-b)P$ the price of capital.

Thus, except for the CPFF case, an increase in turbulence produces an increase in expected cost given risk neutral contractors, while the effect on capital intensity is more speculative, depending on relatively obscure aspects of the production function.

V. THE THEORY—THE RISK AVERSE CASE

Consider next the case of a risk averse contractor. Let $U(\pi)$ denote the monotone increasing strictly concave utilikty funciton for the contractor. Given a revenue function $R(\cdot)$ associated with one of the four contract types above, the contractor chooses K to maximize expected utility:

$$\max_K V = U(\pi_1) + \delta EU(\pi_2)$$

where
$$\pi_1 = R(q_1) - PK - wL_1 \tag{6}$$

$$\pi_2 = R(q_2) - wL_2.$$

The effect of turbulence on capital intensity bias is ambiguous in the risk averse case. By the arguments given earlier, K decreases (increases) as turbulence increases, if U_K is a convex (concave) function of q_2. But $U_{Kq_2q_2}$ is given by

$$U_{Kq_2q_2} = U'\pi_{Kq_2q_2} + U'' \left[2\pi_{q_q}\pi_{Kq_2} + \pi_K\pi_{q_2q_2} \right] + U'''\pi_K\pi_{q_2}^2 \tag{7}$$

When $\pi_{Kq_2q_2}$ is positive, then an increase in turbulence decreases the capital intensity of proudction in the risk neutral case, under FP, IF, or MFP contracting. When there is risk aversion, then even assuming constant or decreasing absolute risk aversion (which implies $U''' > 0$) together with $\pi_{Kq_2q_2}$ positive does not remove the indeterminancy since π_{q_2} is of unknown sign. It is clear that conditions guaranteeing convexity or concavity of U_K will be obscure in terms of economic content.

Thus we have the following:

Proposition 4. Given a risk averse contractor, an increase in turbulence has indeterminate effects on the choice of K, for all DoD contract types. The direction of change in this variable, as well as the quantitative magnitude of the change, will depend in general on the functional forms of the utility and production functions, as well as on the pdf.

Consider next the effect of turbulence on cost. In a world of risk neutral contractors, the cost of turbulence to the contractor is reflected in the EC measure, since it is only expected profits that are of concern to contractors. In a world of risk averse contractors, the appropriate notion of the cost of turbulence to the contractor is the lump sum payment that would be required to restore the contractor's expected utility level to that he achieved before turbulence was introduced into the picture. Is such a lump sum payment always positive? The answer again follows from the Rothschild and Stiglitz result.

Proposition 5. An increase in turbulence increases cost to the contractor, in the sense that there is a decrease in the expected utility of any contractor experiencing turbulence. This hold under risk neutrality or risk aversion, given FP, IF, or MFP contracts.

Proof: Given a monotone increasing concave utility function $U(\pi)$ and given that π_2 is a strictly concave function of q_2, these conditions holding for all K, then for h a mean preserving increase in the spread of f we have

$$\max_K V_h = U(\pi_1) + \delta E_h U(\pi_2) < \max_K V_f = U(\pi_1) + \delta E_f U(\pi_2)$$

from second degree stochastic dominance. Thus the cost to the contractor increases with turbulence given risk averse or risk neutral contractors. In the risk neutral case, the cost to the contractor reduces to EC.

The fact that cost to the contractor increases with an increase in turbulence is not simply an abstract theoretical notion from the point of view of DoD. The contract terms arrived at in negotiations between DoD and a given contractor represent the solution to a bargaining game between a monopsonist and (often) a monopolistics contractor. Just how the gains from trade will be shared between these two parties depends on threat points and like notions of bargaining strength. Given a solution to such a bargaining game, then when turbulence is introduced into the picture, the contractor suffers a loss as indicated in Proposition 5. Turbulence reduces the desirability of DoD contracts to contractors, which should have the effect of shifting bargaining strength away from DoD and to contractors. In the extreme case where DoD has all the bargaining power and contractors are indifferent between undertaking a contract or leaving the defense industry, the introduction of turbulence imposes all of its costs on DoD. In the other extreme case, where DoD is indifferent between signing a contract or going without the item, the costs of turbulence will be borne by the contractor. In the intermediate cases, both DoD and contractors presumably share the costs of turbulence, either under current contracts or under contracts to be negotiated in the future. Since turbulence is costly for contractors under all DoD contracts (except possibly CPFF), the following corollary to Proposition 5 is immediate.

Corollary. Turbulence increases DoD costs under FP, IF, or MFP contracts, unless DoD is on the margin of indifference between executing or not executing a contract.

Calculation of the lump sum payment representing the cost to the contractor of an increase in turbulence can be made as follows. Let α denote a parameter that shifts the pdf f in such a way as to produce a mean preserving incraase in spread. As above, let

$$V = U(\pi_1) + \delta EU(\pi_2).$$

Then we have

$$dV = \left\{ \frac{\partial V}{\partial K} \frac{\partial K}{\partial \alpha} + \frac{\partial V}{\partial \alpha} \right\} d\alpha + U'(\pi_1)dR_1,$$

where $R_1 = pq_1$. By the first order condition, $\frac{\partial V}{\partial K} = 0$. dR_1 is the lump sum payment required to offset the change $d\alpha$, hence $dV = 0$ in solving for dR_1 to obtain

$$dR_1 = -\left\{ \frac{1}{U'(\pi_1)} \right\} \frac{\partial V}{\partial \alpha}$$

$$= -\left\{ \frac{\partial}{U'(\pi_1)} \int_0^\infty U(\pi_2) \frac{df}{d\alpha} dq_2 \right\} d\alpha$$

Integrating by parts twice we have

$$dR_1 = -\frac{\delta}{U'(\pi_1)} \left(\int_0^\infty \left\{ [U''(\pi_2)\pi_{q_2 q_2} + U'(\pi_2)(\pi_{q_2})^2] \int_0^{q_2} \left(\frac{dF(t, \alpha)}{d\alpha} \right) dt \right\} dq_2 \right) d\alpha$$

from which it follows that $dR_1 > 0$, given that the change in α induces a change in f that satisfies second degree stochastic dominance.

Given a change from, say, α_0 to α_1, the payment ΔR_1 required to restore the level of expected utility is given by

$$\Delta R_1 = \int_{\alpha_0}^{\alpha_1} \left\{ -\frac{\delta}{U'(\pi_1)} \right\} \left(\int_0^\infty \left\{ [U''(\pi_2)\pi_{q_2 q_2} \right. \right.$$

$$\left. \left. + U'(\pi_2)\pi_{q_2}^2] \int_0^{q_2} \frac{dF(t, \alpha)dt}{d\alpha} \right\} dq_2 \right) d\alpha \qquad (8)$$

VI. RENEGOTIATION OF DoD CONTRACTS

One common method of compensating contractors for the loss in expected utility they suffer due to turbulence is through renegotiation of an existing contract, as in annual contracting. In the case of fixed price contracts this can come about through a redetermination of the price to be paid, after order quantities are determined. There are legal precedents indicating that when turbulence is DoD induced, DoD might be held responsible for any resulting losses, under CPFF as well as other contracting arrangements.

The most comprehensive study of contracting arrangements of DoD relevant to the renegotiation issue is the RAND study by Morse (1962). Turbulence was a major factor in renegotiations in the post World War II period. One classic case that went through the renegotiation process involved Boeing Aircraft, accused of earning excess profits by the Renegotiation Board in 1952 in connection with its development of the B-47. The case was finally settled in 1962, in a decision in which turbulence played a critcal role. At one point the court said the following:

> Throughout its existence, petitioner has never experienced normal business as that term is generally understood.... In fact, whether petitioner was working to capacity or completely idle has been almost entirely governed by the exigencies of international politics and the safety or danger to the United States engendered thereby. Its business has always been characterized by peaks and valleys and abnormality rather than normalcy. (Morse, p. 131)

Morse's interpretation of the court's decision in favor of the company was this:

> In the court's view the company is the victim of rapid shifts in demand and should not be blamed for inefficiencies in the use of plant or equipment that arise on that score. No distinction is drawn between the variability in demand that is common to most commerce and that which is peculiar to the weapons industry. The implication is that the government must be held almost wholly responsible for such variability. (Morse, p. 132)

In his study of the use of fixed price contracts, Morse found that in 1960, 31% of the fixed price contracts were firm (no later price renegotiation) while only 6% were redeterminable (price subject to later change). However, in dollar terms redeterminable fixed price contracts were only about 10% smaller in total than firm fixed price contracts. Thus renegotiable fixed price contracts (in dollar terms) were roughly as common as firm fixed price contracts, as of 1960. They far exceeded firm fixed price contracts earlier in the post World War II period. It also is of interest that in a study of actual profit rates under incentive type contracts (including firm fixed price and redeterminable fixed price contracts), of 100 contracts, only two actually showed a loss, both being relatively small contracts, with 98 contracts showing a profit, most at a rate higher than the negotiated rate of profit then being paid on CPFF contracts. Thus Morse's study offers some empirical evidence for the importance of renegotiation, even when the contract is of the fixed price variety.

What we will argue is that to the extent that renegotiation is intended to offset potential out of pocket losses due to turbulence, this induces a factor hiring bias that might well be a prime reason for the observed low capital intensity bias of contractors.

The argument is this. Suppose that because of turbulence, the contractor finds that he cannot even cover his variable costs on the order quantity announced by DoD. In such a situation, the contractor has a positive incentive to renege on his contract, unless nonperformance penalties exceed his contemplated out of pocket losses. Presumably this is precisely the time when the contractor is most apt to obtain the most favorable terms in contract renegotiation. We next explore the implications of a model in which the contractor has assurance that in the case of prospective out of pocket losses, DoD will provide compensation sufficient so that the contractor's out of pocket costs are covered. The results we obtain generalize, in an obvious way, the case where there is a subjective pdf over the fraction of his losses that will be absorbed by DoD. We consider the case of a FP contract, but clearly the analysis can be extended to cover the case of IF or MFP contracts. Given our assumptions, the profit function under renegotiation becomes the following:

$$\pi(q_1, q_2, K) = \begin{cases} pq_1 - PK - wL_1 + \delta(pq_2 - wL_2) & \text{for } q_2 \leq \bar{q} \\ pq_1 - PK - wL_1 & \text{for } q_2 \geq \bar{q} \end{cases} \tag{9}$$

where $\bar{q}$ satisfies $p_2\bar{q} - wL_2(\bar{q}, K) = 0$.

(Because g is strictly concave in L, it is only on sufficiently large orders that out of pocket losses can occur due to rising marginal production costs; with a more general production function, renegotiation could take place either at sufficiently low or at sufficiently high order quantities).

In considering renegotiation as an alternative to turbulence in explaining low capital intensities of defense contractors, the appropriate question to ask is "how does the capital choice of a firm operating in nondefense contracting (with renegotiation not available) compare with the choice of the same firm, under the same turbulence conditions, in defense contracting?" Proposition 6 provides the intuitively appealing answer.

Proposition 6. Under renegotiation, the level of capital is less than that which would be chosen by the same contractor under the same conditions without renegotiation. This holds for risk averse or risk neutral contractors, and it holds under FP, IF, or MFP contracting.

Proof: Let $U(\pi_y)$ be the monotone concave utility function of the contractor for $t = 1, 2$, normalized so that $U(0) = 0$, and let f be the pdf. Let K^* denote the level of capital chosen under renegotiation and let K^{**} denote the level of capital chosen when renegotiation is not available. Then we have

$$V_K(K^*) = U_K(\pi_1(K^*)) + \delta \int_0^{\bar{q}} U_K(\pi_2(K^*)) f(q_2) dq_2 = 0,$$

and

$$\tilde{V}_K(K^{**}) = U_K(\pi_2(K^{**})) + \delta \int_0^{\infty} U_K(\pi_2(K^{**})) f(q_2) dq_2 = 0$$

Suppose $K^* = K^{**}$. Then we would have

$$V_K(K^{**}) = (-)\delta \int_{\bar{q}}^{\infty} U_K(\pi_2(K^{**})) f(q_2) dq_2 \leq 0,$$

since $U_K(\pi_2) = U' \frac{d\pi_2}{dK} = U' \left(-\frac{w dL_2}{dK}\right) = \frac{U' w g_K}{g_L} > 0$. Since $V_{KK} < 0$, it follows that $K^* \leq K^{**}$ with strict inequality when $F(\bar{q}) < 1$.

The use of renegotiation as a device to compensate for turbulence induces a capital intensity bias into input hiring because DoD in effect offers a kind of insurance against out of pocket losses, an insurance that produces a moral hazard response of underinvestment in capital on the part of the defense contractor.

Renegotiation does more than this, however. Whether renegotiation is of the crude type indicated in expression (9) or of a more sophisticated type involving partial coverage of out of pocket losses on a probabilistic basis, in any case renegotiation introduces a nonconvexity into the profit function. In turn this means that Proposition 5 no longer necessarily holds. If the compensation paid by renegotiation to the contractor exceeds the costs of turbulence as given in (8), then the contractor would have a preference for more turbulence rather than less, and vice versa. To the extent that contractors can influence the level of turbulence by their own actions, this introduces a new source of inefficiency into the procurement process. In any case, of course, DoD costs still rise with an increase in turbulence; with a renegotiation scheme that overcompensates the contractor, DoD bears more than 100% of the costs of turbulence.

VII. CONCLUSION

This study of the effect of turbulence on cost and a capital intensity bias on the part of defense contractors verifies that turbulence is a source of cost increases for DoD on all contracts other than CPFF, where the results are indeterminate. Turbulence might also be a factor helping to account for the low capital/output ratios of defense contractors, but this can be guaranteed only under conditions that are difficult to interpret economically.

An alternative suggestion is that the possibility of renegotiating defense contracts when out of pocket losses could occur offers an explanation for capital intensity bias. It also can result in a situation in which positive incentives are created for contractors to increase turbulence. Turbulence is also attractive politically, especially as an alternative to cancellation.

APPENDIX

An alternative approach to the issue of the effect of turbulence on expected cost (Propostiion 1 of the paper) is this:

Let $g(L_2, K)$ be a real valued function with continuous second partial derivatives that is monotone incrasing and concave in L_2. Assume the existence of a cost minimizing choice of capital under certainty and under uncertainty for any pdf over q_2. To simplify notation, let $X = q_2$ and $Y = a(X - \mu) + \mu$ where $\mu = E(X)$ and $0 \leq a \leq 1$. Then we have $E(Y) = \mu$ and $V(Y) = a^2\sigma^2$ where $\sigma^2 = V(X)$. We want to show

$$\min_K \{W_1 f(q_1, K) + P_K K + \delta W_2 E_Y[f(Y, K)]\}$$
$$\leq \min_K \{W_1 f(q_1, K) + P_K K + \delta W_2 E_X[f(X, K)]\}$$

Proof:

It suffices to show $E_Y[f(Y, K)] \leq E_X[f(X, K)]$, or $\int f[a(X - \mu) + \mu, K]h(X)dX \leq \int f(X, K)h(X)dX$ for every K. Since $Y = a(X - \mu) + \mu = aX + (1 - a)\mu$, then $f(Y, K) \leq af(X, K) + (1 - a)f(\mu, K)$ by convexity of f in q_2. Therefore $\int f(Y, K)h(X)dX \leq a \int f(X, K)h(X)dX + (1 - a)f(\mu, K)$.

Let $Z = \int f(X, K)h(X)dX - \{a \int f(X, K)h(X)dX + (1 - a)f(\mu, k)\}$.

Then $Z = (1 - a)\{E_X f(X, K) - f(\mu, k)\} \geq 0$ by Jensen's Inequality. Hence we have establisehd the proposition, $E_y[f(Y, K)] \leq aE_X[f(X, K)] + (1 - a)f(\mu, K) \leq E_X f(X, K)$.

In the case of the CES function, the effect of turbulence on the amount of capital hired is the following:

(i) If the production function is CES production function and if the return to scale parameter $\gamma \geq 1$ and the parameter for elasticity of substitution $\alpha \geq 2$, then an increased uncertainty in production requirement will force the firm to invest less in capital.

(ii) If the production function is CES and if the return to scale parameter $\gamma \leq 1$ and the parameter for elasticity of substitution $\alpha \leq 1$, then an increased uncertainty will lead to increase in capital investment.

Proof:

(1) Note that CEC production function is given by:

$$q_2 = [\delta L_2^{-\rho} + (1 - \delta)K^{-\rho}]^{-\gamma/\rho}$$

where

δ is a distribution parameter, $0 < \delta < 1$

γ is a return scale parameter, $\gamma > 0$

ρ is a substitution parameter and is given by $\rho = \frac{1-\alpha}{\alpha}$ with α the elasticity of substitution, $\alpha \geq 0$.

(2) Then $L_2 = f(q_2, K) = \delta^{1/\rho} q_2 - A^{-1/\rho}$ where

$$A = 1 - (1 - \delta) K^{-\rho} q_2^{\rho/\gamma}, \quad 0 < A < 1$$

$$f_{211} = B \left(1 + 2\rho - (\rho + \gamma)A \right)$$

where

$$B = \delta^{1/\rho} \delta^{-2} q_2^{(1+\rho-2\gamma)/\delta} A^{-(1+3\rho)/\rho} K^{-(1+\rho)} (\delta - 1) < 0$$

(3) For (i) it suffices to show $f_{211} > 0$. In particular, we want to show $1 + 2p - (\rho + \gamma)A \leq 0$, or $\frac{2}{\alpha} - 1 - \left(\frac{1}{\alpha} - 1 + \gamma \right) A \leq 0$. Since $\alpha \geq 2$ we have $\frac{2}{\alpha} - 1 - \left(\frac{1}{\alpha} - 1 + \gamma \right) A \leq - \left(\frac{1}{\alpha} - 1 + \gamma \right) A(1-\gamma)A$. Since $\gamma \geq 1$ and $A > 0$, we have $(1 - \gamma)A \leq 0$, thus $f_{211} > 0$.

(4) for (ii) it suffices to show $f_{211} < 0$. In particular we want to show $\frac{2}{\alpha} - 1 - \left(\frac{1}{\alpha} - 1 + \gamma \right) A > 0$. Since $\alpha \leq 1$ we have $\frac{2}{\alpha} - 1 - \left(\frac{1}{\alpha} - 1 + \gamma \right) A > \frac{1}{\alpha} - 1 + (1 - \gamma)A \geq (1 - \gamma)A$. Since $\gamma \leq 1$ and $A > 0$, we have $(1 - \gamma)A \geq 0$, thus $f_{211} > 0$.

ACKNOWLEDGMENTS

This research was supported in part under funding by the Department of the Army, which is not responsible for the opinions or findings of the authors.

The authors would like to thank Bill Gates, Bill Pegram and an anonymous referee for their comments and suggestions. Remaining errors of commission and omission are entirely the authors'.

REFERENCES

Belden, D. "Defense Procurement Outcomes in the Incentive Contract Environment," Stanford University, May 1969, (AD 688 561).

Cummins, J. "Incentive Contracting for National Defense: A Problem of Optimal Risk Sharing," *Bell Journal of Economics and Management*, Spring, 1977, pp. 168-185.

General Accounting Office, *Defense Industry Profit Review*, March 1969, (AD 685 071).

Gates, W. "UH-60A Black Hawk: Development and Procurement Cost History," Jet Propulsion Laboratory, 1983.

Hadar, J. and Russell, W. "Rules for Ordering Uncertain Prospects," *American Economic Review*, 1969, pp. 25-34.

Harris, M. and Raviv, A. "Optimal Incentive Contracts with Imperfect Information," *Journal of Economic Theory*, 1979, pp. 231-259.

Morse, F. "Military Procurement and Contracting: An Economics Analysis," RM-2948-PR, RAND Corporation, June 1962.

Pegram, W. "Capital Investment by Defense and Non-Defense Industries," Jet Propulsion Laboratory, 1983.

Peck, M. and Scherer, F. *The Weapons Acquisition Process*, Harvard University Press: Boston, 1962.

Quirk J. and Terasawa, K. "Sample Selection and Cost Underestimation in Pioneer Projects," *Land Economics,*. Vol. 62, No. 2, May 1986.

Ross, S. "The Economics Theory of Agency: The Principal's Problem," *American Economic Review*, 1973, pp. 134-139.

Rothschild, M. and Stiglitz, J. "Increasing Risk: I. A Definition," *Journal of Economic Theory*, 1970, pp. 225-243.

_____ "Increasing Risk: II. Its Economic Consequences," *Journal of Economic Theory*, 1971, pp. 66-84.

Weidenbaum, M. "Arms and the American Economy: A Domestic Convergence Hypothesis," *American Economic Review Papers and Proceedings*, 1967.

Weitzman, M. "Efficient Incentive Contracts," *Quarterly Journal of Economics*, 1980, pp. 719-730.

Womer, K. N. and Terasawa, K. L. "The Effect of Defense Program Uncertainty on Cost, Schedule, and Capital Investment," *Journal of Productivity Analysis*, forthcoming.

MODELLING THE FIRM-LEVEL MULTIPRODUCT COST STRUCTURE
OF AGRICULTURAL PRODUCTION

Abiodun Ojemakinde
Department of Agricultural Economics and Agribusiness
Louisiana State University

Mark D. Lange
Department of Agricultural Economics and Agribusiness
Louisiana State University

Thomas P. Zacharias
Department of Economics
Iowa State University

Multiproduct cost analysis has been conducted at state, regional or broader levels of aggregation in agriculture. While the theory of the multiproduct firm and the quantitative tools for analysis are well developed there are no published multiproduct farm firm level studies. This is probably largely attributable to insufficient variability associated with firm level input prices thus preventing dual cost analysis.

The purpose of this paper is to examine the multiproduct cost structure of field crop production agriculture at the firm level using neoclassical duality theory. Specifically, we report firm level factor demand and elasticities of substitution (both Allen and McFadden) for fertilizer, capital, labor, chemicals, and seed treating land as a fixed allocable factor. In addition we estimate product specific scale economies and marginal costs. Prior to this analysis, the majority of duality applications in production agriculture have dealt with levels of aggregation well beyond firm level. Beginning with Binswanger's seminal effort, most authors have used secondary data obtained at either the state, regional or national level (Adelaja and Hoque; Lopez; Ray; Shumway (1983, 1986); Weaver). In some cases our firm-level findings are consistent with previous efforts. That is, technology is nonseparable. However, we cannot reject constant returns to scale and homotheticity. In addition, our elasticity of substitution estimates are smaller in absolute value relative to previous reported aggregate studies.

The several firm level studies that may be considered somewhat related to this analysis are discussed in this section. Price elasticities of demand for four variable inputs were reported by Stefanou and Saxena derived from a single output profit function analysis of 131 Pennsylvania dairy farmers. The estimated own input price elasticities ranged from -0.222 to -0.859, however the forage input own price elasticity was estimated as 0.304. Their cross-price elasticities of input demand were relatively inelastic ranging from 0.001 to 0.813 (in absolute value). Multiproduct production function estimates from 70 small family farms in Israel are reported by Just, Zilberman, and Hochman. While this procedure provides production elasticities, no cost information is reported. Cost and output relationships for 24 retail fertilizer plants are analyzed by Akridge and Hertel using a translog cost function. Substantial cost information regarding average incremental cost, marginal cost, economies of scope, and product-specific economies of scale are derived. However, these results are associated with the industrial production of commercial fertilizer and bear little relevance to agricultural field crop production.

Multiproduct Cost, and Elasticities of Input Substitution
and Elasticities of Demand for Inputs

For a given production year, rice and soybean farmers are assumed to minimize short-run cost subject to levels of output set (q), variable input prices (w), and a fixed quantity of land (z).

(1) $C_{min} = c(q_i, w_j, z)$, i, j = 1, 2,...

where C_{min} is minimum variable cost. Agriculture is a competitive enterprise, and farmers, including rice and soybeans producers, are price-takers for inputs and products. Also, production in the short-run is largely determined by factors other than those within the farmer's control. Therefore in the short-run, input and output prices and production quantities are exogenous to farm level decisions.

Relationships among inputs and each input's response to prices have been of interest to economists and agriculturalists, because reliable information about them are useful in policy formulations and optimal input use. Several attempts have been made to estimate possible relationships among inputs and input responses to own- and other input price changes in agricultural production (Ray, Binswanger, Shumway (1983). In addition various forms of input substitution elasticity estimates have been used depending on the amount of information used or assumptions made in estimation (Debertin, et al.). The Allen partial elasticity of input substitution is commonly used, while other forms of input substitution elasticity measures include Morishima and shadow (McFadden) elasticities of substitution. In this study, Allen (partial) and shadow (McFadden) elasticities of input substitution were employed.

Allen partial elasticities of substitution between inputs j and k can be derived from a dual cost function as:

(2) $\sigma_{jk} = [\partial^2 C/\partial w_j \partial w_k \cdot C]/[(\partial C/\partial w_j)(\partial C/\partial w_k)]$

where w_j is the price of the jth input and σ_{jk} is the Allen partial elasticity of substitution between inputs j and k (Uzawa, Binswanger). Inputs are independent if $\sigma_{jk} = 0$; they are substitutes or complements if $\sigma_{jk} > 0$ or $\sigma_{jk} < 0$, respectively. Alternatively, the Allen partial elasticity of substitution can be defined as:

(3) $\sigma_{jk} = \eta_{jk}/S_k$

where $\eta_{jk} = (\partial x_j/\partial w_k)\,(P_k/x_j)$ is the price elasticity of demand for input j with respect to input k price change, and $S_k = x_k\,P_k/C$ is the cost share of input k (Binswanger). For a classical cost function, the shadow elasticity of substitution between factors i and j is (McFadden):

(4) $\delta^*_{ij} = (-C_{ii}/C_i^2 + 2C_{ij}/C_iC_j) - C_{jj}/C_j)/(1/w_iC_i + 1/w_jC_j)$

where $C_i = \partial C/\partial W_i$ and $C_{ij} = \partial^2 C/\partial W_i\partial W_j$.

Multiply (4) by C/C

(4') $\delta^*_{ij} = (S_iS_j/S_i+S_j)\,(-\sigma_{ii} + 2\sigma_{ij} - \sigma_{jj})$

where σ_{ij} is the Allen partial elasticity of substitution defined in (2) and S_i is the cost share of input i. Because the shadow elasticity of substitution uses more information (two input quantities and two input prices) than the Allen partial elasticity of substitution (one input quantity and one input price), the former is considered a better estimate of "true" Hicksian elasticity of substitution than the latter.

The Model

The translog cost function was proposed by Christensen et al. and Diewert (1973) as a cost function consistent in analytic form with several production functions. The translog cost function (written as a second-order Taylor series expansion of an analytical cost function) adopted for this study is shown as:

(5) $\ln C = \ln c + \sum_i^m \alpha_i \ln q_i + \sum_j^n B_j \ln w_j + 1/2 \sum_i^m \sum_h^m \xi_{ih} \ln q_i \cdot \ln q_h$

$+ 1/2 \sum_j^n \sum_k^n \Phi_{jk} \ln w_j \cdot \ln w_k + \sum_i^m \sum_j^n \Omega_{ij} \ln q_i \cdot \ln w_j + \lambda \ln z.$

where C is total variable cost; q_i is the quantities of outputs - rice and soybeans; the w_j are input prices for labor, capital, seeds, fertilizer, and chemicals (herbicides and insecticides); and z is the total acreage in production. This dual cost function is a quadratic approximation to an unknown "true" cost function. The application of duality in economic analysis has grown in popularity largely due to the several merits noted by Diewert (1974), Lau, Pope, and Lopez (1982). These attributes include increased flexibility in estimation, lack of prior restrictions on the underlying objective function, and derivations of systems of input demands and output responses consistent with economic behavior. A drawback associated with the translog function is its failure to meet conditions for global curvature under linear restrictions. Thus, the estimated translog cost function is a local approximation to a cost function.

The specification of the translog cost function allows testing for the characteristics of production. Using Shephard's lemma, logarithmic differentiation of the indirect cost function (5) yields the input cost shares:

(6) $\partial \ln C / \partial \ln w_j = (\partial C / \partial w_j) \cdot (w_j / C) = x_j w_j / C = S_j = \beta_j + \sum_k^n \Phi_{jk} \ln w_k + \sum_i^m \Omega_{ji} \ln q_i$

where S_j is the cost share of input j. With n inputs, there are n-1 independent cost share equations of the form presented in equation (6).

Data Source and Definitions

The analysis presented in this paper is conducted for a sample of rice and soybean farms located in the southwest region of the state of Louisiana. Data were collected from forty-eight farmers for the 1984 production year. Due to missing and incomplete data, four survey respondents were subsequently dropped from the sample. The two outputs were measured as hundredweights (cwt.) of rice and bushels of soybeans.

Five variable inputs and one fixed input were included in the estimation. Total acres in soybeans and rice production was treated as fixed. The decision to treat land as a fixed factor is due to the high level of participation in the rice program for area farmers. In general, farmers will comply with the provisions outlined under the current farm bill in terms of base acreage and set aside provisions. With respect to soybean production, most farmers in the short run follow a fairly stable rotation between soybean acres and rice acres committed to farm program provisions. The five variable inputs were seeds, chemicals, labor, fertilizer, and capital. Total variable cost was then defined as the sum of seeds, chemicals, labor, capital costs, and fertilizer expenditures for 1984 production season.

The hired labor input is estimated by assuming each reported part-time worker is hired an equivalent of twenty full-time weeks in 1984. Each full-time worker is assumed to work forty full weeks in 1984. Survey respondents generally did not supply full information on labor expenses. Unskilled labor wages were taken from Employment and Wages 1984, Louisiana Department of Labor which is reported only for urban areas. The farm labor price for each farm is estimated as the average urban unskilled weekly wage earnings less ninety-six cents per mile to the closest urban center (Lafayette or Lake Charles).

Capital cost is estimated for each farm as the sum of annual machinery depreciation plus opportunity cost of holding the machinery complement. Straight-line depreciation was employed assuming fifteen year useful life span. The opportunity cost of capital is the new purchase price times 10.89 percent interest. Respondents provided machinery manufacturers, descriptions, and ages of capital. New purchase prices are from Official Guide: Tractors and Farm Equipment annual issues and the interest rate of 10.89 percent is the annual average rate on 1 year Treasury notes in 1984. This procedure is equivalent to assuming a well developed capital rental market exists for farm machinery.

Survey information was collected on the seeding rate, cultivar of seed and acres of specific cultivar planted. Using unpublished data obtained from input suppliers seed cultivar prices were multiplied by seeding rate and acres by cultivar to derive total expenditures on seed. Total expenditure on seed was divided by total quantity of seed planted to derive seed price.

Farm firms purchase fertilizer in varying formulations. Survey information was collected on formulations, timing of applications, and acres applied. Using published data on fertilizer formulation prices, total expenditures on fertilizer were computed as the sum of the products of formulation price and the acres of formulation applied (Paxton and Lavergne; Zacharias and McManus). Fertilizer price was fertilizer expenditure divided by total fertilizer applied. Total fertilizer is derived from reported formulations.

Estimation Procedure

Equation (5) and four share equations defined in (6) were jointly estimated by three stage least squares (Zellner's Estimation) technique, with linear homogeneity in input prices and symmetry restrictions imposed a priori. The capital share equation was suppressed as the redundant share equation. Linear homogeneity in input prices requires that:

$$\sum_j^5 \beta_j = 1, \ \sum_j^5 \Phi_{jk} = 0, \ k = 1, \ \ldots, \ 5, \ \text{and} \ \sum_j^5 \Omega_{ij} = 0, \ \text{for} \ i = 1, \ 2.$$

The adding up restrictions on parameters in the input share equations are identical with those for linear homogeneity in input prices for the cost function. As noted by Ray the parameters of the cost function may be estimated directly or through estimations of the share equations as Binswanger provided. Estimation of the full system of cost and n-1 input share equations increases the efficiency of the parameter estimates. The parameter estimates are unaffected regardless of which of the nth input cost share equations is excluded when iteration on the covariance matrix is employed.

Empirical Results

The parameter estimates of the cost function are reported in Table 1. Three sets of parameter estimates are reported in Table 1. The first column reports the translog model estimated with seemingly unrelated regressions without any restrictions on parameters. The second column reports parameter estimates with linear homogeneity in prices and symmetry restrictions imposed. The fourth column reports parameter estimates with linear homogeneity in factor prices, symmetry, homotheticity, and constant returns-to-scale restrictions imposed. These restrictions are consistent with such cost functions and economic theory. We could not reject homotheticity and constant returns-to-scale in production at the 10% level of probability. Symmetry restrictions cause the jointly estimated corresponding parameters of the indirect cost function and the share equations to be (restricted) equal. The constant returns-to-scale (CRS) restrictions require that:

$$\sum_{i}^{2} \Omega_{ij} = 0 \text{ for } j = 1, \ldots, 5; \quad \sum_{i}^{2} \xi_{ih} = 0 \text{ for } h = 1, 2; \text{ and } \sum_{i}^{2} \alpha_i = 1.$$

Table 1. Estimated Parameters[1] of Translog Cost Function.

Variable[2]	Unrestricted SUR	Restricted SUR[3]	Restricted SUR[4]
INTERCEPT	-140.47	5.1844	-1.3132*
	(-1.29)	(1.45)	(-1.87)
lnRICE	8.1571	0.2580	0.5557**
	(1.99)	(0.66)	(32.86)
lnSOYBEANS	3.9266	-0.4701	0.4443**
	(0.36)	(-1.45)	(26.28)
lnRICE*SOYBEANS	-0.0559	0.0137	0.0523**
	(-0.24)	(0.48)	(25.22)
lnRICE*lnRICE	0.0807	-0.0028	-0.0523**
	(0.48)	(0.19)	(-25.22)
lnSOYBEANS*lnSOYBEANS	0.0369	0.0100	-0.0523**
	(0.32)	(0.86)	(-25.22)
lnSEEDS	-1.1277	0.2397	0.3350**
	(-0.11)	(0.57)	(3.82)
lnCHEMICALS	0.3433	0.0134	0.0913
	(0.06)	(0.6)	(1.40)
lnLABOR	28.7843	0.3287	-0.2594**
	(1.57)	(1.11)	(-3.22)
lnFERTILIZER	-6.9315	0.0523	0.6123**
	(-0.51)	(0.19)	(8.72)
lnCAPITAL	-3.5396	0.3659	0.2208*
	(-0.26)	(1.50)	(3.46)
lnSEEDS*lnSEEDS	-1.5695	-0.0419	-0.1433**
	(-2.07)	(-1.28)	(-6.32)
lnCHEMICALS*lnCHEMICALS	-0.0549	0.0076**	0.0050
	(-0.39)	(2.44)	(1.67)
lnLABOR*lnLABOR	-1.2378	-0.0384**	-0.0176*
	(-1.32)	(-4.11)	(-2.04)
lnFERTILIZER*lnFERTILIZER	-1.0539	-0.0063	0.0038
	(-1.63)	(-0.47)	(0.31)
lnCAPITAL*lnCAPITAL	-0.0702	0.0011	-0.0138**
	(-0.25)	(0.33)	(-4.53)
lnSEEDS*lnCHEMICALS	1.3717	0.0308	0.0862**
	(2.68)	(1.31)	(4.86)
lnSEEDS*lnLABOR	1.0185	-0.0582	-0.1267**
	(1.00)	(-1.72)	(-4.86)**
lnSEEDS*lnFERTILIZER	2.4145	0.0295	0.1125**
	(1.67)	(1.11)	(6.19)**
lnSEEDS*lnCAPITAL	-1.0974	0.0399	0.0713**
	(-1.12)	(1.67)	(3.86)
lnCHEMICALS*lnLABOR	-0.1975	0.0528**	0.0619**
	(-0.39)	(2.92)	(5.85)
lnCHEMICALS*lnFERTILIZER	-0.6446	-0.0305	-0.0762**
	(-2.01)	(-1.58)	(-4.43)
lnCHEMICALS*lnCAPITAL	0.0632	-0.0607**	-0.0769**
	(0.23)	(-4.87)	(-6.50)

lnLABOR*lnFERTILIZER	0.7467	0.0157	0.0115
	(0.55)	(0.54)	(0.59)
lnLABOR*lnCAPITAL	0.4027	0.0281	0.0709**
	(0.42)	(1.26)	(5.53)
lnFERTILIZER*lnCAPITAL	-0.0389	-0.0085	-0.0515**
	(-0.04)	(-0.44)	(-2.99)
lnRICE*lnSEEDS	-0.5744	0.0685*	0
	(-1.00)	(2.40)	-
lnRICE*lnCHEMICALS	-0.0884	-0.0029	0
	(-0.42)	(-0.26)	-
lnRICE*lnLABOR	-1.1915	-0.0308	0
	(-1.72)	(-1.56)	-
lnRICE*lnFERTILIZER	0.4564	-0.0008	0
	(0.98)	(-0.05)	-
lnRICE*lnCAPITAL	0.3891	-0.0339*	0
	(1.07)	(-2.43)	-
lnSOYBEANS*lnSEEDS	0.5126	-0.0598*	0
	(0.92)	(-2.26)	-
lnSOYBEANS*lnCHEMICALS	-0.3290	0.0170	0
	(-0.82)	(1.54)	-
lnSOYBEANS*lnLABOR	-0.8310	-0.0057	0
	(-1.02)	(-0.30)	-
lnSOYBEANS*lnFERTILIZER	-0.3876	0.0214	0
	(-0.50)	(1.28)	-
lnSOYBEANS*lnCAPITAL	0.4396	0.0271*	0
	(1.30)	(2.09)	-
lnLAND	0.9085	0.1932	0.8780**
	(1.10)	(0.89)	(6.11)

---

[1] Single asterisk indicates significance at .10; double asterisks indicate significance at .05.

[2] t-ratio in parenthesis.

[3] Homogeneity in factor prices and symmetry restrictions imposed.

[4] Homogeneity in factor prices, symmetry, homotheticity and CRS in production restrictions imposed.

The restrictions for homotheticity require that all output-input price interaction be zero, i. e., $\Omega_{ij} = 0$ for $i = 1$, 2 and $j = 1$, 2, .., 5. This investigation provides information on the independence (or otherwise) of production decisions for outputs, i.e, is the marginal cost ratio independent of factor prices or intensities. The specification for testing separable production is: $\xi_{ih} = -\alpha_i \cdot \alpha_h$; $i \neq h$. Being a nonlinear restriction, the specification is not easily incorporated into (5). However, the fact that the output interaction coefficient ξ_{ih} ($i \neq h$) is nonzero suggested existence of joint production. Existence of non-separable production indicates that the cost function is not additively separable and that optimal relative output quantities are affected by all input prices.

All output coefficients, α_i, are positive and significant at .01, thus implying that total variable cost is an increasing function of each output. Likewise, the input price coefficients, β_j, are positive and significant at the .10 level, except for labor price. However, the factor share equations are positive and elasticity estimates possess correct signs at all observation points. Therefore, the cost function is monotonically increasing in input prices and locally concave. Having imposed homogeneity in input prices and symmetry conditions, the estimated cost function is legitimate.

Elasticity of Factor Substitution

Invoking (2) on (5) and using the derivations provided by Brown and Christensen, the Allen partial elasticities of input substitution between input pairs were estimated as:

$$\hat{\sigma}_{jk} = (\hat{\Phi}_{jk}/\hat{S}_j\hat{S}_k) + 1 \text{ for } j \neq k \text{ and } \hat{\sigma}_{jj} = (\hat{\Phi}_{jj} - \hat{S}_j)/\hat{S}_j^2 + 1 \text{ for all } j, \text{ where the}$$

$\hat{\Phi}_{jk}$ are parameter estimates from (5) and the $\hat{S}_j$ are estimated factor shares. The pairwise elasticities of substitution (Allen partial) are shown in Table 2.

Allen partial elasticities of substitution provide the basis for estimations of price elasticities of demand for inputs and the shadow elasticities of input substitution. Using (3), the price elasticities of demand for inputs are estimated as $\hat{\eta}_{jk} = \hat{\Omega}_{jk} \cdot \hat{S}_k$, for all j and k. The elasticities of substitution between input pairs were estimated as (4'), using Allen partial elasticity estimates. The price elasticities of demand for inputs are reported in Table 3 while shadow elasticities of input substitution are shown in Table 4.

Table 2. Allen Elasticities of Substitution Between Pairs and Inputs[1].

Input Pairs	Mean Estimate	Minimum Estimate	Maximum Estimate
Seeds/Chemicals	0.0703 (5.57)	0.0141	0.5832
Seeds/Labor	-0.0333 (-15.56)	-0.0778	0.0011
Seeds/Fertilizer	0.0866 (9.86)	0.0069	0.3877
Seeds/Capital	0.0842 (11.23)	0.0161	0.3331
Chemicals/Labor	0.1160 (11.69)	0.0099	0.3396
Chemicals/Fertilizer	-0.0633 (-13.46)	-0.1670	0.0055
Chemicals/Capital	0.07165 (-12.14)	-0.2036	0.0192
Labor/Fertilizer	0.0409 (10.36)	0.0009	0.1352
Labor/Capital	0.1321 (11.56)	0.0275	0.4820
Fertilizer/Capital	-0.0394 (-3.05)	-0.5768	0.0117

[1] t-values are in parentheses.

Table 3. Price Elasticities of Demand for Inputs (Mean Estimates)[1].

Demand for			Price of		
	Seeds	Chemicals	Labor	Fertilizer	Capital
Seeds	-1.1218	0.0141	-0.0054	0.0157	0.0177
	(-24.74)	(2.84)	(-13.54)	(7.11)	(8.07)
Chemicals	0.0195	-0.8156	0.0224	-0.0102	-0.0134
	(16.90)	(-126.27)	(8.11)	(11.78)	(-11.32)
Labor	-0.0103	0.0146	-0.9514	0.0076	0.0273
	(-23.65)	(18.58)	(-58.23)	(7.21)	(8.40)
Fertilizer	0.0266	-0.0078	0.0056	-0.8124	-0.0072
	(16.94)	(-21.48)	(20.94)	(-141.41)	(-2.82)
Capital	0.0252	-0.0087	0.0196	-0.0036	-0.8898
	(24.74)	(-18.97)	(22.53)	(-10.40)	(81.30)

[1] t-values are in parentheses.

Table 4. Shadow (McFadden) Elasticities of Substitution Between Input Pairs[1].

Input Pairs	Mean Estimate	Minimum Estimate	Maximum Estimate
Seeds/Chemicals	0.0608 (12.18)	0.0278	0.1592
Seeds/Labor	0.0435 (15.41)	-0.0117	0.0921
Seeds/Fertilizer	0.0689 (30.33)	0.0281	0.1166
Seeds/Capital	0.0802 (15.21)	0.0087	0.1516
Chemicals/Labor	0.0352 (12.62)	0.0103	0.1041
Chemicals/Fertilizer	0.0084 (5.11)	-0.0039	0.4165
Chemicals/Capital	0.0100 (5.51)	-0.0053	0.0377
Labor/Fertilizer	0.0269 (18.14)	0.0107	0.0507
Labor/Capital	0.0501 (11.51)	0.0053	0.1121
Fertilizer/Capital	0.0211 (9.37)	0.0019	0.0633

Scale Economies and Cost

The impacts of output mix and output level on average cost of production are investigated by estimating product-specific and multiproduct economies of scale and marginal cost. The economies of scale and marginal cost estimates are reported in Table 5. Following Ray, the estimated partial scale economy (SCE) for any output is the reciprocal of the variable cost elasticity with respect to that output. An

SCE greater (less) than one indicates that the proportionate increase (decrease) in output is accompanied by a less (greater) than proportionate increase in total costs. Overall scale economy, which is the inverse of the summed reciprocals of the partial scale economies, was constrained to unity, and found to be statistically significant as noted earlier. The SCE estimates reveal the larger product specific scale economies are associated with the soybean enterprise.

Table 5.   Product-Specific and Overall Scale Economies (SCE) and Product-Specific Marginal Cost (MC).

		Mean Estimate	Minimum Estimate	Maximum Estimate
SCE	(Rice)	1.8059	1.2983	2.3115
SCE	(Soybeans)	2.3303	1.7625	4.3524
SOE	(Overall)	1.0		
MC	(Rice)	$8.00	$2.15	$36.80
MC	(Soybeans)	$6.05	$0.34	$23.11

Partial scale economies may be used to obtain marginal costs of each output. Specifically marginal cost is $(\partial \ln C / \partial \ln q_i)\ (C/q_i)$. The reported marginal costs are the means of estimated marginal cost for all farms. These marginal cost estimates provide important information with regard to likely changes in crop production in southwest Louisiana. Louisiana cash prices of soybeans have failed to reach $7.00 in the past two years (1986 and 1987) which has resulted in a decrease in soybean acreage. Given the estimated marginal cost of soybeans a continued decline in the production of soybeans is likely unless central U.S. drought conditions become a more persistent phenomena. The estimated marginal cost of rice indicates producers will continue to produce on all lands qualified for the rice program. Current cash rice prices are sufficient to cover all variable costs, yet the price risk for program non-participants may be sufficient to generally preclude rice production outside the program.

Comparison of Results to Previous Studies

This analysis has provided the first multiproduct farm firm estimates of crop specific economies of scale and marginal cost. As a result, cost comparisons are unavailable. However, estimates of single output firm level input cross-price elasticities reported by Stefanou and Saxena compare quite reasonably in relative magnitudes. Our estimated own input price elasticities, for a differing set of inputs, are noticeably less inelastic than those estimated by Stefanou and Saxena.

Ray's data were developed for U.S. agriculture using a 1939-1977 time series with livestock and crop outputs and five inputs. Given the aggregate nature of his analysis it is not surprising that the estimated elasticities of substitution (Allen) are larger for the U.S. than those reported for southwest Louisiana. However, estimated own price elasticities of input demands are generally less inelastic for this sample of southwest Louisiana farms than Ray's U.S. estimates. The cross-price elasticities reported by Ray are generally larger in absolute value than those estimated for southwest Louisiana. Using Allen partial elasticities of substitution Ray estimated labor and miscellaneous inputs, fertilizer and miscellaneous inputs, and seed, feed and livestock, and miscellaneous inputs to be complementary pairs. The estimated Allen partial elasticities of substitution for this sample of farms indicates chemicals and fertilizer, chemicals and capital, fertilizer and capital, and seeds and labor to be complementary input prices.

Output supply and input demand relations in Texas agriculture was estimated by Shumway using a normalized quadratic profit function for the years 1957-79. Estimated own price elasticities of input demand for Southwest Louisiana farms are less inelastic than those reported by Shumway.

Conclusions

Insufficient variability in input prices across firms has largely prevented farm firm level application of dual cost analysis. Using farm survey data on input application rates with input supplier price data has generated sufficient input price variability across farms. This multiproduct cost analysis indicates soybeans and rice farms in the southwest Louisiana exhibit constant returns-to-scale. Estimated partial economies of scale and marginal costs indicate rice production to be competitive at current cash rice prices while soybeans are barely able to cover marginal costs at current cash prices. Both Allen-partial elasticities of substitution and McFadden shadow elasticities of substitution indicate limited substitutability among inputs. Given price risk it is unlikely producers will be observed to produce outside the rice program.

References

Adelaja, Adesaje, and Anwarul Hogue. "A Multi-Product Analysis of Energy Demand in Agricultural Subsectors." _Southern Journal of Agricultural Economics_ 18 (1986):51-63.

Akridge, Jay T. and Thomas W. Hertel. "Multiproduct Cost Relationships for Retail Fertilizer Plants." _American Journal of Agricultural Economics_, 68 (1986):928-938.

Ball, V. Eldon, and Robert Chambers. "An Econometric Analysis of Technology in the Meat Products Industry." _American Journal of Agricultural Economics_, 64 (1982):699-708.

Berndt, E. R. and L. R. Christensen. "The Translog Function and Substitution of Equipment, Structure, and Labor, in U.S. Manufacturing 1929-68." _Journal of Econometrics_, 1 (1973):81-113.

Binswanger, Hans. "A Cost Function Approach to the Measurement of Factor Demand and Elasticities of Substitution." _American Journal of Agricultural Economics_, 56 (1974):377-86.

Brown, Randall S., and Lauritis R. Christensen. "Estimating Elasticities of Substitution in a Model of Partial Static Equilibrium: An Application to U.S. Agriculture, 1947 to 1974." Modelling and Measuring Natural Resource Substitution, ed. Ernst R. Bendt and Barry C. Field. Cambridge: MIT, 1981.

Brown, Randall, Douglas Caves, and L. R. Christensen. "Modelling the Structure and Production for Multiproduct Firm." Southern Economic Journal, 46 (1979):256-73.

Christensen, L. R., Dale Jorgensen, and L. J. Lau. "Transcendental Logarithmic Production Frontiers." Review of Economics and Statistics, 55 (1973):28-55.

Cowing, Thomas, and Alphons Holtman. "Multiproduct Short-Run Hospital Cost Functions: Empirical Evidence and Policy Implications from Cross-Section Data." Southern Economic Journal, 49 (1983):637-53.

Darrough, M. N. and J. M. Heineke. "The Multi-Output Translog Production Cost Function: The Case of Law Enforcement Agencies." Economic Models of Criminal Behavior, ed. J. M. Heineke. New York: North-Holland, 1978.

Debertin, David L. and Angelos Pagoulatos. "Contemporary Production Theory, Duality, Elasticity of Substitution, the Translog Production Function, and Agricultural Research." University of Kentucky Agricultural Economics Report 40, June 1985.

Diewert, W. E.. "Functional Forms for Profit and Transformation Functions." Journal of Economic Theory, 6 (1973):284-316.

Diewert, W. E.. "Application of Duality Theory." Frontiers of Quantitative Economics, Vol. II, edited by M. D. Intriligator and D. A. Kendrick. New York: North-Holland, 1974.

Fielder, Lonnie and Bergen Nelson. "Agricultural Statistics and Prices of Louisiana 1946-1982." D.A.E. Research Report No. 600, Louisiana Agricultural Experiment Station, 1982.

_____. "Agricultural Statistics and Prices for Louisiana 1978-1983." D.A.E. Research Report No. 631, Louisiana Agricultural Experiment Station, 1984.

Just, Richard E., David Zilberman, and Eithan Hochman. "Estimation of Multicrop Production Functions." American Journal of Agricultural Economics, 65 (1983):770-780.

Lau, Lawrence J.. "A Characterization of the Normalized Restricted Profit Function." Journal of Economic Theory, 12 (1976):131-163.

Lopez, Ramon. "The Structure of Production and the Derived Demand for Inputs in Canadian Agriculture," American Journal of Agricultural Economics, 62 (1980):38-45.

_____. "Applications of Duality Theory to Agriculture." Western Journal of Agricultural Economics, 7 (1982):353-365.

McFadden, Daniel. "Constant Elasticity of Substitution Production Functions." Review of Economic Studies, 30 (1963):73-83.

Paxton, K. W. and David Lavergne. "Projected Cost and Returns: Rice and Soybeans, Southwest Louisiana, 1984. Department of Agricultural Economics Research Report No. 625, Louisiana State University Agricultural Center, Baton Rouge, Louisiana.

Pope, Rulon. "To Dual or Not to Dual." Western Journal of Agricultural Economics, 7 (1982):337-51.

Ray, Subhash. "A Translog Cost Function Analysis of U.S. Agriculture, 1939-77." American Journal of Agricultural Economics, 64 (1982):490-498.

Saez, Roberto, and C. Richard Shumway. "Multiproduct Agricultural Response and Input Demand Estimation in the United States: A Regional Profit Function Approach." Departmental Technical Report No. 85-3. Texas Agricultural Experiment Station, 1985.

Shumway, C. Richard. "Supply, Demand and Technology in a Multiproduct Industry: Texas Field Crops." American Journal of Agricultural Economics, 65 (1983):748-60.

_____. "Supply Relationships in the South - What Have We Learned." Southern Journal of Agricultural Economics, 18 (1986):11-19.

Stefanou, Spiro E. and Swati Saxena. "Education, Experience, and Allocative Efficiency: A Dual Approach." American Journal of Agricultural Economics, 70 (1988):338-345.

Uzawa, H. "Production Functions with Constant Elasticities of Substitution." Review of Economic Studies, 29 (1962):291-99.

Zacharias, Thomas and Brian McManus. "Projected Cost and Returns: Rice and Soybeans, Southwest Louisiana, 1985. Department of Agricultural Economics Research Report No. 635, Louisiana State University Agricultural Center, Baton Rouge, Louisiana.

Weaver, Robert. "Multiple Input, Multiple Output Production Choices and Technology in the U.S. Wheat Region." American Journal of Agricultural Economics, 65 (1983):45-56.

Zellner, A. "An Efficient Method of Estimating Seemingly Unrelated Regressions and Tests for Aggregation Bias." Journal of the American Statistical Association, 57 (1962):585-612.

TRANSACTION COSTS AND THEIR IMPACT ON ENERGY DEMAND BEHAVIOUR

Erich Unterwurzacher[1]
International Energy Agency, OECD, Paris

and
Franz Wirl
Institute of Energy Economics
Technical University of Vienna, Austria
Gußhausstr. 27-29, A-1040 Wien

Abstract: The very recent trends in energy demand are incompatible with empirically fitted price elasticities. Different reasons are conceivable to explain this behaviour - technological progress, public policy etc. This paper argues that transaction costs associated with investment decisions of households - for energy conservation and/or fuel substitution - may have an significant impact. This in turn can explain - at least partially and for some sectors of demand (residential) - the recent energy pattern. The paper provides a theoretical discussion of these aspects and complementary, some empirical examples.

1. Introduction

Traditional econometric models assume energy demand is smooth. Discontinuities are typically not covered. The majority of papers which investigate the prospects for energy conservation empirically apply econometric models and methods. Such models assume that the characteristics of continuity, divisibility and stability apply to energy demand; see the comprehensive treatises of Pindyck (1979) and Bohi (1981). The typical econometric analysis of energy demand fits indirect translog cost and/or utility functions to empirical data of demanded quantities and prices, to obtain the implied elasticities of demand. Further typical applications of these empirical models are: forecasting of energy demand and policy recommendations.

This paper attempts to go beyond the traditional econometric approach. It emphasizes that energy conservation involves transaction costs which may be substantial compared with the potential gain. More precisely the adoption of a new technology requires time, causes

---

[1]This paper represents the personal views of the author and not necessarily those of the IEA or its Member countries.

inconvenience and direct costs, e.g. contracting costs, inconvenience during a period of retrofit, learning costs. These costs - viewed in broader sense - may be substantial in this context. Williamson (1975) introduces the notion of transaction costs. Williamson (1981) applies this concept to describe the behaviour of modern corporations. But transaction costs have so far been neglected as a mean to explain peculiarities of energy demand.

In particular, the presence of significant transaction costs could be one clue to understand the asymmetrical demand behaviour. The current increase in energy demand due to the lower energy prices is much less pronounced as it would be if those elasticities are applied which are derived from data covering the period of rising energy prices. More precisely, empirically fitted energy demand-price elasticities tend to overestimate substantially the recent growth observed in energy demand: total primary energy requirement of the IEA[2] countries continues to grow moderately, 0.7% during 86 (OECD Energy Balances) and 1.9% during 1987 (BP Statistical Review of World Energy 1988), despite the dramatic reductions in fuel prices since the beginning of 1986.

Section 2 describes the concept of transaction costs in the context of energy conservation investments. The impact of these costs on investments and on energy demand are theoretically explored. Section 3 introduces an empirical example based on an techno-economic model and on data available for Vienna, Austria. Section 4 focuses on the consequences for the pattern of energy demand and in particular on the impact on the current evolution of demand due to the recent changes in fuel prices. A final section sums up and makes some suggestions for future research. The consideration of transaction costs as an additional analytical tool for the energy analyst could help to overcome a current methodological weakness and could ultimately improve our understanding of energy demand behaviour.

2. Transaction Costs and Energy Demand - A Theoretical Exposition

Traditional energy demand analysis - as indicated in the introduction - relies on smooth mathematical representations of energy demand. Hence, discrete phenomena and discontinuities are hardly

---

[2]The IEA is an associated body of the OECD (Organization for Economic Cooperation and Development).

covered in this literature (for exceptions see Dubin-McFadden (1984), Cameron (1985), Wirl (1988)). Therefore, transaction costs are also implicitly assumed to be negligible. Indeed, even the above mentioned studies - although deliberately focussing on non-convexities - do not treat transaction costs explicitly. The negligence of transaction costs is acceptable for the transport sector, for most parts of the industry, and probably also for a large fraction of commercial consumers, but seems not suitable for households. The incorporation of these neglected, and not insignificant, cost factors will facilitate a better understanding of the dynamics of energy demand, and will provide - at least theoretically - an explanation for asymmetrical energy demand.

Moreover, this concept could be applied to resolve some of the differences in the public debate on issues of energy conservation. Many conservationists claim that "energy conservation", e.g. in the residential sector, is more efficient from an economic point of view than investments in the supply of energy, e.g. building new power generating capacity. Usually, an techno-economic model of household energy consumption is used to prove the profitability of conservation investments. But ironically, one ends up with the puzzle that numerous consumers may neglect economic incentives and do not realize all possible economic profits.

However, a more cautious deduction might be drawn if one realizes the deficiency of this simple cost-benefit analysis. In short, the profitability of certain investments does not necessarily reflect its economics for individual consumers, if significant costs and/or efforts are involved to realize this profit. In particular, energy conservation investments are prone to incur costs beyond those which are accounted for in a typical cost-benefit analysis. We will summarize all these costs under the heading transaction costs. The following list, which is not exhaustive, will illustrate examples of the costs involved in a retrofit programme intended to conserve energy:

i) Information on energy conservation (fuel prices, "R-values" of windows and insulating materials and the impact on fuel requirements) must be acquired and analyzed in a time consuming manner, although most of the information is publicly available.

ii) The consumer must consult different construction firms to design an optimal retrofit programme, and to select the most efficient company. Furthermore, if grants or other financial support, like (soft) loans or tax write-off, are provided by the government, an additional bureaucratic hurdle has to be overcome.

iii) The fairly complex nature of conservation investments requires high monitoring costs for the consumer to secure the fulfillment of the contract.

iv) Unanimity among the tenants is required in many multi-family buildings (e.g. in Austria and other European countries subject to regulation of apartment rentals). This may end up in a complicated, cumbersome negotiation process even if significant profits are possible for all inhabitants of the building.

v) A landlord who owns and runs the central heating of the building faces the following investment risk: conservation investment will lower the fuel costs which requires additional arguments to defend a fuel bill exceeding actual fuel costs. But the additional revenue is necessary to compensate for the investment outlays. Hence, he will not necessarily pursue an economic conservation programme. Moreover, energy conservation reduces marginal fuel costs and thus increases the incentive to engage in "free riding" where costs are distributed proportionally. This individual ex post opportunism of the tenants may further weaken the economics of the retrofit programme.

vi) The housing market may not appropriately reflect the thermodynamic status of a building. Therefore, this investment will only earn its return if the inhabitant plans to live in this house for a sufficiently long period.

All these costs can be summed up under the label *transaction costs* because they are involved in the course of transacting an energy conservation programme. The term *transaction costs*, as coined by Williamson, e.g. Williamson (1975) considers also ex-post opportunism and fairness, or dignity (Williamson (1984)) as he tends to call it.

Fig. 1 shows the impact of transaction costs - for rising energy prices - on individual conservation investments and **Fig. 2** draws the corresponding energy demand curves. **Fig. 1** shows the individual net benefits, according to the traditional accounting, B_i, i=0,1,2 from conservation investments (I) for three different price levels $p_0 < p_1 < p_2$. Conservation would therefore constitute an economic undertaking even for the low prices p_0, p_1, albeit at a lower degree.

Now suppose that transaction costs amount to T in order to collect this benefit. For simplicity suppose that T is constant for all positive investments I. This implies that energy conservation is economically inefficient when prices are low, e.g. $p=p_0$ or p_1. Only high prices (p_2) warrant the investments for the "optimal" retrofit programme. The consumer will be indifferent whether to invest or not for the benefits corresponding to broken line in **Fig. 1**. Hence, energy behaviour will be discontinuous at the corresponding price level, $p=\tilde{p}$.

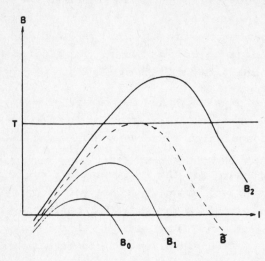

Fig. 1: Optimal Conservation Investment & Transaction Costs

The fact that small price variations are insufficient to cover the transaction costs associated with conservation investments suggests that such variations lead to consumer behaviour geared to short run demand changes, e.g. varying indoor temperature. However, large price increases may trigger an energy conservation programme. In this case the consumer moves along the long run schedule according to the traditional continuous framework. This discontinuity of demand vis a vis fuel prices is shown in **Fig. 2**.

Assume that (E_0,p_0) is an equilibrium point, i.e. (E_0,p_0) is located at the long run demand schedule. Now suppose that p_2 - according to the discussion of **Fig. 1** - is sufficiently large to trigger an investment programme. On the other hand, p_1 is to small to warrant investments. Hence, a price increase from p_0 to p_1 leads to an adjustment along the short run schedule. Therefore, energy demand will exhibit a discontinuity at a price $\tilde{p}\in(p_1,p_2]$ because investments are advisable for the "high" price p_2. In other words (for a given capital equipment), adjustments along the long run relation are rational for prices $p \geq \tilde{p}$; otherwise demand changes are confined to motions along the short run demand relation.

Moreover, this investment is irreversible for both physical (e.g. insulation) and economic reasons. Even if a previous conservation investment was not economical, it will still continue to lower fuel costs. Thus, scrapping it would be suboptimal. Empirical elasticity estimates obtained from time series data over the last twenty years are an equivalent to an average over short run and long run elasticities. Therefore, it is no surprise that these average elasticities are not applicable to the current market situation. Moreover, these elasticities are presumably biased independent of the actual applicability to long run or short run relations. These elasticities are in particular not suitable to predict the energy demand response to the at present low fuel prices, as prevailing demand moves along the short run demand curve, i.e. consumers can afford a higher level of comfort; see **Fig. 2**.

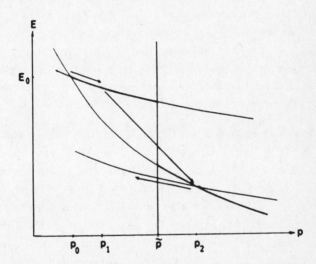

Fig. 2: Energy demand - short vs long run

Fig. 2 describes, in a highly stylized manner, the pattern of energy demand during the last fifteen years, which consists of motions along the short run and long run demand behaviour. The figure shows two short run demand curves associated with initial capital equipment and after a conservation programme. The trends in energy demand before 1973/74, $p \approx p_0$, stem presumably from short run behaviour, as transaction costs dominated by far the minor potential gains from conservation investments. The high fuel prices, $p \approx p_2$, and their persistence for more than a decade from 1974-1985, may have induced considerable conservation efforts, despite the substantial transaction costs. The price collapse since the beginning of 1986 causes demand to increase again, but along a lowered short run demand schedule. Hence, past demand behaviour consists of mixture of motions along short and long run demand curves. The arrows in **Fig. 2** sketch this process. Since current demand is limited to adjustments along the short run demand curve, the application of average price elasticities seems inapplicable, at least for the market segment of residential-heating .

3. Fuel Conservation and Fuel Substitution in Austria

The following empirical examples draw on the economic-engineering framework presented in Wirl (1988). A comprehensive model analyzes fuel requirements for residential heating and considers the following options: choice of comfort (or equivalently indoor temperature; different types of conservation investments (e.g. wall insulation); fuel substitution. Moreover, the framework allows the determination of the optimal decisions on all these aspects. All the examples shown apply to a multi-family dwelling built in the period 1960-1970 (the construction period determines the thermodynamic properties of the building), an infinite planning horizon, myopic price expectations and a real discount rate of 5% per annum.

Fig. 3 shows the economic benefits from optimal conservation programmes if no fuel substitution is feasible or advisable for different fuel price levels. These benefits -except for the case of electricity - appear to be small for the prices prevailing prior to the first oil price shock. A similar conclusion applies to the current (1988) fuel prices. Therefore it may not pay to invest in energy conservation as the small profit, roughly 25$ per 75m² flat[3] (annualized flow, 1985 prices) cannot compensate for the associated transaction costs. Indeed, transaction costs must have exceeded the benefits before 1973, except again for electricity which had its strong market penetration during the decade of high fuel prices, as energy conservation was negligible prior to 1973. However, the high

---

[3]These benefits include the utility gain from higher comfort which results from lower marginal costs; more precisely energy conservation reduces the marginal costs for increasing indoor temperature. Hence, equating marginal utility with marginal costs implies that any conservation programme will increase indoor temperature; see Hirst (1987) for an empirical confirmation of this theoretical finding.

fuel prices of the first half of the eighties raised the economic benefits of conservation programmes substantially (except in the case of district heat). Thus, at last a significant number of consumers considered these benefits as larger than their individual transaction costs and invested in conservation activities.

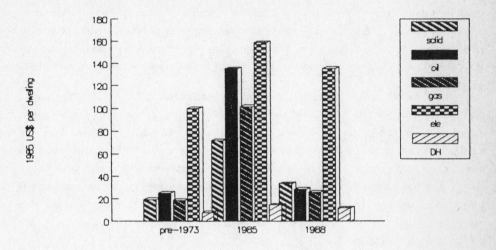

Fig. 3: Economic Benefits from Conservation Programmes

A similar conclusion can be drawn if the economic benefits of fuel substitution are analyzed. Fig. 4 illustrates the benefits of substitution and choice of comfort, based on different price levels. Only the benefits of switching from oil to other energy sources (gas, coal, electricity and district heat) are shown, as those options reflect both, dominant consumers' choice post 1973 and official energy policy. Oil was the main energy source in the early 70's for heating purposes in the residential sector. Therefore, alternatives in the supply strategy are referenced to oil fired heating systems.

The low liquid fuel prices prior to the first oil price shock did not promote fuel substitution. Only switching to gas would result in economic benefits of approximately 50 $ per dwelling (again, expressed at an annualized financial flow). However, the limited supply of gas, in particular in rural areas, limited this substitution. On the contrary, liquid fuels were quite attractive considering its convenience of use, in particular compared with solid fuels.

In contrast, the high liquid fuel prices during the first half of the eighties offered partially substantial benefits for fuel switching (now away from oil). In particular, the fuel substitution to district heat appears attractive. Moreover, this particular fuel substitution served as a substitute for conservation investments which would be rational in case of any other fuel. Therefore, this substitution lowered also the total financial investments. Hence, these benefits overcame - as we know - in a significant number of cases the transaction costs hurdle. In other words, the first half of the eighties were the golden age for the market penetration of district heat. The fact of its relatively slow penetration points again at transaction costs but also at the inefficiencies of public utilities.

The recent fuel prices reveal a picture similar to the sixties and early seventies. No fuel substitution away from oil - the benefits from a substitution to natural gas will in most cases not cover transaction cost - are advisable. Moreover, resubstitution, e.g. from electric heating or solid fuels, may again be advisable[4]. However, any past conservation efforts lowers the benefits from substitution and hence reduces the likelihood that substitution takes place. Hence, again past fuel substitution (own and cross price) elasticities should be cautiously applied.

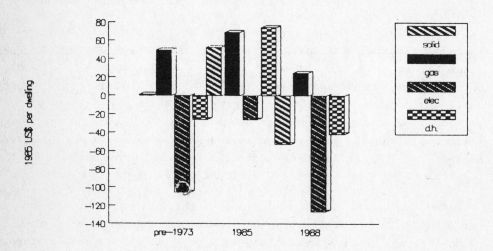

Fig. 4: Benefits from Fuel Substitution, Initial Fuel=liquid

---

[4]These results for other heating systems as initial equipment are not shown in **Fig. 4.** Furthermore, note that the results are not symmetric, i.e. the loss shown for a substitution from oil to electricity does not constitute the gain for the substituting oil for electricity, because of different fixed costs associated to "access" another system.

4. Consequences on energy demand.

The reaction of consumers to the dramatic lowering of fuel prices led - unexpectedly to most of us - to a very moderate increase in aggregate energy demand. Transaction costs are certainly only one explanation for this observed asymmetric demand behaviour. Asymmetric price elasticities can be explained by some other factors, like irreversibility of technological progress and price expectations. Furthermore, government policies foster generally asymmetric behaviour, as energy conservation policies are applied even at the low current energy price levels. These policies give a momentum to investments in energy conservation measures which otherwise would not have been taken place. These effects contributed also to the unexpected "weak" demand reaction to the lowering of energy prices.

But in the case of residential energy demand, transaction costs seem to be the most important factor influencing this asymmetry. Transaction costs may explain some portion of the asymmetric demand behaviour within the industrial sector as well, especially in the case of small enterprises. In these industries there is generally a lower level of technical skill, and a lack of information about energy technologies. This can result in transaction costs which are similar to those in the residential sector.

The consequences of

(a) an increase in energy demand which is still lower than the figure that would be predicted if average elasticities are applied and

(b) a reduced inclination to resubstitute oil

are that the currently balanced energy market will persist for some time, even if energy prices remain at their current low level. Some econometric models which do not take into account this asymmetric consumer reaction (and most existing models do not take this into account) predict an imbalance between supply and demand in the near future, which is likely to be postponed due to a different consumer behaviour as argued above. Particularly for the oil market, sluggish demand reactions help to postpone the (expected) return of higher oil prices. The current buyers' market is likely to last in the medium term. Therefore, it can be projected that oil will not regain its dominant position of the early 70's. Moreover, an asymmetric demand behaviour makes price hikes more costly (to Opec) and could therefore act as a safety valve against another oil price jump.

5. Concluding remarks

This paper tried to find an explanation for the consumer reaction to lower energy prices. Most energy analysts and policy makers have overestimated the consumer reaction to the decrease in energy prices which started in winter 1985, and were surprised by the limited increase of energy and oil demand. Energy policy relies to a great extent on the data which is provided by energy analysts and their models. Overestimating (as well underestimating) of future demand can lead to a misallocation of resources. Now, the projections obtained from econometric demand models tend to overestimate this growth of demand. As analysts we have to adopt and have to look for new techniques to cope with some weaknesses of our present analytical tools. Transaction costs provide one reason for this observed asymmetric behaviour in world energy markets.

The stake for future research are now quite obvious. The empirical application of this paper was confined to a particular example where a great detail of data was available. A broader empirical investigation of residential (and may be also commercial) energy demand seems necessary to support our preliminary findings. In particular qualitative choice models, where it is necessary to surpass a certain treshhold to achieve an impact, could be applied to test the ideas of this paper in broader context and without prohibitive implications on data gathering. Furthermore, it seems appropriate to investigate - theoretically and empirically - other reasons for the current slow response of energy demand to the dramatic reduction in fuel costs.

References:

Bohi Douglas R. (1981), *Analyzing Demand Behavior: A Study of Energy Elasticities*, published for Resources for the Future by John Hopkins Press, Baltimore and London.

Cameron Trudy Ann (1985), A Nested Logit Model of Conservation Activity by Owners of Existing Single Family Dwellings, *Review of Economics and Statistics*, **67**, 205-211.

Dubin Jeffrey and Daniel McFadden (1984), An Econometric Analysis of Residential Electric Appliance Holdings and Consumption, *Econometrica*, **52**, 345-362.

Dubin Jeffrey, Miedema Allen K. and Ram V. Chandran (1986), Price Effects of Energy-Efficient Technologies: A Study of Residential Demand for Heating and Cooling, *The Rand Journal of Economics*, **17**, 310-325.

Hirst Eric (1987), Changes in Indoor Temperature After Retrofit Based on Electricity Billing and Weather Data, *Energy Systems and Policy*, **10**, 1-20.

Pindyck Robert S. (1979), *The Structure of World Energy Demand*, MIT Press, Cambridge, Mass..

Schipper Lee and Andrea N. Ketoff (1985), Residential Energy Use in the OECD, *The Energy Journal*, **6**, No4, 65-85.

Williamson Oliver E., *Markets and Hierarchies: Analysis and Antitrust Implications*, Free Press, New York, (1975).

Williamson Oliver E. (1981), The Modern Corporation: Origins, Evolution, Attributes, *Journal of Economic Literature*, **19**, 1537-1568.

Willimason Oliver E., The Economics of Governance: Framework and Implications, *Zeitschrift für gesamte Staatswissenschafte*, **140**, 195-223, (1984).

Wirl Franz (1988), Thermal Comfort, Energy Conservation and Fuel Substitution: An Economic-Engineering Approach, *Energy Systems and Policy*, **11**, 311-328.

III. Efficiency in Production

RETURNS TO SCALE AND EFFICIENCY IN PRODUCTION: A DISTANCE FUNCTION APPROACH TO
SOUTHERN ILLINOIS HOG FARMS

R. Färe, W. Herr, and D. Njinkeu
Southern Illinois University

1. Introduction

In this paper, we introduce a parametric specification of a ray-homothetic input
distance function. We choose to parametrice our distance function in such a manner
that it becomes log-linear in the parameters. This choice enables us to utilize a
generalized version of Aigner and Chu (1968) to compute the parameters of the
function as solutions to a linear programming problem. The purpose of these
theoretical developments are to formulate a framework for the measurements of scale
elasticity and input efficiency. The analysis follows ideas introduced by Farrell
(1957) and it is applied to the U.S. agricultural sector. The approach followed in
this paper allows for a multiple output technology and does not require knowledge of
prices. In addition, our methodology allows us to explicitly study the notion of
scale elasticity and technical efficiency with respect to output size (in a
multi-output setting) and output mix.

Finally, we apply our methodology to a set of Southern Illinois hog farms over the
period 1980-1987. To preview our results, we find that technical efficiency is in
general high and that increasing returns prevail. Also, we find that there is a
positive relation between farm size and scale elasticity.

2. A Ray-Homothetic Technology

Let $y\epsilon R_+^M$ denote a vector of net outputs and let $x\epsilon R_+^N$ denote a vector of inputs. The
production technology may be modeled by an input correspondence,

$$(2.1) \qquad L: R_+^M \rightarrow L(y) \subseteq R_+^N,$$

where the input requirement set $L(y)$ denotes all input vectors $x\epsilon R_+^N$ that can produce
the output vector $y\epsilon R_+^M$, i.e., $L(y) = \{x\epsilon R_+^N: x \text{ produce } y\}$. Färe and Shephard (1977)
define the input correspondence to be ray-homothetic if it can be written as

(2.2) $L(y) = \dfrac{H(y)}{H(\frac{y}{\|y\|})} \, L(\frac{y}{\|y\|})$,

where $\|y\|$ denotes the norm of y, and where $H: R_+^M \to R_+$ is a scalar valued function, consistent with the properties of L. Moreover, they say that the input correspondence is globally homothetic if it is of the form

(2.3) $L(y) = G(B(y))L(1)$,

where $B: R_+^M \to R_+$ and $G: R_+ \to R_+$ are two functions consistent with the properties of L. In order to relate the two "homothetic" input correspondences, we show next that (2.3) is a special case of (2.2). Let $\lambda > 0$, then it follows from (2.3) that

$$L(\lambda y) = G(B(\lambda y))L(1)$$

and thus

$$L(1) = (G(B(\lambda y)))^{-1}L(\lambda y) = (G(B(y)))^{-1}L(y).$$

Therefore,

(2.4) $L(y) = \dfrac{G(B(y))}{G(B(\lambda y))} \, L(\lambda y)$.

Now, take $\lambda = 1/\|y\|$ and let $G(B(y)) = H(y)$, then (2.4) becomes (2.2). Hence we have shown that (2.3) is a special case of (2.2).

In this paper we will adopt a particular version of (2.3). We assume that B(y) has the property

(2.5) $B(\lambda y) = \lambda^{g(y/\|y\|)} B(y), \ \lambda > 0$,

i.e., the function is ray-homogeneous in outputs. In particular this model allows for the degree of homogeneity to vary with the output mix $y/\|y\|$. (The notion of ray-homogeneity is due to Eichhorn, 1969). The expression (2.5) now yields,

(2.6) $G(B(\lambda y)) = G(\lambda^{g(y/\|y\|)} B(y)), \ \lambda > 0$,

i.e., a ray-homothetic function. This function is a monotone (homothetic) transformation of the ray-homogeneous function (2.5). When (2.6) holds, (2.3) becomes

(2.7) $L(\lambda y) = G(\lambda^{g(y/\|y\|)}B(y))L(1), \lambda > 0.$

We term this input correspondence strongly ray-homothetic to distinguish it from (2.2). Prior to our parametrization, we need to introduce the input distance function. This function is defined as

(2.8) $D_i(y,x) = \sup\{\lambda: x/\lambda \epsilon L(y)\},$

and if $L(y)$ is strongly ray-homothetic it becomes

(2.9) $D_i(y,x) = F(x)/G(B(y)),$

where $G(B(y))$ has the property expressed by (2.6) and where $F(x) = \sup\{\lambda: x/\lambda \epsilon L(1)\}$. (Note that F is homogeneous of degree +1). We also note that since $L(y) = \{x\epsilon R_+^N: D(y,x) \geq 1\}$, (w.7) and (2.9) are equivalent expressions of the technology.

The first objective of this paper is to compute the Farrell input based technical efficiency for each observation. Given the input distance function, this is done by inverting the value of $D_i(y,x)$, since, see Färe, Grosskopf and Lovell (1985, p. 55), the Farrell measure is the inverse of this distance function.

The second objective is to compute returns to scale. This too can be done using the input distance function. Following Färe, Grosskopf and Lovell (1986), the input-based measure of scale elasticity expressed in terms of the input distance function is given by

$$(2.10) \quad \epsilon = -(\lim_{\lambda \to 1} \frac{\partial D_i(\lambda y,x)}{\partial \lambda} \frac{\lambda}{D_i(y,x)})^{-1} = -(\frac{1}{D_i(y,x)} \sum_{m=1}^{M} \frac{\partial D_i(y,x)}{\partial y_m} y_m)^{-1},$$

and the technology exhibit increasing, constant or decreasing returns to scale if $\epsilon > 1, = 1$ or < 1 respectively.

Our parametric choice for the distance function (2.9) is to take $F(x)$ as a translog function, i.e., apply a second order approximation to it, and to take $G(B(y))$ as a ray-homothetic function which is log linear in its parameters. Thus,

$$(2.11) \quad \log D_i(y,x) = a_o + \sum_{n=1}^{N} a_n \ln x_n + \sum_{n=1}^{N} \sum_{j=1}^{N} a_{nj} \ln x_n \ln x_j$$

$$- \sum_{m=1}^{M} (b_m + c_m \frac{y_m}{\|y\|} + d_m \|y\|) \ln y_m = \ln F(x) - \ln G(B(y)),$$

is our choice. The parameters of this model are computed using the linear programming idea of Aigner and Chu (1968). In our framework, if (x^k, y^k), $k = 1, \ldots, K$, denotes an observation, we must solve the linear programming problem

$$\underset{\substack{a_o, a_n, a_{nj} \\ b_m, c_m, d_m}}{\text{Min}} \quad \sum_{k=1}^{K} (\ln F(x^k) - \ln G(B(y^k)))$$

$$\text{s.t. } \ln F(x^k) - \ln G(B(y^k)) \geq 0, \quad k = 1, \ldots, K.$$

$$\sum_{n=1}^{N} a_n = 1, \quad \sum_{n=1}^{N} \sum_{n=j}^{N} a_{nj} = 0, \quad a_{nj} = a_{jn},$$

where the restriction on the parameters are imposed to obtain homogeneity of degree +1 in $F(x)$ and symmetry.

Once the parameters of $D_i(y, x)$ are computed, we can calculate the technical efficiency and the returns to scale. The particular form scale elasticity takes under our parametrization is

$$(2.12) \quad \varepsilon = -\sum_{m=1}^{M} \left(b_m + c_m \frac{y_m}{\|y\|} + d_m \|y\| + d_m \|y\| \ln y_m \right).$$

Expression (2.12) shows that scale elasticity depends on the output mix, i.e., $y/\|y\|$, as well as the size of output, i.e., $\|y\|$. Clearly if $c_m = 0$, $m = 1, \ldots, M$, our technology is globally homothetic, and if in addition, $d_m = 0$, $m = 1, \ldots, M$, the technology is homogeneous.

3. Data and Results

The above framework is used to study the technical efficiency and returns to scale of Southern Illinois hog farms during the period 1980-1986. The data pertaining to hog farms is obtained from Illinois Farm Business Farm Management Service records. A hog farm is defined as one for which the value of feed fed to livestock exceeds 40 percent of the crops returns and hogs received more than half of the value of feed fed.

The hog farms are modeled by a two-output five-input distance function. The two outputs considered are the livestock (hog) output and the non-livestock output. The livestock (hog) output is determined as the gross value of livestock produced composed of livestock return above feed plus the value of feed fed. The gross value of non-livestock output is determined as the sum of crop returns, custom work and other farm receipts. The five inputs are total crop cost, power and equipment cost, labor cost, building cost, and other cost. The number of hog farms included in the study vary between 67 and 88, depending upon the year. The difference in the number of observations between years is due to the fact that the same farm does not meet the definition of a hog farm in every year and some farms enter and exit the service each year.

The value of parameters of the distance function from which the measures of technical efficiency and scale economies are determined are reported in the appendix.

The characteristics of technical efficiency are summarized in tables 1 and 2. Table 1 contains information on the distribution of technical efficiency by year. The mean technical efficiency varies from 82 to 87 percent with the lowest averages found in 1980 and 1981 and the highest averages in 1985 and 1986. These mean technical efficiency indicate that on average all inputs could be reduced by between 13 and 18 percent without reducing output. Most farms have high efficiency scores as more than 50 percent of farms each year have an efficiency score above 80 percent. Except for 1981, comparison of the third quartile and the maximum value indicates that at least 25 percent of the farms each year are more than 95 percent efficient. The least efficient farms have an efficiency score below 50 percent in 1981, 1982, and 1983. As evidenced by the negative skewness coefficient, the least efficient farms are the outliers.

Table 2 gives the correlation coefficient between the measure of technical efficiency and each variable used in the distance function. There is no consistent relationship between the output variables and the measure of technical efficiency. For example only five of the possible 14 correlation between the two types of outputs and technical efficiency for the seven years are significantly different from zero at the 10 percent significance level and of these 3 are negative and 2 are positive. Correlation between the five input categories and the technical efficiency score are basically negative. The negative relationship is observed in all years except 1983 when all correlation are positive. 1983 was unusual in that the payment-in-kind (PIK) program was initiated with substantial acreage reduction. 1983 was also a drought year. Of the remaining 30 possible correlations (5 inputs and 6 years), all are negative except one -- building cost in 1986. Moreover, of the 29 negative correlations only 4 are not significantly different from zero at the 10 percent significance level. The negative correlation between inputs and the measure of technical efficiency is contrary to results obtained by Dawson (1985) and Britton and Hill (1975) and Lund and Hill (1979). Dawson found a positive linear relationship between technical efficiency and inputs while the latter two studies found no consistent relationship between technical efficiency and input or size.

Tables 3 and 4 give similar information for the analysis of returns to scale. In each year the mean coefficient of scale elasticity indicates the presence of increasing returns to scale and except for 1980, minimum values are all larger than 1 indicating the presence of increasing returns to scale on virtually all farms. Except for 1985 and 1986, using the skewness coefficient, the indicated maximum value of scale elasticity constitutes an outlier. About 75 percent of the farms have a coefficient of scale elasticity of 1.30 or less.

Table 4 gives the correlation coefficient between the coefficient of scale elasticity and each variable used in the distance function. Most variables are positively related to the measure of scale elasticity. This could be expected; the larger the input or output the more likely is a farm to enjoy scale economies. Negative correlation coefficients are observed mostly with the non-livestock part of the business -- non-hog output and crop cost. Except for 1981, there is a positive relationship between livestock output and the coefficient of scale elasticity. For the six years in which the correlation is positive, the correlation coefficient is significantly different from zero at the 1 percent significance level.

A special feature of the translog-ray-homothetic distance function is the inclusion of a measure of the size of the farm; size was measured from the output figures. The adoption of a two-output technology also facilitates the analysis of the relationship between the output mix and both returns to scale and technical efficiency. These two features are summarized in table 5. The first two columns give the relationship between size and technical efficiency and scale elasticity, respectively. No consistent pattern could be detected between farm size and technical efficiency. Though most coefficients were negative, only two of the seven coefficients were significant at the 5 percent level and one of these has a positive and the other a negative sign.

A positive and statistically significant correlation at the 5 percent level was observed between size and scale elasticity in all years. The first two columns of table 5 thus suggest that, the smaller firm tend to be more efficient than larger farms although the relationship is at best very weak. And larger farms tend to enjoy scale economies in all year.

The third and fourth columns of table 5 provide the relationship between the output ratio and the measure of technical efficiency and scale elasticity, respectively. There is no consistent correlation between the output ratio and technical efficiency.

However, in 6 of the 7 years there is a negative and statistically significant
correlation between the output ratio and scale elasticity. In 1981 the correlation
is positive but still significant at near the 5 percent level. In the 5 years where
the probability is .01 percent the correlation is smaller than -.76. The negative
association means that as the output mix becomes more oriented towards hogs, scale
economies increase.

The last column of table 5 indicates that there is no consistent relationship
between technical efficiency and scale elasticity.

4. Conclusion

The purpose of this paper is to develop a method for measuring technical efficiency
and returns to scale. The proposed method consists of specifying a distance
function which is further modeled by a ray-homothetic-translog functional form.
Parameters of the distance function are computed via a generalized version of Aigner
and Chu (1968) which, unlike least square techniques, allows computation of the
parameters of a flexible functional form without loss of degrees of freedom.
Another special feature of the proposed approach is the possibility to model a
multi-input-multi-output technology when prices are not available.

The method was applied to Southern Illinois hog farms over the period 1980-1986.
The technical efficiency of hog farms is in general high. Average efficiency score
for each of the years ranged from 82 to 87 percent and the least efficient farms are
the outliers. We observed that technical efficiency tended to be negatively
associated with all variables in the distance function. A consistent negative
association, however, was not found when overall size was measured. No consistent
association was found between technical efficiency and the output ratio. We found
strong evidence of increasing returns to scale on hog farms which is especially
related to the hog enterprise. There is positive association between the
coefficient of scale elasticity and hog output and non-crop variables of the
distance function. This finding is reinforced by the negative correlation between
the ratio of non-hog to hog output with the coefficient of scale economies.

152

Table 1

Description of Technical Efficiency of Hog Farms in Southern Illinois by Year
1980-86

Year	Number of Observations	Mean	Standard Deviation	Minimum Value	First Quartile	Median	Third Quartile	Maximum Value	Skewness Coefficient	Kurtosis Coefficient
1980	76	.8223	.13567	.5634	.7150	.8255	.9526	.9998	-.1567	-1.1669
1981	85	.8178	.14310	.4557	.7119	.8394	.9368	1.0000	-.4631	-.5500
1982	78	.8426	.1239	.4895	.7591	.8331	.9678	.99999	-.4616	-.1830
1983	88	.8637	.1299	.4301	.7944	.8991	.9734	1.0000	-1.1499	.9492
1984	80	.8452	.1187	.5388	.7553	.8523	.9572	.99995	-.3990	-.4030
1985	75	.8713	.1225	.5334	.7787	.8906	.9918	1.0000	-.8043	-.0049
1986	67	.8748	.1099	.5457	.7899	.8830	.9968	1.0000	-.5577	-.2996

Table 2

Correlation Between Technical Efficiency and Each Variable of the Distance Function by Year, 1980-86

Year	y_1	y_2	V124	V131	V135	V138	V144
1980	-.02051 (.8604)	-.00441 (.9698)	-.18637 (.1070)	-.35332 (.0017)	-.21505 (.0621)	-.28192 (.0136)	-.29122 (.0107)
1981	.03164 (.7738)	-.12864 (.2407)	-.15359 (.1605)	-.31804 (.0030)	-.28507 (.0082)	-.25151 (.0202)	-.28827 (.0077)
1982	-.01559 (.8922)	-.19443 (.0881)	-.30864 (.0060)	-.21767 (.0556)	-.16443 (.1503)	-.42687 (.0001)	-.24895 (.0280)
1983	.35013 (.0008)	.39570 (.0001)	.33192 (.0016)	.33564 (.0014)	.13272 (.2177)	.20285 (.0580)	.29579 (.0051)
1984	.05045 (.6567)	.03254 (.7744)	-.17601 (.1184)	-.11226 (.3215)	-.18805 (.0948)	-.25605 (.0219)	-.16667 (.1395)
1985	-.20440 (.0786)	-.28549 (.0130)	-.41657 (.0002)	-.43869 (.0001)	-.37747 (.0008)	-.37151 (.0010)	-.44356 (.0001)
1986	-.03244 (.7944)	-.10387 (.4029)	-.34622 (.0041)	-.29898 (.0140)	.01892 (.8792)	-.30186 (.0130)	-.27870 (.0224)

y_1 = non-hog output   V124 = total crop cost   V135 = building cost   V144 = other cost
y_2 = hog output   V131 = power and equipment cost   V138 = labor cost   p value are indicated in parentheses

Table 3

Description of Returns to Scale on Hog Farms in Southern Illinois by Year, 1980-86

Year	Mean	Standard Deviation	Minimum Value	First Quartile	Median	Third Quartile	Maximum Value	Skewness Coefficient	Kurtosis Coefficient
1980	1.1806	.1782	.9676	1.0519	1.1338	1.2329	1.7633	1.3806	1.4292
1981	1.1682	.0302	1.0955	1.1551	1.1703	1.1757	1.2654	.3111	1.8719
1982	1.2550	.1503	1.0690	1.1612	1.1994	1.3037	1.8237	1.8846	3.7074
1983	1.3015	.0430	1.2081	1.2759	1.2967	1.3234	1.4337	.9874	1.1582
1984	1.2268	.1000	1.1237	1.1552	1.1953	1.2841	1.7292	2.1170	7.0667
1985	1.2404	.0263	1.1794	1.2192	1.2412	1.2625	1.2872	-.1360	-1.0033
1986	1.1795	.0388	1.0686	1.1496	1.1827	1.2089	1.2920	-.1015	.3936

Table 4

Correlation Between Scale Elasticity and Each Variable of the Distance Function by Year, 1980-86

Year	y_1	y_2	V124	V131	V135	V138	V144
1980	-.25292	.59818	-.09908	.05067	.17689	.24470	.05260
	(.0275)	(.0001)	(.3945)	(.6638)	(.1264)	(.0331)	(.6518)
1981	.61249	-.09216	.32301	.27808	.20476	.01506	.30422
	(.0001)	(.4015)	(.0260)	(.0100)	(.0601)	(.8912)	(.0046)
1982	.01633	.79464	.26975	.18965	.31359	.43037	.31059
	(.8871)	(.0001)	(.0169)	(.0963)	(.0052)	(.0001)	(.0056)
1983	.79034	.89358	.73839	.77158	.74021	.77105	.86209
	(.0001)	(.0001)	(.0001)	(.0001)	(.0001)	(.0001)	(.0001)
1984	-.18739	.69540	-.17818	.01367	.28796	.28056	.09834
	(.0960)	(.0001)	(.1138)	(.9042)	(.0096)	(.0117)	(.3855)
1985	-.24460	.46815	-.21110	-.01906	.17757	.26850	.02373
	(.0344)	(.0001)	(.0691)	(.8711)	(.1275)	(.0199)	(.8399)
1986	.20138	.77152	.19066	.42781	.60949	.56241	.44480
	(.1022)	(.0001)	(.1222)	(.0003)	(.0001)	(.0001)	(.0002)

y_1 = non-hog output   V124 = total crop cost   V135 = building cost   V144 = other cost

y_2 = hog output   V131 = power and equipment cost   V138 = labor cost   p value are indicated

Table 5
Correlation Between Size, Output Ratio and the Measure of TE and SE
by years 1980-86

Year	Size · TE	Size · SE	Ratio · TE	Ratio · SE	TE · SE
1980	-.00230	.25697	-.10528	-.8499	.03933
	(.9843)	(.025)	(.3654)	(.0001)	(.7353)
1981	-.07286	.21629	-.02541	.20867	.23013
	(.5075)	(.0468)	(.8175)	(.0553)	(.0341)
1982	-.15550	.64676	.07741	-.76606	-.19319
	(.1740)	(.0001)	(.5005)	(.0001)	(.0901)
1983	.42464	.96344	-.30043	-.31132	.43411
	(.0001)	(.0001)	(.0045)	(.0032)	(.0001)
1984	.05185	.47046	-.07718	-.80364	.06440
	(.6479)	(.0001)	(.4929)	(.0001)	(.5703)
1985	-.27852	.24952	.1660	-.97774	-.15849
	(.0155)	(.0309)	(.1546)	(.0001)	(.1744)
1986	-.09407	.68123	-.01260	-.87217	-.03763
	(.4489)	(.0001)	(.9194)	(.0001)	(.7624)

SE = Scale Elasticity
TE = Technical Efficiency

$$\text{Ratio} = \frac{\text{Non-hog Output } (y_1)}{\text{Hog Output } (y_2)}$$

$$\text{Size} = \left[y_1^2 + y_2^2 \right]^{1/2}$$

Appendix 1: Parameters of the Distance Function

Variable	1980	1981	1982	1983	1984	1985	1986
Crop Cost (x_1)	.648650	.273272	.637472	1.000	.622961	1.153728	.755371
Power, Equipment (x_2)	0	0	-.191543	0	0	-1.037235	0
Building (x_3)	0	.726728	.138484	0	.377039	.494869	.039254
Labor (x_4)	0	0	0	0	0	1.102457	.205375
Other Cost (x_5)	.351350	0	.415587	0	0	-.713819	0
$x_1 x_1$	.420085	.00679923	0	-.291578	-.137961	0	.269985
$x_2 x_2$	0	0	0	0	0	0	0
$x_3 x_3$	-.045407	.277550	.075501	-.181727	.096080	.027464	-.022866
$x_4 x_4$	.407854	.152031	-.336021	-.099578	-.171917	.337397	.062067
$x_5 x_5$	0	.108435	0	-2.009432	.084758	0	.421668
$x_1 x_2$	-.242955	-.249874	-.110567	-.059668	-.020573	-.761822	-.00268351
$x_1 x_3$	.219012	.248342	.145260	-.117624	.193955	.263918	.015109
$x_1 x_4$	-.083017	-.074780	.026447	-.173517	-.144701	.603450	.308503
$x_1 x_5$	-.313124	.069562	-.282274	.496598	-.166641	-.105546	-.590914
$x_2 x_3$	.163738	-.040383	-.285058		-.023657	-.108331	-.066728
$x_2 x_4$	-.299500	-.076363	.130985	-.612113	0	-.409490	-.393842
$x_2 x_5$	.378718	.285853	.043505	.608488	.044230	1.279642	.329797
$x_3 x_4$	-.148542	-.051657	.002058003	.003624519	.006293679	.229844	.062426
$x_3 x_5$	.188800	-.514618	.062239	.259069	-.272672	-.412896	-.121397
$x_4 x_5$	.123206	.050768	.176531	.831794	.310325	-.761200	-.039154
Hog Output (y_1)	0	0	0	.359440	0	.258543	0
Non-Hog Output (y_2)	1.028270	.8112852	.963155	.640560	.764930	.596607	.907801

Appendix 1: Parameters of the Distance Function (continued)

Variable	1980	1981	1982	1983	1984	1985	1986
$y_1/\|y\|$	.030446	.127513	.027623	-.121077	.126924	.025208	.085218
$y_2/\|y\|$	-.150296	-.048054	-.136826	-.152516	.017152	-.089274	-.102470
Size Hog Output	.000001034	$-.395767 \cdot 10^{-5}$	$.367407 \cdot 10^{-5}$	$.966214 \cdot 10^{-6}$	$.212501 \cdot 10^{-5}$	$-.139229 \cdot 10^{-6}$	$-.864018 \cdot 10^{-5}$
Size Non-Hog Output	-.0000010409	$.388352 \cdot 10^{-5}$	$-.376996 \cdot 10^{-5}$	$-.336283 \cdot 10^{-6}$	$-.217834 \cdot 10^{-5}$	$.140232 \cdot 10^{-6}$	$.753951 \cdot 10^{-5}$
Constant Term	0	0	0	3.614708	0	0	0

References

Aigner, D., and S. Chu (1968) "On Estimating the Industry Production Function,"
 American Economic Review, 58:4, 826-839.

Britton, D.K. and H.B. Hill (1975) Size and Efficiency in Farming, Farnborough:
 Saxon House cited by Dawson (1985).

Dawson, P.J. (1985) "Measuring Technical Efficiency From Production Functions: Some
 Further Estimates," Journal of Agricultural Economics 36, 31-40.

Dawson, P.J. (1987) "Farm Specific Technical Efficiency in the England and Wales
 Dairy Sector," European Review of Agricultural Economics, 14(4): 383-394.

Eichhorn, W. (1969) "Eine Verallgemeinerung des Begriffs der Homogenen
 Produktionsfunktion," Unternehmensforschung, 13, 99-109.

Ekanayake, S.A.B. and S.K. Jayasuriya (1987) "Measurement of Firm Specific
 Technical Efficiency: A comparison of Methods," Journal of Agricultural Economics.

Färe, R. (1988) Fundamentals of Production Theory, Lecture Notes in Economics
 and Mathematical Systems, Vol. 311, Springer-Verlag, Berlin.

Färe, R., S. Grosskopf, and C.A.K. Lovell (1985) The Measurement of Efficiency
 of Production, Kluwer-Nijhoff, Boston.

Färe, R., S. Grosskopf, and C.A.K. Lovell (1986) "Scale Economics and Duality,"
 Zeitschrift für Nationalökonomie, 46, 175-182.

Färe, R., and R.W. Shephard (1977) "Ray-Homothetic Production Functions,"
 Econometrica, 45:1, 133-146.

Farrell, M.J. (1957) "The Measurement of Productive Efficiency," Journal of Royal
 Statistical Society, Series A (General), 120, 253-281.

Lund, P.J. and P.G. Hill (1979) "Farm Size, Efficiency and Economics of Size,"
 Journal of Agricultural Economics, 30, 145-158.

Njinkeu, D. (forthcoming) "On Firm Specific Technical Efficiency: A Monte Carlo
 Comparison," European Review of Agricultural Economics.

VARIABLE COST FRONTIERS AND EFFICIENCY:
AN INVESTIGATION OF LABOR COSTS IN HOSPITALS

Patricia Byrnes
Center for Naval Analyses
4401 Ford Avenue
Alexandria, VA 22302

Vivian Valdmanis
School of Public Health
Tulane University
New Orleans, LA 70112

Introduction

Health economists recognize that the rising cost of hospital services is due, at least in part, to features of the industry which create costly resource misallocation that decreases productivity. Organizational structure, lack of competition in the market for health care in some areas, imperfections in factor markets, and government regulation have all been hypothesized to effect the cost minimizing performance of hospitals. A growing body of empirical research which seeks to investigate cost inefficiencies in the health care industry and these predications of the effect of industry structure on performance has resulted. Most of this work has followed one modeling approach: (1) measuring either total cost or technical efficiency with aggregate measures of non- physician labor (2) without examining the technical and allocative components of cost inefficiency (3) and using statistical techniques to estimate a parametric cost or production frontier. In this study additional empirical evidence on inefficiency of hospitals is provided using a different modeling approach.

Previous studies of hospital efficiency and costs have analyzed hospitals on the basis of overall productive efficiency. That is, actual hospital costs are compared to the estimated cost minimizing levels. Cowing and Holtman [5] and Eakin and Kniesner [6] both estimated overall cost minimizing efficiency for hospitals employing the stochastic method of estimating a cost frontier. While these studies provided useful insights into cost efficiency and the structure of the hospital service production relationship, they were limited in two important respects. First, neither study decomposed inefficiency into its technical and allocative component measures. The decomposition of cost inefficiency into these components provides valuable information on the sources of inefficiency. Moreover, the technical efficiency component is measured independent of data on factor prices, hence is free of the well known problems of measuring these variables in the hospital services sector.

A second limitation of these studies is that there was limited analysis of the substitution between labor inputs. Interestingly, both studies found similar results; physician inputs and capital inputs are generally over-utilized given output levels produced by the hospitals. Very little mention was made about non-physician labor which is puzzling given that non-physician labor costs comprise over half (57 percent) of total hospital costs (see [1]).

Other studies, perhaps due to lack of reliable input price data, have focused exclusively on the technical efficiency component, since technical efficiency measurement requires only data on the quantities of inputs and outputs. Banker, Conrad and Strauss [2] compared the non-statistical, linear programming or Data Envelopment Analysis (DEA) approach and stochastic approach to technical efficiency measurement for a sample of North Carolina hospitals. Using DEA, Grosskopf and Valdmanis [11] examined technical efficiency differences between public and non-profit hospital in California. Register and Burning [16], also using the DEA approach, examined technical inefficiency among a nationwide cross-section of non-profit, for profit and public hospitals. These works advanced the use of the non-parametric, nonstochastic approach for analyzing hospitals, however, they did not include measures of allocative efficiency.

This study differs from previous empirical work in three respects. First the performance measure used is different than the measures generally used. Most previous studies have focused on total factor productivity or total cost efficiency or both. While of considerable use, these measures are limited in their ability to focus more neutrally on individual factor efficiency. In particular, the investigation of the hospital's employment of labor inputs may be obfuscated by the hospital's inability to adjust costlessly fixed factors to changes in relative factor prices. To correct for this methodological shortcoming, this study extends the Farrell [9] decomposition of cost efficiency into its allocative and technical components in a short-run or ex-post efficiency framework. The efficiency of the variable factors of production, in this case non-physician labor, are analyzed assuming some factors of production are fixed by ex ante decisions. In this framework, a hospital is not penalized for ex ante mistakes. Rather, the short-run cost inefficiency and sources of that inefficiency, either technical or allocative, are revealed apart from the efficiency loss associated with the fixity of inputs.

The second way in which this study differs is that cost inefficiency is decomposed into it's technical and allocative components. The cost estimates of earlier studies either combined these two or focused on just one component. Information on the source of cost inefficiency allows for exploration of hypotheses that characteristics of the hospital industry create X-inefficiency or managerial slack as well as misallocation of resources given relative prices.

Finally, this study uses the nonparametric DEA approach to model the hospital cost and production relationship. Previous studies, in general, have used an explicit cost function or frontier framework. Consequently their findings are conditioned on a restrictive parametric representation of production possibilities, and they may be misleading if the functional form is inappropriate. Rather than estimate a parametric production or cost frontier using some squared-error minimization criterion, we use linear programming or DEA techniques to bound or envelop the data with a nonparametric production frontier. This approach has the advantage of providing a nonparametric representation of the efficient technology, the structure of which is determined by weak regularity conditions and by the data, rather than the researcher's choice of parametric form. Consequently it minimizes the likelihood that cost performance is masked by specification error.

We apply this approach to a sample of NFP hospitals operating in California in 1982. Since our data are incomplete (as we discuss later), we use this industry to illustrate this method's potential as a tool in both economic analysis of non-profit firms and policy analysis in service sectors.

From a policy perspective, the ex post approach to estimating labor efficiency and costs should be useful. Labor inputs (especially nurses) provide direct patient care; compromising the use of nurses may therefore detract from both patient care and efficiency. The performance measures used here allows us to compare hospital's on the basis of their employment of different types of non-physician labor and compare the substitution between these inputs.

The paper is organized as follows. In section 2 Farrell framework for cost efficiency measurement is reviewed. A discussion of the efficiency in the production of hospital services is included. In section 3 the extension of the Farrell cost efficiency framework is presented and the labor cost efficiency measures in the linear programming (DEA) approach are developed. The hospital data are presented in section 4 and the empirical findings are reported in section 5. Section 6 concludes.

Cost Efficiency and Hospital Service Production

Since Leibenstein, [13] and [14], introduced the theory of X-inefficiency studies of productive inefficiency in a wide variety of industries has resulted. The theory contends that without competition in the product market, X-inefficiency (or inefficiency internal to the firm arising from managerial discretion, non-maximizing behavior and inefficient management techniques) will persist. The NFP hospital sector is one such industry in which conditions existing in the market are conducive for X-inefficiency. For example, the nature of third party reimbursements is one feature of the industry expected to impact X-efficiency performance. Since costs are not passed to the consumer, but reimbursed by insurance, there are no incentives for hospital managers to behave in a cost minimizing manner.

In addition to lack of price competition in the product market, another aspect of the hospital industry which may lead to inefficiency is a non-competitive market for inputs. For example, Sloan and Steinwald [17] and Booton and Lane [3] examine the resource allocation effects of the hospitals' monopsonist control over nurses. In order for a nurse to practice, oftentimes a hospital is the only place s/he can find employment opportunities. Due to this monopsony arrangement, hospitals can suppress wages below what they should have been in a competitive labor market. Further, hospitals can substitute nurses for other labor inputs. Again, features of the hospital input markets, in this example the market for nurses, distort managers decisions so that inputs are not necessarily hired so as to minimize costs.

In order to gauge hospital performance, there have been essentially two types of empirical analysis employed. One estimation procedure compares hospital performance on the basis of costs. The second approach commonly used focuses on the production relationship and compares the total factor productivity of hospitals. In this paper we employ a relatively new approach that follows the work of Farrell [9]. Farrell's framework allows us to put these efficiency notions in context. The importance of Farrell's work is that he focuses on overall cost minimizing efficiency but he provides a decomposition of overall efficiency into two components: allocative and technical efficiency. These concepts are illustrated in figure 1.

Referring to Figure 1, let x_1 and x_2 denote the two inputs used in the production. Let $I'I'$ represent the isoquant or lower bound of the set of all input combinations yielding at least output level u. Given input prices, as reflected in the isocost line labeled C_1, the cost minimizing input combination for output u is at point E.

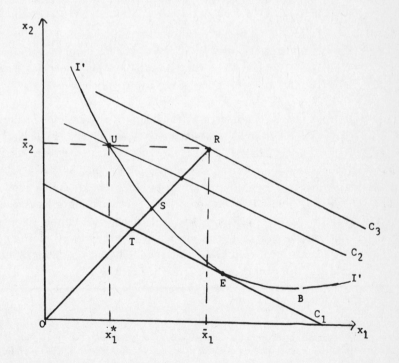

Figure 1: Illustration of Total Cost Efficiency Measures

Farrell proposed measuring the deviation from cost minimization as the ratio of efficient input usage to actual input usage, given observed input proportions. In terms of figure 1, for a firm operating at point R, this overall inefficiency, $OE(u, x, p)$ where, u, refers to output, x refers to inputs, and p refers to input prices, can be measured as OT/OR which in this case is less than one.[1] One minus this measure tells us by how much (in percentage terms) the observed hospital could reduce all inputs proportionately if they were minimizing costs.

By decomposing the overall measure, we find that the technical component of this overall measure is OS/OR in figure 1. Essentially, this technical efficiency measure, denoted $TE(u, x)$, tells us "how far" the firm is from the isoquant. The allocative efficiency component, $AE(u, x, p)$, is measured as OT/OS and captures inefficiency due to the fact that the hospital, even if on the isoquant, with it's factor proportions did not pick the "right" input combination given the relative input prices reflected in C_1. To summarize the Farrell decomposition of overall cost minimizing efficiency:

$$OE(u, x, p) \;=\; TE(u, x) \cdot AE(u, x, p) \tag{1}$$

which is confirmed for the example in figure 1, since

$$OT/OR \;=\; OS/OR \cdot OT/OS \tag{2}$$

In this framework, the performance of hospitals is gauged relative to the minimum costs of that hospital's production. Moreover, differences in actual costs and the estimated minimum cost may be the result of technical inefficiency or allocative inefficiency or both. Note that, it is possible to be technically efficient, that is producing on the isoquant or $TE(u, x) = 1$, but not allocatively efficient. For example, a hospital operating at point B is technically efficient. The combination of inputs does not, however, represent the most effective allocation of inputs given inputs prices.

In the next section we develop measures of efficiency of a subvector of inputs in the linear programming or DEA approach to efficiency measurement. In general these measures allow for cost efficiency analysis in a situation where the level of some inputs are fixed. That is the measures allow for the examination of the efficiency of a subvector of inputs or short-run efficiency. For the case of hospitals, these measures allow us to exploit our data set which is rich in information on non-physician labor and wages and somewhat limited on information on prices for the other inputs. Assuming some inputs are fixed by ex ante decisions and short-run efficiency of hospitals is valid for some policy issues these measures provide information on the inefficiency of labor inputs and the cost savings possible if labor were employed more efficiently.

---

[1] Farrell proposed this "radial" measure to avoid index number problems. We note that although output level u is unobtainable at T, substitution of x_2 for x_1 along $I'I'$ does lead to E, the cost minimizing point, where u is obtainable.

Nonparametric Model of Labor Cost Efficiency

Efficiency of a subvector of inputs is based on the work of Färe [7] and Kopp [12]. Kopp provides an interpretation of single-input measures of efficiency in the Farrell framework and illustrates the parametric statistical method of measurement.[2] Before delving into the specific application–measures of hospital labor efficiency, we illustrate the measure of technical efficiency for a subvector of inputs and its relationship to the technical efficiency of all inputs in Farrell's framework.

Referring to figure 1 of the previous section, in the two input-case, we can define two subvector measures of efficiency-one for the input x_1 and one for the input x_2. We illustrate the subvector measures for input x_1 for the firm operating at point R, producing u employing $\bar{x}_1$ units of x_1 and $\bar{x}_2$ units of x_2. The input x_1 is then the variable input and the fixed input is x_2. Holding x_2 fixed at the observed level, $\bar{x}_2$, the minimum quantity of input x_1 feasible (i.e., u is still obtainable) is x_1^*. Following Färe [7], the measure of technical efficiency for the input x_1 compares the observed usage of input $\bar{x}_1$ to the minimum feasible, holding x_2 at its observed level:

$$TE^1(u, x_1, | \bar{x}_2) = Ox_1^*/O\bar{x}_1 \qquad (3)$$

This measure gives the reduction of input x_1 possible, holding x_2 fixed. Note that relative to the fixed input, the subvector technical efficiency measure is not measured radially. Thus, its measure is not related to total cost in same manner that the technical efficiency measure for all inputs is related to total cost. Increasing the efficiency of the subvector of variable inputs does reduce costs. This cost reduction is illustrated in figure 1, where additional isocost lines, C_2 and C_3, reflecting the original relative input prices have been drawn. The observed level of total cost, at point R, is higher than the efficient cost minimizing level (when all inputs are variable), i.e. $C_3 > C_1$. However, elimination of the inefficiency of the variable factor, given the fixed input level, reduces costs to C_2 which is below the actual level, i.e. $C_3 > C_2$.

The subvector technical efficiency measure is related to variable costs in a similar fashion as the technical efficiency measure for the entire vector of inputs is related to total costs. The Farrell type measure of overall efficiency becomes overall variable cost minimizing efficiency. The decomposition into the technical and allocative components then have variable cost interpretations. The efficiency of a firm is then gauged relative to its ability to produce efficiently in this ex-post world, where some factors are fixed and can not be adjusted. In other words, information on this ex post or variable cost inefficiency and the sources of that inefficiency, (whether technical or allocative) reveals how firm costs can be reduced by eliminating technical inefficiency of variable factors and the hospital's ability to adjust variable factors to their allocative efficient

---

[2]Byrnes [4] illustrates the use of subvector technical efficiency measures in the linear programming framework. This analysis, similar to Kopp's work, extends Farrell's decomposition for the subvector measures in linear programming framework.

level, given the relative prices of variable factors and the inability to adjust fixed inputs.

Empirical implementation of these measures requires specification of the technology in which efficiency is gauged and choice of efficiency measurement. Instead of estimating cost and production functions using statistical techniques (which in general implies that the researcher choose a specific functional form of the underlying technology), we specify and construct a piecewise linear technology from the observed inputs and outputs. We then use linear programming techniques to compute the labor efficiency measures for each hospital in the sample. In other words, we evaluate the efficiency of each hospital relative to the best practice technology determined from all of the hospitals in the sample.

To present the linear programming problems, some notation must be introduced. Let u_{ij} denote the observed quantity of output i of the jth firm, and u_j denote the vector of output quantities for the jth firm. Let x_{ij} denote the quantity of input i of the jth firm, and x_j the corresponding vector of inputs. Assume there are J observations or firms, denote the matrix of observed outputs by U, where U is of order J by M, for M outputs. Partition the vectors of observed inputs into a vector of variable inputs x_j^v and a vector of fixed inputs x_j^f, that is $x_j = [x_j^v, x_j^f]$. Finally, denote the matrix of observed variable inputs by X^v, which is J by V for J firms each having V variable inputs and likewise the matrix of observed fixed inputs by X^f, which is J by F for J observations each having F fixed inputs.

The reference technology in which efficiency is gauged is defined as an input correspondence $L^v(u)$ which is the set of all input vectors, x producing at least output rate u. Following Färe, Grosskopf and Lovell [8] the piecewise linear input correspondence constructed from the observed data can now be written as

$$L^v(u) = \{u \in \Re_n^+ : u \leq z \cdot U, x^f \geq z \cdot X^f, x^v \geq z \cdot X^v, \sum_{i=1}^{J} z_i = 1\} \qquad (4)$$

where, $z = (z_1, z_2, \ldots, z_J)$ denotes the vector of activity parameters.

As an example suppose the sample consists of two firms, each producing one output with two variable inputs and one fixed input. In simple terms, the reference technology is constructed by taking convex combinations of the observed inputs and outputs. In the example, the input correspondence would be constructed as follows:

$$
\begin{aligned}
z_1 \cdot u_1 + & \quad z_2 \cdot u_2 & \geq u \\
z_1 \cdot x_{11} + & \quad z_2 \cdot x_{12} & \leq x_1 \\
z_1 \cdot x_{21} + & \quad z_2 \cdot x_{22} & \leq x_2 \\
z_1 \cdot x_{31} + & \quad z_2 \cdot x_{32} & \leq x_3 \\
z_1 + & \quad z_2 & = 1
\end{aligned}
\qquad (5)
$$

where the fixed input is denoted x_1 and the two variable inputs are x_2 and x_3. The vector of intensity parameters, denoted by $z = (z_1, z_2)$ are used to allow for convex combinations of observed inputs and outputs. Assuming that $u_1 = u_2 = u$ and $x_{11} = x_{12} = x_1$ in our simple example, the constructed reference technology in the variable input space would look something like in figure 2.[3] At A, $x = (x_{11}, x_{21})$ and at B, $x^* = (x_{12}, x_{22})$. If $z = (0, 1)$ we get point A, if $z = (1, 0)$ we get point B and if $z = (1/2, 1/2)$ we get a point along the line segment AB, etc.

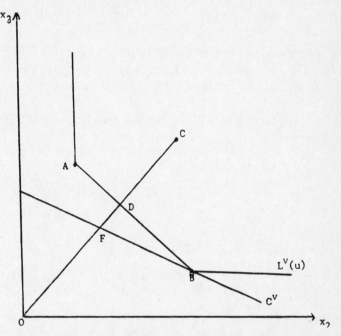

Figure 2: Illustration of Variable Cost Efficiency Measures

In order to calculate the overall level of variable cost efficiency, the cost minimizing combination of variable inputs relative to this technology must be determined. Denote the relative prices of the variable inputs as $p^v = (p_1, p_2, \ldots, p_V)$. The variable cost function relative to $L^v(u)$ for given values of p^v, is determined by:

$$C^v(u, p^v \mid x^f) = minimum \ \{p^v x^v : (x^v, x^f) \in L^v(u)\} \tag{6}$$

The minimum variable cost, $C(u, p^v \mid x^f)$, for the technology is the solution to the following linear programming problem:

$$C^v(u, p \mid x^f) = minimize \ p^v x^v$$
$$s.t. :$$
$$zU \ \geq \ u^o$$
$$zX^v \ \leq \ x^v p^v$$
$$zX^f \ \leq \ x^f$$

---

[3]Note that the $z's$ are restricted to be non-negative and must sum to unity.

$$\sum_{i=1}^{J} z_i = 1 \tag{7}$$

Given the estimated minimum variable cost, $C^v(u, p^v \mid x^f)$, for the observation and the actual variable cost, $p^v x^v$, overall efficiency for the variable inputs is defined as the ratio of minimum variable costs to observed variable costs:

$$OE^v(u, x^v, p^v \mid x^f) = \frac{C(u, p^v \mid x^f)}{p^v x^v} \tag{8}$$

In figure 2, for a firm operating at point C, this is given by the ratio, OF/OC. It gives the amount by which the variable inputs could be proportionally decreased so that variable costs will be minimized and the same output level be produced.

The measure of technical efficiency of the variable factors, denoted $TE^v(u, x^v \mid x^f)$, is obtained by solving the following linear programming problem:

$$
\begin{aligned}
minimize \quad & \lambda \\
s.t. : \quad & \\
zU \geq \; & u^o \\
zX^v \leq \; & \lambda x^v \\
zX^f \leq \; & x^f \\
\sum_{i=1}^{k} z_i = \; & 1
\end{aligned}
\tag{9}
$$

The λ parameter is used to determine the amount by which observed variable inputs can be proportionally reduced, while still producing the output level, given the level of the fixed inputs. This corresponds to the ratio OD/OC in figure 2 for observation C. Essentially, this measure of technical efficiency for the variable inputs tells us "how far" in variable input space the hospital is from the isoquant. A measure of allocative efficiency for the variable inputs is $AE^v(u, x^v, p^v \mid x^f)$ is defined as the ratio of the overall to the technical efficiency measure. In figure 2 allocative inefficiency is measured as OF/OD and captures inefficiency due to the fact that the hospital, even if on the variable input isoquant, given its variable input proportions did not pick the "right" input combination given the relative input prices reflected in the isocost line C^v. To summarize, the Farrell decomposition of variable cost minimizing efficiency into its variable input technical and allocative components is given by:

$$OE^v(u, x^v, p^v \mid x^f) = TE^v(u, x^v \mid x^f) \cdot AE^v(u, x^v, p^v \mid x^f) \tag{10}$$

which is confirmed for the example in figure 2, since

$$OF/OC = OD/OC \cdot OF/OD \tag{11}$$

In the next section, this approach is applied to a sample of not-for-profit (NFP) hospitals.

Data

The not-for-profit (NFP) hospital data used in this study are obtained from the California Health Facilities Commission (CHFC) survey for fiscal year 1983. The sample consists of 123 community (non-teaching) NFP hospitals. Hospitals in the survey reporting complete and consistent data are included in the sample.

The focus of this analysis is on the inpatient portion of hospital care, hence the specification of both the inputs and outputs pertain to only inpatient services. Even by limiting the analysis to inpatient care only, the production of hospital inpatient is modeled in a multiple output production framework. This multiple output framework allows for variation in labor usage and labor costs for different types of services. Table 1 gives sample descriptive statistics of the inputs and outputs used in the analysis.

The three outputs (measured as number of discharges) are: medical, surgical acute (ACUTE) discharges; medical, surgical intensive care (ICU) discharges; and maternity (BIRTHS) discharges. Not all outputs were produced by all the hospitals in our sample. As revealed by the minimum values for the ICU and BIRTHS variables (see table 1), for some hospitals, these services were not part of their patient mix in 1983.

Table 1

Input and Output Variables: Descriptive Statistics
(Sample Size = 123)

Variable	Mean	Standard Deviation	Minimum Value	Maximum Value
ACUTE	7779.85	4913.68	367.00	32005.00
ICU	359.80	381.21	0.00	2526.00
BIRTHS	1417.26	1326.48	0.00	6159.00
RN	281383.44	231645.57	12200.00	1288208.00
MGT	29073.38	32296.27	2.00	225948.00
TECH	17384.70	38095.52	2.00	384211.00
AIDE	82118.44	63762.18	2520.00	333766.00
LPN	65238.05	53207.83	3538.00	354187.44
DOC	306.91	342.99	16.00	2446.00
BEDS	266.77	152.32	38.00	943.00

Turning to the specification of inputs, five variable inputs and two fixed inputs are specified. We focus on the efficiency of non-physician labor, holding capital and physician labor fixed. This specification follows the short-run specification of the hospital production process of other researchers (Friedman and Pauly [10]).

The CHFC data distinguish between productive hours in inpatient care versus labor input for ambulatory care, the former is used in our specification. The five variable inputs are the five non-physician labor variables: registered nurse (RN) hours; management and administrative personnel (MGT) hours; technical services personnel (TECH) hours; aides and orderlies (AIDES) hours; and licensed practical nurse (LPN) hours. All hours are measured in full-time equivalence hours. Unfortunately, data are not available for licensed practical nurses (LPNs) from the survey. The LPN hours were estimated using the RN hours for each hospital and a county specific index of the fraction of LPN hours to RN hours.[4]

The two fixed inputs are the number of physicians and the average staffed beds. The number of physicians include staff physicians and physicians with admitting privileges. The primary reason we focus on only non-physician labor costs, holding the number of physicians fixed is that physicians usually bill patients separately for their services. Obtaining data on physician costs is not possible. The final fixed input is the number of staffed beds. Following Pauly and Wilson [15], staffed beds are used instead of licensed beds, since staffed beds are those which are fully staffed and operational to serve patients.

The variables described in table 2 are the hourly wages for the five non-physician labor inputs and the total variable costs. For each type of non-physician labor (including LPNs) the average hourly wage rate was reported in the survey. For our sample, non physician labor costs range from under 500 thousand to over 24 million dollars. The average hospital in the sample employed 5.5 million dollars of non-physician labor to provide inpatient care in 1983.

The composition of total non-physician labor costs can be determined from the descriptive statistics of the cost shares of each type of labor given in table 3. The cost of registered nurses account for just under two-thirds, on average, of non-physician labor costs. For the hospitals in this sample, aides and orderlies salaries account for the next largest share, 12 percent on average. Expenditure on LPNs, for the average hospital is 11 percent of non-physician labor costs. Management salaries account for 8 percent of total non-physician labor costs, with the technical staff portion accounting for the least, only 3 percent, on average. There is less variation in the share of LPN costs than the other components, this is due to the fact that the LPN hours was constructed from an index that varies by the county the hospital operates.

---

[4]The county-specific fraction of LPN hours to RN hours was obtained from the AHA Guide to Hospital Statistics.

Table 2

Input Price Variables: Descriptive Statistics
(Sample Size = 123)

Wage Rate (Dollars)	Mean	Standard Deviation	Minimum Value	Maximum Value
RN	13.15	1.25	7.98	16.58
MGT	14.53	1.30	11.02	20.27
TECH	10.69	3.00	5.69	26.81
AIDE	7.05	1.01	5.42	9.75
LPN	8.94	0.91	6.92	13.50
TVC	5.5M	4.2M	0.4M	24.1M

Table 3

Descriptive Statistics of
Actual Labor Cost Shares

Labor Type	Mean	St. Dev.	Min Val	Max Val
RN	0.66	0.09	0.33	0.86
MGT	0.08	0.05	0.00	0.31
TECH	0.03	0.06	0.00	0.49
AIDE	0.12	0.07	0.01	0.36
LPN	0.11	0.03	0.04	0.17

Empirical Results

Using the specification described in section 3, we compute three measures of efficiency the overall measure and its components, technical and allocative efficiency. These measures are defined in a framework of minimization of the non-physician labor costs. For all of the measures, efficiency occurs when the value of the measure is unity, i.e, hospitals characterized as overall efficient ($OE = 1$), use the efficient mix of non-physician labor which minimizes the variable costs of production of services. Technically efficient hospitals, ($TE = 1$), used the least amount of non-physician input among other hospitals in the sample with similar mix of services and fixed inputs. One minus the measure gives the amount by which the non-physician labor inputs could be proportionately decreased if the hospital had performed as well as other similar hospitals in the sample.

Before proceeding to the results, several general comments about the linear programming method of computing efficiency measures need to be discussed. First, these measures gauge the performance of hospitals relative to the best practice frontier technology which is constructed from the observations in the sample. Thus, these are relative and not absolute measures of performance. Second, this method essentially compares a given hospital to those hospitals in the sample which are most like it in terms of the level and mix of the three hospital services specified and the level and mix of the fixed and variable inputs specified. Finally, as in any empirical study, the results are only as good as the data. If there are systematic biases in the measurement of the variables, these will be reflected in the measures of performance. This last problem is of particular concern since the linear programming method used here does not explicitly include an error term for measurement or sampling error. With these remarks in mind we turn to the performance measures.

Table 4 gives summary statistics of each measure for the sample. We find that average overall efficiency defined in this variable cost minimizing framework is approximately 0.72. On average, if inefficient hospitals would have performed as well as other similar hospitals, the cost of non-physician labor could have been about 28 percent lower. Less than a quarter of the hospitals in our sample (30) operated with minimum variable (non-physician) labor costs.

Table 4

Summary of
Efficiency Measure Results

Efficiency Measure	Mean	St. Dev.	Median	Minimum Value	Number Efficient
Overall	0.72	0.21	0.71	0.28	30
Allocative	0.83	0.14	0.85	0.31	30
Technical	0.87	0.18	1.00	0.32	65

The overall variable cost minimizing measure is a composite of both technical and allocative inefficiency. Thus, the relative size of those measures provides evidence of the source of deviations from minimum labor costs. Our findings reveal that, average hospitals deviated from allocative efficiency by 17 percent. Similarly, independent of the relative wages, average hospitals could reduce labor inputs by 13 percent (1.00-0.87). Since many more hospitals are characterized as technically efficient, 65 hospitals compared to only 30 hospitals which are allocatively efficient, these findings suggest that except for those thirty hospitals, the hospitals in our sample are apparently choosing the "wrong" combination of non-physician labor given the relative prices of these inputs and the levels of the fixed inputs. Therefore, one could conjecture that hospitals are minimizing total costs and that the choice of fixed inputs constrains the hospitals to certain mix of non-physician labor that does not allow them to minimize variable costs.

With these methods employed here, we are capable of calculating the average labor shares which would result if each hospital performed as efficiently.[5] Table 5 provides

---

[5] These solution to the linear programming problem provides the efficient labor shares.

a description of the estimated efficient shares of each type of non-physician labor in minimum non-physician labor costs. These values can be compared to average actual input shares of hospitals in the sample, provided in Table 3. Comparison of these two tables reveals that, on average, non-physician labor costs could be decreased if the share of registered nurses decreased slightly and the share of aides were slightly increased.

Table 5

Descriptive Statistics of
Efficient Labor Cost Shares

Labor Type	Mean	St. Dev.	Min Val	Max Val
RN	0.62	0.07	0.45	0.86
MGT	0.08	0.03	0.00	0.28
TECH	0.03	0.05	0.00	0.22
AIDE	0.16	0.07	0.02	0.35
LPN	0.12	0.02	0.06	0.19

We would like to shed further light on the measures by comparing them to more "traditional" measures of performance. Table 6 compares measures of average product (output per unit of input) and average cost measures of efficient and inefficient hospitals in our sample. The best practice (efficient) hospitals, in terms of both allocative and technical efficiency, have on average lower average variable cost (cost per discharge) and higher average products (output per bed and output per physician).[6] It is encouraging that our results are consistent with more traditional measures.

Table 6

Characteristics of Efficient/Inefficient Hospitals

	Number of Hospitals	Variable Cost per Discharge	Discharge per Bed	Discharge per Physician
Allocative				
Efficient	30	475	42.5	62.5
Inefficient	93	611	35.2	41.4
Technical				
Efficient	65	515	40.5	49.1
Inefficient	58	649	32.3	43.7

---

[6]Correlation coefficients between each measure and these traditional measures of performance are always the correct sign and generally statistically significant.

Conclusion

The purpose of this paper is to study the labor costs of hospitals via an innovative approach. The nonparametric production frontier approach, popularized by Farrell, is applied to a sample of not-for-profit (NFP) hospitals operating the state of California in 1983. The approach allows for the estimation of the cost minimizing level of labor given the level of output (hospital services) and fixed inputs. Actual labor costs for each hospital are compared to the estimated cost minimizing level to reveal the level of allocative efficiency which exits in the hospital choice of labor mix. Because the estimated level of labor costs are derived from a production frontier, both technical and allocative "mistakes" on the part of the hospital can be examined.

Analysis of the labor cost efficiency of hospitals in our sample revealed that if the average inefficient hospitals would have performed as well as the best practice in the sample, non-physician labor costs would decrease by 28 percent. Deviations from allocative and technical efficiency are on average the same size, although the hospitals in our sample are more likely to be allocatively inefficient.

A further extension of this work should include the measurement of the long-run cost efficiency and it's components for the hospitals in our sample. Unfortunately reliable data on total costs and the physician wage and capital prices are not available. With existing data, we could estimate the technical efficiency of all inputs, that is, assuming all inputs are variable. Moreover, techniques have been developed (see Byrnes [4]) to compare this measure to the subvector technical efficiency measures computed here. From this analysis the technical efficiency loss associated with the fixity of inputs can be gleaned by comparing the subvector and total input measures.

Given our findings, this method appears useful in empirical analysis of efficiency in industries where analysis of the efficiency of a subvector of inputs is of interest or when examination of ex post efficiency is the appropriate tool for policy analysis.

References

[1] American Hospital Association *Hospital Statistics* Chicago, IL. (1987)

[2] Banker, R. D., R. Conrad and R. Strauss, "A Comparative Application of Data Envelopment Analysis and Translog Methods: An Illustrative Study of Hospital Production." *Management Science* 32 (1986)30-44.

[3] Booton, L. D. and J. Lane, "Hospital Market Structure and the Return to Nursing Education." *Journal of Human Resources* 20 (1984):184-196.

[4] Byrnes, P. "Ownership and Efficiency in the Water Supply Industry: An Applica-

tion of the Nonparametric Programming Approach to Efficiency Measurement." Ph.D. Dissertation, Southern Illinois University, Carbondale, IL., (1985)

[5] Cowing, T. and A. Holtman "The Multiproduct Short-Run Hospital Cost Function: Empirical Evidence and Policy Implications From Cross-Section Data." *Southern Economic Journal* 49 (1983):637-53.

[6] Eakin, B. K. and T. J. Kniesner "Estimating a Non-Minimum Cost Function for Hospitals." *Southern Economic Journal* 54 (1988):583-597.

[7] Färe R. "Efficiency and the Production Function." *Zeitschrift fur Nationalokonomie* 35 (1975):317-24.

[8] Färe R., S. Grosskopf and C.A.K. Lovell *The Measurement of Efficiency of Production.* Boston: Kluwer Nijhoff, 1985.

[9] Farrell, M.J. "The Measurement of Productive Efficiency." *The Journal of the Royal Statistical Society* 120, Series A, Part 3. (1957):253-281.

[10] Friedman, B. and M. Pauly "Cost Functions for a Service Firm with Variable Quality and Stochastic Demand: The Case of Hospitals." *Review of Economics and Statistics* 63 (1981):620-624.

[11] Grosskopf, S. and V. Valdmanis "Measuring Hospital Performance: A Non-parametric Approach." *Journal of Health Economics* 6 (1987):89-107.

[12] Kopp, R.C. "Measurement of Productive Efficiency: A Reconsideration." *The Quarterly Journal of Economics* 96 (1981):477-503.

[13] Leibenstein H. "Allocative Efficiency Versus X-Efficiency." *American Economic Review* 56 (1966):392-415.

[14] Leibenstein H., "On the Basic Proposition of X-Efficiency Theory." *American Economic Review* 68 (1978):328-332.

[15] Pauly, M. and P. Wilson "Hospital Output Forecasts and the Costs of Empty Hospital Beds." *Health Services Research* 21 (1986):403-428

[16] Register, C.A. and E.R. Burning "Profit Incentives and Technical Efficiency in the Production of Hospital Care." *Southern Economic Journal* 53 (1987):899-914.

[17] Sloan, F. and B. Steinwald *Insurance, Regulation and Hospital Costs.* Lexington, MA: Lexington Books, 1980.

COSTING OUT QUALITY CHANGES:
An Econometric Frontier Analysis of U.S. Navy Enlistments

Richard C. Morey
QA/IS Department, University of Cincinnati
Cincinnati, OH 45221-0130, U.S.A.

Abstract

The required quality mix of U.S. Navy enlisted recruits, i.e. the proportion who have a High School Degree and who score in the upper percentiles on the Armed Services Entrance Exams, can have pervasive impacts on the size of the recruiting budget needed and its composition. Additionally, the recruiting environment, e.g. the unemployment rate, the size of the eligible population, competition from other services, service policies concerning the management of its Delayed Entry Program, etc., as well as the cost per recruiter, overhead costs associated with placement cost of advertising, etc. also will affect the total budget needed and the proper utilization of each resource. This effort focuses on forecasting the recruiting cost impacts of contemplated changes in the quantity and quality mix of U.S. Navy recruits. The approach utilized is econometric, utilizing the so-called Translog frontier estimation technique, involving estimating systems of equations. The data base is at the monthly, regional level for FY84-FY86. The effort estimates the recruiting cost impacts of varying the quality mix as well as the recruit substitution possibilities without increasing recruiting costs. The costs impact of varying key demographics is also estimated. The results generally agree with the conventional wisdom of Dod manpower planners. The general approach is applicable to settings other than military recruiting where it is of interest to estimate the budget impacts of varying the quality or quantity of outputs.

1.0 INTRODUCTION

The U.S. Navy spends several hundreds of millions of dollars annually to recruit male, nonprior service, enlisted, active duty personnel. These expenditures take the form of salaries and benefits for recruiters (4,047 man years of recruiters in FY86), recruiter's field level support for items such as secretaries, office space, travel, etc. ($41M in FY86), Naval Recruiting Command headquarters' expenditures (approximately $21M in FY86 for the enlisted side) and Navy advertising (national and local advertising totaling $16M in FY86 for enlisted personnel) (see Morey and McCann, [1980] and [1983], for more background on Navy recruiting).

The above resources are expended to obtain five different categories of recruits, the categorization being based on quality. The recruit quality rating has two distinct components: possession of a High School Diploma or not, and their percentile score on the Armed Forces Qualification Test (AFQT) (see Figure 1).

Over the period FY84-FY86, numbers and percentages in the various categories for varied substantially as seen in Table 1. We observe the substantial variation in the percentages obtained by year, especially pronounced for the lower quality categories. This variation is due to changes in total quotas, resources allocated, competition from other services, and changing demographics.

One of the ongoing issues being faced by the Services is the relationship between the incoming quality of the recruit and soldier performance (see e.g. Armor et al. [1982], Horne [1987], and Scribner et al. [1986]). The Services have always valued the attaining of a High School Diploma by a recruit as it is highly correlated with the recruit's tendency to complete his term of service. In addition, Schinnar et al.

Figure 1: **RECRUIT QUALITY MATRIX**

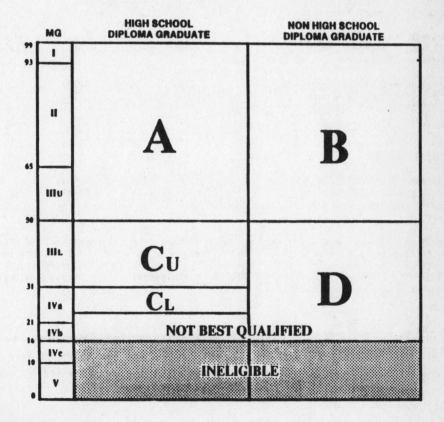

[1988] regress the performance of the Army recruit against incoming quality characteristics. They find that the effect of the test score is positive and highly significant. As a result of these and other studies, the Army (CBO study, [1986]) has had as
its recruiting goals at least 88.5% of all male recruits having a High School Diploma,
and between 65% and 69% being in the top three Mental categories (I-IIIU). Additionally, the goals in the Army's POM (Program Objectives Memorandum) planning process for
FY89-FY94 are for at least 90% HSDG's and at least 63% in the top three Mental
categories (Toomepuu [1989]). However, this quality is not free. The Congressional
Budget Office [1986] estimated that over the 5 subsequent year period, the Army would
have to spend additionally between $410M and $785M to reach the quality levels
desired.

TABLE 1: VARIATION IN QUALITY MIX OF MALE, 17-21 YEAR OLD, NON-PRIOR SERVICE (NPS),
ACTIVE DUTY RECRUITS OVER FY84-FY86

	FY84	FY85	FY86	Total over 3 Years
1) Total of Male, 17-21 years old NPS, Active duty contracts	64,413 (100%)	66,970 (100%)	79,313 (100%)	210,696 (100%)
2) A Cell, Male 17-21 years old NPS Active duty contracts (HSDG and Mental Categories I-IIIU)	36,742 (57%)	32,345 (48.3%)	36,915 (46.5%)	106,002 (50.3%)
3) C_u cell, Male 17-21 years old, NPS Active duty contracts (HSDA and Mental categories IIIL)	15,492 (24%)	17,205 (26%)	21,073 (27%)	53,770 (25.5%)
4) C_ℓ cell, male 17-21 years old, NPS Active Duty contracts (HSDG and Mental category IVA)	7,286 (11%)	7,442 (11%)	9,004 (11%)	23,732 (11.3%)
5) B cell, male 17-21 years old, NPS, Active Duty contracts (NHSDG and Mental categories I-IIIU)	4,887 (8%)	9,971 (15%)	9,276 (12%)	24,134 (11.5%)
6) D cell, male 17-21 years old, NPS, Active Duty contracts (NHSDG and Mental categories IIIL, IVA and IVB)	16 (.02%)	7 (.01%)	3,045 (3.8%)	3,068 (1.5%)

*The numbers shown are the unrenormed contract figures; the renorming has the effect of
slightly lowering some of the higher quality totals in the FY84 and FY85 time periods.
In order to provide some feeling for the impact of renorming in the aggregate, the
unrenormed test scores indicated that 45.28% of the recruits were A cell, whereas the
renormed test scores increased this to 47%.

Given the possibly austere military budgets on the horizon, Dod planners realize
that more of the male quotas may have to draw from the lower quality categories. Since
many of the Non A cell categories are also becoming supply limited, deliberate planning

planning and resource allocation strategies will be needed which recognize the multi-dimensional output character of the problem.

In this setting, this paper develops and exercises an econometric approach, using actual Navy monthly/regional recruiting data over the time period FY84-FY86, designed to deal with the following scenario:

i)   Given exogenous enlistment goals by type (i.e., number and mix), for some upcoming Fiscal year;

ii) Given a hypothesized recruiting environment for the year in question consisting of: size of eligible population, percent Black, and unemployment rate;

iii) Given hypothesized levels of non-controllable resources (joint Dod advertising expenditures, military/civilian pay ratios, etc.) expected for the year in question;

iv) Given the prices per unit for each type of recruiting resource, e.g., cost of a recruiter man year, overhead factors for a placement dollar of local advertising, overhead rates for a placement dollar of national advertising, etc.;

v)   Given the Navy's policy regarding management of its Delayed Entry Program (DEP)*, i.e. initial levels and mix at the beginning of the year in question, average sizes of DEP and composition** of DEP throughout the year, and "compactness"** of DEP;

then, what is the minimum total recruiting cost needed to meet the levels of enlistments required? Also what is the budget's sensitivity to changes in the postulated quality mix, what substitutions among different recruit quality categories may be possible, and what are the budget impacts of varying demographics?

---

*Each of the Armed Services' Recruiting Commands enables a potential recruit to delay his actual shipping date (called his accession date) for up to a year from the time he signs an obligation to enter a given Service. If a recruit chooses to delay his shipping date beyond a month of his time of signing, he enters the so-called Delayed Entry Program; for more background, see Morey [1985].

**The mix of quality in the DEP pool can have an impact on recruiting efforts since recruits who have made a decision to enlist often encourage their peers to inquire about the Service as a possible option and can become a type of recruiter aide. By compactness of DEP, we are referring to the distribution of recruits in the Delayed Entry Program by accession date, i.e. 1 month out, 2 months out, etc. If the short term needs of the Navy are not coming out of DEP, then there is more "direct ship" pressure on recruiters with the result that the quality of the recruits falls.

Naturally such estimates are heavily caveated since they are complex and convoluted functions of the recruiting environment, competition from other services, the incentive mechanisms available, quotas, management of the Delayed Entry Program, etc. These difficulties notwithstanding, only when these types of estimates are available can the country rationally deal with the cost/quality tradeoffs personnel in the Armed Services.

In this setting the thrust of this effort is to exercise a well accepted, econometric frontier approach, using recent cross sectional/longitudinal Navy recruiting data provided by the U.S. Navy Recruiting Command. We will be particularly interested in assessing the impacts of quality and quantity changes in quotas on recruiting costs. The approach will utilize simultaneous equation regression analysis (see Zellner, [1963]) to capture dynamic interactions and to help induce efficiency.

2.0 THE MODEL

We shall view the recruiting process as a production process, the outputs of which are produced and sold by means of production inputs (i.e. resources to be allocated) in a specified recruiting environment, together with non-resource management decisions (related to the management of the Delayed Entry Program). The multiple outputs will be the numbers of five different types of enlistments the Navy desires. The production inputs to be costed out individually will be recruiters, Navy national advertising, local advertising and field level support cost. These are "public" in nature in the sense that they influence production of all outputs, and are not allocable to a specific type of enlistment. The recruiting environment will consist of size of eligible population, local unemployment rate, percent black in region, etc. and resources uncontrollable by the Navy (e.g. Joint Dod advertising expenditures and military/civilian pay ratios). Additionally Navy policy variables related to the management of its Delayed Entry Program will also be included.

A formal optimization problem can then be stated as:

Let $Y = (y_1, y_2, y_3, y_4, y_5)$ represent an exogenous vector of enlistments required for a given upcoming fiscal year. Let $X = (x_1, x_2, x_3, x_4)$, a vector, represent the efficient level of each of the four controllable resources (recruiters, field level support cost, Navy national advertising, local advertising) required to be expended to meet Y. Also let Z be a vector of environmental and policy variables, e.g., size of 17-21 year old population, percent of eligible population that is black, unemployment rate, level of Joint DOD military advertising, military/civilian pay ratios, seasonal variables, size and distribution of DEP of each type at the beginning of the horizon, etc. Then a production technology is represented by a production possibilities set $T(Y,X,Z) \leq 0$ which shows all (X,Z) vector combinations capable of producing each Y vector. Finally, suppose the controllable resource vector X has per unit costs given by the vector $P = (p_1, p_2, p_3, p_4)$. Then the cost allocation optimization problem is: given Z and Y, select X so as to minimize PX subject to $T(Y,X,Z) \leq 0$. The solution to the above is an optimal resource utilization vector $X(Y,P,Z)$ and minimized total resource cost $K(Y,P,Z)$ $= P \cdot X(Y,P,Z)$. The resource cost function $K(Y,P,Z)$ describes the minimum total cost required to produce outputs Y, at resource unit costs P, in the environment Z.

For the theory above to be applied to the Navy problem, it is necessary to endow the minimum incentive cost function with a functional structure and to specify an estimation technique. The structure should be sufficiently flexible to impose no properties on recruiting technology that are unwarranted by the data. It should also be sufficiently simple to be tractable empirically in light of the size of the data base, relative to the number of included explanatory variables.

A flexible second-order logarithmic specification, known as translog, (see e.g. Christenson, Jorgenson and Lau [1973]) has been applied to health care (see e.g. Banker et al. [1986]), electric power generation (see Christensen and Greene [1976]) and Army Recruiting (see Lovell and Morey [1989]). A simplified translog incentive cost function can be written as:

$$\ln K = a_0 + \sum_{i=1}^{5} a_i \ln y_i + \sum_{i=1}^{4} b_i \ln p_i + \sum_{i=1}^{5} c_i (\ln y_i)^2 + \sum_{i=1}^{31} g_i \ln z_i \qquad (3)$$

Where y_j = number of enlistments of type j
$(j=1,2,3,4,5)$;

p_i $(i=1,2,3,4)$ denotes the cost per unit for each of the four types of resources consumed;

z_i $(i=1,2,\ldots,31)$ include environmental variables (size of eligible population, percent Black, local unemployment rate, monthly dummy variables, and dep characteristics),

and K denotes the total recruiting costs, $\sum_{i=1}^{4} p_i x_i$ where x_i $(i=1,2,3,4)$ is the level of the level of utilization of the ith monetary resource. Necessary conditions for the efficient utilization of each monetary resource result from an application of Shepard's Lemma (see e.g., Varian [1984]) which can be stated as:

$$x_i^* = \frac{\partial K^*}{\partial p_i} \quad \text{(the asterisk denotes the optimal values of } x_i \text{ and } K) \tag{4}$$

By adding the equations of (4), to that of (3), efficient utilization of each resource type is promoted. In addition, since the cost function (3) is logarithmic, from (4), we have $\partial(\ln K)/\partial(\ln p_i) = (\partial K/\partial p_i)(p_i/K) = p_i x_i/K$ for all i. Hence the optimal _fraction_ of the total resource cost that should be allocated to the ith resource, from (3) and (4), is given by:

$$p_i x_i/K = b_i \quad (i=1,2,3,4) \tag{5}$$

where b_i is the coefficient of $\ln p_i$ in equation (3).

It should be stressed that the left sides of (3) and (5), in the econometric estimation, utilize the observed values. The right sides, exclusive of the error terms, represent the efficient levels. The residual error terms in both types of equations represent the differences between the two. When the intercept term of equation (5), namely b_i, is constrained to have exactly the same estimated value as the coefficient of $\ln p_i$ in (3), we are imposing the necessary conditions for allocative efficiency in the Navy's allocation of resources. Since the mean of the residuals of (3) and (5) will be zero, we will be assuming that, on average, over the period observed, the Navy has been allocating recruiting resources efficiently. Hence in estimating the recruiting costs impacts of changes in the quality mix of Navy recruits, it will be based on the resource mix strategies actually in use by the Navy Recruiting Command over the period FY84-FY86.

The statistical problem then is to estimate the parameters in the system of equations, (3) and (5). A systems estimator is called for. Several are available, the most popular of which is Zellner's "Seemingly Unrelated Regressions" technique (1963). In this two-step method, each equation is estimated separately by ordinary least squares, after which the ordinary least squares residuals are used to form a consistent estimator of the covariance matrix. This estimator is unbiased, consistent, and asymptotically efficient.

We observe the following important uses of the model:

i) From (3), $\dfrac{d(\ln K)}{d(\ln y_j)} = a_j + 2c_j \ln y_j \quad (j = 1,2,3,4,5) \tag{6}$

is the elasticity of the quantity of the jth type of enlistment on the minimum total recruiting cost. Observe that these are not constant (as in a Cobb-Douglas specification) but vary, based on the level of enlistments desired of the particular type.

ii) From (i), $\dfrac{a_j + 2c_j \ln y_j}{a_k + 2c_k \ln y_k}$

is the rate of possible substitution between enlistments of type j and k, at the level of enlistments of y_j, y_k, <u>keeping the total recruiting cost fixed</u>.

iii) b_i, i.e., the right side of (5), is the percent of the total recruiting cost that should be spent on resource i, on average;

iv) g_i represent elasticities of the ith environmental factor on the total minimum level of recruiting costs.

3.0 SUMMARY OF DATA AVAILABLE

The data base utilized is at the monthly, regional level for the three-year period, FY84-FY86. Since there are six Navy recruiting regions, a total of 36 x 6 = 216 monthly-region cells results. Also during this period, there was a total of nearly 211K net* enlistments of the male, nonprior service, active duty type.

The detailed data elements by month and region are:

i) For male, nonprior service, active duty enlistments, we have <u>net</u> production and <u>DEP sizes</u> broken down for each of the five types of recruits displayed in Figure 1.

ii) The number of actual recruiters present by month by region;

iii) DEP "compactness" profiles, i.e., at the beginning of a given month for each region for each of the next 12 outmonths, the percent of the total accession goal (for male, nonprior service, active duty enlistments) anticipated to be met by deliveries from the DEP bank. (This is a 36x12x6 data base);

iv) The level of headquarters and field level support costs by region by quarter;

v) The level of national advertising placement cost by month by region;

vi) The level of local advertising expenditures by area by quarter;

---

*Adjusted for attrition while in DEP; attrition factors are of the order of 6-9%.

vii) The ratio of military pay to civilian pay (for 1st year recruits) by month by
     region;

viii) Size of the 17-21 year old, male population by region by year;

ix) Percent of the 17-21 year old, male population that is Black, by region by
    year.

Table 2 shows the variation in the above measures at the national level. It is
this variability, particularly at the cross sectional level in so-called "natural"
experiments, that enables regression analyses to sort out the separate effects of each
factor. Table 2 deals with ranges for the key demographics and resources.

4.0 KEY INSIGHTS FROM EXERCISING MODEL

The parameter estimates, from Section 2's model specification exercised on the
data summarized in Section 3, appear in the Appendix. Consider now some of the key
quantitative insights, using the estimated parameters of the cost allocation model.

i) the coefficient a_1, related to the logarithm of enlistments of type A (HSDG,1-
    IIIU) is .604 and barely significant (at the 12% level)*, whereas the coefficient
    c_1, related to the square of the logarithm of the same type of enlistments, is
    $-.04$ and insignificant (i.e. its t value is -1.26). Hence from (6), the elas-
    ticity of A type (HSDG,1-IIIU) enlistments on the recruiting cost needed, is
    estimated to be .604, i.e. every 1% increase in the quota of A cell, nonprior
    service, male, active duty enlistments is predicted to increase the total
    recruiting costs needed (exclusive of Navy Recruiting Headquarter's cost, joint
    Dod advertising, and military pay) by .604%. The fact that the elasticity is
    less than 1 is because not all of the recruiting cost is devoted to this one type
    of enlistment. Also it is interesting to note that, at least over the ranges of
    FY84-FY86, the elasticity is constant since c_1 is insignificant.

ii) The coefficient of a_3, related to the logarithm of C_u cell enlistments, (HSDG,
    IIIL) is -1.18 and very significant, as is c_3, estimated to be .116. From (6),
    evaluating the elasticity at the <u>regional</u>, <u>monthly mean</u> for FY84-86, an estimated
    average elasticity for male, nonprior service, active duty HSDG, IIIL type

---

*Its t value is 1.54. In other regression runs, when allocative efficiency conditions
were relaxed or when recruiter costs were omitted, the coefficient a_1 was very significant. That unexpected marginal significance may be due in part to colinearity since
the square of the same variable was also included as an explanatory variable to
capture possible nonconstant elasticities.

enlistments on recruiting cost of .098 results. Note this elasticity is dependent on the _level_ of enlistments of the type needed and _increases_ (as impacted)
as the quota for HSDG, IIIL enlistments increases.

iii) The coefficient a_3 for HSDG, IVU cell enlistments is -.12 and very significant;
similarly the corresponding c_4 is .014 and very significant. Evaluating the
elasticity at the mean again for FY 84-FY86 yields an average elasticity for the

Table 2: Averages and Ranges over 3-year Period

	National	Average	Range
1)	National Unemployment Rate	.0736	.659-.0887 (34% range from lowest to highest
2)	Size of 17-21 year old male population (nationwide)	8.571M	8.465M-8.860M (4.6% range)
3)	Size of Black, 17-21 year old population (nationwide)	1.167M	1.145M-1.184M (3.4% range)
4)	NRC monthly local advertising expenditures	$115K	$96K-$185K
5)	National total support cost/month (field and headquarters) for enlisted personnel*	$5.82M	$3.85M-$10.26M
6)	Average ratio of military/ civilian pay for 1st year recruits	1.227	1.152-1.284 (11.5% range)
7)	Number of recruiters (nationwide)	3671	3274-4443 (36% range)
8)	Navy national _annual_ advertising placement cost for enlisted personnel (nationwide)	$7.42M	$4.587M in FY84 to $10.064M the FY86
9)	Joint Dod Advertising placement cost (in FY86 dollars)	$17.00 M	14.7M in FY86 and $19.67M in FY84
10)	Average dep size (male, non-prior service, 17-21 year old, active duty)	29,948	26.3K in FY86 and 35.02K in FY84
11)	Total number of net, male, 17-21 year old, non-prior service, active duty contracts	70,232	64.413K in FY84 and 79.313K in FY86
12)	Percent HSDG, 1-IIIU	50.6%	46.5% in FY86 to 57% in FY84
13)	Percent non HSDG, 1-IIIU	11.67%	8% in FY84 to 15% in FY85
14)	Percent HSDG, IIIL	25.67%	24% in FY84 to 27% in FY86
15)	Percent HSDG, IVA	11%	no variation
16)	Percent non HSDG, IIIL and IVA	1.28%	.01% in FY86 to 3.8% in FY86

quota of HSDG, IVA enlistments on recruiting cost of .0085, and is increasing with increasing quotas.

iv) For non-HSDG, I-IIIU cell enlistments, a_2 is -.003 but insignificant, whereas c_2 is -.0004 and significant. Hence the cost elasticity related to this type of enlistment is slightly negative but very significant, suggesting this type of enlistment is not supply limited, but rather is demand limited. Additionally, as this type of enlistment has typically been used to "backfill" to meet quotas, their occurrence has typically been associated with fewer quality contracts and hence lower costs. The slight negative sign is indicative of this substitution phenomenon.

v) Finally, for non HSDG, IIIL, a_5 is .002 and very significant, whereas c_5 is insignificant.

vi) The sum of the elasticities for all types of male, non-prior service, active duty enlistments, evaluated at the monthly, regional mean over the 3 year period, is about .757. This result may reflect the fact that recruiting costs are incurred for activities outside the recruitment of male, non-prior service, active duty individuals. In particular, the recruitment of women, male prior service recruits, reservists, minorities, etc. all consume resources. An improved specification of the model would include these as outputs also. We also observe that this total elasticity, related to male, non-prior service, active duty enlistments, is increasing with the total level of such enlistments and that diminishing returns (i.e. an elasticity of greater than one) sets in quickly as the quotas are increased.

vii) Impact of Exogenous Variables:

a) Percent Black in male, 17-21 old population: As this percent increases, recruiting cost increases, the elasticity being .031 and very significant. This is to be interpreted that, given the quality mix of recruits coming in over FY84-FY86, (i.e. nearly 76% HSDG and Mental category I-III), an increase in the average percent of the eligible population that is black would increase the total recruiting resources needed. This result is very intuitive.

b) Unemployment: As unemployment increases, the recruiting cost decreases, the elasticity being -.048 and very significant. This is very consistent with the well-known fact that higher unemployment generally aids recruiting.

c) **Ratio of Military/Civilian Pay**: As the ratio of military to first year civilian pay increases, recruiting costs go down, as expected, the elasticity being -.068. This coefficient is however statistically insignificant, perhaps due to small variations in the measure or errors in its measurement.

d) **Joint DOD Advertising Expenditures**: As Joint advertising expenditures increase, Navy recruiting costs would decrease as expected (the elasticity is -.0002 but it is insignificant).

e) **Navy Recruiting Command NRC Headquarter's Expenditures**: As the model was run at the regional level and since much of the Headquarter's expenditures is difficult to reduce (e.g., civilian budgets), we excluded NRC's Headquarters expense from the dependent variable (recruiting cost) but included it as an environmental variable. Its impact was as expected, i.e., as NRC Headquarters expense increased, other recruiting costs decrease, the elasticity being -.002 (significant at the 17% level).

f) **The size of eligible male population** had a negative and very significant elasticity at -.526, signaling the expected decrease in recruiting cost needed if the eligible population base were to expand.

g) **The relative prices per unit for each type of resource** are the most significant factors in the model. The results indicate a change in the price of local advertising, relative to the price of a recruiter, has an elasticity of .0094; for national advertising (normalized by price per recruiter), the price elasticity was .067, whereas the corresponding normalized price elasticity for recruiter field level support was .235.

viii) Next, consider the key substitution possibilities <u>with no change in the recruiting cost</u> from (7). To illustrate, the elasticity for HSDG, 1-IIIU cell enlistments had earlier been estimated to be .604, whereas the estimate of the elasticity for HSDG, IIIL enlistments (evaluated at the overall mean level) was .098. Hence the ratio of .604/.098 or 6.16 is to be interpreted that a 1% decrease in the highest quality enlistments (A cell) can be substituted (or offset) by a 6.16% increase in the lower quality enlistments (C_ℓ cell), at no increase in recruiting cost. As there were on average 490.75 of the highest quality enlistments obtained over FY84-86 (in each region and month) and 248.935 of the C_ℓ cell enlistments, we estimate that the recruiting efforts associated with a drop of 4.91 HSDG, 1-IIIU male, active duty, nonprior enlistments can be used instead to obtain .0616 (248.935) = 15.334 more HSDG, IIIL enlistments with no change in costs; hence a substitution rate of 3.123 results.

Following this logic, the following substitution matrix results for the HSDG categories:

SUBSTITUTION RATES WITH NO CHANGE IN RECRUITING COSTS
(utilizes elasticities estimated at overall mean for period FY84–FY86)

	(1–IIIU)	(IIIL's)	(IVA's)
1–IIIU	1	3.123	15.88
IIIL	.32	1	5.08
IVA*	.063	.197	1

The substitution rate between the HSDG, 1–IIIU cell and the HSDG, IIIL cell (the total comprising about 76% of all Navy, male, nonprior service, active duty recruits), agrees approximately with the Army's estimate (see [CBO Report, 1986]) that a "high quality" recruit is about 4 times more difficult to obtain than a "low quality" recruit.

A very important related issue is the substitution rate between HSDG enlistments and non–HSDG enlistments, matched on given mental categories. For example, using the combined of elasticities for HSDG, IIIL and HSDG, IVA's versus the corresponding for non–HSDG IIIL's and IVA's, we estimate the cost to recruit a HSDG individual in these mental categories could alternatively be used to yield about 4.15 nonHSDG recruits in the same mental categories. These estimates and the ones for other mental categories suffer from the practice of the services to meet monthly enlistment quotas, when short, by "backfilling" from the perceived, demand limited pool of recruits. Hence the substitution estimates given between the HSDG recruit versus the nonHSDG recruit should be viewed as illustrative.

xi) Finally consider the impact on costs of changes only in the mix of recruits. To aid in the presentation of these results, consider as the scenario an "average" year (based on FY84–FY86) in which 70,232 net, male, nonprior service, Active Duty enlistments would have been obtained. The "average year would have: 50.3% (35,327) A cell; 25.5% (17,909) C_u cell; 11.3% (7,936) C_ℓ cell; 11.5% (8,077) B cell; and 1.5% (1,053) D cell. The total recruiting costs would have been $163.99M (in FY86 dollars), exclusive of headquarter costs.

Then, consider the yearly cost impacts of increasing the yearly A cell HSDG, 1–IIIU's, by 1% (i.e. adding 353 more) by decreasing the C_u cell, (HSDG, IIIL's), by 353 recruits so that the yearly totals are unchanged. Then from the elasticity of A cell quotas on total recruiting cost, increasing the A cell by 1% is estimated to increase total recruiting costs by .604%. At the same time, reducing C_u cell enlistments by 353 recruits represents a 1.97% drop in the original

level of 17,909. Hence, since the elasticity for C_u cell enlistments (evaluated
at the mean) is .098, the savings from the reduction of 1.97% fewer C_u cell contracts is 1.97 (.098) = .19%. Hence the overall net increase in total recruiting
costs is estimated to be .604% - .19% or .414%. This would be about $.679M if
the recruiting costs were at the average of $163.99M.

Considering other possibilities, we can develop the following matrix where the
entries in the matrix depict the net change in cost if a 1% increase in the type of
enlistment represented on the vertical axis were to occur, assuming it were offset by
the same number of enlistments of the type represented on the horizontal axis, so that
the total number of enlistments obtained was unchanged.

RECRUITING COST IMPACT (percentage-wise) OF CHANGE IN QUALITY MIX OF RECRUITS ONLY

	A cell	C_u cell	C_ℓ cell
A cell (HSDG, 1-IIIU)	0	+.414% ($.679M)	+.566% ($.928M)
C_u cell (HSDG, IIIL)	-.204% (-$.334M)	0	+.079% ($.129M)
C_ℓ cell (HSDG, IVA)	-.124% ($.203M)	-.035% (-.057M)	0

Note, finally a 1% increase in the C_ℓ cell, with the quantity taken from the A
cell, would involve a savings of .124% (or about $.203M). This number is low since a
1% increase in C_ℓ cell contracts (for our average year scenario) would only be 79 extra
C_ℓ enlistments and hence 79 fewer A cell enlistments.

5.0   CONCLUSIONS

It is very important that Dod manpower planners have the ability to predict the
likely cost impacts of changes in the quality mix of recruits. The Armed Services have
moved to increasingly sophisticated weapon systems with their accompanying need for
higher quality recruits. To be able to perform credible, defensible, scenario by
scenario, costing analysis would be valuable input into the continuing debate regarding
the Services' requests for upgrading the incoming quality of recruits.

This paper has developed and exercised, using actual data for a recent period, a
well-accepted econometric approach for accomplishing this. The approach yields individual elasticities, by type of recruit, on total recruiting costs as well as elasticities associated with varying key environmental factors such as the unemployment
rate, the size of the eligible population, etc.

A number of caveats need to be stated at this point. First, while the modified translog specification used is quite flexible, it is not non-parametric. Hence other specifications could change the results. Collinearity and omitted variables are always of concern, especially when quotas and allocation patterns tend to move in tandem and where more demographic information would be desirable. These caveats notwithstanding, the estimates coming from the exercise appear quite reasonable and agree with the conventional wisdom on the direction of the impacts. Secondly, our key thrust has been to cost out contemplated changes in quality and quantity, together with the impacts of changing recruiting environment, if the Navy were to continue its past patterns of allocating its total budget. Of substantial interest would be to uncover any allocative inefficiencies in the Navy's trading off of recruiters, support costs and different types of advertising. These issues can be attacked if one does not make the standard assumptions that the necessary conditions for allocative efficiency were met on average. Lovell and Morey [1989], in a Translog analysis of enlistment incentives for the Army, found what appear to be substantial allocative inefficiencies related to the Army's past use of enlistment bonuses and the Army College Fund, especially as they were applied to the non-Combat Arms MOS's.

Clearly, much more effort is needed in this difficult and pervasive problem area, not only regarding the costs associated with recruit quality and quantity changes, but also on the impacts such changes would have on the performance and readiness of the Armed Services. Econometric approaches, such as the one illustrated here, can be useful in providing quantitative insights and in identifying the data bases needed in the future.

This paper utilizes data and analysis performed under the sponsorship of the Navy Manpower, Personnel and Training R&D Program of the Chief of Navy Research Under Contract N00014-86-K-0732 with the Office of Naval Research (see Morey, [1988]).

REFERENCES

1. Armor, D.J., Fernandez, R., Bers, K. and Schwarzback, D., "Recruit Aptitudes and Army Job Performance: Setting Enlistment Standards for Infantrymen," Rand Corporation Report R-2874-MPRL, 1982.

2. Banker, R.D., Conrad, R.F., and Strauss, R.P., "A Comparative Application of Data Envelopment Analysis and Translog Methods: An Illustrative Study of Hospital Production," Management Science, 32, No. 1, 1986.

3. Christensen, L.R., Jorgenson, D.W. and Lau, L.J., "Transcendental Logarithmic Production Frontiers," Review of Economics and Statistics, 55: 28-45, 1973.

4. Christensen, L.R. and Greene, W.H., "Economies of Scale in U.S. Electric Power Generation," Journal of Political Economy, May, 1976.

5. Congressional Budget Office," Quality Soldiers; Costs of Manning the Active Army," June, 1986.

6. Horne, D.K., "The Impact of the Soldier Quality on Army Performance," Armed Forces and Society, Vol. 13, No. 3, 1987.

7. Lovell, C.A.K. and Morey, R.C., "The Allocation of Consumer Incentives to Meet Simultaneous Sales Quotas: An Application to U.S. Army Recruiting," (under review in Management Science), 1989.

8. Morey, R.C. "Impacts of Size, Composition and Compactness of the Delayed Entry Pool on Enlistment Contract Production: Efficient Allocation of Recruiting Expenditures and Optimal Dep Management," Office of Naval Research Final Report, Duke University, February, 88.

9. Morey, R.C. "Managing the Armed Services' Delayed Entry Programs to Improve Productivity in Recruiting," Interfaces, Sept.-Oct., 85, Vol. 15, No. 5, pp. 81-90.

10. Morey, R.C. and McCann, J. "Armed Forces Recruiting Research: Issues, Findings, and Needs," Naval Research Logistics Quarterly, December, 83, Vol. 30, No. 4, pp. 697-719.

11. Morey, R.C. and McCann, J.M. "Evaluating and Improving the Recruiting Process for the Navy," Management Science, Vol. 26, No. 12, December, 1980, pp. 1198-1210.

12. Schinnar, A.P., Wood, L., Nord, R., Schmitz, E. and Durongkavenoj, P. "Recruit Quality, Soldier Performance, and JA Assignment," (submitted to Journal of Productivity, 1988).

13. Scribner, B.L., Smith, D.A., Baldwin, R.H., and Phillips, R.W., "Are Smart Tankers Better? AFQT and Military Productivity," Armed Forces and Society, 12/2, 1986.

14. Toomepuu, J. (Chief, Research and Studies Division, U.S. Army Recruiting Command), private communication, 1989.

15. Varian, H., Microeconomic Analysis, Second Edition, New York: W.W. Norton and Company, 1984.

16. Zellner, A. (1963). "Estimations for Seemingly Unrelated Regression Equations: Some Exact Finite Sample Results," Journal of the American Statistical Association, 63, 1180-1200.

APPENDIX

THIRD STAGE PARAMETER ESTIMATES FROM EXERCISING SIMULTANEOUS EQUATION

REGRESSION MODEL ON REGIONAL-MONTHLY DATA FROM FY84-FY86

Basic Scenario: Recruiter's cost on a per man-year basis (salary and benefits) were estimated at $32,000 in 1986 dollars*; also the necessary conditions for allocative efficiency were imposed. The dependent variable is the logarithm of total Navy recruiting cost, less Navy Recruiting Command's Headquarter cost.

Variables	Parameter Estimates and t Ratios from Model
Intercept	1.22 (.92)
ln(contracts of A type)	.604 (1.53)
ln(contracts of B type)	-.003 (-.97)
ln(contracts of C_u type)	-1.18 (-3.83)
ln(contracts of C_ℓ type)	-.12 (-1.79)
ln(contracts of D type)	.002 (7.37)
$(\ln(\text{contracts of type A}))^2$	-.04 (-1.26)
ln(price per unit for local advertising/price per recruiter)	.0094 (63.98)
ln(price per unit for Navy National Advertising/price per recruiter)	.067 (19.65)
ln(price per unit for Field Level support cost/price per recruiter)	.235 (103.7)
$(\ln(\text{contracts of type B}))^2$	-.0004 (-1.58)
$(\ln(\text{contracts of type } C_u))^2$	.116 (4.04)
$(\ln(\text{contracts of type } C_\ell))^2$	.014 (1.74)
$\ln(\text{contracts of type D})^2$	-.0002 (-.53)
ln(Size of dep of type A) 2 months earlier	.929 (1.89)
ln(Size of dep of type B) 2 months earlier	.032 (3.87)
ln(Size of dep of type C_u) 2 months earlier	-.829 (-1.66)
ln(Size of dep of type C_ℓ) 2 months earlier	.0033 (.75)
ln(dep of type A two months earlier)·ln(# of recruiters)	.573 (7.84)
ln(dep of type C_u two months earlier)·ln(# of recruiters)	-.581 (7.37)

* Estimate provided by Controller, U.S. Navy Recruiting Command.

APPENDIX continued

ln(dep size of A type 2 months earlier)^2	-.29 (-9.12)
ln(dep of size of C$_u$ type 2 months earlier)^2	.311 (9.03)
ln(Size of eligible male population)	-.526 (-9.36)
ln(percent of eligible population that's Black)	.031 (2.47)
ln(level of Joint Dod Advertising expenses)	-.0003 (-.04)
ln(level of Navy Recruiting Command Headquarters cost)	-.0016 (-1.36)
ln(local unemployment rate)	-.048 (-1.71)
ln(ratio of military/civilian pay ratio)	-.069 (-.49)
ln(Percent of this month's accession goal covered by dep)	-.09 (-1.94)
ln(percent of last month's accession goal covered by dep)	.046 (.93)
ln(percent of accession goal 2 months ago covered by dep)	-.028 (-.49)
ln(percent of accession goal 3 months ago covered by dep)	-.097 (-1.99)
January Monthly dummy	-.025 (-1.36)
February Monthly dummy	.13 (6.78)
March Monthly dummy	.09 (4.51)
April Monthly dummy	.15 (5.01)
May Monthly dummy	.133 (2.81)
June Monthly dummy	.019 (.34)
July Monthly dummy	-.039 (-.56)
August Monthly dummy	.056 (1.06)
September Monthly dummy	.188 (4.06)
October Monthly dummy	.171 (9.06)
November Monthly dummy	.098 (5.41)

IV. Recent Developments in Cost Modeling

COST MODELING FOR DESIGN JUSTIFICATION

James S. Noble[1] *and J.M.A. Tanchoco*[2]
School of Industrial Engineering, Purdue University
West Lafayette, Indiana 47907 U.S.A

Abstract

Product cost models are usually developed after the product design has been completed. As a result, the economic trade-offs made throughout the design process are often made on an ad-hoc basis. As an alternative, a product cost model can be developed for use through the design process. This procedure will give more accurate cost information and will enhance decision making during the design process. This simultaneous development of the product design and cost model is termed **design justification,** implying the design is economically and functionally justified as it is developed. In this paper a framework is presented for design justification and the results from a prototype of a system are given.

1. Introduction

There are several reasons for accurately tracking and measuring the benefits and costs of a product. First, and of primary importance, it is necessary to determine the economic feasibility of a product in order to assure its financial success. Second, it is desirable to insure that the allocation of funds are made to economically viable products. This requires knowledge of the economic and functional performance of the product.

Measuring costs and benefits can be achieved using a variety of approaches.

Benefits can be measured in several ways:

1. *The dollar value of product sales or production.* This is possible when the result of the design is an easily determined product or system.

2. *Arbitrary measure of performance (i.e. system flexibility).* This is used when the direct benefit from the design is hard to determine.

3. *Neglect of all benefit.* This can be used when comparing several alternative designs that have equal benefit. Thus, cost is implied as the primary determinant.

Likewise, there are several approaches to developing cost models:

---

[1] Graduate Research Assistant pursuing Ph.D. degree in Industrial Engineering
[2] Associate Professor of Industrial Engineering

1. *Budget constraint analysis.* This entails using the budget from each design function to develop the cost model (Meisl 1988).

2. *Bill of Materials analysis.* This method requires the cost model to be developed by working down the bill of materials for the product or system (Leshuk, p.22 Fabrycky 1984).

3. *Parametric modeling.* This consists of developing the empirical relationships between certain cost parameters and selected physical or performance parameters (Daschbach 1988).

All of these approaches must be, or typically have been, applied at the end of the design phase and tend to be primarily an estimation of the actual cost/benefit. Thus, the cost/benefit information usually does not have any impact on the design process. The potential benefit that could be derived from including cost/benefit information during the design process has been alluded to by several in the past. Fleischer and Khoshnevis give the results of a West German survey showing that by including value analysis in the product life cycle an average of 33 percent savings in cost could be obtained of which 65 percent of this was found in the design phase (Fleischer 1986). Both Boothroyd and Wierda maintain that the decisions made by a product designer determines approximately 75 percent of the eventual cost of the product (Boothroyd 1988, Wierda 1988).

In this paper, the development of cost models during the design process is discussed. The term *design justification* is used to denote the concept that the design is economically and functionally justified as the product is developed. The result is a design that better meets the desired functional characteristics and an accurate cost model for the product. The developed model contains both cost and benefit factors.

2. Literature review

The amount of literature that   directly addressed this issue has been limited in the past. Only recently has interest in integrated product design and cost modeling developed. However, an abundance of literature exists on the separate areas of design and justification. Figure 1 shows the range and relationships among the areas of research in economic analysis. The areas of cost/benefit estimating, economic modeling and design are treated independently.

An example of an early attempt to integrating the design and justification processes was done by Manheim (Simon 1969). He used a "developing cost model" for a highway system to aid design decisions. Gustavson (Gustavson 1984) used the cost components of an assembly system to be the driving force behind an automatic design generation model. A static cost

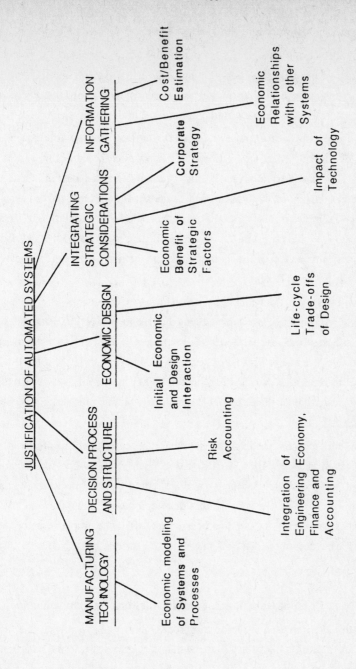

Figure 1 - Justification Research Areas

model was used in which inputs were given to generate the optimal system.

A benefit/cost model design concept was proposed by Blank and Carrasco (Blank 1985). Their concept consisted of providing an economic model for each stage of the systems development and implementation. The economic models suggested would evolve with, and be used throughout, the conceptual, design, construction and implementation phases.

Another approach to cost/benefit and design integration has been to link cost models to design databases. Fleischer and Khoshnevis proposed a knowledge-based design system linking design, process planning and cost analysis within a computer-aided design (CAD) system (Fleischer 1986). Wierda reviewed the types of cost models that could be used to aid in product design and gave some examples of research on how these could be linked with CAD systems to enable the designer to see the cost impact of design decisions (Wierda 1988). Boothroyd developed an actual implementation of a system to estimate the machining cost that can be used during the design of the product (Boothroyd 1988).

Griffin (Griffen 1988), and Fad and Summers (Fad 1988), suggest that the parametric method for cost modeling should be used throughout the design process. Griffin states that the use of cost models in design must be viewed as "evolutionary", implying that the model detail must match the state in which the project is in. Fad and Summers (Fad 1988, p.166] state, "Too many developers fail to recognize that cost has historically been treated as an inevitable result caused by a required design rather than a variable that can be planned for strategically and used to control design."

The need for integrating cost models and the design process has been proposed and discussed before (Fad 1988, Fleischer 1986, Griffin 1988, Wierda 1988). The specifics of implementing this concept and how a developing cost model could be used in design has not been addressed. This paper shows how the concept of a developing cost model can actually be used to integrate cost/benefit information and the design process. The implemented model is a specific application for the design of EMI/RFI shields.

3. Design Justification - Concept Development and Framework for Implementation

Traditional cost models are used in the design process in one of two ways. One way is that the cost estimate is made from a budgetary limit, which is passed down to the designer. In this case the designer can often become preoccupied with the cost constraint and becomes restricted in coming up with the best functional design.

The other way, as is most often the case, the designer is allowed to develop the product and then the cost model is developed to match it. In this case little thought is initially made by the designer about cost. The functionality of the product is primarily considered. Often, the design is later rejected based on cost considerations and then the whole design process is reinvestigated to determine where cost might be reduced. This more typical situation is illustrated in figure 2. In this case, the technologies and engineering constraints, which are known, are used to construct what is deemed to be a good design (PLAN A1 in figure 2). After the cost model is developed the proposed PLAN A1 is analyzed. As a result of the analysis the design is either accepted or rejected based upon the criteria set. If the design is rejected, the reasons are given and the plan is returned for modification or the plan is completely redone. As can be seen, unless the design is initially accepted the cycle tends to be inefficient and time consuming.

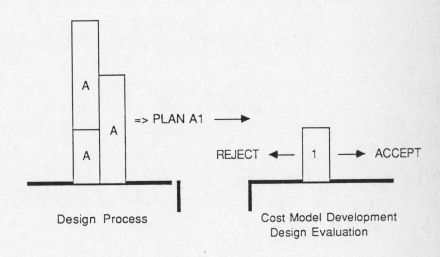

Figure 2 - Present Design and Justification Interaction

The basic concept of design justification is that there is a need to have meaningful interaction between design and economic justification at all major points of design trade-off. This will result in greater attention focused on the design factors which will enhance product performance with respect to the best cost efficiency. It will also allow for the product cost model to be developed incrementally with the design. Thus it can be used as a decision tool throughout the entire design process. The added information within the design process enables the most economical and functionally acceptable design to be developed. Figure 3 illustrates the design justification interaction. The underlying concept is to allow for the design and cost model development to take place concurrently, resulting in the best design possible from both a functional and economic perspective.

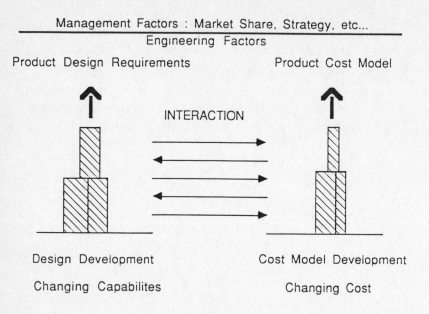

Figure 3 - Proposed Design Justification Interaction

The development of the cost model, within the design justification concept, can be illustrated using a crystal (i.e. design) which expands three dimensionally. Consider a project for which a preliminary cost model is developed. This model can be represented as a balloon around the design. This preliminary model could be developed from a budget constraint analysis or a similar past design.

The design process begins with the expansion of the "design crystal" not significantly impacting the cost model balloon (figure 4a). As design decisions are made the cost model balloon changes to reflect these changes. Some changes have little impact on the overall size of the balloon and others cause the balloon to expand to accommodate the design. The changes due to a design decision which are made to the cost model are always maintained so that they may be considered in conjunction with future design and cost model changes. When the cost model is expanded to what is deemed to be a critical level (figure 4b), the past design decisions and associated cost model modifications are brought into consideration.

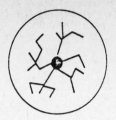 Begin product design, initial cost model balloon.

Figure 4a - Cost Model Balloon Stage 1

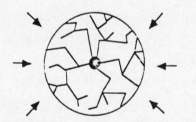 The cost model balloon expands for consideration of all design trade-offs.

Figure 4b - Cost Model Balloon Stage 2

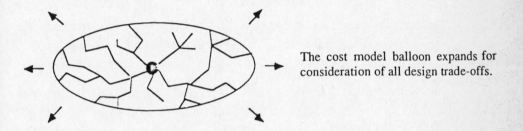 The cost model balloon shrinks as the analysis shows design trade-offs that can be implemented to maximize the overall benefit.

Figure 4c - Cost Model Balloon Stage 3

By searching and combining design trade-offs previously encountered, an effort can be made to reduce the overall cost, yet maintain the greatest benefit (figure 4c). The goal of this search is to maximize the benefits and still keep the overall cost model balloon within a reasonable boundary.

While developing a system to aid design justification, it was found that the system environment is determined to a large extent by the way in which information is presented to the decision maker. The current trend in design and cost model methodologies is to work toward quantifying all information about a design in order to aid in the computer analysis of the design process. However, in doing this, the creativity, intuition and previous knowledge of the designer can be "quantified out" of the process.

Therefore, the proposed framework for the development of cost models to aid in the design of a product, requires an environment consisting of the following:

1. The ability to analyze and present quantifiable information. Quantifiable means that the information can be determined with certainty.

2. The presentation of uncertain or incomplete information in such a manner that the decision maker is able to process and integrate information throughout the design process.

3. The decision maker is the decision mechanism that drives the design process.

The implementation of this environment makes several components necessary for design justification to occur. These components are: a knowledge base, an analysis procedure for design evaluation and cost model development, and a presentation medium that supports differing types of interaction.

A knowledge base is necessary so that a body of design knowledge can be accessed throughout the design process. A knowledge base is a collection of facts, data and component interactions within the design sphere. The knowledge base by its structure leads the designer down the feasible technical path of alternatives for the product design. Conducting a search of the knowledge base makes it is possible to obtain the necessary information required to develop a design from an engineering and economic perspective.

The quantitative analysis component provides the decision maker with the opportunity to experiment with quantifiable design information and to develop the associated cost model for the design. The analysis relies upon information provided by both the knowledge base and the decision maker and consists of the ability to evaluate both the engineering and economic aspects of the design.

The final component is an engineering workstation that facilitates interaction between the knowledge base, quantitative analysis and decision maker. The workstation provides graphical capabilities so that the information can be assimilated by the decision maker. This platform makes the decision maker an essential component in the entire decision making process.

4. Prototype Implementation of Design Justification Concept

A prototype implementation of such a design justification environment was developed. The product used to test the design justification concept was an EMI(electromagnetic interference)/RFI(radio frequency interference) shield for an electrical metering device (figure 5).

Figure 5 - An EMI/RFI Shield

The need for this product evolved after recent advances in electrical metering devices which resulted in the use of solid state electronics as the measuring mechanisms in meters rather than mechanical components. These meters are typically used in environments that are characterized by large amounts of electromagnetic and radio waves. These electromagnetic and radio waves affect the solid state electronics by altering the specified performance characteristics. Therefore, to ensure accurate electrical metering, a shield for the metering device is necessary.

The major function of the shield is to reduce the EMI/RFI in the metering circuitry. The effectiveness of such a physical barrier relies primarily on the conductivity of the material used. There are three ways in which sufficient conductivity can be obtained in the shield:

1. Use of a conductive metal material.

2. Use of an engineering plastic/conductive material composite.

3. Use of an engineering plastic coated with a conductive material.

The design process required for an EMI/RFI shields consist of selecting the shields performance requirements, structural material and associated forming process, and the shielding material, with its associated application process.

The required design justification system components were implemented on a SUN 3/50 workstation using the C programming language interfaced with the X windowing system (Debord 1987). The information flow within the implemented design justification environment is shown in figure 6. The supporting knowledge base consist of current material and equipment costs, and provides the feasible technical path resulting from choosing a given manufacturing technology or material. The knowledge base was obtained through the input of two design engineers and published materials on material properties and costs. The system allows the designer to concurrently consider the engineering and cost ramifications of selecting different product components and processes. A cost model consisting of the fixed and variable costs is updated and developed along with the design. Appendix 1 describes the specific cost model used. In the design of an EMI/RFI shield, the fixed cost component considered consists of material forming equipment and shielding application equipment. The variable cost component consists of the structural and shielding materials and their forming and application cost, respectively.

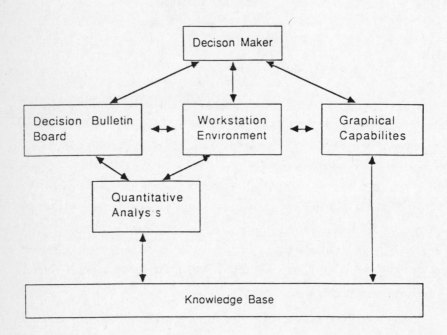

Figure 6 - Implemented Design Justification Information Flow

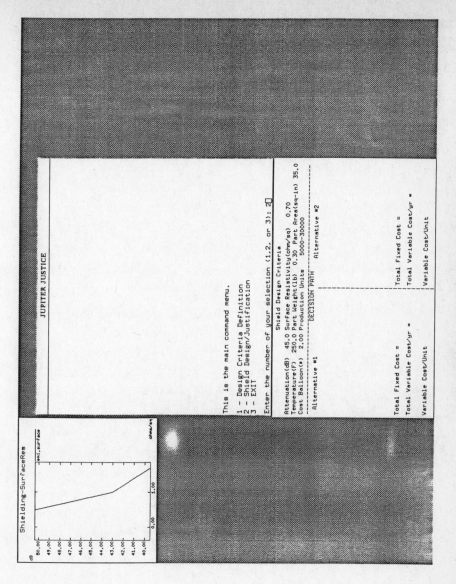

Figure 7 - Design Justification Example 1

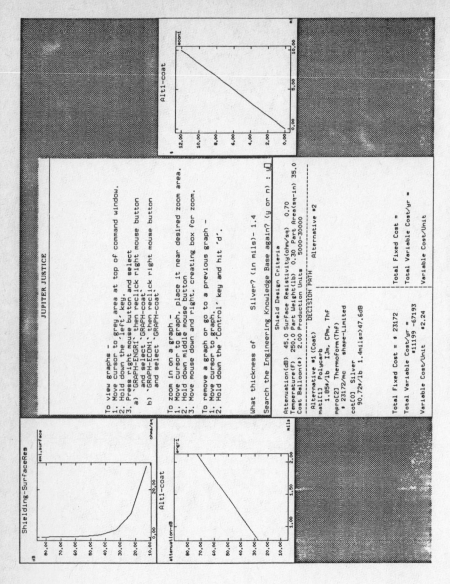

Figure 8 - Design Justification Example 2

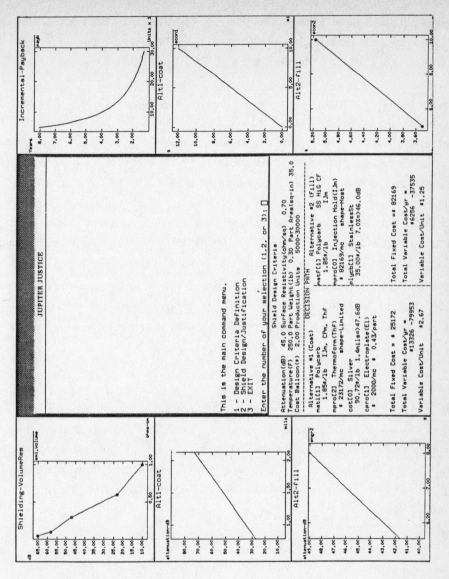

Figure 9 - Design Justification Example 3

Figures 7, 8, and 9 show several of the steps that occur when using the design justification system and the associated cost model development. Figure 7 shows the results of selecting the initial design criteria. During criteria specification graphs relating different material properties to shielding ability are presented. The other information is supplied by the user. Figure 8 shows the decisions made for the engineering plastic, material forming process, and the selection of the thickness of shielding material that is needed to obtain the desired shielding performance in the development of design alternative one. Engineering information is graphed on the left and economic data is graphed on the right allowing for both factors to be considered in the decision. The developing cost model is given at the bottom of the decisions listed for alternative one. Figure 9 depicts the result of a complete iteration of using the design justification system. Two EMI/RFI shield alternatives have been developed along with their associated cost models. An incremental payback comparison between the two alternatives has been conducted and is plotted over the specified production range in the upper right corner of the screen.

The developed prototype design justification system is a specific application of the design justification concept. Its present use is confined to the company with which it was developed. However, the framework proposed could be extended to solving more general design problems.

5. Conclusion

The need for considering the economic ramifications along with engineering factors of design trade-offs within the design process has been shown. The development of a cost model throughout the design process allows for this to be achieved. Using an integrated environment, it is possible to assist the designer in both of these related tasks. The proposed framework for design justification was implemented and was shown to aid in the design of a functionally and economically better product.

6. Acknowledgements

The work reported in this paper was partially supported by a David Ross Grant from Purdue University. The Landis and Gyr, Inc. of Lafayette, Indiana is also acknowledged for providing the product information.

7. References

Blank, L. and H. Carrasco, 1985, "The Economics of New Technology: System Design and Development Methodology," *Proc., 1985 Int. Industrial Engineering Conf.,* pp. 161-167, Los Angeles, CA.

Boothroyd, G., 1988, "Estimate costs at an early stage," *American Machinist,* vol. 132(8), pp. 54-57.

Daschbach, J.M. and H. Apgar, 1988, "Design Analysis through Techniques of Parametric Cost Estimation," *Engineering Cost and Production Economics,* vol. 14(2), pp. 87-93.

Debord, L. J., 1987, *Using X - An Introduction to the X Window System,* School of Electrical Engineering, Purdue University, West Lafayette, IN.

Fad, B.E. and R.M. Summers, 1988, "Parametric Estimating for New Business Ventures," *Engineering Cost and Production Economics,* vol. 14(2), pp. 165-176.

Fleischer, G.A. and B Khoshnevis, 1985, "Incorporating Economic Impact Assessment into Computer-Aided Design, *Proc., 1986 Int. Industrial Engineering Conf.,* pp. 163-174, Dallas, TX.

Griffin, J.J., 1988, "Whole Life Cost Studies: A Defense Management Perspective," *Engineering Cost and Production Economics,* vol. 14(2), pp. 107-115.

Gustavson, R.E., 1984, "Computer-aided Synthesis of Least Cost Assembly Systems," *Proc., 14th Int. Symposium on Industrial Robots,* pp.95-106, Gothenburg, Sweden.

Fabrycky, W.J., Ed., 1984, *Proc. Research Planning Conf. on Engineering Economics,* Dept of IEOR - Virginia Polytech Inst and State U., Mountain Lake, Virginia.

Meisl, C.J., 1988, "Techniques for Cost Estimating in Early Program Phases," *Engineering Cost and Production Economics,* vol. 14(2), pp. 95-106.

Noble, J.S., 1988, "A Unified Decision Environment for Product Design and Economic Justification," M.S.I.E. Thesis, School of Industrial Engineering, Purdue University, West Lafayette.

Simon, H.A., 1969, *The Sciences of the Artificial,* Massachusetts Institute of Technology, Cambridge, MA.

Throne, J., 1979, *Plastics Process Engineering,* Marcel Dekker, NY.

Wierda, L.S., 1988. "Product Cost-Estimation by the Designer," *Engineering Costs and Production Economics, vol. 13(3), pp. 189-198.*

APPENDIX 1 - IMPLEMENTED COST MODEL FOR EMI/RFI SHIELD DESIGN

The following is the complete cost model developed and implemented in the design justification environment for EMI/RFI shields.

A. GENERAL COST MODEL

$$TC = F + Vx$$

where,

$$Fixed\ cost = F = MFE + SAE$$
$$Variable\ cost / unit = V = PM + SM + FP + SP$$
$$x = production units$$

MFE, SAE, PM, SM, FP and SP are defined below.

B. SPECIFIC COST MODEL
1. FIXED FACTORS

a) MFE - material forming equipment

$$MFE = (mold/cavity\ (\$)) + (primary\ m/c\ (\$)) + (ancillary\ m/c\ (\$))$$

where,

$$log[mold/cavity\ (\$)] = A_m\ log[part\ weight\ (lb)] + B_m$$

$$log[primary\ m/c\ cost\ (\$)] = A_p\ log[part\ weight\ (lb)] + B_p$$

$$ancillary\ m/c\ cost\ (\$) = C_a\ (primary\ m/c\ cost)$$

Values for capital cost for each process are obtained from Throne (Throne 1979). The values for the parameters A_m, B_m, A_p, B_p, C_a are dependent on the type of forming process. The capital cost was converted from the 1973 dollars used by Throne to 1987 dollars.

b) SAE - shielding application equipment

$$SAE = 2000$$

2. VARIABLE FACTORS

a) PM - plastic materials (possibly filled)

$$PM = (material\ cost\text{-}\ \$/lb)(partweight)$$

b) SM - shielding materials

$$SM = (cost\ \$/lb)(coating\ area\text{-}\ sq\text{-}in)\left[\frac{coat\ thickness\text{-}\ mils}{1000}\right](coat\ density\text{-}\ lb/sq\text{-}in)$$

c) FP - forming process

$$FP = 0$$

In the model used for this paper, the variable cost of the forming process is assumed to be zero.

d) SP - shielding process

$$SP = \frac{(cost/sq\text{-}ft)}{144}(area\text{-}\ sq\text{-}in)$$

THE EFFECT OF TECHNOLOGY ON THE SUPPORTABILITY AND COST OF AVIONICS EQUIPMENT

Daniel B. Levine, Stanley A. Horowitz, Joseph W. Stahl

Institute for Defense Analyses
1801 N. Beauregard Street
Alexandria, Virginia 22311

INTRODUCTION AND CONCLUSIONS

Introduction

In keeping pace with recent advances in electronics, the military services have shifted from solid state devices (transistors) to micro-miniaturized devices (chips) in the design of avionics. By employing micro-miniaturized electronics, those who design military aircraft have sought to take advantage of the intrinsically higher reliability of chips. At the same time, designers have taken advantage of micro-miniaturized components to build more performance into avionics systems. However, in the views of some, the means used to increase performance have had negative effects on supportability, which counters the positive intrinsic effect.

The reliability and maintainability of avionics have strong effects on cost. Pound-for-pound, avionics is generally recognized as the most expensive, complex and sophisticated part of an aircraft. In some modern aircraft, the avionics may cost as much as 30 percent of total flyaway cost, and avionic support costs for some older aircraft reportedly approach three-fourths of total support costs [1]. Reliability and maintainability also affect decisions about the provisioning of spares and the size and location of repair facilities.

Finally, the relationship between micro-miniaturization and supportability has an important bearing on overall operational performance. To the extent that modern avionics systems are unreliable and difficult to maintain, the military services will suffer from lower aircraft sortie rates, lower combat performance for a given force of aircraft, and lower performance from a given total budget spent on tactical aircraft. If pushing hard on the forefront of technology does, in fact, exact a high premium in reduced reliability and maintainability, policy planners may wish to consider this tradeoff in deciding how much performance to design into future aircraft.

The principal question for this study is whether the net effect of micro-miniaturization on reliability has been positive or negative.[1] Has the intrinsically high reliability been outweighed by lower reliability

---

[1] This work was supported by IDA's fund for central research. The authors wish to thank Mr. Seymour Deitchman for suggesting the topic and encouraging the work, Dr. Stephen Balut for his valuable suggestions and comments on the analysis, and Mr. Robert Simmons for his substantial contributions to the form and style of the paper.

and higher cost from the push to higher performance? Has maturation of the new technology increased reliability and decreased cost enough to counteract these effects, if they exist?

To determine the net effect, we will relate reliability to technology and maturity without holding constant the intervening variable of cost. The net effect will be the combined result of the "intrinsic" and "performance" effects. We will then relate technology to cost, and cost to supportability. We will also estimate the extent to which the relationship between cost and reliability depends on technology and maturation.

These relationships will be estimated using statistical regression techniques, which avoids the need for a detailed, or "micro" model and allows us to focus on the overall relationships.

Conclusions

We find no evidence that the transition from solid state to micro-miniaturized devices lowered the supportability of avionics equipment. The picture was mixed when the new technology was first introduced: reliability rose but maintainability fell even more, which yielded an unfavorable net effect on repair time per operating hour. But as the new technology matured, reliability improved, and maintainability, though still lower than before the transition, improved as well, which gave a favorable effect on repair time per operating hour.

When cost is included in the analysis, the evidence points to the conclusion that, at least in the case studied, as technology matures, the services may be able to achieve both greater reliability and higher performance in avionics equipment without paying a higher price for them.

DATA

The data on 33 items of avionics equipment are listed in Table 1, and the variables in the table are defined in the remainder of this section. The items of equipment range from low-cost automatic direction finders, radar altimeters and TACANs to high-cost radars, computer sets and ECM equipment. The dates of manufacture span the period 1965 to 1978. The items were installed in the Air Force F-4C, F-4D, F-4E, F-4G, RC-135A, C-130B, C-130E, F-15A, F-15C, C-141A, C-5A, and F-111E, and in the Navy F-18.

For some of the electronic items, we obtained the reliability and maintenance data from the Air Force Logistic Command's D056 Log Reports for August 1979 through January 1980 [2] and the cost data from a proprietary data base. For the remaining items, we obtained the reliability and maintenance data from the Navy VAMOSC-Air Reports for October 1985 through September 1986 [3] and the cost data from a data base prepared by Information Spectrum, Inc. The variables are defined as follows:

Number (No.). Some of the data are proprietary, so we have omitted the detailed designations (AN/ numbers) of the items and simply numbered them for convenience.

Reliability (REL). Reliability was calculated by dividing total operating hours by the total number of failures. "Total" means summed over all the aircraft in which the item was installed, and for the entire period of data collection.

Maintainability (REP). Maintainability was calculated by dividing non-depot repair time by the total number of failures. (Our focus is on estimating the effect of technology on maintainability in the squadron.) Repair time is measured in man-hours, and includes the time spent on unscheduled maintenance at the organizational level plus the time spent on all maintenance at the intermediate level, both scheduled and unscheduled. Although repair time for scheduled maintenance at the organizational level is not included, it only amounts to less than 1 percent of the total, according to detailed data we were able to obtain for 8 of the 33 items of equipment.

Procurement Cost (COST). Cost is the estimated cost of the 100th unit procured, measured in thousands of FY 1978 dollars.

Technology (TECH). TECH is a dummy variable used to discriminate between the items built with solid state technology and those built with micro-miniaturization: TECH = 0 for solid state technology; TECH = 1 for micro-miniaturization.

Experience (EXP). EXP is a dummy variable used to capture the effect of maturation on supportability: EXP = 0 for those items whose data were obtained from the 1979-80 reports and which were built with solid-state technology and earlier micro-miniaturization; EXP = 1 for the remaining items, whose data were obtained from the 1985-86 reports and which were built with later micro-miniaturization technology. We will be able to use this variable to make a judgment about the reliability of the F-18, since all the 1985-86 data are for this aircraft, and this aircraft alone.

Type of Equipment (TYPE). The last seven columns are dummy variables used to describe the type of equipment as defined by the second letter (the Equipment Designator) in the item's AN/ designation: T1 = electro-mechanical, T2 = countermeasure, T3 = radar, T4 = radio, T5 = special types, T6 = visible light, and T7 = data processing. For example, an AN/APG-65 is a radar ("P" stands for radar in the AN/ code) and is represented by setting T3 equal to 1 and all the other T's equal to zero. A few items lacking an AN/ designation were represented by setting all seven T's to zero.

Table 1. Data on Avionics Equipment

No.	REL	REP	COST	TECH	EXP	T1	T2	T3	T4	T5	T6	T7
1	805.4	9.9	1.8	0	0	0	0	0	1	0	0	0
2	69.6	13.0	7.4	0	0	0	0	1	0	0	0	0
3	32.3	12.5	14.4	0	0	0	0	0	1	0	0	0
4	49.6	20.6	18.1	0	0	0	0	1	0	0	0	0
5	52.2	19.3	21.5	0	0	0	0	1	0	0	0	0
6	55.5	8.9	23.8	0	0	0	0	0	0	1	0	0
7	70.9	16.7	47.9	0	0	0	0	0	0	1	0	0
8	59.3	34.8	97.6	0	0	0	0	0	1	0	0	0
9	29.6	13.6	140.8	0	0	0	0	0	0	1	0	0
10	57.3	30.9	152.0	0	0	0	0	1	0	0	0	0
11	35.0	25.8	156.4	0	0	0	0	1	0	0	0	0
12	6.5	14.3	338.6	0	0	0	0	1	0	0	0	0
13	13.8	27.3	350.7	0	0	0	0	1	0	0	0	0
14	13.8	34.2	498.2	0	0	1	0	0	0	0	0	0
15	202.7	44.4	30.0	1	0	0	0	0	0	0	0	0
16	341.9	29.6	40.9	1	0	0	0	0	0	0	0	0
17	244.4	24.9	42.2	1	0	0	0	0	0	1	0	0
18	697.5	66.0	53.0	1	0	0	1	0	0	0	0	0
19	379.1	32.2	53.7	1	0	0	0	0	0	0	0	0
20	80.1	40.1	87.3	1	0	0	0	0	0	0	1	0
21	81.6	41.0	164.6	1	0	0	0	0	0	1	0	0
22	63.4	28.2	219.8	1	0	0	0	1	0	0	0	0
23	86.3	36.0	235.0	1	0	0	1	0	0	0	0	0
24	156.6	46.7	490.0	1	0	0	1	0	0	0	0	0
25	20.8	48.9	1,015.9	1	0	0	0	1	0	0	0	0
26	20.7	23.2	534.9	1	1	0	0	1	0	0	0	0
27	75.7	16.0	97.8	1	1	0	0	0	0	0	0	1
28	59.6	23.4	128.7	1	1	0	0	0	0	1	0	0
29	132.3	15.7	77.8	1	1	0	0	0	0	0	1	0
30	758.8	22.3	10.6	1	1	0	0	1	0	0	0	0
31	2,608.4	36.3	6.6	1	1	0	0	1	0	0	0	0
32	2,455.0	33.4	14.2	1	1	0	1	0	0	0	0	0
33	878.6	74.6	205.9	1	1	0	1	0	0	0	0	0

SUPPORTABILITY

In this section we estimate the net effects of technology and experience (maturation) on supportability. First we estimate the effects of micro-miniaturization and maturation on reliability. Then we estimate their effects on maintainability. Finally, we examine their combined effect on a measure of supportability in which our measures of reliability and maintainability are combined.

Reliability

The dependence of reliability on technology is shown in Table 2. The dependent variable is the (natural) logarithm of reliability. We found that using the log form of reliability and maintainability (and cost in later regressions) yielded closer fits with the data.[2]

The fact that the coefficient of TECH is positive bears on the central question of the study. It indicates that, holding the other variables constant, the shift from solid state to micro-miniaturized devices probably led to an improvement in reliability, not the reverse. The size of the coefficient indicates that the improvement was an increase of 75 percent. (Reliability improved by a multiplicative factor of $e^{.56}$ = 1.75, a rise of 75 percent.)

The coefficient of TECH has fairly low statistical significance, however. The t-statistic of .86 corresponds to a 40-percent level of significance, meaning that the true coefficient of technology could have been zero and there would still have been a 40-percent chance of obtaining data yielding a coefficient as large, in absolute value, as the one actually estimated. This percentage fails to meet the criterion of 10 percent often used in empirical studies.

Table 2. Net Effect of Micro-Miniaturization on Reliability
(Dependent variable: log REL)

Independent Variable	Coefficient	t-statistic	Significance (Percent)
Constant	5.14	5.40	<1
TECH	0.56	0.86	40
EXP	1.34	2.14	4
T1	-2.51	-1.64	11
T2	-0.10	-0.11	91
T3	-1.63	-1.79	9
T4	-0.39	-0.33	75
T5	-1.36	-1.46	16
T6	-1.73	-1.52	14
T7	-2.71	-1.79	9
$R^2 = .53$			

---

[2] The values of R^2 for the regression in Table 2 and other regressions reported in this paper are fairly low; this means we are missing some of the important determinants, and the regressions would give imperfect forecasts. Our intention, however, is not to forecast the dependent variables, but rather to estimate their dependence on the explanatory variables that we *have* included in the equations – and these dependencies can be estimated and significant inferences drawn even if R^2 is low.

Significance levels notwithstanding, the coefficient of TECH must be regarded as the best estimate that can be made with the data and specification of the regression equation. Taking everything together, we can certainly say that the analysis offers no support whatever for a judgment that replacing transistors with chips *lowered* reliability.

The positive (and statistically significant) coefficient of EXP suggests that reliability improved even further, by a factor of 3.8 as the micro-miniaturization technology matured. Taken together, the coefficients of TECH and EXP thus imply that, in the long run, shifting from solid state to mature micro-miniaturization led to a huge rise in reliability, by a factor of almost 6.7 ($e^{.56}$ x $e^{1.34}$ = 6.7).

Maintainability

Although items with micro-miniaturization technology seem to fail less often, Table 3 implies that they take longer to fix: the coefficient of TECH is positive (higher technology leads to longer repair time) and the estimate is highly significant. The numerical value of 0.70 implies that, holding the other variables constant, the shift from solid state to micro-miniaturized technology has led to an approximately 100 percent increase in repair time per failure.

Table 3. Net Effect of Micro-Miniaturization on Maintainability
(Dependent variable: log REP)

Independent Variable	Coefficient	t-statistic	Significance (Percent)
Constant	2.85	9.58	<1
TECH	0.70	3.39	<1
EXP	-0.32	-1.60	12
T1	0.68	1.41	17
T2	0.46	1.63	12
T3	0.12	0.43	67
T4	-0.07	-0.18	86
T5	-0.20	-0.69	50
T6	-0.17	-0.47	64
T7	-0.46	-0.97	34
R^2 = .63			

As before, added experience seems to have had a beneficial (though not highly statistically significant) effect, tending, in this case, to lower repair time per failure. It did not, however, completely counteract the negative effect of technology: taking the two changes together, the time spent on repair rose by 46 percent.

Note also that some of the "T" variables in Tables 2 and 3 have sizable coefficients and t-statistics, which shows that it was important to control for the type of equipment.[3] The coefficients of T1, for example, confirm the suspicion that electro-mechanical items have poorer reliability and higher repair time.

Total Repair Time

Our results, so far, indicate that, regarding the ability of the military services to support their avionics equipment, the transition from solid-state to micro-miniaturization technology was a mixed blessing: Micro-miniaturized equipment fails less frequently but takes longer to fix when it does fail. Experience (maturation), however, improves both reliability and maintainability.

We need to tie these threads together and consider the joint effect of micro-miniaturization technology and maturity on reliability and maintainability. First of all, we can combine reliability and maintainability into repair time per operating hour: repair time per operating hour equals failures per operating hour multiplied by repair time per failure, which equals (1/REL) x REP. Next, we can calculate the effect of technology on this composite measure by combining the changes in 1/REL and REP obtained from the regression coefficients in Tables 2 and 3 (we are referring to *multiplicative* changes in this section): change in repair time per operating hour equals change in failures per operating hour multiplied by change in repair time per failure, which equals $(1/e^{.56})$ x $e^{.70}$ = .57 x 2.01 = 1.15. Thus, the transition to micro-miniaturization seems to have had an adverse, but rather small, effect on repair time per hour, increasing it by 15 percent. The failure rate was cut almost in half (the .57 factor), but the doubling of repair time per failure was more than enough to counteract it. However, factoring in the effects of experience from Tables 2 and 3 changes the picture: change in repair time per operating hour = $(1/(e^{.56}$ x $e^{1.34}))$ x $(e^{.70}$ x $e^{-.32})$ = .15 x 1.46 = .22.

Thus, once the micro-miniaturization technology had matured, it required 78 percent less repair time per operating hour than did solid state items. Repair time was still higher than before the transition to micro-miniaturization (although now only 46 percent as opposed to 100 percent before maturation had taken place), but the failure rate was now lower by a huge factor of seven (1/.15).

COST

Up to now, we have focussed attention on the net effect of technology on supportability, neglecting the individual contributing factors mentioned earlier (the intrinsic reliability of chips and the move toward building more performance into electronic systems).

---

[3] We re-ran the regressions without the type dummies that had poor t-statistics. Most of the changes were negligible and in no case did the coefficient of the important variables – technology, experience, and cost – change sign or general magnitude.

In the remainder of this report, we present three additional analyses that are designed to cast light on these contributing factors. We estimate the effect of micro-miniaturization and maturation on cost, the effect of cost on supportability, and the extent to which the cost-reliability relationship depends on technology and maturation.

Micro-Miniaturization

Has micro-miniaturization been accompanied by higher cost, as many believe? The figures in Table 4 suggest "yes, but only initially": The coefficient of TECH is positive, but it is outweighed by the negative coefficient of EXP. The coefficient of TECH (implying that cost initially rose by a sizable factor of 2.8) is consistent with the hypothesis that the military services took advantage of the size and weight savings of micro-miniaturization to incorporate greater performance into their electronic equipment, which drove up the cost. (There might also have been an intrinsic effect in either direction, due to a difference in cost of constructing a given component with micro-miniaturized or solid state technology.)

The fact that the coefficient of EXP is higher and opposite in sign to the coefficient of TECH suggests that as the new technology matured, it became possible to achieve the higher performance without paying a higher price. Engineering changes, improved production techniques, learning, and market forces may have been some of the specific factors leading to the reduction in cost.

Table 4. Effect of Micro-Miniaturization on Cost
(Dependent variable: log COST)

Independent Variable	Coefficient	t-statistic	Significance (Percent)
Constant	2.66	2.29	3
TECH	1.03	1.30	21
EXP	-1.23	-1.60	12
T1	3.55	1.90	7
T2	1.51	1.36	19
T3	1.59	1.44	16
T4	-0.05	-0.04	97
T5	1.30	1.15	26
T6	1.33	0.96	35
T7	2.11	1.14	27

$R^2 = .29$

Supportability

For a given technology, does higher cost lead to lower supportability? The negative sign and highly significant coefficient of log COST in Table 5 confirm the suspicion that costly, high-performance equipment is indeed less reliable. Technology is included in the regression and thus held constant, and so the coefficient of cost measures the extent to which reliability depends on changes in cost that were not brought about by changes in technology. We therefore assume that the cost variable in Table 5 is primarily performance related. Because reliability and cost are both in the log form, the coefficient of log COST implies that a 10-percent increase in cost leads to a 6.8-percent reduction in reliability, for items with a given technology.[4]

Table 5. Effect of Cost on Reliability
(Dependent variable: log REL)

Independent Variable	Coefficient	t-statistic	Significance (Percent)
Constant	6.95	11.57	<1
Log COST	-0.68	-6.99	<1
TECH	1.26	3.27	<1
EXP	0.51	1.35	19
T1	-0.10	-0.10	92
T2	0.93	1.72	10
T3	-0.55	-1.01	32
T4	-0.42	-0.63	53
T5	-0.48	-0.87	39
T6	-0.83	-1.26	22
T7	-1.28	-1.43	17
$R^2 = .85$			

Higher cost is associated with worse maintainability as well (Table 6). The coefficient of log COST implies that a 10-percent increase in cost led to approximately a 1-percent increase in repair time per failure.

---

[4] Although we assume that two independent variables–cost and technology–are systematically related, we have reported the results of ordinary least squares regression in Table 5 because we obtained nearly identical results when we estimated the log COST and log REL equations simultaneously with two-stage least squares regression.

Table 6. Effect of Cost on Maintainability
(Dependent variable: log REP)

Independent Variable	Coefficient	t-statistic	Significance (Percent)
Constant	2.61	8.27	<1
Log COST	0.09	1.81	8
TECH	0.60	2.96	1
EXP	-0.20	-1.02	32
T1	0.35	0.71	49
T2	0.32	1.14	27
T3	-0.02	-0.08	93
T4	-0.06	-0.17	87
T5	-0.32	-1.13	27
T6	-0.29	-0.84	41
T7	-0.66	-1.41	17

$R^2 = .68$

Reliability Versus Cost and the Case of the F-18

It is interesting to view the figures in Table 5 from a different perspective: how the relationship between cost and reliability has been affected by technology and experience. This is shown in Figure 1, which depicts the original data points and the relationships between reliability and cost implied by the regression equation in Table 5. In Figure 1, "Solid State" corresponds to setting both TECH and EXP to zero in Table 5; "Micro-Min. (Earlier)," to setting TECH to 1 and EXP to zero; and "Micro-Min. (Later)," to setting both TECH and EXP to 1. In generating the regression curves in the figure, the dummy variables for type of equipment were set at their mean values, which is why the curves are not the best fits to the reliability and cost data points.

The positive and sizable coefficient of TECH in Table 5 is represented, in Figure 1, by a substantial upward shift of the reliability-cost curve arising from the initial move from solid state to micro-miniaturized technology. In other words, the services were able to achieve higher reliability for a given cost.

The coefficient of EXP, while positive, is much smaller than that of TECH. The reliability-cost curve thus continued to rise as the new technology matured, but by a smaller extent than that resulting from the initial move to micro-miniaturization. The maturation effect is substantial, especially given the fact that the plot is logarithmic. However, the t-statistic of the coefficient of EXP indicates that we cannot be as confident of the maturation effect as of the initial shift.

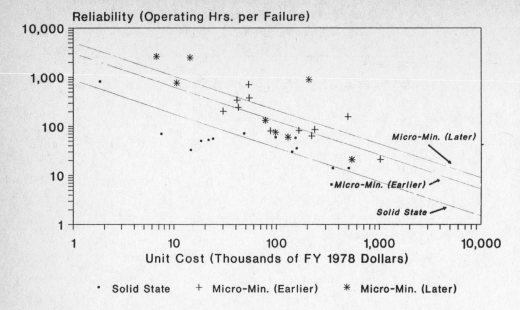

Figure 1. The Effect of Micro-Miniaturization on the Reliability-Cost Curve

The information in Figure 1 bears on two issues regarding the F-18's reliability. (The F-18 items were all constructed with mature, "later" micro-miniaturization technology represented by the top curve.) The first question is, to what extent does the F-18's electronics use an improved technology relative to previous aircraft? The results we have just discussed indicate that the use of mature micro-miniaturization did seem to offer the aircraft's designers a somewhat better reliability-cost tradeoff to work with. The evidence is mixed because the coefficient of EXP is substantial but the statistical significance is not high (Table 5).

The second question concerns the region of the reliability-cost curve that the F-18's designers chose to work at. During the development of the F-18, the Navy made a deliberate effort, costing approximately $100 million, to achieve a high level of reliability for the aircraft's avionics through improved design and restraint in pushing for higher performance.

Were the Navy's efforts successful? The fact that the data points for the F-18 (indicated by stars) generally lie higher than the points for the earlier micro-miniaturized items (indicated by plus signs) suggests "yes": The items installed in the F-18 are somewhat more reliable than those used in the other aircraft.[5] Moreover, the fact that the F-18 items lie generally to the left–lower in cost–supports the notion that the Navy achieved the simplicity and restraint it sought in the design effort.

---

[5] It is difficult to pick out the two collections of points in Figure 1 and compare the values of reliability by eye, especially because it is a log-log plot. However, we tested the hypothesis that the two distributions have the same mean and

In summary, the higher reliability of the F-18 items is due to two causes: the more mature micro-miniaturization afforded the Navy a better reliability-cost (i.e., reliability-performance) tradeoff, and the Navy chose to seek the upper-left side of the tradeoff by investing in greater simplicity and using some restraint in seeking higher performance.

REFERENCES

[1] Air Force Audit Agency, Department of the Air Force, Summary Report of Audit, *Impact of New Management Concepts on Support and Maintainability of Avionic Equipment* (87381), 23 March 1979.

[2] *Maintenance Actions, Manhours and Aborts by Work Unit Code for Various Aircraft*, AFLC-PCN D056B5006, RCS: Log-MMO (AR) 7170, August 1979–January 1980.

[3] VAMOSC-Air F/A-18, FY 1986.

ROCKET PROPULSION COST MODELING

Arve R. Sjovold, Damon C. Morrison
Tecolote Research, Inc.
5266 Hollister Avenue, Santa Barbara, CA 93111

1.0 INTRODUCTION

The advent of the Strategic Defense Initiative has focused a great deal of attention on the United States capability to place large masses in orbit. Both the likely sizes and the numbers of satellites that may be required for SDI strongly suggest the need for a new generation of launch vehicles with low cost a priority requirement.

Just as important, the Challenger disaster has focused intense scrutiny on our manned space program and the reliance we have placed on a single launch vehicle program with which to implement it. A great deal of consideration is now being given to alternative launch methods, including greater use of expendable launchers and new launch vehicles for our space program.

It is also important to note that whatever programs are put forth to satisfy these emerging requirements, they will have to be conducted within tight budgetary constraints and in competition with other national programs for limited government revenues. Thus, demonstration of the ability to meet cost objectives will be essential, and competent cost estimates will be indispensable.

In support of these pursuits in general and in two cases in specific, namely, the Advanced Space Propulsion System (ASPS) and the Advanced Launch System (ALS), Tecolote has been engaged in research to develop better cost models for rocket propulsion. The ASPS program established the need for a liquid rocket engine cost model with which to estimate the costs of development and production of a small thrust, orbital transfer vehicle. The ALS established the need for development and production cost models for both liquid and solid rocket motors of high thrust.

Although there have been previous investigations and developments of rocket engine cost models, most of these models were tied to few real data points and incorporated subjective factors to capture variations in complexity and the like. These models may produce reasonable estimates only in the hands of a skilled analyst with a great deal of rocket engineering experience. Thus, our perusal of the existing models indicated a need for a more objective model, one that requires little if any subjective factors for its application.

The initial effort was dedicated to support the cost estimating requirements of the ASPS program. The ASPS program sought to develop a low thrust, liquid propellant vehicle to inject satellites from low earth orbits to geosynchronous orbit, a mission previously performed by such engines as Centaur and Agena. The ASPS vehicle, however, had to use a storable propellant and was required to meet certain weight and volume requirements peculiar to the Space Shuttle.

In searching for useful CERs or models with which to make an ASPS estimate, we found none that we could assure would be adequate to treat the designs likely to be proposed. Particular concern addressed the possibility that the Shuttle constraints would force designs of high thrust-to-weight ratios, with consequent sophisticated technology or manufacturing methods. Therefore, we initiated an effort to collect as much data on historical pump-fed, liquid engine systems from which to gain additional insight and to derive CERs or, at least, a reasonable cost estimate.

A data base was generated for the ASPS effort, but it comprised basically "vintage" rocket engines; by that we mean engines developed and produced primarily in the late 1950s and 1960s. Some data was available on the Space Shuttle Main Engines (SSME), a more recent development, as well as current RDT&E data on a small, pump-fed system, the XLR-132.

This data base was used to develop a CER appropriate to vintage systems, but was inadequate in explaining SSME technology. Nonetheless, a reasonably satisfactory estimate for an ASPS engine was generated using this information. The same data base was used to generate an ancillary CER relating engine weight to thrust, but again this CER was appropriate only to vintage systems and was incapable of explaining SSME technology or the ultra large engine, the Apollo F-1.

Immediately following the ASPS effort, support was required in the development of cost estimates for the ALS. The preliminary designs for the ALS, however, required the use of both large, solid motors and large, pump-fed liquid engines. To support this effort, additional data was gathered on both solid and liquid rocket engine systems.

With the additional liquid engine data we reinvestigated the ASPS CER development to see what could be done to explain the costs of those engines that could not be considered part of the vintage system CER. The solid rocket engine cost data was incorporated with previous solid cost data held at Tecolote and a new effort at CER development was initiated.

The model developments reported herein meet the requirement for totally objective models. The development process begins with a revisit of historical data on all the programs from Atlas to the current Space Shuttle main engines and Peacekeeper motors. The normalization of raw data with regard to escalation was recalculated wherever possible. A new methodology was applied to the investigation of cost-quantity relationships (learning curves) and new approaches to the development of strong engineering hypotheses relating cost and rocket engine parameters were tried and tested. As a result, CERs for production and development costs of pump-fed liquid engines and solid rocket motors have been developed which have unusually high explanatory power and are consistent with sound engineering understanding of what should drive rocket engine costs.

The article is organized as follows. The next section describes the salient features of the data bases and the efforts to collect additional data. (The data is described in more detail, engine-by-engine, in a detached appendix which is proprietary and therefore not included here.) This section also reviews the characteristics and methodologies of existing cost models. Section 3 of the article discusses the development of the methodology focusing on the limitations imposed by the data base and new approaches to handling the effects of cost-quantity relationships. Section 4 deals with the development of hypotheses for CER development, while section 5 reports the results of regression testing of those hypotheses.

2.0 DATA COLLECTION

An important part of the data collection effort was devoted to existing rocket engine models to understand their strengths and weaknesses.

2.1 LIQUID ENGINE MODELS

We discovered two liquid engine cost models, one developed by Rocketdyne and one by Marshall Space Flight Center. Each of these entities also has solid motor cost models as does Tecolote. With regard to the liquid engine models, neither was supported by an extensive data base. Both model developments relied on strong engineering hypotheses calibrated to two or three data points. There was general agreement on engine weight as a paramount cost driver, but in both cases the models used stratifications to explain the cost of engines of extraordinary characteristics such as the SSME. Convincing arguments can be made why a simple weight-based CER which explains ordinary or vintage systems well is inadequate to explain SSME, J-2, and even F-1. In fact, in our initial effort in support of ASPS, the same rationale was adopted. It was thought that engines of the sophistication of the SSME would lie in a cost strata well above the vintage systems but exhibit the same sensitivity to weight as the vintage systems.

Rocketdyne[*] uses this rationale to create a basic weight sensitivity based on H-1 and F-12 production costs and then creates two new strata, one exemplified by the J-2 engine which utilizes LOX (Liquid Oxygen) and LH_2 (Liquid Hydrogen) as propellants, and the second by the SSME which is characterized as staged combustion, also employing LOX and LH_2. The resultant CERs were obtained with data after normalization for both quantity and production rate based on engineering understanding of the manufacturing processes. The CER development was carried out with cost data normalized to Theoretical First Unit (TFU), a practice which we feel is fraught with difficulty if statistical techniques are to be employed in the CER development.

The Marshall Space Flight Center model follows pretty much the same rationale. The technique for establishing the basic weight sensitivity of unit costs was not presented in the material we had available, but the Marshall model ended up with one strata for the F-1 and a separate strata for the three LOX/LH_2 systems, Centaur, J-2, and SSME. The Marshall model develops these CERs with data normalized to TFU and relies strongly on engineering hypotheses for its support. However, the CERs purport to be the result of statistical regression analyses but with four data points it is difficult to test the engineering hypotheses.

Based on our review of these two liquid engine cost models, we concluded that engine weight was a paramount cost driver, but little insight was developed as to what particular quantitative factors could be used to explain engines of different strata. The Rocketdyne model also utilizes a normalization curve for engine chamber pressure, acknowledging its importance as a secondary cost driver. But chamber pressure was not used as a quantitative factor to explain the separation between strata. The fact that both of these models were based on few historical cost data points and relied strongly on engineering hypotheses that could not be readily tested by statistical regression analyses led us to conclude that

---

[*]Our understanding of the Rocketdyne model was developed through a personal briefing by Rocketdyne personnel.

they were primarily of use only to those that had sufficient engineering understanding of the underlying hypotheses. We were also concerned with some of the normalizations that were performed on the data. Normalization for quantity was performed assuming a nominal 90 percent learning curve, but there was no demonstration of the validity of this particular value. Similarly, we were concerned with the normalization for production rate. Finally, our greatest concern was with the lack of a sufficiently large data base with which to test various cost hypotheses.

2.2 SOLID MOTOR MODELS

A similar situation prevails with respect to cost models for solid rocket motors. Tecolote has performed extensive investigations on solid rocket motors and has developed CERs for unit production costs. Typically, most investigations stratify strategic missiles from tactical missiles. Although with solids there is a generally richer data base, the quality of the CERs is not necessarily high. Our investigation for this effort is centered on large, solid motors which are best represented by the class of strategic systems in our data base. Strategic systems and large space boosters must pay more attention to motor mass fractions than tactical systems, and thus more sophisticated and expensive manufacturing techniques are pursued to achieve high mass fractions.

Within the class of strategic systems, total impulse or gross motor weight appears as a paramount cost driver. Propellant weight is almost as good, since with uniformly high mass fractions propellant weight and gross weight are very highly correlated. Some success has been achieved in showing through regression analyses that differences in motor case material are significant. Generally, non-steel motor cases, that is, glass filament or titanium, cost more than steel cases.

The Rocketdyne model development discusses the significance of nozzle cost and thrust vector control system costs to total motor cost. They find that the costs of these two subsystems is usually more than half the motor cost. The Rocketdyne model incorporates adjustments for production rate and quantity. Rocketdyne apparently has two model forms. In one form, unit production cost is a function of gross motor weight, a performance adjustment factor related to specific impulse, a degree of newness factor (binary in form), a learning curve factor, and a production rate factor. The alternative form substitutes motor inert weight for motor gross weight. Attempts to include nozzle complexity or mass fraction efficiency as explanatory variables were unsatisfactory. Apparently, either gross weight or inert weight are so highly correlated with nozzle weight that either of these parameters captures much of the cost explained by nozzles and TVC subsystems. The model form incorporating motor inert weight was selected as their best fit and the relationship is based on 17 strategic programs.

Tecolote's previous investigations have led to CERs for solid motors which use total impulse or motor gross weight as primary cost drivers. Statistical significance was demonstrated between motors with steel and non-steel cases, but this was over the whole class of tactical plus strategic systems. Since non-steel motor cases are found only in strategic systems, the non-steel CERs represent, in effect, strategic systems. However, some strategic systems utilize steel cases, so their characteristics are not represented in the non-steel CERs. Tecolote's best fit for non-steel motors occurs with gross weight as the primary cost driver and a variable comprising the product of chamber pressure and motor diameter as a secondary variable. However, CERs using total impulse or propellant weight in combination with secondary variables are nearly as good. A data base comprising 10 engines was used in the development of this CER, the largest engine being the Poseidon first stage. The Tecolote CERs are of adequate quality--a standard error of ±.27 in log space--but given the limited range of the primary independent variable, motor gross weight, they produce large prediction errors for points outside the data range. The ALS motors are likely to be seven times as heavy as the first stage Poseidon.

The Rocketdyne model apparently includes Peacekeeper costs in its data base. Peacekeeper first stage is about one-third as large as the expected ALS motors, so that model may be more useful with regard to the prediction interval of the independent variables. However, an extrapolation beyond the data base of this magnitude with a CER of modest standard error is probably unreliable.

Although the Rocketdyne model included Peacekeeper in its data base, which may have rendered it of some use to the ALS exercise, Tecolote did not have access to the calibrated forms or the data bases of this model. Tecolote's model was insufficient with respect to the prediction range of the primary cost driver, but with suitable additions to the data base it was likely that an acceptable model for ALS applications could be generated.

2.3 DATA BASE

Since one of the objectives of this effort was the development of CERs that are as objective as possible, we required a data base size sufficient to support statistical regression testing of model hypotheses. As much as possible, we wanted to avoid the inclusion of subjectively derived complexity factors that, because of a sparse data base, could not be tested statistically.

Liquid rocket engines naturally divide into two main groups, those that are pressure fed and those that are pump fed. Although the thrust chamber assemblies of these two groups appear to have much in common, the design considerations governing the use of pressure-fed systems are significantly different such that they take on slightly different characteristics. In addition, as engine systems they are less complex, lacking turbo pumps and gas generators. Nonetheless, if cost data can be collected at the subsystem level (i.e., thrust chamber assembly, pump, gas generator, pressurizing system, etc.), data from the pressure-fed engines could be used to broaden the data base of those subsystems in common with pump-fed systems. Since our initial data-gathering efforts quickly demonstrated that it would be very difficult to get cost data at the subsystem level for either pressure-fed or pump-fed systems, we have excluded pressure-fed systems from this study. At some later time, it may be appropriate to direct an effort toward the development of a pressure-fed engine model.

For solid rocket motor model development, we concentrated on motors used in strategic systems and for launch boosters for space applications; tactical solid motors were excluded, although some of the model forms discovered in this study may also be useful to a study of tactical motors.

Both the liquid and solid propulsion data base costs have been normalized to FY87 dollars using the NASA escalation indices. The liquid data reflect costs at the price level (fee included). It is important to note that the solid propulsion model is based on costs at cost level (fee not included). The reason for the difference is that in the liquid case most of the costs collected were at the price level. Most of the solid costs didn't include fee. We wanted to reflect the data in as pure a form as possible. Thus, if a majority of the data points had fee, then the models reflected costs with fee. This minimized the additional error present when one assumes additional costs not present in the raw data. Where fee needed to be included or excluded, 10 percent was assumed. Both include General and Administrative costs.

2.3.1 Liquid, Pump-Fed Data Base

For this study, a data point was considered to be an engine system comprising one thrust chamber assembly with nozzle and injector, a turbo pump, a gas generator or some other mechanism to power the turbo pump, gimbal hardware, nozzle skirts, valves, piping, and miscellaneous hardware. In general, the hardware list included those items listed in the Liquid Propellant Engine Manual for the individual engines. This definition is consistent with previous investigations and is coincident with the engine hardware boundaries employed in defining deliverable engine subcontracts. Thus, no adjustments to cost data were required to make cost data consistent with the normal hardware definitions of the engines. The data points collected for this study are listed in table 2.1, except that the unit cost data has been deleted for publication in this article.

For all but the Agena and RL-10, the only production cost data that was available was the average unit cost for the approximately total buy or, as in the case of the J-2 and SSME, a first unit cost extrapolated from actuals. Although we obtained production cost histories by year for Agena and RL-10, the production histories were characterized by changes in rates and breaks in production. For these two engines, the production histories were distilled into a single representative average cost for each engine to put them on an equal basis with the remaining data points.

For all the data points, technical, descriptive data was taken from the Liquid Engine Propulsion Handbook. Production rate information was collected from various sources including contractors, Jane's Satellite volume, and Aerospace Corporation documents to which we had access.

For engine development costs, we were able to obtain data for only eight systems. Also, for Atlas and Titan systems the development costs were for a complete engine set per missile. In the case of Atlas, an engine set comprised two boosters and a sustainer; for Titan, an engine set is two boosters and one second stage.

Table 2.1 summarizes the data base developed for liquid, pump-fed engines. Details for each engine are presented in a detached, proprietary appendix, which also contains the proprietary cost data.

2.3.2 Solid Rocket Motor Data Base

The solid motor data base developed for this study comprised 19 data points for production and 8 for development. Each data point is defined as one solid motor consisting of a case, liner, insulation, propellant, igniter, nozzle, nozzle extensions, and thrust vector control hardware. This is the usual definition consistent with the hardware boundaries for solid motor subcontracts. By this definition, each stage of a multistage missile represents a potential data point.

TABLE 2.1
Liquid Rocket Engines

Liquid Production Costs

LIQUID ROCKET ENG'S

	CAC COST $M	QUANTITY	WEIGHT LBS	THRUST K LBS	# COOLANT TUBES
1 agena		5	296	17.0	260
2 thor		400	2028	195.0	292
3 atlas sus		200	1108	80.0	240
4 atlas booster		400	1495	185.0	292
5 saturn 1 h1		164	2011	225.0	292
6 rl-10 a3-3		100	273	15.0	360
7 titan 3 s-1		66	1672	235.6	160
8 titan 3 s-2		33	1144	100.0	148
9 saturn f1		98	18684	1750.0	178
10 saturn j2		1	3477	230.0	360
11 ssme		1	7000	512.0	390
12 rs-27		14	2261	223	292

LIQUID ROCKET ENG'S

	Pc	Pc*TUBES	PUMP PSI	PPSI*TBS	RATE/YR
1 agena	535	139100.0	949	246740.0	12
2 thor	588	171696.0	913	266596.0	32
3 atlas sus	706	169440.0	1036	248640.0	23
4 atlas booster	578	168776.0	898	262216.0	46
5 saturn 1 h1	707	206444.0	1020	297840.0	30
6 rl-10 a3-3	400	144000.0	990	356400.0	15
7 titan 3 s-1	783	125280.0	1376	220160.0	14
8 titan 3 s-2	831	122988.0	1222	180856.0	7
9 saturn f1	1122	199716.0	1856	330368.0	16
10 saturn j2	718	258480.0	1238	445680.0	24
11 ssme	3260	1271400.0	6800	2652000.0	3
12 rs-27	678	197976.0	1017	296964.0	7

Liquid Development Costs

	UNIT PROD COST @ Q=150	# PROTO'S	DEV COST M$87
1 AGENA	.649	2	
2 ATLAS (SUS. + BOOST)	4.240	38	
3 RL-10	.701	75	
4 TITAN II (S-1,S-2)	4.021	23	
5 F1	9.323	56	
6 J2	3.656	38	
7 SSME	10.456	17	
8 TITAN I (S-1,S-2)	4.092	47	

Much of the solid motor production cost data was in hand at Tecolote, although distributed among several sources. The Tecolote data was traceable to raw lot cost data in all cases but the Titan IIIC and Titan 34D data points. These two data points were furnished to Tecolote by the contractor as first unit costs (as we understand them they are extrapolated from actuals).

Technical data for these motors was retrieved from the solid rocket motor manual and information readily available from contractors, such as the Titan IIIC handbook. Production rate data was calculated from production lot histories. The rate was calculated to be representative of the main plateau of the production profile. Table 2.2 summarizes the data for solid rocket motors with the exclusion of the proprietary cost data.

Development cost data was obtained from the ICBM Flyaway Cost Model for the five Minuteman data points and from Cost Performance Reports for the points labeled "System A, B, and C." The number of development prototypes was retrieved from the Missile Handbook and corroborated by other data. The detailed data base and proprietary costs for rocket motor developments is also presented in the detached appendix.

2.3.3 Escalation

During the course of our effort to estimate costs for the proposed ASPS, we discovered that OSD official inflation indices for procurement (e.g., "3020" indices) appeared to underestimate cost escalation for rocket engines. A review of Aerospace industry indices in the government's publication of producer price indices indicated that indeed OSD general procurement indices were lower. Inquiries with rocket engine manufacturers confirmed this finding; escalation indices used in-house by Rocketdyne were very close to those used by NASA for its projects which were significantly higher than OSD indices. Rocketdyne indicated that the NASA indices should be satisfactory for this effort, and those are the indices we have used.

The need for accurate indices is quite important to this study effort because the data points span at least 25 years in manufacturing intervals. In order to aggregate as large a sample as possible, we have assembled within the same data base, engines developed and produced in the late 50s such as Atlas along with the most recently developed SSME. To the degree that inflation indices are in error, either excess random error or systematic bias can be introduced into regression results under these circumstances.

TABLE 2.2
Solid Rocket Motor Production Cost Data

Solid Production Costs

	CAC 87 $M	QUANTITY	TOTAL WT K LBS	# NOZZLES	NOZZLE WT LBS	D1	D2
1 MM I,II,III STAGE 1		2249	50.3	4	948	1	1
2 MM I STAGE 2		925	11.7	4	390	1	1
3 MM II,III STAGE 2		1324	15.5	4	350	1	2.718
4 MM I,II STAGE 3		1547	4.2	4	169	1	2.718
5 MM III STAGE 3		698	7.9	1	227	1	2.718
6 POLARIS A2 STAGE 1		350	22.2	4	604	1	1
7 POLARIS A2 STAGE 2		350	8.5	4	309	1	2.718
8 POLARIS A3 STAGE 1		667	23.9	4	1440	1	2.718
9 POLARIS A3 STAGE 2		667	9.5	4	172	1	2.718
10 POSEIDON C3 STAGE 1		547	41.9	1	761	1	2.718
11 POSEIDON C3 STAGE 2		547	17.1	1	424	1	2.718
12 TITAN 3C,D STAGE 0		1	498.4	1	7922	1	1
13 TITAN 34D STAGE 0		1	542.6	1	7747	1	1
14 SYSTEM A		71	107	1	1535	2.718	1
15 SYSTEM B		71	60.6	2	1485	2.718	1
16 SYSTEM C		71	17.5	2	479	2.718	1
17 TRIDENT 1 S-1		602	41.9	1	*	2.718	1
18 TRIDENT 1 S-2		579	18.9	1	*	2.718	1
19 TRIDENT 1 S-3		583	4.1	1	*	2.718	1

D1 and D2 are case material stratification variables. See page 35 for details.

Solid Development Costs

	EST CAC150 NZWT	TOTWT	# PROTOS	FSED $M
1 MM I,II,III STAGE 1	1.914	2.153	125	
2 MM I STAGE 2	1.357	1.025	125	
3 MM II,III STAGE 2	1.301	1.706	48	
4 MM I,II STAGE 3	.981	.877	125	
5 MM III STAGE 3	.745	.559	46	
6 SYSTEM A	4.043	2.958	21	
7 SYSTEM B	4.851	3.257	21	
8 SYSTEM C	3.128	1.730	21	

*Note: CAC_{150} are estimates using the resultant model CERs.

3.0 METHODOLOGY

Our review of previous model developments and the available data has produced concerns with several aspects of the methodologies used in these model developments. The methodological problems are posed by small, inconsistent data bases and the normalizations of cost data that are usually performed.

The normalizations are performed to correct for the effects of quantity on cost and the effects of inflation. In addition, some investigators have performed additional normalizations for minor technical variables that are believed to effect cost based on engineering understandings. The difficulty in this process is that there is often insufficient data to establish confident normalization factors such as learning slopes.

3.1 EFFECTS OF INCONSISTENT DATA BASES

The data bases are typified by inconsistent WBS reports and holes in the data base such that even if WBSs can be mapped one into the other, they may not be homogeneous. This leads to a situation where for a particular WBS line there may be too few data points upon which to perform regression analyses. This leaves the investigator with the most practical option of performing regression analyses at the highest level of indenture at which there is a sufficiently large data base.

We have found with liquid rocket engine data that there is virtually no visibility in cost at the subsystem level. For some of the more recent engines such as SSME, there is subsystem cost data, but by far the majority of the cost data is for older systems that we have characterized as vintage such as Atlas, Thor, Titan, and Agena. It is also noteworthy that a data base comprising vintage and more recent systems spans more than 25 years of rocket engine development such that the effects of any advances in technology are also embedded in the data. Thus, for liquid rocket engines we are left with the position that model development must proceed from analyses at the total engine cost level with the consequence that little cost insight can be gained on the effects of technology advance at the subsystem level. We found that solid rocket motor data is in much the same state, although there are probably more cases for which subsystem data may be available.

As a consequence of this general condition, all of our regression analyses on production costs are conducted at the total engine level. With regard to development costs for liquid engines, we have already noted that some data points represent sets of engines and analyses were conducted at that level in those cases.

3.2 EFFECTS OF QUANTITY ON PRODUCTION COST

Typically in cost analysis, the data base contains observations, or data points, over a wide range of costs and quantities. Often there may not be any overlap in production quantities for independent observations which nominally belong to the same set (e.g., tactical air-to-air missiles may vary over a wide range of quantities). Standard practice in the industry is to normalize costs to a standard production quantity using learning curve methodology. Quite often the standardized quantity is one, referred to as the first theoretical unit or TFU (i.e., T_1).

If the data base contains lot data for each data point, a learning curve is fitted to each data point to establish its T_1, which then becomes the basis for CER development in which cost is regressed against hypothesized cost driving performance or descriptive parameters. There are good theoretical and practical arguments as to why this is a poor methodology.

On the theoretical side, the choice of T_1--the intercept from a learning curve regression analysis--is generally not a real point, that is, there rarely is a first lot of just one. Moreover, in the most common case, T_1 is far removed in the quantity dimension from the body of the data. The consequence of choosing T_1 under these circumstances is that T_1 is a very uncertain value based on the confidence intervals for the regression line used to establish it. Viewed in another way, T_1 can be said to have a large variance. Using a set of T_1's to develop a CER necessarily introduces more random variation to the dependent variable. From the statistical point of view, there is nothing special about T_1 or about any intercept, for that matter. The intercept is merely an artifact of the fit and the choice of origin for the variables used in the fit. In fact, the intercept can be made to disappear if the means of all the variables are chosen, through a translation of axes, as the origin for the regression exercise.

Even though T_1 has no significance statistically, considerable engineering significance has been attributed to it as the "theoretical first unit" in a production series. However, this significance may be misplaced. If, for example, a particular production series is characterized by a few early small lots such that the statistical criticisms against choosing T_1 are less significant, one must be cognizant of the effect pricing, as opposed to cost, may pay in early lots. The way in which a manufacturer prices his early lots may depend strongly on the long-term view of production lots for the item. Thus, early lots may exhibit a learning curve more representative of a pricing strategy than a cost incurrence effect. One may assume that pricing strategies vary across the manufacturers.

One approach that may be used to avoid the statistical and practical criticisms associated with using T_1 as the basis of regression analyses is to standardize the dependent variable, unit cost, at a quantity near the "center of gravity" of the data base. In this approach, each manufacturer's lot cost history is used to generate a unit cost at a reasonably central quantity. This unit cost may be calculated from a learning curve obtained from regression on the lot history or may be simply interpolated between the adjacent lot plotting points. Clearly, where the chosen central quantity is not within the range of the lot plotting points, the value must be calculated from extrapolation of the lot history or by prediction from the learning curve. This approach has the advantage of constraining the CER regression analysis to the domain of the raw data as nearly as possible.

In the circumstances surrounding this study, lot histories were not available for most of the liquid engines; all that was available were average unit costs for the quantities that had been produced to the time of the data collection (e.g., 1970 for those data abstracted from the Aerospace report). Some lot data was available for two engines, Agena and Centaur, but the production history in both cases was characterized by many breaks.

The approach selected, given the constraints on the data, was to use the average unit cost at the quantity shown in the raw data base and to introduce a quantity variable in the CER regression analyses. That is, instead of first normalizing for quantity, the quantity effect on cost was determined simultaneously with the effects of the other independent variables hypothesized as drivers for the CER development. The CER equation takes the general form (for the log-linear form):

$$CAC(Q) = a \ Q_1^{\ b}(x_1^{\ c} x_2^{\ d} \dots x_n^{\ m}) \epsilon$$

where:

$CAC(Q)$ = cumulative average unit cost at quantity Q

x_i = the other independent variables

$a, b, \dots m,$ = the coefficients to be determined

ϵ = the error term

For a successful regression result of this form, the exponent may be assumed to reflect an industrywide learning effect, and if the data includes several manufacturers, it may be further assumed that variations in pricing strategy have been averaged out. This method also has the advantage that no data point contains any unnecessary components of random variation by having used an extrapolated point not within the range of the raw data.

In the case of solid rocket motors, there was considerably more lot data available, but not in all cases. Trident and Peacekeeper data was for just one quantity. Also, the quantities varied a great deal, so it was decided to use the same approach described above for liquid engines. Thus, for solids the imputed learning curve slope by this method can be assumed to reflect an industrywide learning effect, a virtue when doing independent cost estimates for a program before the production contractor has been selected.

3.3 REGRESSION CALCULATIONS

All regression calculations were performed with Tecolote's statistical package, TECOSTAT, developed as part of the automated cost estimating tools comprising ACEIT,[*] a comprehensive software package for cost estimators. The TECOSTAT package performs the usual linear and log-linear multiple regressions, but is tailored to the needs of the cost analyst. It provides all the standard measures of fit plus useful heuristic measures of fit that allow the cost analyst to readily compare the quality of fits generated from different spaces (e.g., a fit done in arithmetic space with one done in logarithmic space).

For these model developments, the log-linear regression forms were used almost exclusively, owing to the ranges in the dependent variable. Most of the unit cost data exhibits a range of almost two orders of magnitude, and under such circumstances it is best to assume that random errors are in proportion to the cost magnitude, which case is implicit in choosing the log-linear form.

4.0 HYPOTHESIS DEVELOPMENT

Our first efforts in support of the ASPS program resulted in showing the importance of engine weight for a pump-fed liquid engine as a cost driver. This was consistent with the findings of previous researchers, and our additional studies testing thrust as a possibility indicated that weight was indeed better. However, our preliminary model for the ASPS was unable to explain such engine designs as the J-2 and the SSME, both of which were liquid hydrogen-liquid oxygen fueled, and thought, therefore, to belong to a different subset. This subset did not explain why the model did not

---

[*]Automated Cost Estimator Integrated Tools

fit the F-1 engine, which in design should have been similar to the engines in the set used to develop the model. Thus, the task was to find explanatory variables besides weight that could explain these other data points.

With regard to solid rocket motors, previous investigations both from within Tecolote and outside had demonstrated several first-order cost drivers of nearly equal merit: total motor weight, propellant weight, or total impulse, to name those most prominent. Our original approach, therefore, was to build on these efforts and attempt to find additional design parameters that, combined with any of these first-order drivers, could help to explain more of the variance in unit costs. Most of these previous investigations had produced models of barely adequate estimating error for the purposes of most independent cost estimating needs. Furthermore, for the ALS program, which anticipates the development and production of large solid motors, there was concern with the predictability of the then available CERs to a region significantly beyond the range of the data base. To address such circumstances, it is important to have a CER with good statistical fit and based on a sound engineering hypothesis. Because the existing CER fits were not tight, the task was to find additional variables which, when used with any of the known primary cost drivers, made good engineering sense.

With these positions as a point of departure, we set out to develop hypotheses for regression testing beginning with liquid engines and production data and following with solid motors and production data. These efforts are described in the next subsections, which are then followed by a discussion of the hypotheses developed for development costs for both liquid and solid engines.

4.1 LIQUID ENGINE HYPOTHESES - PRODUCTION

During the ASPS studies, we investigated relationships between weight and thrust. For the vintage systems it was found that thrust was a good predictor for engine system weight, but the relationship could not explain the J-2, SSME, or F-1 engines. Again we believed that the J-2 and SSME belonged to a different subset by virtue of their liquid hydrogen fuel requirements, but we were unsatisfied that the F-1 could not be explained, since it was of more conventional design employing LOX-RP-1 (Liquid Oxygen and Rocket Propellant 1) as propellants. It seemed intuitive that the same variables that could explain F-1 weight would probably be useful to help explain F-1 costs which, as pointed out in section 3, were also not consistent with the vintage system CER developed for ASPS. The lack of consistency of F-1, SSME, and J-2 with the weight-thrust CER from the ASPS study is presented in figure 4.1. Shown in the figure is the regression line and the points used to develop it along with the F-1, SSME, and J-2 points as identified. Clearly all three of these engines are heavier than their developed thrust might indicate.

A perusal of other design parameters suggested that chamber pressure may have some explanatory power. From an engineering standpoint, this makes sense, since higher pressures will cause most of the plumbing to have thicker walls and thus be heavier. At this point, we began a review of the engineering design of regenerative cooled, pump-fed engines and the design trade-offs that are usually considered.

The primary focus of the design is the management of the thermal load on the thrust chamber and throat sections due to the high combustion temperatures. Figure 4.2, taken from reference 9, depicts the profile of the thermal load and, in the adjacent frame, the typical pressure profile of the coolant from pump discharge, through the tubular coolant passages, back up to the injector. Clearly the greatest thermal loads are on the combustion chamber and throat sections. Once the gases have expanded suffi- ciently, their temperatures have lowered appre-ciably such that in designs calling for high expansion ratios, the last section of the nozzle can be made with a skirt not requiring regenerative cooling. Such a skirt can be cooled by radiation or under certain constraints by ablation. Since a tubular-walled nozzle skirt should weigh more than a radiative-cooled nozzle skirt, attention should focus on the tubular-walled portions of the design to discover weight-driving parameters. Now the SSME has a high expansion ratio nozzle, yet does not employ a radiative-cooled skirt. This is probably due to the fact that it operates at an extremely high chamber pressure such that the gases must be expanded further before they reach the limit below which a radiative-cooled skirt can be used effectively. Thus, the SSME has a large nozzle surface area that is regeneratively cooled. The total thermal load and the length of the coolant passages in this design require an extraordinarily high pressure drop to maintain a high coolant flow velocity. This is evidenced by comparing the ratios of pump discharge pressure of the coolant flow to chamber pressure for the various engine designs. The vintage systems employ chamber pressures in the 700 to 800 psi range, and pump discharge pressures are approximately 1.5 times as high when the propellants are LOX/RP-1 or storable. The SSME has a chamber pressure of 3000 psi and a pump discharge pressure over 2.2 times that. The Centaur, which has a relatively low chamber pressure but also uses liquid hydrogen as the coolant, also has a pump discharge-to-chamber pressure ratio over 2.2.

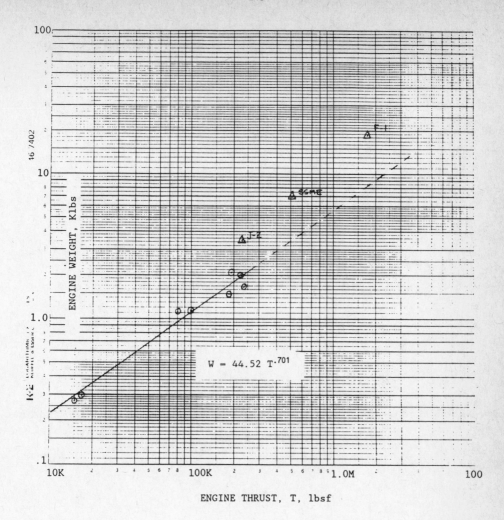

Figure 4.1.   Liquid engine weight vs. thrust, vintage systems.

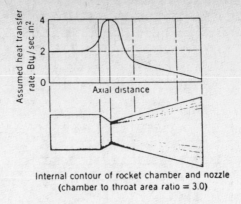

Figure 4.2a. Typical rocket thrust chamber cooling load
as a function of characteristic length,
throat area, and nozzle area ratio.

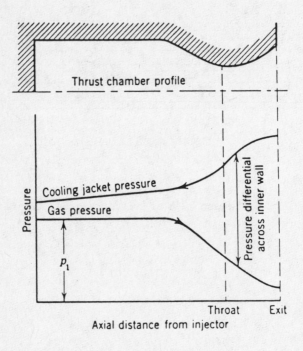

Figure 4.2b. Typical coolant pressure profile.

From this analysis we concluded that the weight of the thrust chamber assembly including the cooled portion of the nozzle should be sensitive to the magnitude of the pump discharge pressure of the coolant flow for which the tubular wall must be designed. Since the thrust and chamber pressure of the engine dictates the nominal size of the thrust chamber and thrust already has been shown to be a primary driver for engine weight, we hypothesized that the remaining unexplained variations in weight could be explained by the size of the cooled portions of the nozzle. To test this hypothesis, we constructed a variable as the product of pump discharge pressure (P_{PD}) and the area of the cooled surface of the nozzle (A_N):

$$P_{PD} \cdot A_N$$

The pump discharge pressure was obtained directly from the liquid engine propellant handbook, and A_N was calculated from dimensional information for the nozzle assuming the expansion geometry of the nozzle could be approximated using the equation for surface area for the frustum of a cone. The hypothesized relationship is:

$$W = a \, T^b (P_{PD} \cdot A_N)^c \epsilon$$

where:

W = engine weight

T = thrust

$P_{PD} \cdot A_N$ = as explained above

a,b,c = coefficients to be fit

ϵ = a multiplicative error term appropriate for a log-linear fit

This hypothesis was tested by regression, and the results are given in figure 4.3. The model is clearly successful in explaining the weights of a wide variety of engine designs. There is no need to create a separate stratum for liquid oxygen-liquid hydrogen engines. It is noteworthy that the exponent on thrust remained essentially the same with the incorporation of the additional variable indicating that it is truly independent with high explanatory power.

The success of the weight model caused us to focus attention on the design features of the tubular-walled chamber for likely cost drivers. It is intuitive that the use of pump discharge pressure in the weight model also picks up the increased weight of the pumps made necessary by the higher pump pressures. Thus, pump discharge pressure should be a cost driver, at least from the standpoint of capturing pump costs. Chamber pressure would not be as good, since the ratio of discharge pressure to chamber

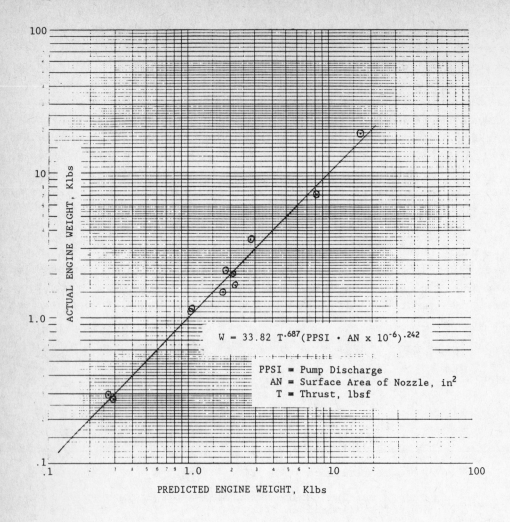

Figure 4.3. Liquid engine weight actuals vs. predicted, vintage and new designs.

pressure varies significantly, and it is the discharge pressure that the pump must be designed for.

The complexity of the cooled wall thrust chamber is not represented by the weight alone. Two chamber assemblies of the same dimensions may have nearly the same nominal weights, yet one may have a few but larger passages while the other may have many but smaller passages. Clearly, the design with a larger number of passages should cost more to produce, but probably offers more control in the thermal management. Clearly there is a sophisticated design trade-off among the size, number, pressure, flow, and weight of the passages to achieve the thermal management requirement. We believe that the parameter which best reflects this trade-off is the resulting number of tubes (coolant passages) used in the design through the chamber and throat sections. (Some designs with higher expansion ratios may use a higher number of passages for the aft end of the nozzle, but the thermal loads are way down in this section and thus tube number does not necessarily reflect complexity here.)

Based on the above analysis, we hypothesized the following model form for the production cost of liquid, pump-fed engines.

$$CAC(Q) = a \ Q^b \ W^c \ (P_{PD} \cdot N_T)^d \ \epsilon$$

where:

$CAC(Q)$ = Cumulative average unit cost at quantity, Q

W = engine system weight

$P_{PD} \cdot N_T$ = a composite variable of pump discharge pressure times the number of coolant passages in the chamber-throat sections

a,b,c,d = coefficients to be fit

ϵ = a multiplicative error term

We also hypothesized the following alternative model form using chamber pressure (P_c) instead of discharge pressure:

$$CAC(Q) = a \ Q^b \ W^c \ (P_c \cdot N_T)^d \ \epsilon$$

We also tested these two forms with the variables P_c, P_{PD}, and N_T separated:

$$CAC(Q) = a \ Q^b \ W^c \ P_{PD}^d \ N_T^e \ \epsilon$$

$$CAC(Q) = a \ Q^b \ W^c \ Pc^d \ N_T^e \ \epsilon$$

Later in the investigation a study of the residuals indicated a correlation with production rate. Thus, we tested the two alternative model forms with a rate parameter included:

$$CAC(Q) = a \ Q^b \ W^c \ (P_{PD} \cdot N_T)^d \ R^e \ \epsilon$$

$$CAC(Q) = a \ Q^b \ W^c \ (P_c \cdot N_T)^d \ R^e \ \epsilon$$

where R = production rate.

4.2 SOLID ROCKET MOTOR HYPOTHESES - PRODUCTION

The study of solid rocket motor designs began with a review of the design parameters of the engines in the data base. The work by Meisl of Rocketdyne had indicated the high significance of the nozzle and thrust vector control (TVC) systems to total motor cost. In reviewing the design parameters associated with the nozzle, we were immediately struck by the fact that several of the motors in the data base were designed with four nozzles. We reasoned that if a nozzle was as expensive an item as Meisl maintained, then four nozzles should cost more than a single nozzle of the same weight or delivering the same impulse. Accordingly, we hypothesized that number of nozzles, N, should be a cost driver to be included with one of the primary drivers of gross motor weight (W), propellant weight (W_p), or total impulse (I_T):

$$CAC(Q) = a \ Q^b \ W^c \ N^d \ \epsilon$$

$$CAC(Q) = a \ Q^b \ W_p^{\ c} \ N^d \ \epsilon$$

$$CAC(Q) = a \ Q^b \ I_T^{\ c} \ N^d \ \epsilon$$

It was also possible that nozzle weight might be a significant driver, since the number of nozzles does not indicate whether they are large or small, and there is some room for nozzle weight to vary significantly without producing commensurate variations in any of the three primary alternative drivers. Accordingly, we hypothesized a nozzle weight (W_N) driver to be used with or in lieu of the three primary drivers, together with the number of nozzles:

$$CAC(Q) = a \ Q^b \ W^c \ N^d \ W_N^{\ e} \ \epsilon$$

or

$$CAC(Q) = a \ Q^b \ N^c \ W_N^{\ d} \ \epsilon$$

If, in the course of regression testing, it was found that number of nozzles and nozzle weight were competing to explain much the same portion of variance, one would be dropped in favor of the other.

Finally, previous studies had indicated the likelihood that variation in motor case material may have a significant effect on cost. Some of the newer rocket motors have gone to the use of exotic materials with high strength-to-weight ratios to obtain significant reductions in inert weight and corresponding gains in mass fraction. A perusal of the design data indicated that there may be three significant categories of material with regard to their cost impacts. These are steel, kevlar, and all other, mainly glass filament wound. Thus, additional model forms were hypothesized by including two dummy variables to define three possible strata. These stratifying variables were tested with all the previous hypothesized model forms, and the following equation demonstrates the general form the equations take when the stratifying variables are included:

$$CAC(Q) = a \; Q^b \; W^c \; N^d \; W_N^f \; e^{gD_1} \; e^{hD_2} \; \epsilon$$

where the stratifying variables take on the values given by:

	D_1	D_2
Steel	0	0
Kevlar	0	1
Other	1	0

4.3 DEVELOPMENT MODEL HYPOTHESES - LIQUIDS AND SOLIDS

For both liquids and solids the available data bases include less points than the corresponding production data bases. With small data bases there is not much opportunity to include but a few explanatory variables in the model. The model form we have chosen for development cost equations is taken from an approach that is used often at Tecolote and forms the basis of several of its most successful development models.

The technique relies upon the well-established idea of prototype-to-production ratios. In the Tecolote models, a standardized estimate of unit production cost is used to predict the cost of fabrication of the development prototypes. Once prototype fabrication costs are established, other development cost categories are scaled from them. The form of the relationship between production unit cost and prototype hardware fabrication is as follows:

$$FAB = a \; (UC)^b \frac{[(N_p + .5)^c - (.5)^c]}{c}$$

where:

FAB = the hardware fabrication cost of N_p prototypes

$$UC = \text{a unit production cost standardized to a given}$$
$$\text{quantity and rate}$$

$$a,b,c = \text{coefficients to be determined}$$

The term dealing with the quantity of prototypes is the approximation to the cumulative cost of the first N_p units learning along a curve $N_p{}^b$ where

$$b = c-1 .$$

This equation form requires non-linear regression calculations and visibility to hardware fabrication costs within the total development cost. The latter condition could not be met for our study since we had only total development costs for the most part. Since the non-hardware development costs have been shown from other systems to scale fairly reliably from prototype hardware fabrication costs, we elected to regress total development cost against a standardized unit hardware production cost and the number of prototypes. To avoid the need for a non-linear regression package, we adopted an approximate form suitable for log-linear regressions. The hypothesized model for development costs is:

$$C_{DEV} = a \ (UC)^b \ N_p{}^c \ \epsilon$$

For the standardized unit cost, we selected a quantity and rate well within the data base and used the most successful production model equation to estimate this cost for each data point. We chose for the standardized unit cost the value at CAC(150) at a rate of 10/year. Thus, with this specific choice for unit cost, the model equation is:

$$C_{DEV} = a \ [CAC(150)]^b \ N_p{}^c$$

Other variables that may affect the cost of development independent of the variables included above are development duration, number of hot firing tests, and any unique requirements, such as a significant amount of delivered software. Unfortunately, none of this data was available to the study, so these variables could not be tested.

5.0 RESULTS

In this section we present the results of regression testing of the alternative hypotheses that were presented in section 4. We begin with the presentation and analysis of the results for liquid engine production costs, since the liquid engine systems were the first to be addressed and formed the basis for the overall methodology. Following the presentation of liquid engine system results, we present the analysis and results for

the solid motor production costs followed by the analysis and results for
both development cost models.

5.1 LIQUID ENGINE PRODUCTION MODELS

The model form incorporating pump discharge pressure and the number
of coolant passages proved to be the best model form. The model also includes
a rate parameter which was found to be significant and proved in the course
of the study to be helpful in improving the quality of the fit with regard
to the other variables, indicating that the rate variable is capturing truly
independent variance.

Table 5.1 summarizes the regression results for the model forms found
to be most promising. A comparison of standard errors and R^2_{ADJ} indicate
that case 1 is the preferred model form. The t-statistics (shown in parentheses under each coefficient) are at a maximum for all the coefficients and
the quantity and rate coefficients are well within reasonable bounds based
on experience with other systems. Case 2 is presented to show the effect
if the composite variable is split into two independent variables. Even
with the additional degree of freedom, no increase in explanatory power
is gained. The t-statistics for quantity, rate, and weight are lower, strongly
suggesting that the composite variable is indeed superior. We also wanted
to determine if pump discharge pressure has more explanatory power than
chamber pressure, either as part of a composite variable or as an independent
variable. Cases 3 and 4 are the counterparts to cases 1 and 2, with chamber
pressure replacing pump discharge pressure. It is clear that chamber pressure
performs less well, indicating that in those cases where discharge pressure
is extraordinarily high relative to chamber pressure (as in the Centaur
and SSME, for example), the difference is significant. (Recall from section
4 that pump discharge pressure and chamber pressure are highly correlated
in conventional liquid oxygen-RP-1 and storable designs, but depart when
liquid hydrogen is used as a fuel.)

The results summarized in table 5.1 are based on calculations with
all the data points except the H-1 engine system. The H-1 is a significant
outlier by statistical measures. Its inclusion in the calculations still
supports case 1 as the preferred model, changing the coefficients slightly
but producing a poorer quality, but acceptable fit. The coefficient on
the rate term is marginal, however, and overall standard error increases
from .1276 to .2126. Compared to the standard error calculated without
H-1, the H-1 data point is approximately five standard deviations from the
regression line. When H-1 is included in the calculations, it is still
identified as a significant outlier. Since the inclusion of H-1 does not

TABLE 5.1

Summary of Regression Testing Alternative
Hypotheses - Liquid Engines, Production*

Case	Regression Equation (T-statistics)	D.F.	R^2_{ADJ}	s.e.
1. Composite Variable of Pump Discharge and Number of Passages $$CAC(Q) = aQ^b R^c W^d (PPSI \cdot N_T)^e$$	$$CAC(Q) = .00124\, Q^{-.251} R^{-.132} W^{.618} (PPSI \cdot N_T)^{.347}$$ $$(-9.67)(-1.89)(16.81)\qquad (4.31)$$	6	98.95%	.1276
2. Separate Variables for Pump Discharge and Number of Passages $$CAC(Q) = aQ^b R^c W^d (PPSI)^e (N_T)^f$$	$$CAC(Q) = .00131\, Q^{-.246} R^{-.180} W^{.641} (PPSI)^{.262} (N_T)^{.4351}$$ $$(-8.65)(-1.76)(12.54)(1.75)\qquad (2.78)$$	5	98.85%	.1335
3. Composite Variable of Chamber Pressure and Number of Passages $$CAC(Q) = aQ^b R^c W^d (PSI \cdot N_T)^e$$	$$CAC(Q) = .00101\, Q^{-.252} R^{-.136} W^{.594} (PSI*N_T)^{.395}$$ $$(-8.43)(-1.71)(12.96)\qquad (3.59)$$	6	98.63%	.1457
4. Separate Variables for Chamber Pressure and Number of Passages $$CAC(Q) = aQ^b R^c W^d (PSI)^e N_T^f$$	$$CAC(Q) = .00125\, Q^{-.244} R^{-.207} W^{.638} (PSI)^{.247} (N_T)^{.503}$$ $$(-7.78)(-1.86)(9.61)\ (1.27)\qquad (3.09)$$	5	98.60%	.1473

*CAC costs are at price level (i.e., Fee is included). Bold box refers to the recommended CER. Units for the variables are as identified in table 2.1.

alter the basic conclusion regarding significant cost-driving variables, and because of its extremity is likely to bias the coefficients slightly, we believe the model equation calculated without H-1 is the preferred model.

It is noteworthy that the liquid engine model developed here is capable of explaining the costs of the widest range of engine designs without the need for stratifying variables as is the general case for all previous investigations. The success in specifying pump discharge pressure and design parameters of the thrust chamber and nozzle (i.e., number of passages and nozzle surface area) to explain both engine weight and cost must lend credence to the hypothesis that these variables implicitly capture engine complexity over the widest range. The literature has established that these design variables are at the center of engine design trade-offs so there is good reason to believe that the model is a good predictor of costs.

5.2 SOLID MOTOR PRODUCTION MODELS

Although we found one superior model form, we present two model forms as recommended for use because of difference in the primary driving variable in each equation. The preferred model uses the weight of the nozzle assembly (including thrust vector control hardware) as the primary driving variable. However, because nozzle weight is not always a readily obtainable design parameter, we include a second model form using total motor weight as the primary driver. Table 5.2, summarizing the regression results, compares these two model forms along with two variations on the nozzle weight form. Case 1 is the model with total motor weight as the driver, and Case 2 is the model using nozzle weight. Both models include the number of nozzles as a driver. Based on the comparison of standard errors, case 2 is clearly superior to case 1 and is the preferred model to use if information on nozzle weight is in hand.

One significant difference between the two model forms is in the number of significant strata found in the data. When using total weight as the driver, significant differences are found for motors of steel, glass, and kevlar cases. These strata are defined by the dummy parameters D_1 and D_2, which take on the following values:

	D_1	D_2
Steel	0	0
Kevlar	0	1
Other	1	0

TABLE 5.2

Summary of Regression Testing Alternative
Hypotheses – Solid Motors[*]

Case (T-statistics)	Regression Equation	R^2_{ADJ}	s.e.
1. Total Motor Weight with Two Strata $CAC(Q) = aQ^b W_T^c N_N^d e^{fD_1} g^{D_2}$	$CAC(Q) = .397Q^{-.215} W_T^{.509} N_N^{.557} e^{.705D_1} e^{.367D_2}$ $\quad(-4.82)\ (7.04)\ (5.27)\ (4.02)\ (2.36)$	94.97%	.2140
2. Nozzle Weight with One Stratum $CAC(Q) = aQ^b W_N^c N_N^d e^{fD_1}$	$CAC(Q) = .267Q^{-.215} W_N^{.388} N_N^{.281} e^{.951D_1}$ $\quad(-7.23)\ (7.06)\ (4.25)\ (10.42)$	98.03%	.1371
3. Nozzle Weight with Two Strata $CAC(Q) = aQ^b W_N^c N_N^d e^{fD_1} g^{D_2}$	$CAC(Q) = .242Q^{-.217} W_N^{.399} N_N^{.293} e^{.977D_1} e^{.047D_2}$ $\quad(-6.95)\ (6.37)\ (3.94)\ (8.66)\ (0.43)$	97.87%	.1425
4. Nozzle Weight with One Stratum and Production Rate $CAC(Q) = aQ^b R^c W_N^d N_N^f e^{gD_1}$	$CAC(Q) = .499Q^{-.124} R^{-.239} W_N^{.371} N_N^{.324} e^{.708D_1}$ $\quad(-1.94)\ (-1.59)\ (7.07)\ (4.79)\ (4.04)$	98.27%	.1284

[*]CAC cost is at the cost level (i.e., Fee not included). Bold box refers to the recommended CERs.

When using nozzle weight, only kevlar is distinguished as a stratum separate from all other. Case 3 shows what results when both dummy variables are introduced; the slight difference between steel and glass is insignificant and the fit is not improved, despite the allowance of one additional degree of freedom.

We also attempted to establish a rate effect. Case 4 demonstrates the result when rate is introduced in the model form with nozzle weight. Although the overall standard error decreases, the t-statistics for both the quantity and dummy variables are greatly diminished from case 2 values. The t-statistic on quantity is barely significant, and that for rate is insignificant at the 95 percent confidence level (one-tailed test). Furthermore, the exponent on quantity has been shifted significantly. This instability in the coefficient is most likely due to high correlation between quantity and rate variables in the data base. Most of the data points are for the production of strategic missiles for which it appears that large procurement quantities are matched by roughly proportional production rates. Thus, if there is a rate effect in the production of solid motors, it cannot be discovered within the set of data compiled here due to the high correlation between rate and quantity. Therefore, it must be assumed that the quantity term in either case 1 or 2 captures both the inherent quantity effect and whatever rate effect may be operating.

For the purposes of cost estimating, both model forms are reasonably good fits and are recommended. It is believed, however, based on the preceding analyses, that the model form incorporating nozzle weight is engineeringly more accurate.

5.3 DEVELOPMENT MODELS, SOLIDS, AND LIQUIDS

The sparse data bases for development costs limited the ability to test many variables together. The regression analyses were therefore limited to tests of the production-to-prototype model forms hypothesized in section 4.

Successful regression models were found for both liquid and solid engines. The driving variables in both cases are the cumulative average unit cost at quantity 150 and, in the case of liquids a rate 10 per year, and the number of FSED prototypes to be fabricated. The CAC(150) cost is calculated from the appropriate production model recommended in subsections 5.1 and 5.2 above. Table 5.3 presents the regression results of the calculations performed by the Tecolote statistical package.

TABLE 5.3

Summary of Regression Hypotheses
Liquid and Solid Engines, Development

Case	Regression Equation (T-statistics)	D.F.	R^2_{ADJ}	s.e.
1. Liquid Engine Development with Production Cost and Number of Prototypes. F-1 Deleted. Development Cost = a CAC^b_{150} Proto's^c	Dev Cost = 52.947 $CAC^{.939}_{150}$ Proto's$^{.618}$ (10.22) (6.69)(5.11)	6	94.19%	.3371
2. Solid Engine Development with Estimated Production Cost (Based on Total Weight) and Number of Prototypes. Development Cost = a $TWCAC^b_{150}$ Proto's^c	Dev Cost = 17.360 $TWCAC^{1.030}_{150}$ Proto's$^{.756}$ (6.35) (7.30) (7.22)	7	90.63%	.1967
3. Solid Engine Development Estimated Production Cost (Based on Nozzle Weight) and Number of Prototypes Development Cost = a $NZ*CAC^b_{150}$ Proto's^c	Dev Cost = 5.389 $NZCAC^{1.103}_{150}$ Proto's$^{.991}$ (3.42) (8.35) (9.07)	7	92.69%	.1737

All CERs listed here are recommended.

For the liquid engine development model, it appeared that the F-1 was an outlier; the result in table 5.3 is based on calculations with F-1 data deleted. Although the standard error is relatively large (s.e. = .33) compared to the production model, this is most often the case. Improvement in the model will require a larger data base and more information on programmatic characteristics of the development efforts than we were able to obtain. Again it is worth noting that no stratification of the data for exotic fuels was necessary to achieve a satisfactory model.

For solid motor development costs, two model forms were developed. The table presents the regression results when the cost drivers are the number of prototypes and the CAC(150) derived from the production model based on total motor weight, or on the basis of the production model using nozzle weight. Both regression calculations produce models with reasonably good fit statistics. The standard errors are less than .20 (~ equivalent to 20 percent), which is quite good for a development model. The model calculated using the weight-based production cost as a driver produces exponents on the cost drivers that are in good agreement with conventional wisdom and past experience on other development models. Development cost is a linear function of unit production cost (i.e., CAC(150)$^{1.03}$ which can be taken as linear within the error in establishing the exponent) and the exponent on number of prototypes implies a learning slope on multiple prototype fabrication well within previous experience. The exponent value of .756 corresponds to a unit cost learning slope of -.244, which is equivalent to about 84 percent. In contrast, the model form using nozzle weight to obtain the unit production cost driver implies no learning (the exponent on number of prototypes is .991, which is essentially 1.0, implying a learning slope of 100 percent). Both model forms should produce accurate results for conditions within the range of the data base. However, for estimating cases involving numbers of prototypes beyond the range of the data base, we are inclined to recommend the model with the weight-based unit cost driver owing to the more reasonable value for the learning exponent.

BIBLIOGRAPHY

1. Marshall Space Flight Center, Launch Vehicle Cost Model, Volume 1, Cost Estimating Relationships, PRC Systems Services, PRC D-2264-H, October 1986.

2. Claus J. Meisl, Missile Propulsion Cost Modeling, Journal of Parametrics, Volume V, No. 4, December 1985.

3. Liquid Propellant Engine Manual, Chemical Propulsion Information Agency.

4. Jane's Spaceflight Directory, 1987. Jane's Yearbooks.

5. STS Cost Methodology, Volume III, Supporting Data, Aerospace Corp., TOR-0059 (6759-04)-1, August 31, 1970.

6. Rocket Motor Manual, CPIA M1, Chemical Propulsion Information Agency.

7. ICBM Flyaway Cost Model, SAMSO, Doc. No. 787, May 1979.

8. Ted G. Nichols, U.S. Missile Data Book, 1982, Sixth Edition, Data Search Associates.

9. George P. Sutton, Rocket Propulsion Elements, Fourth Edition, John Wiley & Sons.

10. Jane's Weapon Systems, 1987-1988, Jane's Yearbooks.

11. A. J. Kluge, Cost Models and Support Data for Solid Rocket Motors (U), Tecolote Research, Inc., TM-128, April 1980 (Conf).

12. A. J. Kluge, R. A. Nordsieck, A. R. Sjovold, Strategic Defense Initiative Components Cost Analysis, Tecolote Research, Inc., CR-0068, June 1985.

SCHEDULE ESTIMATING RELATIONSHIPS FOR TACTICAL AIRCRAFT

Bruce R. Harmon, Lisa M. Ward, and Paul R. Palmer
Institute for Defense Analyses
1801 N. Beauregard Street
Alexandria, Virginia 22311

INTRODUCTION

Background

Representatives of the Office of the Secretary of Defense (OSD) are responsible for review of service acquisition programs prior to their inclusion in the defense program that is submitted to the president and subsequently to Congress. Parts of this process involve the review of proposed acquisition schedules. A need exists for tools for OSD action officers to use when engaged in such reviews. The research documented in this report was initiated to provide methods for assessing the reasonableness of proposed acquisition schedules for tactical aircraft programs. The research was performed at the Institute for Defense Analyses (IDA) under the sponsorship of the Assistant Deputy Under Secretary of Defense (Air Warfare).

Approach

Historical experience is the appropriate starting point for the development of a schedule assessment tool. Such a tool should reproduce typical schedules while accounting for schedule variations among programs.

Schedule, technical and cost data on historical tactical aircraft programs were collected. Emphasis was placed on the full scale development (FSD) phase of the acquisition cycle. Of relevance were not only schedule interval data but also the program and technical parameters to which schedule intervals may have been related. Our approach to data analysis is to decompose overall program schedules into five schedule intervals for which estimating relationships can be found. The primary technique in defining and testing these relationships is linear regression analysis.

DATA COLLECTION AND PRESENTATION

Data were collected in some detail for nine fighter and attack aircraft programs. Criteria for selecting which aircraft programs to include focused on the newness of the program, its importance in historical perspective, and the expected availability of data.

All fighter and attack programs with development occurring from the early 1970s to early 1980s are included in the database. These programs include the F-14, F-15, A-10, F-16, F/A-18, and AV-8B.

A limited amount of data was collected for the Navy's S-3 program, which was in development during this same era. Although not strictly a fighter or attack aircraft, the S-3 antisubmarine warfare (ASW) aircraft has characteristics similar to a medium attack plane, including weight and speed and the ability to locate and destroy surface targets.[1] The S-3 is of interest because it is the most recent Lockheed-California aircraft development and was developed and produced through a teaming arrangement with Vought.

Earlier aircraft programs in the database include the F-4A and the F-111A. The F-4 program, from which the most ubiquitous fighter aircraft of the 1960s and 1970s sprang, serves as a historical benchmark. The F-111 program is included because it was the major fighter development of the 1960s, ushering in many technological advances. The F-111 also represents the high end of the fighter spectrum in terms of weight and range. Earlier programs of interest for which data availability was deemed insufficient included the A-6 and A-7 attack aircraft.

Table 1 presents information characterizing our nine tactical aircraft programs and their associated aircraft. Presented are program and aircraft technical characteristics that might have an effect on schedule intervals. These programs represent a rich variety in terms of both program and aircraft attributes, while staying in the relatively narrow confines delineated by fighter/attack aircraft. Five different prime contractors are represented. Three aircraft programs, the A-10, F-16, and AV-8B, used flying prototypes prior to and during full scale development.[2] Three programs, the S-3, F/A-18, and AV-8B, employed contractor teaming arrangements during development and production.[3] Off-the-shelf engines were used in the F-4, F-14, A-10, F-16, and AV-8B programs. Aircraft attributes are also diverse; this reflects both the mix of missions represented and technological advances that occurred over the time period of these programs.

Sources of the data included OSD, the military services, contractors, third parties (studies and databases at IDA, RAND, etc.), and the open literature. Cost and technical data were obtained principally from government sources and the prime contractors. Most cost and technical data were originally compiled in a report documenting IDA research on aircraft development costs [1]. Schedule data for major milestones were obtained from Selected Acquisition Reports, contractors, and the services were also compiled in these reports. The most important sources of schedule and test data were the prime contractors. Requests for data were sent to the prime contractors asking for detailed milestone, testing, and aircraft delivery information.

Our primary concern is with FSD program milestones and the schedule intervals derived from them. Other types of data are also of interest. Statistics characterizing development flight test are important; flight test duration is determined by the number of flight test aircraft, the rate at which they can

---

[1] One indication of the similarity between the S-3 and attack aircraft is the use of the S-3's TF34 engine in the A-10.

[2] The F/A-18 is not considered a prototype program because of the large differences between the YF-17 prototype and the eventual F/A-18 design. The YF-17 prototype was never used in flight testing during the FSD program.

[3] The F-111 development was a joint Air Force/Navy program with Grumman having primary responsibility for the Navy's F-111B version of the aircraft. As only a very small portion of F-111A development involved Grumman, it is not included under the teaming/joint venture classification.

Table 1. Program and Aircraft Characteristics

Characteristics	F-4A	F-111A	F-14A	S-3A	F-15A	A-10A	F-16A	F/A-18	AV-8B
Program Characterisitcs									
Military Service	USN	USAF	USN	USN	USAF	USAF	USAF	USN	USMC
Prime Contractor	MCAIR	GD	Grumman	Lockheed	MCAIR	Republic	GD	MCAIR	MCAIR
Prototype	No	No	No	No	No	Yes	Yes	No	Yes
Teaming/Joint Venture	No	No	No	Yes/Vought	No	No	No	Yes/Northrop	Yes/BAe
Engine Development	No	Yes	No	Yes	Yes	No	No	Yes	No
Number of FSD Aircraft	7	17	12	8	20	6	8	11	4
Aircraft Characteristics									
Empty Weight (lbs.)	25,458	46,172	39,037	27,260	26,795	22,141	14,062	23,014	13,086
Combat Weight (lbs.)	36,817	59,620	53,156	38,192	35,140	38,543	17,522	31,300	22,950
Maximum Speed (kn.)	1150	1262	1170	447	1434	389	1172	1029	533
Thrust/Weight Ratio*	.88	.62	.78	.49	1.34	.47	1.24	1.03	.92
Mission Radius (nmi.)	410	800	520	458	650	250	295	360	192
Advanced Materials (% of airframe structure wt.)									
Titanium	9	2	30	3	36	10	2	13	8
Composites	0	0	1	0	3	0	4	10	26

*At combat weight.

Source: *Military Aircraft Development Cost*, Vol. I, *Summary Report*, Institute for Defense Analyses.

fly, and the number of test hours that must be flown. As the timely availability of funding for FSD and the ability of prime contractors to apply resources to development tasks affect the overall pace of full scale development, FSD contract expenditure profiles are considered another important class of data.

Schedule intervals in the concept exploration, and demonstration and validation phases prior to FSD are often highly dependent upon political factors and thus are not emphasized in our data collection or analyses. However, prototype developments and paper competitions leading to FSD contract awards seem to have consistent patterns across programs and are therefore included.

Development Program Schedules

In presenting program schedule data we look at both the overall development program, with emphasis on full scale development, and major subsystem development, which often includes pre-FSD hardware prototyping. In order to compare across programs, milestone dates are normalized to a common milestone, that milestone being full scale development start. FSD start is used because it represents the most unambiguous base point common to all programs; normalized milestones are expressed as months from FSD start. Table 2 presents major milestones for the nine programs, expressed both as calender dates and in their normalized form.

Milestone I (or its equivalent for programs started before the institution of the DSARC review process) shows much variation over the programs under consideration. There is much room for interpretation when determining the equivalent of Milestone I for earlier programs; in all cases we have agreed with the Milestone I equivalents put forth in RAND's schedule interval study [2]. In searching for a less ambiguous pre-FSD milestone, we looked at milestones associated with the beginning of competition or other activity leading to the award of an FSD contract. For the three programs with flying prototypes this milestone is the start of prototype development.[4] In the case of the non-prototype programs this milestone is the request for proposals (RFP) beginning competitive paper studies leading to the award of an FSD contract.[5] Having consistent and comparable pre-FSD milestones will help us determine the overall schedule effects of prototyping *vis a vis* the more traditional development approach, where paper studies play the dominant role in determining what contractor/aircraft design will be selected for full scale development and production.

The remaining milestones tend to be self-explanatory. Critical design review (CDR) is achieved when the government concurs that the detail design of the airframe meets design specifications. The large variation in months to CDR indicates that the CDR process may differ between programs and/or

---

[4] The YA-10 and YF-16 prototypes were the winners of flyoff competitions. The YAV-8B prototype was only a part of a competition in the sense that at the time of its development there were alternative aircraft under consideration to fulfill the Marines' attack requirements.

[5] The F-4 program is an exception; its pre-FSD period represents the time from the original contract award to McDonnell Aircraft until the final specification of the aircraft design was decided upon by the Navy. Design specifications are usually decided upon at the start of FSD.

Table 2. Program Milestones

Milestones	F-4A	F-111A	F-14A	S-3A	F-15A	A-10A	F-16A	F/A-18	AV-8B
Calendar Dates									
Milestone I	10/54	2/60	11/67	11/65	4/65	12/69	9/71	9/71	3/76
Pre-FSD Activity Start (RFP or prototype start)	10/54	9/61	6/68	1/68	9/68	12/70	4/72	10/74	3/76
Contract Award/FSD Start	7/55	11/62	1/69	8/69	12/69	3/73	1/75	12/75	4/79
Critical Design Review	4/57	9/63	7/70	1/72	4/71	5/74	4/75	4/77	7/80
First Flight	5/58	12/64	12/70	1/72	7/72	2/75	12/76	11/78	11/81
First Production Delivery	6/59	4/67	5/72	4/73	11/74	11/75	8/78	5/80	11/83
24th Production Delivery	2/61	1/68	10/73	7/74	9/75	1/77	7/79	5/82	6/85
Initial Operational Capability	7/61	4/68	12/73	2/74	9/75	10/77	6/80	1/83	8/85
Months From FSD Start									
Milestone I	-9	-33	-14	-45	-56	-39	-40	-51	-37
Pre-FSD Activity Start (RFP or prototype start)	-9	-14	-7	-19	-15	-27	-33	-14	-37
Contract Award/FSD Start	0	0	0	0	0	0	0	0	0
Critical Design Review	21	10	18		16	14	3	16	15
First Flight	34	25	23	29	31	23	23	35	31
1st Production Delivery	47	53	40	44	59	32	43	53	55
24th Production Delivery	67	62	57	59	69	46	54	77	74
Initial Operational Capability	72	65	59	54	69	55	65	85	76

contractors. The most unambiguous milestone is first flight. Delivery of the first production aircraft is more ambiguous as it can be affected by the number of test aircraft built.[6] For example, this milestone is reached 59 months after FSD start for the F-15 program; this relatively long time period reflects the large number of flight test articles procured under the F-15 FSD contract. The definition of initial operational capability (IOC) tends to differ from program to program, but is usually related to the activation of the first squadron of aircraft. These differing definitions make comparisons among programs difficult and provide the motivation for formulating a new milestone. The date of the 24th production delivery was chosen as a milestone analogous to, but less ambiguous than, IOC. The 24th production delivery represents the equivalent of the first Air Force squadron or Navy carrier wing; Air Force fighter squadrons have traditionally been made up of 24 aircraft while Navy carriers have fighter wings consisting of two squadrons of 12 aircraft each. Comparing this milestone with IOC reveals that the delivery of the 24th production aircraft in most cases occurs before IOC. The two exceptions are the F-15, where the two milestones occur in the same month, and the S-3, where the 24th production delivery occurs after IOC. The latter exception may be explained by the much smaller size of ASW squadrons.

Figure 1 displays in graphical form FSD milestones as expressed in months from FSD start. Averages for all programs are plotted on the horizontal axis and values for individual programs are plotted on the vertical axis. Points above the 45-degree line represent values higher (longer time intervals) than the group average for a given milestone; those below that line represent values lower (shorter time intervals) than this average. For these milestones, dispersion around the mean is greater for milestones which occur later in the program; the one exception is for the CDR, problems with which we noted above. The most "average" programs are the F-111 and the S-3. All of the MCAIR programs take longer than average for most milestones from first flight on. Programs with shorter than average interval durations include two of the three prototype programs, the A-10 and the F-16. The F-14, which was a very high-priority program for the Navy, is also of below average length.

Development Flight Test

Detailed flight test data were collected on six programs. These include the F-111A/E, F-14A, F-15A, F-16A, F/A-18, and AV-8B. Detailed data were not available for the F-4, S-3, or A-10 programs. Table 3 displays flight test statistics for the six programs. Emphasis is on development flight test (DT&E). The approach is not only to look at the overall length of the flight test programs, but also to examine the determinants of that length. These determinants include the number of test aircraft, the utilization rate of these aircraft as measured in flights and flight hours per month, and the total number of flight hours flown. We compiled these measures for both the total test fleet and for different classes of test aircraft as defined by their test missions.

---

[6] This may not pose an analytical problem as long as there is consistency across programs in the use of programmed test aircraft and early production aircraft. This is generally the case, but there are exceptions, which are explored below.

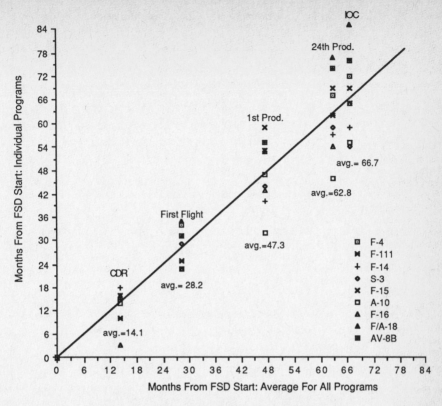

Figure 1. Full Scale Development Milestones

These classes consist of air vehicle test aircraft, avionics/systems test aircraft, armament/weapons-delivery test aircraft and reliability and maintainability (R&M) test aircraft. Air vehicle test aircraft are those used to test the basic soundness of the flight vehicle design and include flutter, structural integrity, stability and control, airframe performance, propulsion performance, flying qualities, spin, and high angle-of-attack test aircraft. This class tends to dominate the test fleets both in number of aircraft and flight hours flown. Avionics/systems and armament/weapons-delivery classes are more narrowly defined and their numbers tend to reflect the mission of the aircraft. R&M aircraft were only used in the F-14, F-16, and F/A-18 DT&E programs.

Certain clarifications should be made about the above data. Aircraft months used to calculate flight hours per month are based on the total time individual aircraft are in the test program, including down time.[7] Generally, all test aircraft will not participate for the entire length of the DT&E program. One important determinate of test program time not addressed in the above data is the length of participation for individual aircraft.

---

7   Some definitions of aircraft months exclude downtime for modification or ground testing.

Table 3. Development Flight Test Statistics

	F-111	F-14	F-15	F-16	F/A-18	AV-8B
Air Vehicle Test Aircraft						
Number of Aircraft	15	5	6	6	6	2
Number of Flights	1,695	779	1,851	1,293	1,698	866
Number of Flight Hours	2,697	1,312	1,664	1,637	2,365	1,037
Hours/Flight	1.59	1.68	.90	1.27	1.39	1.20
Hours/Aircraft Month	6.6	10.7	10.7	15.5	12.7	17.1
Avionics Test Aircraft						
Number of Aircraft	5	4	3	1	1	1
Number of Flights	549	745	691	333	350	423
Number of Flight Hours	1,017	1,169	819	488	591	478
Hours/Flight	1.85	1.57	1.19	1.47	1.69	1.13
Hours/Aircraft Month	10	11.3	15.2	24.4	19.4	17.4
Armament Test Aircraft						
Number of Aircraft	4	1	2	1	2	2
Number of Flights	277	110	512	91	707	644
Number of Flight Hours	313	164	372	174	952	523
Hours/Flight	1.13	1.49	.73	1.91	1.35	.81
Hours/Aircraft Month	5.7	8.6	6.9	12.0	17.0	8.9
R&M Test Aircraft						
Number of Aircraft	-	1	-	2	3	-
Number of Flights	-	32	-	358	677	-
Number of Flight Hours	-	40	-	280	1013	-
Hours/Flight	-	1.25	-	.78	1.50	-
Hours/Aircraft Month	-	8.0	-	18.1	32.2	-
Total Flight Test						
Number of Aircraft	24	11	11	10	12	5
Number of Flights	2,521	1,666	3,054	2,075	3,432	1,933
Number of Flight Hours	4,027	2,685	2,856	2,581	4,922	2,038
Hours/Flight	1.60	1.61	.94	1.24	1.43	1.05
Hours/Aircraft Month	7.2	10.7	10.9	16.5	16.2	13.9
DT&E Length (months)	91	45	44	48/25[a]	40	68/37[a]

[a]Length if DT&E performed by prototype aircraft is ignored.

Note that the numbers of test aircraft in Table 3 differ from those in Table 1. Table 1 gives the number of test aircraft originally programmed for and bought under the FSD contract, whereas Table 3 gives the number of test aircraft actually used in the development flight test program. In the case of the F-111, the large difference reflects F-111A production aircraft that were diverted to the test program and the three F-111E test aircraft that were included. For the F-14 program, the Table 3 does not include the two aircraft used by Hughes Aircraft in the development of the AWG-9/Phoenix weapons control system or the single F-14B aircraft used for testing of the F401 engine. In addition to the nine F-14A DT&E aircraft programmed for use by Grumman, a production aircraft was used to compensate for unplanned attrition, while a second production aircraft was used for radiation/electromagnetic compatability testing.[8] This brings the total to 11, as shown in Table 3. In the F-15 program, nine category II or initial operational test and evaluation (IOT&E) aircraft were purchased under the FSD contract and are thus not reflected in the

---

[8] In all, three F-14 test aircraft were lost. The first aircraft (#1) crashed on its second flight. That aircraft and the one that replaced it (#1X, formerly #12) are treated as a single aircraft in our calculations.

DT&E statistics.[9] In the case of the F-16 and AV-8B programs, the difference is accounted for by the prototype aircraft used during the FSD program. For the F/A-18 the difference is due to a test aircraft that had crashed being replaced by an early production model.

Our main focus is on the flight-hour rates achieved by the various classes of test aircraft for the different programs. Looking at just the air vehicle test aircraft, we see a clear pattern where the heavier and more complex aircraft achieve lower flight-hour rates. This pattern is also evident for avionics and armament aircraft, but there are anomalies for these classes. In the case of avionics aircraft, the AV-8B would be expected to achieve a higher rate, and in the case of armament aircraft, the F/A-18, and to a lesser extent the F-16, would be expected to reach lower rates. There is no clear explanation for the former, but the latter may be due to the more diverse uses of the armament aircraft in both the F-16 and F/A-18 flight test programs. This is particularly true in the case of the F/A-18 where the armament aircraft were also used extensively for avionics testing. Looking across classes for individual test programs, we see another pattern. The highest flight-hour rates are achieved for avionics aircraft (when we exclude R&M aircraft from the analysis), while the lowest rates are achieved by armament aircraft. The one anomaly is caused by the unusually high flight-hour rates evident for F/A-18 armament aircraft. Only three programs had R&M aircraft. No general pattern for this class of aircraft is evident. However, for both the F-16 and F/A-18, R&M aircraft achieve flight-hour rates higher than the program average, and for the F/A-18, these aircraft achieve a rate far higher than the other classes of aircraft.

By decomposing the test fleet into different classes of aircraft, we gain better insight into the determinants of flight-hour rates. If we were to look at only total program rates, such an analysis would be distorted. For example, the unusually high flight-hour rate evident for the F/A-18 program is in large part a result of the three R&M aircraft in the test fleet, and the relatively low flight-hour rate of the AV-8B program (given the small size and simplicity of the aircraft) is the result of the heavy emphasis on armament aircraft in the test fleet.

Early Production

Data were collected characterizing the early production periods for a portion of our sample programs. Detailed data on production lead times were collected for five programs, including the F-111, F-15, F-16, F/A-18, and AV-8B. Detailed data were not available for the F-4, S-3, F-14 or A-10 programs.

Production times are measured as the number of months from long-lead release for a given lot of aircraft to the the first aircraft delivery for that lot. For the FSD lots we consider FSD start as equivalent to long-lead release. Table 4 presents production times and other data describing the FSD and first three

---

9   Of these nine aircraft, only seven were actually used in category II testing. In addition to these seven aircraft, seven of the 11 DT&E aircraft were also used in category II testing and were responsible for most of the category II flight hours.

Table 3. Lot Data

Lot	Quantity	Cumulative Quantity	Long-Lead Release (LL)	Months From 1st Flt. to LL	1st Delivery	Production Time in Months	Last Delivery	Delivery Time in Months	Monthly Delivery Rate
F-111									
FSD	17	17	11/62	8	12/64	25	12/66	25	0.7
FY 1965	7	24	8/65	10	4/67	20	7/67	4	1.8
FY 1965/66	11	35	10/65	16	7/67	21	11/67	5	2.2
FY 1966	14	49	4/66		12/67	20	3/68	4	3.5
F-15									
FSD	20	20	12/69	3	7/72	31	11/74	29	0.7
FY 1973	30	50	10/72	14	11/74	25	12/75	14	2.1
FY 1974	62	112	9/73	26	12/75	27	7/76	8	7.7
FY 1975	72	184	9/74		8/76	23	4/77	9	8.0
F-16									
FSD	8	8	1/75	0	12/76	23	6/78	19	0.4
FY 1977	16	24	12/76	6	8/78	20	5/79	10	1.6
FY 1978	89	113	6/77	19	6/79	24	5/80	12	7.4
FY 1979	145	258	7/78		6/80	23	5/81	12	12.1
F/A-18									
FSD	11	11	12/75	-11	11/78	35	2/80	16	0.7
FY 1979	9	20	12/77	4	5/80	29	7/81	15	0.6
FY 1980	25	45	3/79	16	9/81	30	10/82	14	1.8
FY 1981	79	124	3/80		11/82	32	11/83	13	6.1
AV-8B									
FSD	4	4	4/79	-6	11/81	31	6/82	8	0.5
FY 1982	12	16	5/81	6	11/83	30	1/85	15	0.8
FY 1983	21	37	5/82	23	12/84	31	10/85	11	1.9
FY 1984	26	63	10/83		10/85	24	10/86	13	2.0

procurement lots for five programs. Lots are characterized by lot quantity, the cumulative quantity associated with the last delivery in that lot and the delivery rate for aircraft in that lot.

In examining production times, we saw that they were closely related to the time from FSD start to first flight (production time for the FSD lots). We also saw that production time increased with increasing lot size and decreased with cumulative quantity when lot sizes were stable.

Full Scale Development Costs Over Time

As development times cannot be separated from the rate at which resources are applied to the development program, FSD costs over time were collected for all nine programs. Of interest are expenditures for the FSD prime contracts. The source of these data for most programs is Contractor Cost Data Reporting (CCDR) system reports. These data were available at six-month intervals. The two exceptions were the F-4 program, where monthly data were taken from MCAIR documents, and the S-3 program, where annual data were collected from Navy sources. In all cases costs were converted into constant dollars. These data were originally compiled in the set of reports documenting the IDA research on military aircraft development costs.

DATA ANALYSIS

The five program intervals analyzed are as follows: (1) length of pre-FSD activity, (2) period from FSD start to first flight, (3) length of development flight test, (4) early production time, and (5) total FSD program length (as defined by the period from FSD start to the delivery of the 24th production aircraft). The last four intervals typify full scale development.

The relationships between the intervals relevant to full scale development are depicted in Figure 2, where the F-15 program is used as an example. Pre-FSD activity is not included in Figure 2. First flight marks the culmination of early design and manufacturing activity and initiates the development flight test program. During flight testing, information is gathered to be used both in refining the aircraft design and in supporting production decisions. The concurrency of development and production can be seen in the overlap of development flight testing and early production activity. This production activity is characterized by production times for the early procurement lots as expressed as the interval between long-lead release and the delivery of the first production aircraft. The measure of overall FSD program length brackets its constituent intervals and serves to characterize the program as a unified whole.

In applying regression analysis, schedule intervals measured in months were treated as dependent variables and regressed against those independent variables thought to influence these intervals. The adequacy of these regression models was tested using standard measures of statistical significance and model fit. Models whose parameter estimates carried intuitively incorrect signs (for example, if the model indicated decreasing intervals with increasing aircraft weight) were rejected.

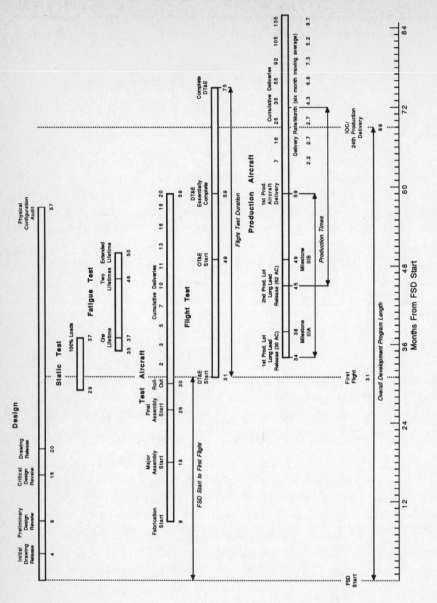

Figure 2. F-15 Program Schedule

Expected determinants of schedule interval length were tested. Pre-FSD activity was expected to be longer for programs with prototypes. Time to first flight was expected in increase with measures of aircraft size and technical complexity, such as weight and speed. Program structure variables were also of interest. We expected that the existence of a prototype program would decrease the time to first flight while cntractor teaming in development was expected to lengthen this interval. Production times were expected to shorten with the cumulative quantity produced, much in the same way as costs decrease with cumulative quantity. Overall FSD program length was expected to be determined by the same types of variables as time to first flight. Another expected determinant was the expenditure rate of full scal e development costs.

The one interval for which length was not directly estimated was the span of the development flight test program. Here the dependent variable was the flight-hour rate achieved by the flight test aircraft. Given this valuse and information about the number and employment of test aircraft, and the required number of flight hours, the length of the flight test program can be determined. It was expected that flight-hour rate would decrease with the size and complexity of the aircraft being tested. The test missions for which individual aircraft were used were also expected to affect flight-hour rate.

Pre-FSD Activity

The primary goal in analyzing this program interval is to gain insight into the schedule penalties associated with the development of a flying prototype prior to the full scale development program. As explained in Chapter III, the analogous program interval to prototype development time for non-prototype programs is the period from the RFP to the award of the FSD contact. These intervals describe the length of what we call "pre-FSD activity" in our database.

In our regression analysis, values for the length of pre-FSD activity (PFSD) for nine programs are regressed against an indicator variable (PROTO) whose value is one for prototype programs and zero for non-prototype programs. The resulting equation and associated measures of statistical significance and model fit are presented below.

$$\text{PFSD} = 13.0 + 19.33 \text{ (PROTO)}$$
$$(.0002) \quad (.0005)$$
$$N = 9 \qquad R^2 = .84 \qquad \text{Adjusted } R^2 = .81 \qquad \text{SEE} = 4.55$$

Significance levels are in parentheses below the parameter estimates. N is the number of observations and SEE is the standard error of the estimate. This regression model indicates pre-FSD activity lasting 13 months for non-prototype programs and an additional 19.33 months (32.33 months) for prototype programs. The relatively high R^2 shows that most of the variation in pre-FSD activity can be explained by the existence or non-existence of a prototype program. Figure 3 illustrates the relationship between the actual values for the nine programs and values predicted by the above equation. The predicted values are equal to the average for each of the two different groups of data.

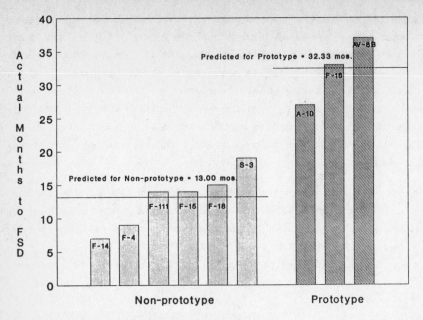

Figure 3. Pre-FSD Activity

The interpretation of these results is that, all other things being equal, having a prototype program lengthens the time to full scale development start by a little more than a year and a half. This does not mean that the existence of a prototype will lengthen the entire program by that amount. In fact, the early experience gained through a prototype tends to shorten full scale development time. This tendency is quantified in the analyses of other program intervals.

Time to First Flight

In developing a regression model to estimate the time required to achieve first flight from the start of FSD, many different specifications were tested.

Attempts to use aircraft characteristics as explanatory variables were unsuccessful. Variables such as weight and speed traditionally used in cost estimating relationships were either statistically insignificant or carried the wrong sign. A possible reason for the failure of technical characteristics to explain the variance in this interval is the relatively narrow focus of the sample population. For example, the heaviest aircraft in our sample is the F-111 (time to first flight, 25 months) with an empty weight of 46,000 pounds, while the lightest aircraft in our sample, the AV-8B (time to first flight, 31 months), has an empty weight of 13,000 pounds. If we were to define our population to include bomber and heavy transport aircraft this range would be much larger; i.e., the B-1 bomber has an empty weight of 190,000 pounds and took 56 months to achieve first flight.

A more fruitful approach involved using program and contractor variables to predict time to first flight. In the most satisfactory model time to first flight (TFF) is regressed against three indicator variables that carry the value of either one or zero. These include variables that identify programs that had McDonnell Aircraft as the prime contractor (MCAIR), programs that employed prototyping (PROTO), and programs that involved major subcontractor/contractor teaming arrangements (TEAM). The resulting equation and measures of statistical significance and model fit are presented below.

$$TFF = 25.1 + 6.9 \text{ (MCAIR)} - 2.7 \text{ (PROTO)} + 2.9 \text{ (TEAM)}$$
$$(.0001) \quad (.002) \qquad (.065) \qquad (.060)$$
$$N = 9 \qquad R^2 = .93 \qquad \text{Adjusted } R^2 = .89 \qquad SEE = 1.6$$

The regression results show all parameter estimates significant at the .10 level. Figure 4 plots time to first flight predicted by the above equation against program actuals. Values above the 45-degree line are overestimated by the model, while values below that line are underestimated. The interpretation of this equation is that a baseline program (a non-MCAIR program without teaming or a prototype) will require 25 months to reach first flight; a MCAIR program, 7 months longer; a program with a prototype, 3 months shorter; and a program with teaming, 3 months longer. Looking at the predicted values in Figure 4, we see six classes of programs – "baseline" programs (F-111, F-14), programs distinguished only by prototyping (A-10, F-16), a single program distinguished only by teaming (S-3), two MCAIR programs with neither prototyping nor teaming (F-4, F-15), a single MCAIR program with only teaming (F/A-18), and another MCAIR program with both prototyping and teaming (AV-8B).

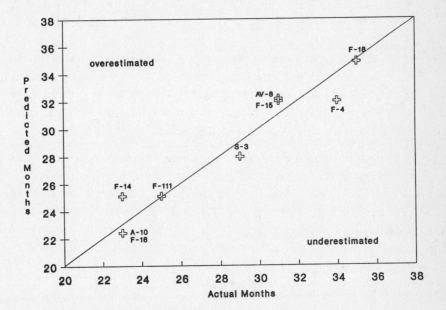

Figure 4. Predicted Vs. Actual Time From FSD Start to First Flight

Perhaps the most striking result is the extra length associated with MCAIR programs. A possible explanation is that McDonnell's development philosophy dictates a longer and more thorough design effort prior to first flight. Another factor could be longer manufacturing flow-time associated with building the development aircraft. This longer time to first flight should not *a priori* be considered negative. Spending more time prior to first flight may help reduce the number of problems surfacing later in the program when they are more difficult and costly to correct. Conversely, having aircraft flying earlier in the program facilitates the early accumulation of flight test data. Discussions with McDonnell representatives indicate that they are aware of the higher than average duration of their programs and that they are implementing changes in order to shorten schedule intervals. It is not within the scope of this study to draw conclusions about the optimal length of the schedule intervals under consideration.

More expected are the parameter estimates for the prototype and teaming variables. Having designed and built a prototype prior to FSD would provide a contractor with a head start in FSD. The added length for teaming programs may be due to both the organizational difficulties such an arrangement might create and the complications associated with transporting major subassemblies from plant to plant.

Flight Test

The approach to analyzing flight test duration consists of two steps. First, regression analysis is employed to estimate flight-hour rates using data presented in Chapter III. Given an average flight-hour rate, flight test program length can be derived from the following relationship:

$$\text{Flight test duration} = f\left[\frac{\text{Required number of flight test hours}}{\text{(Monthly flight-hour rate)} \times \text{(Number of test aircraft)}}\right],$$

where the required number of flight test hours and the number of test aircraft are taken as exogenous. This basic equation must be modified to reflect the sequential delivery of the test aircraft (programmed test aircraft are not all available at the start of the test program) and the fact that, once delivered, test aircraft do not all remain in the test fleet for the full duration of the program. It is more appropriate to tackle this second step in Chapter V, where we apply our analyses to a hypothetical program.

As pointed out above, relationships exist between aircraft weight and test mission, and average flight-hour rates. To quantify these relationships, regression equations predicting average monthly flight-hour rate for three test missions were estimated. These missions include air vehicle test (AHM), avionics test (AVHM), and armament test (ARHM). Average flight-hour rates for the F-111, F-14, F-15, F-16, F/A-18, and AV-8B programs were regressed against aircraft empty weight (EWT). A multiplicative specification was employed. The three equations and associated measures of statistical significance and model fit are presented below.

$$AHM = 5486 \ (EWT)^{-.61}$$

$$(.002) \qquad (.007)$$

$$N = 6 \qquad R^2 = .86 \qquad \text{Adjusted } R^2 = .83 \qquad SEE = .14$$

$$AVHM = 4915 \, (EWT)^{-.57}$$
$$(.005) \qquad (.019)$$

$$N = 6 \qquad R^2 = .78 \qquad \text{Adjusted } R^2 = .73 \qquad SEE = .17$$

$$ARHM = 330 \, (EWT)^{-.36}$$
$$(.054) \qquad (.14)$$

$$N = 5 \qquad R^2 = .56 \qquad \text{Adjusted } R^2 = .42 \qquad SEE = .21$$

Figure 5 plots average flight-hour rates against empty weight. Also included are the regression lines defined above.

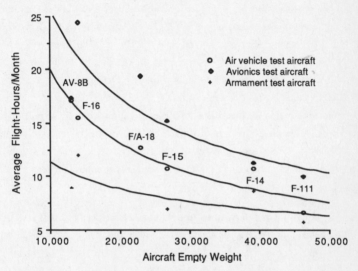

Figure 5. Flight-Hour Rate Vs. Aircraft Empty Weight

Only five data points were used in estimating flight-hour rates for armament aircraft; the F/A-18 data point was dropped because of the ambiguities in the definition of armament test aircraft in that program. Because of the low number of data points used to estimate these equations, caution should be used in their application.

Early Production

In analyzing early production data the primary concern was finding the determinants of production time for the early production lots. To do this, data presented in Table 4 were used to estimate an equation for production time (PT). In specifying the independent variables for this regression equation, three different effects were addressed. The first was the correlation between time to first flight and production time. To take this into account, two of the three variables used in the time-to-first-flight equation, the MCAIR and teaming indicator variables, were incorporated. The second effect noted was the increase in production times as lot quantities increase. This was addressed by including lot quantity (Q) as an explanatory variable. The third effect was learning, where production times are expected to decrease as cumulative quantities increase. Cumulative quantity (CUMQ) was included in the specification and was measured at the last delivery of the prior lot; for the FSD lot it was measured at unit one. Production time for the FSD lot (time to first flight) is analogous to the first unit cost (T_1) of a manufacturing learning curve. An exponential specification was used. The equation and associated measures of statistical significance and model fit are presented below[10].

$$PT = 19.3 \ (Q)^{.094} \ (CUMQ)^{-.063} \times 1.16 \ (MCAIR) \times 1.21 \ (TEAM)$$

$$(.0001) \quad (.0009) \qquad (.0002) \ (.0036) \qquad\qquad (.0004)$$

$$N = 22 \qquad R^2 = .88 \qquad \text{Adjusted } R^2 = .85 \qquad SEE = .07$$

In addition to the twenty lots presented in Table 4, another lot was added for both the F/A-18 and AV-8B, bringing the total number of data points to 22. This equation shows McDonnell production times to be 16% longer than for other contractors; this indicates that the schedule disadvantage MCAIR programs suffer for time to first flight flight (7 months more than a baseline of 25 months as predicted by our equation for that interval) decreases for production times. The opposite relationship is evident for programs incorporating teaming. The parameter estimate for Q indicates longer production times for larger lot sizes. A possible explanation for this is that larger lot quantities complicate production planning and material procurement. A learning hypothesis for production time is supported by the parameter estimate for cumulative quantity. Production times estimated from this equation are illustrated in Figure 6. Presented are plots of predicted production time against cumulative quantity for several lot sizes based on a non-MCAIR program without teaming.

Because this equation was derived from data characterizing the initial part of the production program, it should not be applied to later production lots. We found that the relationships illustrated above do not hold for later lots.

Overall FSD Program Length

Overall FSD program length is defined as the time from FSD start to the delivery of the 24th production aircraft. This is a more consistent measure of FSD length than is time to initial operational capability. In estimating a regression equation for FSD length two steps are followed. First, a measure characterizing FSD expenditure profiles is estimated for each program. This measure is then used as an explanatory variable in a regression equation for estimating the time to the 24th production delivery.

We realize that FSD program length cannot be divorced from the rate of FSD program expenditures. This expenditure rate may be affected by both the availability of funding (demand side) and the rate at which the prime contractor can apply resources to development tasks (supply side). The literature in applied R&D management notes an empirically derived relationship between time and the buildup of R&D expenditures. When plotted this relationship resembles a logistic distribution or

---

[10] In reporting equations with multiplicative specifications, the exponential terms associated with 1/0 indicator variables are converted into a multiplicative form to ease interpretation. The form shown above is not strictly correct as the value of the equation becomes 0 when the value of the indicator variable is 0. The correct interpretation is that the value of the terms representing a given effect (i.e., 1.16 (MCAIR) becomes 1 when the value of the indicator variable is 0).

biological growth curve. Traditionally these curves have been fitted to expenditure data with functions incorporating second- and third-order polynomials. Norden [3] presents an alternative specification that yields a parameter estimate having a clear interpretation related to development time. The function to be fitted to the data is as follows:

$$Y = K(1 - e^{-At^2}),$$

where

Y = cumulative expenditure at time t
K = total expenditure at the end of development
t = time from program start
A = shape parameter governing time to peak expenditure rate.

Given data for cumulative expenditures over time, A can be estimated using non-linear least squares; t is measured in months for our data. Data for K and Y can be scaled to any baseline without changing the parameter estimates of A.

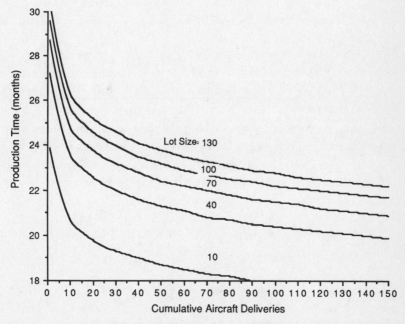

Figure 6. Production Time Vs. Cumulative Deliveries for Varying Lot Sizes

The higher the value for A, the sooner expenditure rate will peak and the higher that peak will be. "Demand side" interpretations of A would be that programs with high values are "crash" programs, while programs with low values are low priority programs subject to funding stretch-outs. "Supply side" interpretations would be that programs with high values of A are associated with the ability of the prime contractor to apply resources at a high rate relative to the total expenditure required (K), while programs with low values of A would show opposite tendencies.

Table 5 shows estimates of A and their associated standard errors for eight full scale development programs. Because only fragmentary data were available for the AV-8B program, it was not included in this analysis. The relative A values for the above programs are generally intuitively satisfying. The F/A-18 is a good example of a stretched-out program; the F-14, a crash program. The A-10 program shows the highest value of A, possibly because of carry over from the prototype program and its very low development cost. Figure 7 shows four examples of expenditure profiles generated from the estimated A values. Cumulative expenditures are normalized to their proportion of total FSD cost.

Table 5. Non-Linear Regression Results for A

Program	Parameter estimate	Standard error
F-4	.00068	.000007
F-111	.00070	.000023
F-14	.00107	.000892
S-3	.00105	.000019
F-15	.00074	.000012
A-10	.00253	.000079
F-16	.00075	.000020
F/A-18	.00064	.000009

Given values for A, the next step was to incorporate this variable into a regression equation estimating FSD program length (T24). Additional variables in the regression equation included MCAIR and prototype indicator variables. An exponential specification was employed. The equation and associated measures of statistical significance and model fit are presented below.

$$T24 = 22.1 \, (A)^{-.141} \times 1.15 \, (MCAIR) \times .89 \, (PROTO)$$
$$(.0011) \quad (.054) \quad (.035) \qquad\qquad (.075)$$

$$N = 8 \qquad R^2 = .95 \qquad \text{Adjusted } R^2 = .91 \qquad SEE = .05$$

The regression results show all parameter estimates significant at the .10 level. Figure 8 plots FSD program length predicted by the above equation against program actuals. Values above the 45-degree line are overestimated by the model and values below that line are underestimated.

FSD program length for MCAIR was estimated to take 15% longer than for other contractors. This translates into FSD length about eight months longer than the average for other contractor's programs, which in turn closely reflects MCAIR's schedule disadvantage at first flight. Prototype programs were estimated to take 11% less time than programs without prototypes. This translates into an

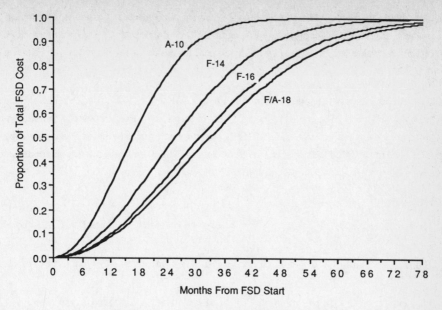

Figure 7. Example Expenditure Profiles

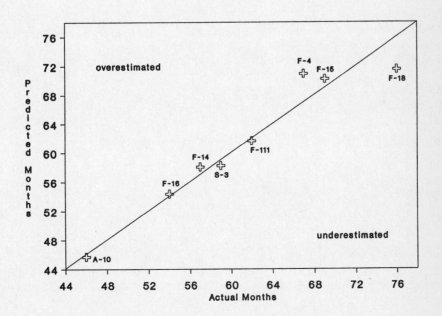

Figure 8. Predicted Vs. Actual Program Length

FSD length about seven months shorter than the average for non-prototype programs. According to our estimates, the schedule advantage of prototype programs at first flight more than doubled by the end of the FSD program. A sizable portion of the extra time required for prototype programs prior to FSD was made up during FSD.

The equation estimating total FSD program length has at least two uses. It can provide a quick method of assessing the total length of proposed FSD programs given that proposed expenditure profiles are also available to the analyst. Another, and perhaps more interesting use is that of a consistency check on schedule assessments produced from an integrated set of the three interval estimates addressed above.

REFERENCES

[1]   Harmon, Bruce R., et al., *Military Aircraft Development Costs*, Volumes I-V, IDA Report R-339, September 1988.

[2]   Smith, G. K., and E. T. Friedmann, *An Analysis of Weapon System Acquisition Intervals, Past and Present*, The RAND Corporation, R-2605, November 1980.

[3]   Norden, Peter V., "Useful Tools for Project Management," *Management of Production*, M. K. Starr (ed.), Penguin, 1963, pp. 71-98.

V. Production Lot Sizing

LOT SIZING AND WORK-IN-PROCESS INVENTORIES IN SINGLE STAGE PRODUCTION SYSTEMS

Avijit Banerjee and Jonathan S. Burton
Drexel University, Philadelphia, PA

ABSTRACT

This work modifies the classical deterministic production lot size model for single stage manufacturing systems, by incorporating the effects of work-in-process inventories. The results obtained from the relatively simple single input case are used to develop a heuristic solution algorithm, involving an efficient search technique, for obtaining a solution for the model under the more general and complex multiple inputs scenario. This solution procedure is illustrated through a numerical example.

1. INTRODUCTION

Inventory management is one of the key cost control areas in production systems. Within this area, the lot sizing problem has received considerable research attention, since the development of the economic order quantity (EOQ) concept by Harris in 1915 [7]. An early modification of the EOQ model involved the incorporation of a finite production rate, resulting in the well-known classical production lot size (PLS) formula. Through the years, the single stage PLS model has been greatly embellished and has found applications under a wide variety of conditions (see [12] for a survey). Most of these applications, however, suffer from a serious drawback, in that they do not consider the effects of work-in-process (WIP) inventories.

It should be mentioned that the past two decades have seen significant progress in multistage lot sizing research, which do incorporate WIP effects [5], [8]. While some of the work in this area have focused on developing optimum seeking algorithms with simplifying assumptions, much effort has gone into developing heuristic procedures involving less restrictive assumptions [2],[6]. In recent years, Billington et al. [3] and Moily [9], among others, have made substantial contributions to the capacitated multi stage lot sizing problem.

Nevertheless, most of this work cited above tend to ignore the effects of the gradual conversion of input to output at a finite rate within each production stage. In contrast, we explicitly consider the effects of WIP inventories that result from such gradual conversion of input to output, albeit in single stage production environments.

In a recent study, Banerjee and Burton [1] examined the implications of such transformation processes in terms of WIP inventories and studied their influence on the lot sizing decision in single as well as multistage environments. However, their assumption of lot-for-lot ordering seriously restricts the applicability of the results obtained. Although for the sake of simplicity, our attention is confined to single stage systems under deterministic conditions, we relax the lot-for-lot assumption here, in an attempt to generalize some of the results of the aforementioned work.

In the following section, we state our assumptions and the notational scheme used. Subsequently, we present our analyses, models and a numerical illustration . Finally, the last section of this paper contains a summary and some concluding remarks.

2.   ASSUMPTIONS AND NOTATION

The following major assumptions are made in our work:
(1) a product is manufactured autonomously in a single stage batch system and stored in a single location;
(2) the input items (e.g. materials, parts, etc.) are ordered independently of one another and the entire order quantity of each input is received at the same time;
(3) the production and storage environment is deterministic, i.e. the demand and production rates, lead times, cost parameters, etc. are all known and constant through time;
(4) stockout situations for the end item as well as the inputs are unacceptable and not permitted;
(5) no quantity purchase price discounts are available for the input items procured from external sources;
(6) the planning horizon is infinite;
(7) there are no constraints on storage space and capital invested in inventories.

The inventory items in any production system are arranged in a hierarchical manner, with the number of levels in this hierarchy de-

pending on the number of manufacturing stages. In single stage systems, representing the simplest of cases, there are two such levels,
with the end items or finished products occupying the upper level,
while the input items necessary for production are at the lower level.
In our terminology, the top (i.e. end item) level is labeled 0 and the
bottom (i.e. input item) level is labeled 1. Accordingly, the finished
product and the input items are termed, respectively, level 0 and
level 1 items.

In addition, we use the following notational scheme:

D = demand rate for the end item in units per period;

P = end item production rate in units per period;

S_0 = fixed setup cost for producing an end item batch;

C_0 = total production cost (exclusive of setup cost) per unit
($/unit) for the end product;

S_j = fixed ordering cost for the jth input item in $/order
($j = 1, 2, \ldots, m$);

C_j = purchase price of input item j in $/unit;

r = the inventory holding charge, expressed as a fraction of
item value;

T = total inventory cycle time for the end item (periods);

t = production time per cycle required by the end item in
periods;

Q_0 = production lot size for the end item in units;

Q_j = order quantity for input item j in units;

TRC = total relevant cost.

Note that, of necessity, $P \geq D$. Also, without loss of generality,
we assume that the manufacture of each unit of the product requires
one unit of input j. For instance, if 5 lbs. of a raw material and 2
units of a part are required to produce a unit of an end item, a
"unit" of the material is specified to be 5 lbs. and 2 units of the
part are defined as one "unit" of this input, in order to satisfy this
assumption. As mentioned above, it is further assumed that each input
is procured independently, in order to avoid the complexities associated with the joint ordering of multiple items.

3. ANALYSES AND MODELS FOR A SINGLE INPUT ITEM

In order to facilitate the analysis, we first consider situations
where only a single input is required to manufacture the final product

(in other words, m = 1). The results thus obtained are extended to the more general multiple inputs case, discussed in the next section.

In deriving the optimal production lot size for an end item under deterministic conditions, the total relevant cost per period has traditionally been expressed as

$$TRC'(Q_0) = (D/Q_0)S_0 + (Q_0/2)(1 - D/P)rC_0 ,$$

where the first term represents the setup cost and second term reflects the inventory holding cost per period [12]. From this cost function the optimal batch size can be easily obtained, i.e.

$$Q_0 = \sqrt{[2DS_0/rC_0(1 - D/P)]}, \tag{1}$$

which is the classical PLS formula. This formula, however, ignores the presence of WIP inventories and their influence on the lot sizing decision.

If the effects of such inventories are taken into account, the PLS formula above is no longer valid. Figure 1 shows the inventory time plots for the finished and input items, depicting the case of a single input ordered on a lot-for-lot basis, which we shall assume for the moment. Based on the results of a prior study [1], the total relevant cost per period, taking into account the inventory cycles of both items at the two levels simultaneously, is

$$TRC(Q_0) = (D/Q_0)(S_0 + S_1) + (Q_0 r/2)[C_0(1 - D/P) + DC_1/P].$$

From this expression, the optimal batch size, incorporating the effects of WIP, is given by

$$Q_0^* = \sqrt{\frac{2D(S_0 + S_1)}{r[C_0(1 - D/P) + DC_1/P]}} . \tag{2}$$

The assumption of lot-for-lot ordering implies that the optimal order quantity for the input item is $Q_1^* = Q_0^*$. If we now relax this restrictive assumption, two distinct cases are possible. First, it may be optimal if the input item order lot size is a fraction of the batch size for the final product (i.e. $Q_1 = Q_0/n$), or, secondly, the optimal policy may be to let the order quantity of the procured item be a multiple of the production lot size for the end item (i.e. $Q_1 = kQ_0$). It can be easily shown that if the latter case is optimal, k must be a positive integer (see Rosenblatt and Lee [3] for proof). In contrast, if the former case is optimal, there may be no such restriction on the value of n. If n is allowed to be a non-integer, however, the model and its analysis becomes substantially more complex than the results obtained here. Thus, for simplicity, it

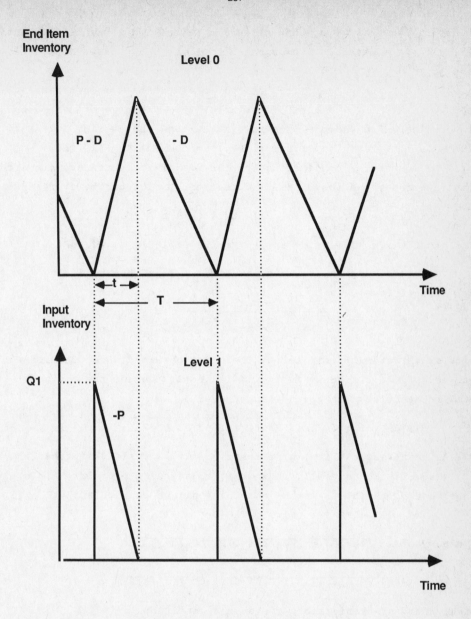

FIGURE 1: INVENTORY TIME PLOTS FOR LOT-FOR-LOT ORDERING

is assumed in this paper that n is also restricted to a positive integer. With this caveat, we examine each of these two cases separately.

Case 1: $Q_1 = Q_0/n$

Figure 2 shows the inventory time plots of the product and the input with n=3 (i.e. 3 lots of the input item are ordered per production cycle) as an example. Generally speaking, the average inventory of the level 1 item is $(Q_0/2n)(t)(D/Q_0) = (Q_0/2n)(Q_0/P)(D/Q_0) = DQ_0/2nP$. Therefore, considering both levels of the inventory hierarchy simultaneously, the total relevant cost per period can be expressed as

$$TRC(Q_0,n) = DS_0/Q_0 + (Q_0/2)(1-D/P)rC_0 + nDS_1/Q_0 + DQ_0rC_1/2nP$$

or $\quad TRC(Q_0,n) = (D/Q_0)(S_0+nS_1) + (Q_0r/2)[C_0(1-D/P) + DC_1/nP] \qquad (3)$

For minimizing TRC, we set the first partial derivative of (3) with respect to Q_0 equal to 0 at $Q_0 = Q_0*(n)$ and obtain

$$Q_0*(n) = \sqrt{\frac{2D(S_0 + nS_1)}{r[C_0(1-D/P) + DC_1/nP]}} \qquad (4)$$

which is structurally similar to the model obtained under the lot-for-lot assumption (2). Substituting (4) into (3), we get the optimal total relevant cost as a function of n, i.e.

$$TRC(Q_0*,n) = \sqrt{2Dr(S_0+nS_1)[C_0(1-D/P)+DC_1/nP]}. \qquad (5)$$

As mentioned earlier, n is restricted to a positive integer in (5). Also, it can be easily shown that equation (5) is convex in n. Consequently, if (5) is minimized at $n = n*$, we can state that
$$TRC(Q_0*,n*) \le TRC(Q_0*,n*+1).$$

In other words, $\sqrt{2Dr[S_0+n*S_1][C_0(1-D/P)+DC_1/n*P]}$

$$\le$$

$$\sqrt{2Dr[S_0+(n*+1)S_1][C_0(1-D/P)+DC_1/(n*+1)P]},$$

which, after simplification, yields the condition

$$(S_0C_1/S_1C_0)[D/(P-D)] \le n*(n*+1). \qquad (6)$$

To determine the optimal production lot size, we first find the smallest integer, n*, that satisfies inequality (6); then substitute $n = n*$ into (4) to obtain $Q_0*(n*)$, representing the end item batch size that minimizes the total relevant cost. The optimal input item order quantity is simply obtained as $Q_1* = Q_0*(n*)/n*$.

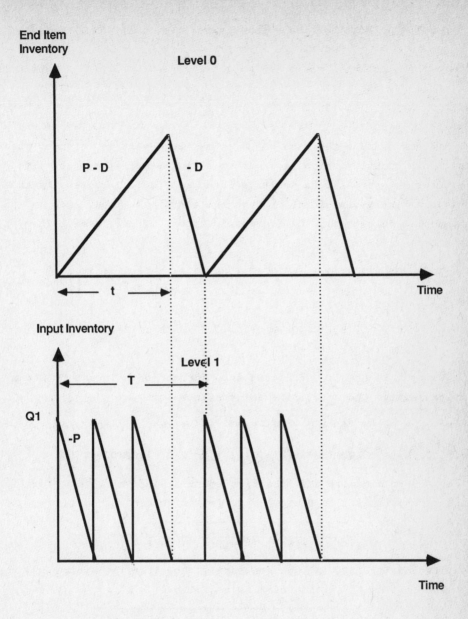

FIGURE 2: INVENTORY TIME PLOTS OF Q1= Qo/n (n = 3)

Proposition 1: For the single input case (i.e. m=1), $n^* > 1$, iff

$$S_0 C_1 / S_1 C_0 > 2(P/D-1).$$

Proof: Substituting $n^*=1$ in (6) we get $S_0 C_1 / S_1 C_0 \leq 2(P/D-1)$, which is the necessary and sufficient condition for n^* to be unity. It then follows that $n^* > 1$ iff $S_0 C_1 / S_1 C_0 > 2(P/D-1)$.   Q.E.D.

Case 2: $Q_1 = kQ_0$

We now examine the case where it may be desirable to order the input in a quantity which is a multiple of the end item's lot size, i.e. $Q_1 = kQ_0$, where k is a positive integer. Figure 3 represents the inventory time plots of the product and its single input with k=3 as an example. In general, the average inventory of the level 1 item is given by:

$$
\begin{aligned}
I_1 &= (D/Q_1)[Q_0 t/2 + (k-1)Q_0 T + Q_0 t/2 + (k-2)Q_0 T + \ldots\ldots \\
&\qquad\qquad + \ldots\ldots + 2Q_0 T + Q_0 t/2 + Q_0 t + Q_0 t/2] \\
&= (D/kQ_0)[kQ_0 t/2 + Q_0 T\{(k-1) + (k-2) + \ldots\ldots+ 1\}] \\
&= (D/kQ_0)[(kQ_0/2)(Q_0/P) + Q_0 (Q_0/D)\{k(k-1)/2\}] \\
&= (Q_0/2)(D/P + k -1).
\end{aligned}
$$

Using this result and taking into account both inventory items simultaneously, the total relevant cost now is

$$TRC(Q_0, k) = DS_0/Q_0 + Q_0 rC_0 (1-D/P)/2 + DS_1/kQ_0 + Q_0 rC_1 (D/P+k-1)/2$$

or $TRC(Q_0, k) = (D/Q_0)(S_0 +S_1/k)+(Q_0 r/2)[C_0 (1-D/P)+C_1 (D/P+k-1)]$ (7)

As before, to minimize TRC, the first partial derivative of (7) with respect to Q_0 is set to 0 at $Q_0 = Q_0^*(k)$ to obtain

$$Q_0^*(k) = \sqrt{\frac{2D(S_0 + S_1/k)}{r[C_0 (1-D/P) + C_1 (D/P +k -1)]}} .$$ (8)

Substituting (8) into (7), we can easily show that the minimum total relevant cost as a function of k is as follows:

$$TRC(Q_0^*, k) = \sqrt{2Dr(S_0 +S_1/k)[C_0 (1-D/P) + C_1 (D/P+k-1)]}.$$ (9)

As in the previous case, k is a positive integer in equation (9), which can easily be shown to be convex in k. Therefore, if (9) is minimized at $k=k^*$, $TRC(Q_0, k^*) \leq TRC(Q_0, k^*+1)$. Substituting first $k = k^*$ and then $k = k^*+1$ in (9) and simplifying, the following condition for optimum k is derived:

$$(S_1 C_0 -S_1 C_1)(1-D/P)/S_0 C_1 \leq k^*(k^*+1).$$ (10)

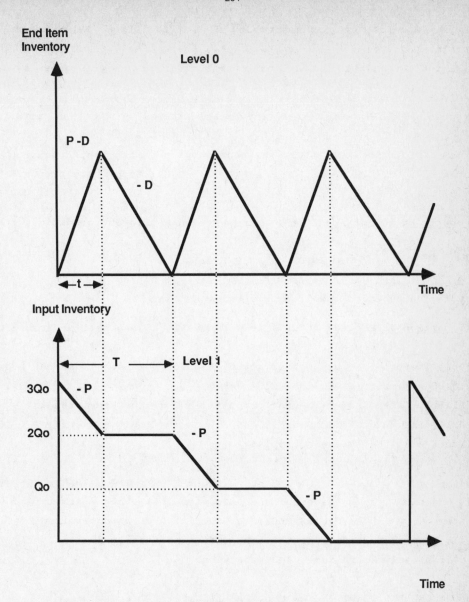

FIGURE 3: INVENTORY TIME PLOTS FOR Q1 = kQo (k=3)

The minimum positive integer valued k^* that satisfies (10) is then substituted into (8) to compute $Q^*(k^*)$, the optimal production lot size for the end item. The input item's order quantity is given by $Q_1^* = k^* \cdot Q_0^*(k^*)$.

Proposition 2: For the single input case (i.e. $m = 1$) $k^* > 1$, iff
$$S_0 C_1 / (S_1 C_0 - S_1 C_1) < (1/2)(1-D/P).$$
Proof: Letting $k^* = 1$ in (10), the necessary and sufficient condition for $k^* = 1$ is $S_0 C_1 / (S_1 C_0 - S_1 C_1) \geq (1/2)(1-D/P)$, from which proposition 2 follows. Q.E.D.

Proposition 3: For $m = 1$, the necessary and sufficient conditions for lot-for-lot input item ordering are:
$$S_0 C_1 / S_1 C_0 \leq 2(P/D - 1) \tag{11}$$
$$\text{and} \quad S_0 C_1 / (S_1 C_0 - S_1 C_1) \geq (1/2)(1-D/P). \tag{12}$$
Proof: The proof follows from propositions 1 and 2. Q.E.D.

Proposition 4: For any input item, if $n^* > 1$, k^* vanishes and vice versa.
Proof: The proof is by contradiction. From proposition 1, we can show that $n^* > 1$, iff $S_0 C_1 D / 2 S_1 C_0 > P-D$. \tag{13}
Similarly, after some algebra, proposition 2 may be rewritten as
$k^* > 1$, iff $2 S_0 C_1 P / (S_1 C_0 - S_1 C_1) < P-D$. \tag{14}
Since $P \geq D$, the following apply:
$$2 S_0 C_1 P / (S_1 C_0 - S_1 C_1) \geq 2 S_0 C_1 D / (S_1 C_0 - S_1 C_1),$$
and $2 S_0 C_1 P / (S_1 C_0 - S_1 C_1) > S_0 C_1 D / 2(S_1 C_0 - S_1 C_1) > S_0 C_1 D / 2 S_1 C_0$.
If condition (13) holds simultaneously with (14), then from the above statement we can derive $2 S_0 C_1 P / (S_1 C_0 - S_1 C_1) > P-D$, which contradicts (14). Thus both conditions (13) and (14) cannot hold simultaneously, i.e. if $n^* > 1$, k^* vanishes and vice versa. Q.E.D.

4. MODEL AND SOLUTION FOR MULTIPLE INPUTS

So far, our analyses have been limited to cases involving a single procured item (i.e. $m = 1$). Now we extend our discussion to the case of multiple input items (i.e. $m > 1$). In order to derive the model for $m > 1$, cost functions (3) and (7), developed earlier, need to be combined in a way that allows the order quantity of input item j to be (a) a multiple of Q_0, (b) a fraction of Q_0, or (c) equal to Q_0. Since we know from proposition 4 that some k_j and/or n_j values will be zero, incorporating both of these for any j in the model will result in some of the terms to be divided by zero, rendering them meaning-less. Therefore, we define $\underline{M} = (M_1, M_2, \ldots, M_m)$ for the m inputs and use (3) and (7) to express the generalized cost function as follows:

$$TRC(Q_0, \underline{M}) = (D/Q_0)(S_0 + \sum_{j=1}^{m} S_j/M_j) + (Q_0 r/2)[C_0(1-D/P)$$

$$+ \sum_{j=1}^{m} M_j C_j (D/P + Max\{M_j, 1\} - 1)] \qquad (15)$$

Determining the optimal lot sizes for the end product and each of the input items in this situation involves the minimization of the R.H.S. of (15), subject to restrictions on M_j, such that either M_j or $1/M_j$ is a positive integer for j = 1, 2, ..., m. Note that in (15) the use of a single lot size multiplier, M_j, and the restrictions on it for any j, embodies all three possible input item order quantity scenarios mentioned above. Clearly, for any $M_j > 1$, the corresponding $k_j = M_j$; and for any $M_j < 1$, the corresponding $n_j = 1/M_j$. For those j when $M_j = 1$, $n_j = k_j = 1$, implying lot-for-lot ordering.

The formulation above represents a mixed integer, nonlinear, constrained optimization problem, which may be difficult to solve efficiently, particularly for large problems. Therefore, to tackle this problem, we develop a heuristic solution algorithm incorporating a search procedure, outlined below.

The following first order optimality condition is derived from (15) by setting its first partial derivative with respect to Q_0 to 0 at $Q_0 = Q_0^*(\underline{M})$. This expresses the optimal production lot size as a function of $\underline{M}$ i.e.

$$Q_0^*(\underline{M}) = \sqrt{\frac{2D(S_0 + \sum_{j=1}^{m} S_j/M_j)}{r[C_0(1-D/P) + \sum_{j=1}^{m} M_j C_j (D/P + Max\{M_j, 1\} - 1)]}} . \qquad (16)$$

Furthermore, substituting (16) into (15), the minimum TRC as a function of $\underline{M}$ may be written as

$$TRC[Q_0^*, (\underline{M})] = \sqrt{[2Dr(S_0 + \sum_{j=1}^{m} S_j/M_j)\{C_0(1-D/P)}$$

$$+ \sum_{j=1}^{m} M_j C_j (D/P + Max\{M_j, 1\} - 1)\}]} . \qquad (17)$$

Our suggested heuristic algorithm for minimizing the total relevant cost function (15) proceeds as follows:

Step 1: Based on proposition 1, if $S_0 C_j / S_j C_0 > 2(P/D-1)$, for $j = 1, 2, ..., m$, calculate n_j using inequality (6), then set the corresponding M_j values to $1/n_j$. Similarly, based on proposition 2, if $S_0 C_j / (S_j C_0 - S_j C_j) < (1/2)(1-D/P)$, for $j = 1, 2, ..., m$, calculate the corresponding k_j values using (10) and set these $k_j = M_j$. For each of the input items that does not satisfy either of the above conditions, set the corresponding n_j, k_j and M_j to unity. The remaining n_j and k_j values are set to 0.

Step 2: Substitute the M_j values (for $j = 1, 2, ..., m$) determined in step 1 into (17), to obtain the current best TRC value, say TRC_0.

Step 3: This step describes our search procedure used:
  (a) for $j = 1, 2, ..., m$, increase each nonzero n_j by 1 independently and successively to compute a series of new TRC values after resetting the corresponding M_j to $1/n_j$.
  (b) repeat step 3(a), successively decreasing each of the n_j values by 1;
  (c) repeat steps 3(a) and 3(b) for the nonzero k_j values. resetting each time $M_j = k_j$ as appropriate.
  (Note that in steps 3(a) through 3(c), if any n_j (or k_j) is reduced from 1 to 0, the corresponding k_j (or n_j) is changed from 0 to 2 resetting the corresponding M_j accordingly.)

Step 4: If the smallest TRC found in step 3 is less than TRC_0, then TRC_0 is set equal to this value and we return to step 3; otherwise the search is terminated.

5. NUMERICAL EXAMPLE AND COMPUTATIONAL EXPERIENCE

In order to illustrate the heuristic algorithm described above, suppose that the following data are available for one of the products manufactured in a single stage production system:

$S_0 = \$500/setup$, $C_0 = \$100/unit$, $P = 6000$ units/year, $D = 2000$ units/year and $r = \$0.25/\$/year$.

Input Item, j :	1	2	3	4	5	6
S_j (\$/order) :	100	80	75	60	50	70
C_j (\$/unit) :	1	1	2	4	40	45

Using steps 1 and 2 of our algorithm, we obtain the following results:

j :	1	2	3	4	5	6
n_j :	–	–	–	1	1	1
k_j :	4	3	2	1	1	1

$TRC_0 = \$8972.52$, $Q_0 = 342.90$.

The application of steps 3 and 4 indicates the best improvement in TRC if n_5 is increased from 1 to 2, yielding

j :	1	2	3	4	5	6
n_j :	–	–	–	1	2	1
k_j :	4	3	2	1	–	1

$TRC_0 = \$8959.82$, $Q_0 = 365.71$.

Returning to steps 3 and 4, further reduction in TRC is achieved by decreasing k_1 from 4 to 3, leading to

j :	1	2	3	4	5	6
n_j :	–	–	–	1	2	1
k_j :	3	3	2	1	–	1

$TRC_0 = \$8959.21$, $Q_0 = 369.45$.

From this stage, another iteration does not result in any further improvement in TRC, hence, the algorithm terminates. In fact, we solved this problem by complete enumeration and verified that our solution is indeed optimal. Finally, using the n_j and k_j values obtained in the last iteration, the lot sizes for the respective input inventory items can be calculated without difficulty.

If the classical PLS model, ignoring the effects of WIP inventories, is employed in this example, the product's manufacturing batch size would be 346.41. The actual total cost resulting from this lot size, taking into account the WIP effects, would, of course, be dependent upon the order quantities of the input items. If these items are procured on a lot-for-lot basis, the actual total relevant cost would be $9627.32, representing a cost penalty of 7.5%. Thus, it may be desirable, from an optimization as well as practical standpoint, to incorporate the effects of WIP in making production batch sizing decisions.

In order to gain some insights into the efficiency and effectiveness of our heuristic solution procedure, we randomly generated a set

of 120 problems, varying the number of input items from 2 to 8. We
We solved each of these problems using our heuristic, as well as by
complete enumeration for obtaining the optimum. In the case of 113 of
these problems, the solutions yielded by the heuristic technique were
optimal. For the remaining 12 problems, the resulting cost penalties
were less than 1% in all cases. In addition, the CPU time required by
our algorithm was between 2% to 5% of that required for complete enumeration. In view of these observations it appears that the suggested
heuristic is relatively fast and effective in finding at least near-
optimal solutions.

6. SUMMARY AND CONCLUSIONS

In this paper we have analyzed the effects of WIP inventories on
lot sizing decisions in single stage systems under deterministic conditions. Initially we developed optimal lot sizing models for the single input case, relaxing some of restrictive assumptions made in earlier work in this area. Then we formulated a nonlinear, mixed integer,
constrained optimization model for the more general multiple inputs
situation.

Although optimum seeking techniques, such as branch and bound,
may be employed for solving this problem, we suspect that such
approaches may not be very efficient, particularly for relatively
large problems. For this reason, we suggest a heuristic algorithm involving a simple search procedure. Our algorithm is illustrated
through a numerical example and we show that the solution thus obtained is superior to the one resulting from the application of the
classical PLS model. One advantage of our approach is that, considering the WIP effects, we are able to simultaneously derive the production and purchase lot sizes, respectively, for an end item and the input items necessary to manufacture it. Furthermore, our computational
experience, although limited, indicates that the suggested heuristic
is quite fast and leads to optimal or near-optimal solutions.

For future directions of research in this area, we suggest extension of our analyses to more complex multistage systems, relaxing the
integer requirements on the n_j values. No doubt, such extensions may
prove to be difficult to analyze. Nevertheless, it is hoped that the
insights obtained from our work will be able to facilitate future research in this important field.

REFERENCES

1. Banerjee, A. and Burton, J.S., "Single and Multistage Production Lot Sizing with Work-In-Process Inventory Considerations", paper presented at the 5th International Symposium on Inventories, Budapest, Hungary, August, 1988.

2. Biggs, J. R., Goodman, S. H. and Hardy, S. T., "Lot Sizing Rules in a Hierarchical Multi-Stage Inventory System", Production and Inventory Management, First Quarter (1977), pp. 104 - 115.

3. Billington, P. J., McClain, J. O. and Thomas, L. J., "Heuristics for Multi-Level Lot-Sizing with a Bottleneck", Management Science, Vol. 32, No. 8 (1986), pp. 989 - 1006.

4. Crownston, W. B., Wagner, M. H. and Williams, J. F., "Economic Lot Size Determination in Multi-Stage Assembly Systems", Management Science, Vol. 19, No. 5 (1973), pp. 517 - 526.

5. De Bodt, M. A., Gelders, L. F. and Van Wassenhove, L. N., "Lot Sizing Under Dynamic Demand Conditions: A Review", Engineering Costs and Production Economics, Vol. 8, No. 3 (1984), pp. 165 - 187.

6. Graves, S. C. "Multi-Stage Lot Sizing: an Iterative Procedure", in Schwarz, L. B. (ed.), Multi-Level Production/Inventory Control Systems: Theory and Practice, New York: North Holland, 1981, pp.95-109.

7. Harris, F., Operations and Costs, Chicago: A. W. Shaw, 1915.

8. Lambrecht, M. R., Vander Eecken, J. and Vanderveken, H., "Review of Optimal and Heuristics Methods for a Class of Facilities in Series Dynamic Lot-Sizing Problems", in Schwarz, L. B. (ed.), Multi-Level Production/Inventory Control Systems: Theory and Practice, New York: North Holland, 1981, pp. 69 - 94.

9. Moily, J. P., "Optimal and Heuristic Procedures for Component Lot-Splitting in Multi-Stage Manufacturing Systems", Management Science, Vol. 32, No. 1 (1986), pp. 113 - 125.

10. Rosenblatt, H. M. and Lee, H. L., "Improving Profitability with Quantity Discounts Under Fixed Demand", IIE Transactions, Vol. 17, No. 4 (1985), pp. 388 - 395.

11. Steinberg, E. and Napier, H. A., "Optimal Multi-Level Lot Sizing for Requirements Planning Systems", Management Science, Vol. 26, No. 12 (1980), pp. 1258 - 1271.

12. Tinarelli, G. U., "Inventory Control: Models and Problems", European Journal of Operational Research, Vol. 14 (1983), pp. 1 - 12.

OPTIMAL STRATEGIES FOR INVESTMENT IN SETUP COST REDUCTIONS IN A JUST-IN-TIME ENVIRONMENT

Dr. David F. Rogers
Department of Quantitative Analysis and Information Systems
College of Business Administration
University of Cincinnati
531 Carl H. Lindner Hall
Cincinnati, Ohio 45221-0130

ABSTRACT

Setup cost reductions in a Just-In-Time environment typically allow for reduced inventories, increased capacity, and greater flexibility because of the resulting reduced lot sizes. This study is a detailed analysis of investing in a one-time cost to reduce the setup cost (and time) in the classical (Wilson) economic order quantity lot-size model. A present value approach is employed and the number of periods required to recoup the initial investment is derived.

1. Introduction and Literature Review

Just-In-Time (JIT) production systems have been the focus of much recent attention in the manufacturing management literature (see Hall [1983] and Schonberger [1982]). A major conceptual element of these production systems involves investment to reduce the cost (and time) involved in each manufacturing setup with the goal of reducing lot sizes and inventories. This paper is a further probe of the tradeoff between the cost of the initial investment to reduce the setup cost in the classical (Wilson) Economic Order Quantity (EOQ) model and the savings associated with reduced setup costs within the EOQ model.

1.1 Financial Decision Making for Ordering Policies

Ordering policies are partially responsible for the large inventories that constituted 18% of all assets of U.S. manufacturing firms in 1985 (Hill and Sartoris [1988]). Several authors have considered various aspects of optimal economic and financial decision making as related to ordering policies. A seminal paper by Hadley [1964] compares the average annual cost with the discounted cost over all future time periods of procuring units and holding inventory. He notes that only a negligible difference exists between the average annual cost and the discounted cost criteria for most inventory problems that might reasonably be encountered but adds that significant differences may be obtained in extreme cases.

Beranek [1967] considered the financial implications of lot-size inventory models. He notes several examples for which different repayment arrangements give rise to different order quantities because the carrying costs are not proportional to the true average inventory. Haley and Higgins [1973] considered inventory policy and trade credit financing and showed that, in general, optimality requires simultaneously determining order quantities and payment time decisions. Trippi and Lewin [1974] were among the first to consider the present value of discounted costs over an infinite horizon within the classical EOQ framework. They concluded that their approach that explicitly considers the time value of money is much more robust to errors than the classical, average cost per unit time model. Thompson [1975] derived similar results as those of Trippi and Lewin [1974]. He also considered deterioration, obsolescence, personal property taxes, insurance costs, and storage costs by formulating the inventory problem as a capital budgeting problem. Gurnani [1983] considered an economic analysis for several different inventory systems and concluded that higher interest rates and longer planning horizons may contribute to a larger discount rate that may bring about significant changes in order quantities. However, several derivational errors that exist in this paper as well several faulty arguments were uncovered by Kim and Chung [1985].

Rummel [1985] examined physical flows and cash flows to make inventory decisions in a present value framework. Kim, et al. [1986] provided both empirical and theoretical results for determining order quantities by using a net present value approach versus the classical EOQ model and note significant differences. Thorstenson [1988] provides a thorough survey of this area forming a bridge between inventory theory and the theory of finance.

1.2 Setup Cost Reduction Strategies for Just-In-Time Production

Likewise, several authors have been concerned with setup cost reductions in order to facilitate a JIT objective of zero inventory. In fact, this philosophical approach to production was practiced by Kiichiro Toyoda (now Toyota) of Japan as early as 1938 when its first large-scale automobile plant was built. The institution of JIT production "with delivery of the right part, at the right time, in the right amount" made storage facilities unnecessary (Toyota Motor Manufacturing, U.S.A., Inc. [1988]). JIT remains the foundation of the Toyota process because it enhances efficiency and enables quick response to change. Raia [1986] noted that reductions in setup times from three days to four hours on some operations lead to a decrease of work-in-process inventory of as much as 70% at Harley-Davidson. General Motors and Toyota have also witnessed similar phenomena in their production facilities.

The focus of this paper is upon the financial implications of reducing the setup cost within the classical EOQ lot size model. Extensions to the classical EOQ lot size model to accommodate a JIT approach have been previously considered. Porteus [1985] examined optimization of a modified EOQ total cost function that includes a one-time investment of reducing the setup cost. Amortization is considered for the investment to reduce the setup cost but not for the remaining cost per unit time. Porteus [1986b] considered the discounted present value criterion for setup, purchase (production), and holding costs amortized as well as the one-time investment to reduce the setup cost. He derived results for the case when the one-time investment to reduce setup costs is a logarithmic function.

The remainder of this paper involves a present value approach to considering the reduction of the setup cost in the EOQ model and proceeds as follows. Section 2 contains a basic optimization problem for reducing setup costs and several different forms of this model are considered. In Section 3 another optimization problem will be considered for which a criterion of minimization of the present value of an annuity rather than the average cost per unit time is employed. This model allows for an additional analysis that yields the payback period, the time necessary to recoup the one-time investment cost to reduce setup costs. Section 4 is a summary and discussion of avenues for future research.

2. A Basic Optimization Model for Setup Reduction

In this section the classical EOQ lot-size model is extended to minimize the annual amortized investment cost of changing (lowering) the setup cost plus the annual average inventory related costs by optimizing over both the order quantity and the setup cost as Porteus [1985] suggests. The classical (Wilson) EOQ lot-size model (Hadley and Whitin [1963]) is derived from the following total annual cost function that includes holding, setup, and purchasing (or production) costs:

$$TC(Q) = hQ/2 + KD/Q + bD \quad , \tag{1}$$

where h = the marginal holding (carrying) cost rate,
$\quad Q$ = the manufacturing (or purchasing) lot size,
$\quad K$ = the cost of a machine (or order) setup,

D = the average annual demand rate, assumed deterministic and known,

b = the per unit production (or purchasing) cost, and

TC(Q) = the total cost of ordering Q units.

The first order condition for a minimum point for TC(Q) is

$$\partial TC(Q)/\partial Q = h/2 - KDQ^{-2} = 0 \quad , \tag{2}$$

and solving for Q yields the optimal order quantity

$$Q^* = (2KD/h)^{1/2} . \tag{3}$$

Note that $\partial^2 TC(Q)/\partial Q^2 > 0$ and thus Q^* is a global minimum of a convex function.

Now consider investing resources to reduce the setup cost per setup. Let C(K) be the investment cost function for this reduction. The firm's cost of capital, i, is assumed given and thus iC(K) is the annual amortized cost of investing in $K setup. The total annual amortized investment cost as a function of K, TC(K), is derived by substituting (3) into (1) and adding iC(K):

$$TC(K) = \frac{h(2KD/h)^{1/2}}{2} + \frac{KD}{(2KD/h)^{1/2}} + bD + iC(K) \tag{4}$$

$$TC(K) = (KDh/2)^{1/2} + (KDh/2)^{1/2} + bD + iC(K) \tag{5}$$

$$TC(K) = (2KDh)^{1/2} + bD + iC(K) . \tag{6}$$

We desire to find the optimal value of K, say K^*, to minimize TC(K). A matter of concern is the form of TC(K) and this is dependent upon C(K). The cases of C(K) being linear, concave, and convex will be considered.

2.1 Linear and Concave Investment Cost Functions

Suppose the investment cost function, C(K), is linear in K over a fixed, specified interval from K=0 to the current value of K, denoted K' (and thus iC(K) is also linear), C(K')=0. Let $A = (2KDh)^{1/2}$ and note that

$$\partial A/\partial K = Dh/(2KDh)^{1/2} > 0 \quad , \text{ and} \tag{7}$$

$$\partial^2 A/\partial K^2 = -(Dh)^2/(2KDh)^{3/2} < 0 . \tag{8}$$

Thus A is monotonically increasing at a decreasing rate and is a concave function over [0,∞).

Since iC(K) is linear over the interval [0,K'], and thus concave, TC(K) will likewise be concave over the interval [0,K'], since the summation of two concave functions yields a concave function as illustrated in Figure 1 below. Note that TC(K) is not concave over the interval $[0,\infty)$. Values beyond K' (increases in the setup costs) are assumed uninteresting.

To minimize TC(K) in general requires comparing TC(K=0) with TC(K=K'), since TC(K) over the interval [0,K'] is concave and the minimum of a concave function lies at one of its extreme points. The following three cases may arise:

Case #1: TC(K=0) < TC(K=K')

The optimal policy is to reduce the setup cost to zero and incur iC(0). Of course, a setup cost of zero may be unrealistic in many cases. However, some setup times have been drastically reduced from several hours to only a very few minutes. For these cases, a comparison of the smallest feasible K and K' would be needed.

Case #2: TC(K=0) > TC(K=K')

The best policy is to not make an investment (iC(K') = 0) and no change in K is necessary.

Case #3: TC(K=0) = TC(K=K')

According to the model, reducing K to zero and incurring iC(0) or leaving K=K' are both optimal. Additional system performance information such as the effects upon product quality would be needed to determine which of these options to pursue.

Note that the less realistic case of C(K) being concave over [0,K'] yields identical results as for the linear case.

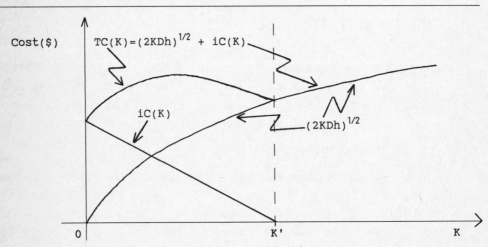

Figure 1: TC(K) and its Components Over K for Linear iC(K)

2.2 Convex Investment Cost Functions

A possibly more realistic form for the investment cost function would be convex as pictured in Figure 2. A convex C(K) is often intuitively more appealing because the marginal cost to reduce K might naturally increase as K approaches zero. The assumption is made that it is infinitely expensive to reduce K to zero and thus iC(K) is asymptotic to the cost axis. Furthermore assume that C(K') = 0 for K' the current setup cost.

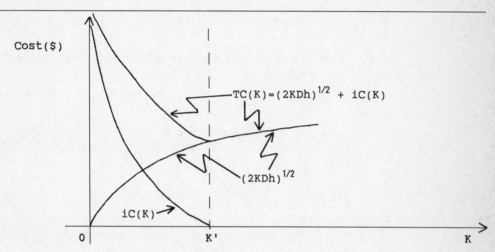

Figure 2: TC(K) and its Components Over K for Convex iC(K)

Analyzing the case for a convex C(K) is more difficult because TC(K) now consists of the sum of a convex and a concave function. Less in general can be claimed about the convexity/concavity of TC(K) without knowing the specific form of C(K). For C(K) known and convex, consider the following cases over the interval [0,K']:

Case #1: $\left| \dfrac{\partial^2 iC(K)}{\partial K^2} \right| > \left| \dfrac{\partial^2 (2KDh)^{1/2}}{\partial K^2} \right|$, for all $K \varepsilon [0,K']$.

The convex function iC(K) dominates the concave function $(2KDh)^{1/2}$ and TC(K) will be convex over the entire interval [0,K']. The optimal value of K, say K^*, will be $K^*=K'$. Figure 2 depicts this case.

Case #2: $\left| \dfrac{\partial^2 iC(K)}{\partial K^2} \right| < \left| \dfrac{\partial^2 (2KDh)^{1/2}}{\partial K^2} \right|$, for all $K \varepsilon [0,K']$.

This case is impossible under the assumption that C(K) is asymptotic to the vertical axis. The function iC(K) will always dominate near K=0 yielding at least a small region of convexity.

Case #3:
$$\left| \frac{\partial^2 iC(K)}{\partial K^2} \right| > \left| \frac{\partial^2 (2KDh)^{1/2}}{\partial K^2} \right| \quad , \quad \text{for } K\epsilon[0,K\text{''}), \ 0 < K\text{''} < K',$$

and

$$\left| \frac{\partial^2 iC(K)}{\partial K^2} \right| < \left| \frac{\partial^2 (2KDh)^{1/2}}{\partial K^2} \right| \quad , \quad \text{for all } K\epsilon(K\text{''},K'] \ .$$

The convex function iC(K) dominates the concave function $(2KDh)^{1/2}$ over [0,K'') yielding a region of convexity but $(2KDh)^{1/2}$ dominates iC(K) over (K'',K'] yielding a region of concavity. However, the optimal K, K^*, will lie in the convex region because the concave function over the interval [0,K'] is always increasing. To find K^*, solve for K in the following first-order condition:

$$\partial TC(K)/\partial K = (Dh/2K)^{1/2} + iC'(K) = 0 \ . \tag{9}$$

To summarize these three cases, if a critical point, K^*, exists on the interval [0,K'] for TC(K), then reduce K to K^* and incur $C(K^*)$. Adjust Q^* to be

$$Q^* = (2K^*D/h)^{1/2} \ . \tag{10}$$

If there are no critical points over [0,K'] then do not change the current K=K'.

Consider the following example with h=2, D=5, K'=16, $C(K)=10K^{-1/2}-2.5$, i=.1, b=50, and thus $TC(K)=(2KDh)^{1/2} + bD + i(10K^{-1/2}-2.5)$ and the initial $Q^*=8.94$ from (3). The first-order condition is

$$\partial TC(K)/\partial K = (Dh/2K)^{1/2} - 5iK^{-3/2} = 0 \ , \tag{11}$$

and solving for K^* yields

$$K^* = i(50/Dh)^{1/2} = .2236 \ . \tag{12}$$

Since $0 < K^* < K'$, reduce K to K^*, adjust Q^* to $Q^*=1.06$, and incur $C(K^*)=18.65$ and $TC(K^*)=253.98$. With a specific form for C(K) given, it is now possible to consider the sensitivity of K^*. The value of K^* will increase with increases of i and will decrease with increases in D and/or h. For example, if i increases to .11, the optimal setup cost increases to $K^*=.246$. Suppose h=3 and the original i=.1 is employed: $K^*.1825$. A complete sensitivity analysis of K^* with respect to i, D, and h (supported graphically) would be of paramount importance for any actual case studies.

Finally, the "well-behaved" linear, concave, and convex functions previously considered for C(K) may not be applicable for many actual situations. "Ill-behaved" functions with $j=1,\ldots,m$ discontinuity points, denoted K_j, and any mixture of different regions of linearity, concavity, and convexity might actually arise as portrayed in the example in Figure 3. One possible approach is to approximate the "ill-behaved" C(K) with a "well-behaved" function and proceed with the appropriate previous analyses. Another approach is to consider each of the $j=1,\ldots,m$ discontinuity points, $TC(K_j)$, and any critical points of TC(K) between any two K_j and choose the K^* from these points that minimizes TC(K).

Both "well-behaved" and "ill-behaved" C(K) may be rationalized in different situations. A "well-behaved" C(K) function (or a "well-behaved" portion of an "ill-behaved" C(K)) may arise from adding more simultaneous worker minutes to the setup task. The discontinuities of the "ill-behaved" case may be exemplified by the necessity of purchasing additional equipment to continue reducing K.

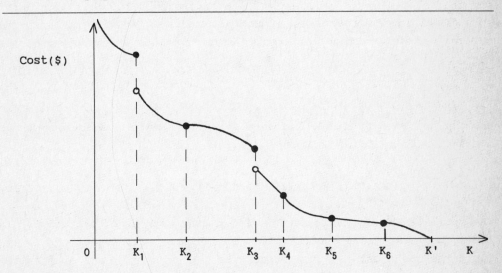

__Figure 3:__ C(K) Depicted with Several Discontinuity Points and Different Regions of Linearity, Concavity, and Convexity

3. A Present Value Optimization Model

An optimization model for reducing setup costs (and time) within the classical EOQ framework with the criterion of minimization of the present value of a future annuity is presented in this section. Following the convention of Section 2, the optimization problem is restated with respect to K as in (4)-(6) and the one-time investment required to reduce K, C(K), is added. The assumption of periodic compounding is made. The formula for calculating the present value of a future annuity (or a series of equal payments that occur at equally spaced intervals for a predetermined period of time) is given as (Bierman and Smidt [1988]):

$$A_{n|} = \frac{1-(1+i)^{-n}}{i} ,\tag{13}$$

where $A_{n|}$ is a symbol representing the present value of a dollar per period, for n periods, discounted at the firm's cost of capital, i.

The basic formulation for the present value of an annuity (PV_A) is to minimize

$$PV_A(TC(Q)) = \left[\frac{1-(1+i)^{-n}}{i}\right] [hQ/2 + KD/Q + bD] .\tag{14}$$

Further analysis of this model for an infinite horizon are compared to the average cost model to determine the number of time periods necessary for the investment in reducing K to be recovered. The multiplier of i for C(K) employed in Section 2 is omitted because C(K) is a cost incurred at time zero and is thus in terms of present value. From (6) we obtain

$$PV_A(TC(K)) = \left[\frac{1-(1+i)^{-n}}{i}\right][(2KDh)^{1/2} + bD] + C(K) ,\tag{15}$$

and for a given n, i, D, and h the optimal K^* is sought by methods similar to those found in Section 2.

It is of special interest to examine (15) as $n\to\infty$:

$$\lim_{n\to\infty} PV_A(TC(K)) = (1/i) [(2KDh)^{1/2} + bD] + C(K) .\tag{16}$$

The optimal $K=K^*$ may be found for (16) by the methods of Section 2. In fact, the first-order condition of (6) and (16) with respect to K will yield the identical K^*. Now substitute $K=K^*$ into (15) and examine the following relation:

$$\left[\frac{1-(1+i)^{-n}}{i}\right][(2K^*Dh)^{1/2}+bD]+C(K^*) = \left[\frac{1-(1+i)^{-n}}{i}\right][(2K'Dh)^{1/2}+bD].\tag{17}$$

Solving (17) for n yields n^*, the break-even point for the number of periods it will take the investment in reducing setup costs, $C(K^*)$, to payoff. Solving (17) for n produces:

$$n^* = \frac{\ln(\Delta S) - \ln[\Delta S - iC(K)]}{\ln(i+i)} \qquad (18)$$

where $\Delta S = (2K'Dh)^{1/2} - (2K^*Dh)^{1/2}$ is the recurring change in the total cost due to a reduced setup cost.

By incorporating (13) we now have a further criteria by which decisions can be made. If n^* is very large, management may forego investing in $C(K^*)$ in anticipation of a drastic change in one of the parameters, e.g., a forecasted decrease in D.

Continuing with the example from Section 2, recall that h=2, D=5, K'=16, $C(K)=10K^{-1/2} - 2.5$, i=.1, b=50, and $TC(K)=(2KDh)^{1/2} + bD + i(10K^{-1/2}-2.5)$. Previous results revealed $Q^*=8.94$, $K^*=.2236$, $C(K^*)=18.65$, and $TC(K^*)=253.98$. Solving (18) with this information yields $n^*=1.32$ periods. Therefore, if the life of the demand for the product under consideration is greater than 1.32 time periods (usually years), then the investment should be made to reduce K. The value of n^* for this example will decrease with increases in h and/or D, e.g., if h=3 then $n^*=1.065$. In general, the effects of a change in i upon n^* are indeterminable because it appears in both the numerator and the denominator of (18). If i increases to .11, then n^* increases to 1.43 time periods. Thorough sensitivity analyses for changes in n^* given changes in i, D, and h would also be a very important feature of a thorough real-world study.

4.   Summary and Future Research Directions

The major tenets of JIT will eventually manifest changes in virtually every traditional facet of production and service organizations. In this paper the effects of a one-time investment to reduce the setup cost in the classical (Wilson) EOQ lot-size model have been thoroughly analyzed. Previous approaches to this problem have been extended by employing present value analyses to determine the number of periods required to recover the initial investment.

Directions for future research are abundant. The present value approach taken here is but one of several possible ways of incorporating the time value of money. Continuous compounding, finite horizons, and entirely different present value formulations are only a few of the different approaches that may be employed. Criteria other than the minimization of present values may be considered such as the return on investment criterion considered by Schroeder and Krishnan [1976]. The effects upon the present value analysis of the total cost as a function of K for various values of the production cost, b, would be an interesting study.

Keller and Noori [1988] extended the work of Porteus [1985] to include probabilistic demand during lead time for the lot-size reorder point, (Q,r), model. Results are derived with demand during lead time assumed to be distributed either uniformly or exponentially for the cases of logarithmic cost functions and power cost functions. Raturi and Singhal [1988] also consider setup reductions in the (Q,r) model under the objective of maximizing the value of the firm using the capital asset pricing model (CAPM). Their results indicate that setup cost reductions lead to increasingly less accurate policies unless present value analyses are employed. Zangwill [1987a, 1987b, and 1988] and Gerchak [1988] have considered setup reduction in a dynamic lot-sizing model under the assumption of nonstationarity of both product demands and costs from period to period. Indeed, many combinations of problem settings and assumptions should be reinvestigated to consider setup cost reductions.

Setup reduction has been shown to increase the effective machine capacity (Spence and Porteus [1987]). Production systems have been shown to benefit from lower setup costs by improved quality control (Porteus [1986a, 1988]). These initial prototype studies should provide an impetus to integrate setup reduction analyses into virtually every aspect of manufacturing.

Empirical data should be collected for future studies to determine the actual form of the investment cost function. The effect upon lot-sizes of reducing setup costs should be of particular concern. Since these investment cost functions are usually estimates of hypothetical cost functions, it would be interesting to examine the robustness of the solution with errors in the estimates.

Finally, note that setup cost reduction is a critical element of JIT but the entire benefits of a JIT system will not be realized without the integration of the other JIT elements, e.g., pull scheduling, level loading, preventive maintenance, etc. Future mathematical analyses should be performed with consideration of all of the JIT philosophies.

REFERENCES

Beranek, William, "Financial Implications of Lot-Size Inventory Models", Management Science, Vol. 13, No. 8, pp. B401-B408, April, 1967.

Bierman, Harold Jr. and Smidt, Seymour, The Capital Budgeting Decision: Economic Analysis and Financing of Investment Projects, Seventh Edition, The Macmillan Company, New York, New York, 1988.

Gerchak, Yigal, "Can a Reduction in Set Up Costs Indeed Increase Total Costs?", Management Science, Vol. 34, No. 10, pp. 1271-1272, October, 1988.

Gurnani, Chandan, "Economic Analysis of Inventory Systems", International Journal of Production Research, Vol. 21, No. 2, pp. 261-277, 1983.

Hadley, G. and Whitin, T.M., Analysis of Inventory Systems, Prentice-Hall, Inc., Englewood Cliffs, New Jersey, 1963.

Hadley, G., "A Comparison of Order Quantities Computed Using the Average Annual Cost and the Discounted Cost", Management Science, Vol. 10, No. 3, pp. 472-476, April, 1964.

Haley, C.W. and Higgins, R.C., "Inventory Policy and Trade Credit Financing", Management Science, Vol. 20, No. 4, Part I, pp. 464-471, December, 1973.

Hall, Robert W., Zero Inventories, Dow-Jones Irwin, Homewood, Illinois, 1983.

Hill, Ned C. and Sartoris, William L., Short-Term Financial Management, Macmillan Publishing Company, New York, New York, 1988.

Keller, Gerald and Noori, Hamid, "Justifying New Technology Acquisition Through its Impact on the Cost of Running an Inventory Policy", IIE Transactions, Vol. 20, No. 3, pp. 284-291, September, 1988.

Kim, Yong H. and Chung, Kee H., "Economic Analysis of Inventory Systems: A Clarifying Analysis", International Journal of Production Research, Vol. 23, No. 4, pp. 761-767, 1985.

Kim, Yong H., Philippatos, George C., and Chung, Kee H., "Evaluating Investment in Inventory Policy: A Net Present Value Framework", The Engineering Economist, Vol. 31, No. 2, pp. 119-136, Winter, 1986.

Porteus, Evan L., "Investing in Reduced Setups in the EOQ Model", Management Science, Vol. 31, No. 8, pp. 998-1010, August, 1985.

Porteus, Evan L., "Optimal Lot Sizing, Process Quality Improvement and Setup Cost Reduction", Operations Research, Vol. 34, No. 1, pp. 137-144, January-February, 1986a.

Porteus, Evan L., "Investing in New Parameter Values in the Discounted EOQ Model", Naval Research Logistics Quarterly, Vol. 33, pp. 39-48, 1986b.

Porteus, Evan L., "Optimal Inspection, Lot Sizing and Setup Reduction", Research Paper No. 912, Graduate School of Business, Stanford University, Palo Alto, California, July, 1988.

Raia, Ernest, "Just-in-Time USA", Purchasing, pp. 48-62, February 13, 1986.

Raturi, Amitabh S. and Singhal, Vinod R., "The Effect of Risk on Cycle and Safety Stocks", Working Paper OM-1988-002, Department of Quantitative Analysis and Information Systems, College of Business Administration, University of Cincinnati, Cincinnati, Ohio, July, 1988.

Rummel, Jeffrey L., "Cash Flow Analysis for Inventory Decisions", Working Paper Series No. QM85, Graduate School of Management, University of Rochester, Rochester, New York, June, 1985.

Schroeder, Roger G. and Krishnan, Ramakrishnan, "Return on Investment as a Criterion for Inventory Models", Decision Sciences, Vol. 7, No. 4, pp. 697-704, October, 1976.

Schonberger, Richard J., Japanese Manufacturing Techniques, Free Press, New York, New York, 1982.

Spence, Anne M. and Porteus, Evan L., "Setup Reduction and Increased Effective Capacity", Management Science, Vol. 33, No. 10, pp. 1291-1301, October, 1987.

Thompson, Howard E., "Inventory Management and Capital Budgeting: A Pedagogical Note", Decision Sciences, Vol. 6, No. 2, pp. 383-398, April, 1975.

Thorstenson, Anders, Capital Costs in Inventory Models - A Discounted Cash Flow Approach, PROFIL Series No. 8, Production-Economic Research in Linkoping, Linkoping Institute of Technology, Linkoping, Sweden, 1988.

Toyota Motor Manufacturing, U.S.A., Inc., "Fact Sheet: Toyota Motor Corporation History", Georgetown, Kentucky, 1988.

Trippi, Robert R. and Lewin, Donald E., "A Present Value Formulation of the Classical EOQ Problem", Decision Sciences, Vol. 5, No. 1, pp. 30-35, January, 1974.

Zangwill, Willard I., "Eliminating Inventory in a Series Facility Production System", Management Science, Vol. 33, No. 9, pp. 1150-1164, September, 1987a.

Zangwill, Willard I., "From EOQ Towards ZI", Management Science, Vol. 33, No. 10, pp. 1209-1223, October, 1987b.

Zangwill, Willard I,, "Rejoinder to the Note by Yigal Gerchak", Management Science, Vol. 34, No. 10, pp. 1272-1273, October, 1988.

PROCESS CONTROL WITH LOT SIZING

Michael H. Peters
Quantitative Business Analysis Department
Louisiana State University
Baton Rouge, LA 70803

Introduction

One of the widely used statistical approaches to maintaining control of a process is the control chart. To use this tool, the designer must determine three parameters: the sample size to be taken from the output of the process, the control limits on the chart, and the number of units to be produced between samplings (the intersample interval). The general procedure is administered as follows: near the end of the intersample interval a number of units are taken from the output of the process; the sampled units are inspected; if the resulting information does not fit within the prescribed control limits, the process is stopped and investigated for the presence of an assignable source that may be altering the output of the process. There are two basic versions of single sample control charts used for process control: variables charts ($\bar{x}$-chart and Cusum chart) and attributes charts (p-chart, np-chart and c-chart).

A significant amount of research has been performed on the economic design of sampling plans for process control (see Montgomery 1980 for survey). In most of these works, it is assumed that the product volume passing through the process is infinite, or at least very large. There are many production situations when the volume produced of a product can not be considered infinite, i.e., the process performs operations on different products with various lot sizes. Indeed, these lot sizes are frequently small.

When the volume is assumed to be infinite (very large), the sampling plan is not considered a function of the lot size, but the optimal sample size and control limits are a function of lot size (Hald 1960). Thus, there is a lot size for a given product on a particular process below which the process control procedure described above is not economically justified. This quantity will be referred to as the threshold. For lot quantities smaller than this threshold, the expected costs incurred under the near-optimal sampling scheme (taking and inspecting the sampled units, investigating and correcting the process, and defective units exiting the process) are greater than the expected cost with no sampling (defective units exiting the process). The objective of this study is to investigate the behavior of this threshold relative to changes in various quality-related costs and process parameters for the production situation. The results should be of interest to designers and users of statistical process control systems particularly in production environments where small lot sizes are a goal, such as just-in-time (JIT) and zero inventory (ZI).

Several researchers have investigated the relationship between sampling plans and lot sizes. Krupp (1985), Chung (1987), and Baker (1987) examined sampling plans in a ZI environment. Their works focus on the acceptance sampling mode of quality control rather than process control, i.e., the sampling procedure provides information about the quality of the process output after production of the lot is completed, but does not provide information about the state of the process during the production of the lot. Sampling plans are based on MIL standards tables, or variations thereof, rather than economics. Porteus (1986), Rosenblatt and Lee (1986), and Lee and Rosenblatt (1987) have investigated the effect of process quality on lot size using economic-based models. In their models, the process is assumed to be reset to the in-control state only at the beginning (or end) of a production run (lot size), and there is no sampling of process output during the production run. The focus is on determining the optimal lot size or the optimal machine inspection schedule.

To perform this investigation, a cost-based model was developed and is described in the next section. In Section 3, the procedure used for determining the threshold for a set of system costs and parameters is presented. The results of this study are given in Section 4 followed by concluding remarks.

2. Model Development

In this section, a model that approximates the expected cost per unit time is developed. It is similar to the model presented by Montgomery, Heikes and Mance (1975). Using this model and the objective of minimizing the expected cost per unit time, a near-optimal sampling plan can be computed for a particular set of system costs and parameters, and specified lot size. This, in turn, is used to determine the volume at which the cost per unit time under the near optimal plan is approximately equal to the cost per unit time under no sampling, i.e., the threshold.

Assume that a process performs operations on a variety of products with various lot sizes. When the process is set up to produce a quantity of a particular item, it is assumed that it is in control. The proportion of defective units produced is p_0 when the process is in this in-control state. The process can be placed in an out-of-control state by any one of s possible assignable sources of variation from the in-control state. These sources are assumed to be associated with the process itself and its environment. When the process is in one of the out-of-control states evoked by an assignable source, the proportion defective produced by the process is p_i where $p_i > p_{i-1}$ for $i = 1,2,\ldots,s$. It is assumed that the time that the process remains in the in-control state is an exponentially distributed variable with a mean λ^{-1}. Once the process is disturbed by an assignable source during an intersample interval, it is assumed the process is free from further occurrence of additional assignable sources during that interval, i.e., there is a maximum of one process shift during an intersample interval. The process is not self-correcting, so it stays out of control until detected.

The control procedure assumed in this study employs an np-chart to assess the state of the process during the production of a lot. The intersample interval is k units and the sample size is n units. This means that after (k-n) units have been produced, the next n units are taken as a sample. Thus, the last n units processed prior to the end of the intersample interval will be inspected and should provide the most current information about the state of the process. If the number of nonconforming units in the sample is less than or equal to the upper control limit, c, the process is allowed to continue uninterrupted. The lower control limit is considered to be zero. If the number of nonconforming units exceeds c, the process is considered to be out of control. The process is stopped, investigated and, if necessary, corrected back to the in-control state. If the process is in state i, the expected cost of investigation and correction is A_i and the expected time required to conduct the investigation and correction steps is t_i. It is assumed the investigation and correction steps are error free. This sampling procedure is repeated until production of the lot is completed.

The number of samples taken over the production of a lot quantity of Q units, f, is one minus the smallest integer that is greater than or equal to Q/k. The number of units produced after the last sample is denoted by r and is equal to Q-fk.

When the sampling plan (n,c and k) is used to control the quality of the process, the expected quality control related costs incurred during the production of Q units are

$$(c_f + c_v n)f \qquad \text{(sampling costs)}$$

$$+ \sum_{t=1}^{f} \sum_{j=0}^{s} A_j q_j \alpha_j^t \qquad \text{(expected investigation and correction costs)}$$

$$+ c_d \left(k \sum_{t=1}^{f} \sum_{j=0}^{s} p_j \gamma_j^t + r \sum_{j=0}^{s} p_j \gamma_j^{f+1} \right) \qquad \text{(expected cost of nonconforming units exiting the system) (1)}$$

where

c_f = fixed cost of taking a sample,

c_v = variable cost of sampling,

c_d = expected cost of a nonconforming unit exiting the system,

q_j = probability that the sampling procedure outlined aboveindicates the process is out of control when the process is in state j,

α_j^t = probability that the process is in state j at the time the sampling procedure is applied after t intersample intervals have elapsed,

γ_j^t = probability that the process is in state j at any time during the tth intersample interval,

γ_j^{f+1} = probability that the process is in state j at any time after the last sample.

The expected time to produce the lot is

$$ET = Q/R \qquad \text{(production time)}$$

$$+ \ fnv \qquad \text{(sampling time)}$$

$$+ \ \sum_{t=1}^{f} \ \sum_{j=0}^{s} t_j q_j \alpha_j^t \qquad \text{(expected investigation and correction time)} \qquad (2)$$

where

R = production rate,

v = sampling time per unit.

The expected net profit per unit time can be approximated by Equation 1/Equation 2. In general, the objective is to find the sampling plan that minimizes the expected cost per unit time given a lot size.

If there is no sampling during the production of the lot, the first and second terms of equation (1) become zero and the quality-related cost is

$$c_d \ Q \ \sum_{j=0}^{s} p_j \gamma_j^1 . \qquad \text{(expected cost of nonconforming units exiting the system)} \qquad (3)$$

The development of the vector $\hat{\gamma}^t$ is presented later in this paper. In this case an intersample interval of Q is used to compute the elements of $\hat{\gamma}^1$ since no samples are taken during production of the lot. The time to produce Q units is Q/R, therefore the expected net cost per unit time is approximated by

$$\frac{c_d \ Q \ \sum\limits_{j=0}^{s} p_j \gamma_j^l}{Q/R}.$$

(4)

If the expected cost per unit time under no sampling (Equation 4) is less than the expected cost per unit time under minimum cost sampling, sampling during the production of the lot is not economically warranted. The maximum volume where this condition occurs is considered the threshold.

2.1 Development of Vectors $\hat{q}$, $\hat{\alpha}^t$ and $\hat{\gamma}^t$

To develop the vectors $\hat{q}$, $\hat{\alpha}^t$ and $\hat{\gamma}^t$, it is necessary to introduce some additional notation and assumptions.

Let P_{ij} be the probability that the process shifts directly from state i to state j during the production of k units. The assumption is made that the sample size is small compared to the intersample interval, thus the probability of a shift during the production of sampled units is negligible. The probability of the process remaining in control during the production of k units is

$$P_{00} = 1 - \int_0^{k/R} \lambda e^{-\lambda t} dt = e^{-\lambda k/R}.$$

(5)

The probability of shifting to an out-of-control state is $1 - e^{-\lambda k/R}$. Although there are different ways of distributing this probability among the s out-of-control states, the method presented by Knappenberger and Grandage (1969) is used here. The transition probabilities to the out-of-control states are based on binomial probabilities and are calculated using

$$P_{0j} = \binom{s}{j} \frac{1 - e^{-\lambda k/R}}{(1-(1-\pi)^s)} \pi^j (1-\pi)^{s-j}, \qquad j = 1,2,\ldots,s.$$

(6)

This distribution is indexed by the parameter π where $0 < \pi < 1$. Increasing π increases the likelihood of the process shifting to one of the out-of-control states.

For the case when the process is not in control at the time of sampling, an assumption similar to that made by Montgomery et al. (1975) is made. That is, "the probability of a shift to a further out-of-control state is proportional to the probability of a shift to that out-of-control state from the in-control state." Thus,

$$P_{ij} = \begin{cases} \dfrac{P_{0j}}{1-P_{00}}, & j > i > 0 \\[2em] \dfrac{\displaystyle\sum_{w=1}^{j} P_{0w}}{1-P_{00}}, & j = i > 0 \\[2em] 0, & j < i > 0. \end{cases} \tag{7}$$

2.1.1 Vector $\hat{q}$

The vector $\hat{q}$ contains the probabilities that the sampling procedure will indicate that the process is out of control when the process is in state i.

If the sample size is greater than one-tenth of the lot size, it is assumed that the number of nonconforming units follows a hypergeometric distribution with parameters n, Q and p_i. Thus,

$$q_i = \sum_{x=c+1}^{\infty} \frac{\binom{p_i}{x}\binom{Q}{n-x}^{Q-p_iQ}}{\binom{Q}{n}}, \qquad i = 0,1,\ldots,s. \tag{8}$$

If the sample size is less than one-tenth of the lot size, the number of nonconforming units, c, in a sample of size n is assumed to be binomially distributed with parameters n and p_i. Thus,

$$q_i = \sum_{x=c+1}^{\infty} \binom{n}{x} p_i^x (1-p_i)^{n-x}, \qquad i = 0,1,\ldots,s. \tag{9}$$

2.1.2 Vector $\hat{\alpha}^t$

An element α_j^t is the probability that the process is in state j at the time the sampling procedure is applied after t intersample intervals have elapsed. To develop this vector, a matrix B is computed. An element of this matrix, b_{ij}, is the probability of a transition from state i to state j during the production of k units. The elements of this matrix can be calculated by examining three different situations.

In the case where the process is in state i at sample x and is in a better state j at sample x+1 (j<i), the probability of a transition is the product of the

probability that the result from sample x indicates the process is out of control, thus the process is immediately reset to state 0, and the probability of the process shifting from state 0 to state j during the intersample interval.

$$b_{ij} = q_i P_{0j}, \qquad 0 \leq j \leq i. \qquad (10)$$

In the case where the process is in state i at sample x and at sample x+1 is in the same or a worse state j ($j \geq i$),

$$b_{ij} = q_i P_{0j} + (1-q_i)P_{ij}, \qquad j \geq i \geq 0. \qquad (11)$$

The second term accounts for the situation when the sample x result indicates that the process in not out of control. The process remains in state i immediately after sample x, but may shift to state j during the intersample interval.

The vector $\hat{\alpha}^t$ is calculated using

$$\hat{\alpha}^t = \hat{\alpha}^0 [B]^{t-1} \qquad (12)$$

where $\alpha_j^0 = P_{0j}$.

Matrix B is the transition matrix of an irreducible, aperiodic, positive recurrent Markov chain. In the case of a relatively small lot quantity, the maximum value of t would be relatively small. As the lot size approaches ∞, t approaches ∞, and this vector would contain the steady-state unconditional probability of the process being in a particular state at the time a sample is taken, regardless of the initial state.

2.1.3 Vector $\hat{\gamma}^t$

γ_i^t is the probability that the process is in state i at any time during the tth intersample interval. To calculate this probability, Δ, the average proportion of the intersample time interval that elapses before a shift occurs, given a shift between sample x and x+1, is needed. According to Duncan (1956),

$$\Delta = \frac{1-(1+\lambda k/R)e^{-\lambda k/R}}{1-e^{-\lambda k/R}} \left(\frac{R}{\lambda k}\right) \qquad (13)$$

Using this and previous results,

$$\gamma_i^t = \alpha_i^{t-1} P_{ii} + \Delta\alpha_i^{t-1} \sum_{h=i+1}^{s} P_{ih} + (1-\Delta) \sum_{l=0}^{i-1} \alpha_1^{t-1} P_{1i}, \qquad 0 \geq i \geq s. \qquad (14)$$

The first term is the probability that the process is in state i after t-1 intersample intervals and remains in state i until the end of the interval t. The second term is the probability that the process is again in state i after t-1 intersample intervals have elaspsed, but shifts to a higher (worse) state h during the tth interval. This is weighted by the proportion of the interval the process spends in state i. The probability of being in a lower (better) state after t-1 samples and shifting to state i during interval t is the third term. As with the second term, the third term is weighted by the proportion of the interval the process spends in state i.

When i=0, the last term is zero since state 0 can not be reached from any higher state. The second term is zero when i=s because there can be no direct transitions from state s.

3. Solution Procedure

In this section, the procedure used to find the threshold volume for a particular set of system parameters is outlined.

First, a near-optimal sampling plan and its associated cost were obtained for a value of Q using a pattern search technique. Since computational experience has indicated that the solution is sensitive to starting values, for each value of Q the search procedure was applied four times using a different starting point in each case. Second, the cost for that quantity was calculated when no sampling was used. Using a binary split search procedure, the lot size where the costs under the sampling and no-sampling situations were approximately equal was found. A maximum percentage difference between the near-optimal sampling cost and the no-sampling cost was provided to determine when to terminate this search. The percentage used in this study was .1%. Because the difference function was relatively flat and lumpy, partially because the decision variable must be integers, this procedure resulted in a maximum cost lot quantity that satisfied the maximum difference condition as well as a minimum lot quantity that satisfied the same condition. Thus for a particular problem, a range was determined for the threshold volume. This range was plotted on the figures discussed in the next section. In most cases, the range was very narrow.

To investigate the relationship between the threshold and selected system costs and parameters, a subject cost/parameter was varied while holding the others constant, and the threshold value found for the resulting system.

Base values for the system costs and parameters used in this study are presented in Table 1. Values for investigation and correction time were given for the in-control state and out-of-control state s, and intermediate values were assumed to be linear functions of p_j. In this study, s=3. The investigation and correction cost was directly proportional to the investigation and correction time.

Table 1

Base Values for System Parameters

c_f = \$10.00	R = 100 units/hour
c_v = \$1.00/unit	π = .800
c_d = \$5.00/unit	λ = 1.00/hour
A_0 = \$6.67	p_0 = .01
A_3 = \$40.00	p_1 = .10
t_0 = 10.0 minutes	p_2 = .15
t_3 = 60.0 minutes	p_3 = .25
v = .05 minutes/unit	

4. Results

Fourteen problem sets were investigated. Four of the problem sets were generated by varying four quality-related cost parameters separately, fixed cost of sampling (c_f), variable cost of sampling (c_v), cost of a defective unit (c_d), and investigation and correction costs (A), over a wide range while holding all other problem parameters constant. Three more problem sets were developed by separately varying three process parameters, production rate (R), mean time to process shift (λ^{-1}), and shift parameter (π).

The resulting threshold ranges for the cost parameters are plotted in Figure 1. Figure 2 contains the results for the three process parameters. In both figures, the parameter values are plotted as percentages of their base values. A summary of the results is presented in Table 2.

The data in Figure 1 indicates that the inspection related costs have opposite effects on the threshold volume – directly proportional to c_v and inversely proportional to c_f. In both cases, the relationship is practically linear over much of the range, and it terminates abruptly. The overall effect of increasing the cost of a defective unit (c_d) is to decrease the threshold. The relationship between threshold volume and c_d is somewhat hyperbolic in shape. Investigation and correction time (cost) has a similar relationship to the threshold. In both cases, the function truncates at a maximum value for that variable.

The threshold appears to be sensitive to all three of the process parameters investigated. As seen in Figure 2, the relationship between the threshold and π is inversely proportional and somewhat hyperbolic in shape. Threshold volume and λ are related in an inversely proportional, hyperbolic fashion. There is a similar relationship between the threshold and production rate. In both cases, λ and R, the threshold volume truncates to zero when a maximum value of the variable is reached.

As can be seen, the volume above which statistical process monitoring is economically justified is affected by the values of certain system costs and parameters. Although the results for this study are specific to the set of costs and parameters assumed, the general relationships hold across a wide variety of cases. While some of the general relationships found between threshold volume and system costs and parameters may be discernable from a "common sense" standpoint, e.g., it becomes more important to monitor a process as the cost of a defective unit increases, the shape, and even direction, of some of these relationships is not easily deduced.

The results of this study provide some explicit insights to these relationships which should aid the designer of quality control systems. By knowing the general direction and shape of these relationships, the designer is in the position to know when monitoring is economically warranted on a process for particular lot size and when it is not. The cost model can be used to find a near optimal sampling plan in the case where sampling is justified.

****

FIGURE 1
THRESHOLD VS COST PARAMETERS

****

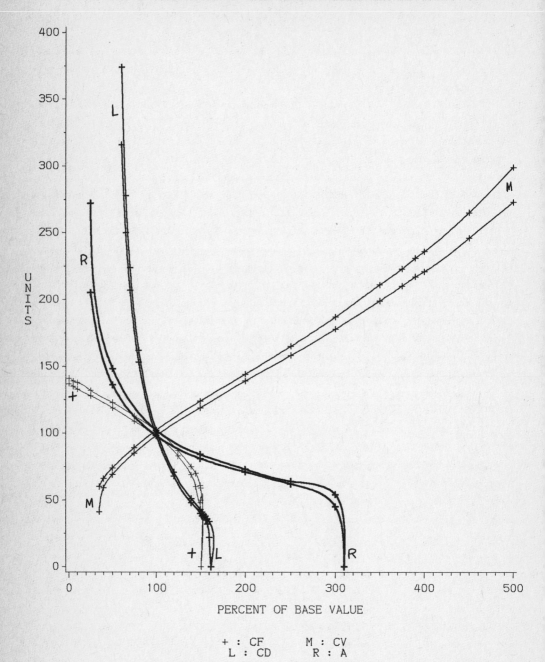

+ : CF   M : CV
L : CD   R : A

****
FIGURE 2
THRESHOLD VS PROCESS PARAMETERS
****

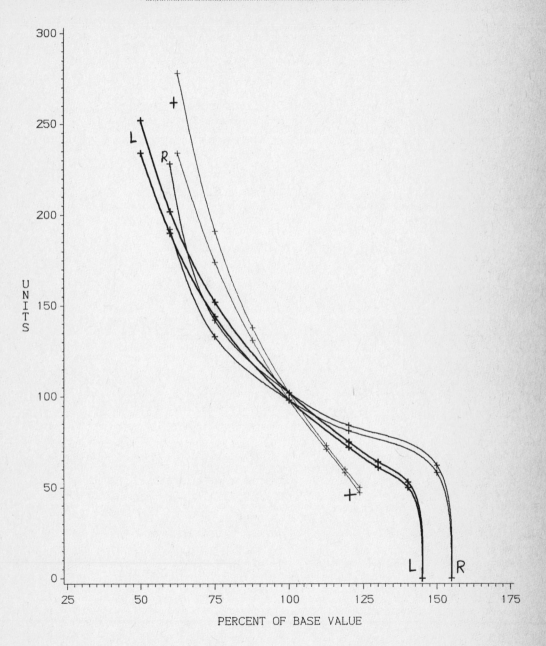

+ : PI   R : R   L : LAMBDA

Table 2

Summary of Results

Parameter	Affect on Threshold
c_f	inversely proportional, linear over a range, then decreases rapidly
c_v	directly proportional, somewhat linear after reaching minimum value for c_d
c_d	inversely proportional, hyperbolic up to maximum value for c_d
A_j/t_j	inversely proportional, hyperbolic up to maximum value for t_j
π	inversely proportional, somewhat hyperbolic, truncated at $\pi = 1.00$.
R	inversely proportional, hyperbolic up to maximum value of R
λ	inversely proportional, hyperbolic up to maximum value of λ

REFERENCES

Baker, R.C., "The Marriage of Zero Inventories and Conditional Sampling Procedures, "Production and Inventory Management, 28, 1 (1987), 27-30.

Chung, C., "Quality Control Sampling Plans under Zero Inventories: An Alternative Method," Production and Inventory Management, 28, 2 (1987), 37-42.

Duncan, A.J., "The Economic Design of x-Charts Used to Maintain Current Control of a Process," Journal of the American Statistical Association, 51, 274 (1956) 228-242.

Hald, A., "The Compound Hypergeometric Distribution and a System of Single Sampling Inspection Plans Based on Prior Distributions and Costs," Technometrics, 2, 3 (1960), 275-372.

Knappenberger, H. and A.H.E. Grandage, "Minimum Cost Quality Control Tests," AIIE Transactions, 1, 1 (1969) 24-32.

Krupp, J.A.G., "Reconciling Quality Control Sampling Plans and Zero Inventories," Production and Inventory Management, 26, 3 (1985) 143-148.

Lee, H.L. and M.J. Rosenblatt, "Simultaneous Determination of Production Cycle and Inspection Schedules in a Production System," Management Science, 33, 9 (1987), 1125-1136.

Montgomery, D.C., R.G. Heikes and J.F. Mance, "Economic Design of Fraction Defective Control Charts," Management Science, 21, 11 (1975), 1272-1284.

Montgomery, D.C., "The Economic Design of Control Charts: A Review and Literature Review," Journal of Quality Technology, 12, 2 (1980), 75-87.

Porteus, E.L., "Optimal Lot Sizing, Process Quality Improvement and Setup Cost Reduction," Operations Research, 34, 1 (1986), 137-144.

Rosenblatt, M.J. and H.L. Lee, "Economic Production Cycles with Imperfect Production Processes," IIE Transactions, 18, 3 (1986), 48-55.

VI. Mathematical Programming Models for Cost Analysis

Evaluation Of Computer Assisted Telephone Interviewing
As A Survey Methodology By Means Of
Cost Models And Mathematical Programming

William F. McCarthy

The University Of Maryland, Graduate School, College Park, MD.

(Former Special Assistant, U.S. Bureau of the Census, Washington, DC.)

Computer assisted telephone interviewing (CATI) is now considered a valid methodology for survey interviewing. It offers a number of advantages over the current data collection methodology. Among these advantages are efficient survey management (more accurate and timely operations information), reduced data collection and processing time, improved data quality, improved interviewer training and monitoring, reduced problems in recruiting and retaining an interviewing staff, and reduced costs associated with development, printing, and data keying of paper questionnaires (Nicholls,1978,1983;Groves, 1983; Groves and Mathiowetz, 1984; Nicholls and Groves, 1986; McCarthy, 1988 A.).

Since 1981, the U.S. Bureau of the Census has been conducting studies to evaluate CATI in order to see if it is a feasible methodology for conducting surveys. Recently, two studies conducted by the author, have looked at the use of CATI. One, Study A, looked at the use of CATI as a partial means of data collection for the National Crime Survey (NCS), a current demographic survey (McCarthy, 1988 A). The other, Study B, looked at the use of CATI as the major means of a new approach in collecting demographic, economic, health, and census sample data (Herriot, Bateman, and McCarthy, 1988).

This paper will discuss the techniques that were used to aid the decisionmakers in determining whether or not the use of CATI is feasible for both applications mentioned. Section 1 briefly outlines how cost modeling and sensitivity analysis were used to compare the costs of using CATI in conjunction with the current data collection methodology against the costs of only using the current data collection methodology (the current methodology uses paper questionnaires via personal visit and telephone interviews); Section 2 describes how mathematical programming was used to optimally design a survey sample that integrates the use of CATI; Section 3 presents the results of the analyses.

1. Cost Modeling

When investigating the feasibility of a new survey methodology, the cost of implementing and using it needs to be assessed. In general, cost modeling can help the decisionmakers to identify a preferred course of action from among other possible alternatives. The first part of this section will discuss how the cost models were developed. Following this will be a discussion of how the cost models were utilized to analyze costs.

1.1 Overall Development of the Cost Models

One cost model was developed to analyze the production requirements and costs for conducting surveys with CATI in conjunction with the current data collection methodology (Model I), another cost model was developed for the current data collection methodology (Model II). Model II was used as a benchmark for comparison purposes. Each model consisted of two components: 1) one that specifies the production requirements of conducting a survey; and 2) one that determines the resulting costs that are generated by the production requirements.

Basically, the production requirements entail the workload distribution (the average number of interviews (cases) assigned to CATI or the current data collection methodology), the staff distribution (the number of interviewers, supervisors, etc., that are required to meet the demands of some specified workload distribution), time constraints (the amount of time available to conduct a particular survey), the night differential requirement, salary and benefit requirements of the staff, and assumptions about the unit costs for interviewed and noninterviewed cases (for both CATI and the current data collection methodology), and other associated fixed and variable costs for such things as sample design and selection, development of training materials (for the staff), telephone costs for both CATI and the current data collection methodology, questionnaire development and printing (for CATI this requires software development as well), data keying, programming, data analysis, and publication of the results.

The resulting costs that are generated are in the identical format of the cost reports put out by the Bureau's Budget Office. These cost reports, in addition to other reports, are used by the decisionmakers to keep track, and analyze, the costs associated with conducting surveys.

In order to permit meaningful comparisons between Model I and Model II, both models were developed within the framework of a system cost element list (McCullough, J.D., 1965; Quade, 1966; Fisher, 1970; Massey, Novick, and Peterson, 1972). A cost element list aligns the elements of the two models in such a way to permit meaningful comparisons. In addition, the list also provides that all costs associated with a system are identified and included.

In general, each of the cost models had the following framework (based on a system cost element list):

Production-Requirements

Each of these	Workload distribution	X
is considered	Staff distribution	X
an element.	Time constraints	X
	Etc.	X

Resulting Costs

Each of these	Direct costs	X
is considered	Applications & overheads	X
an element	Etc.	X
Overall Unit Cost	(Total cost/Total number	X
	of cases assigned)	

Where X= some quantitative value based on data or formulae.

Refer to Attachment 1 for a partial listing of the cost categories/elements that were used; Attachment 2 gives an example of the corresponding cost formulae used.

Once the cost models were developed on paper, they were translated into microcomputer-based models. In particular, the spreadsheet package Lotus 1-2-3, and later Symphony, were used. For details on the advantages of using such a spreadsheet approach, refer to Baker, Clark, Frund, and Wendell (1987).

1.2   How the Costs Models Were Utilized

For Study A, the model which produced the lowest overall cost was considered as a likely data collection methodology to use. However, since efficiencies were not built into either model, it was felt that sensitivity analyses should be done, on both models, to get a sense of what the overall total cost might be under different sets of assumptions that concerned efficiencies. In particular, the objective was to see how sensitive the models were with respect to variations in one or more of the key cost elements (variations caused by the application of different sets of efficiency assumptions).

For Study B, further analyses were conducted to determine which data collection methodology would be optimal in the sense of maximizing productivity, minimizing costs, etc. For these particular analyses, mathematical programming was used. In general, linear and/or integer programming was employed. The results of the micro-computer-based models and the mathematical programs, in conjunction with sensitivity analyses, were used to generate costs that would be used in Study B. In particular, the costs from Model I were later used in a constrained nonlinear program that ultimately determined the overall costs for collecting data when CATI was used as the major means of data collection.

2. The Use of Mathematical Programming to Optimally Design
   A Survey Sample That Integrates The Use of CATI

The primary reason for using CATI in a maximum sense, is due to several reasons:
1) the advantages it has over the current data collection methodology mentioned in the
beginning of the paper; and 2) the fact that telephone interviews tend to be relatively
inexpensive (Lepkowski and Groves, 1986).

Unfortunately, surveys that just use a telephone sample are vulnerable to coverage bias, i.e. the inability of telephone surveys to represent non-telephone households
can cause bias problems for certain demographic, socio-economic characteristics
(Thornberry and Massey, 1978). In order to remove this coverage bias and yet ensure
the maximum use of the cheaper CATI methodology, a dual frame approach is used to
construct a survey design which combines a telephone sampling frame with an area or
address (household) sampling frame, which would cover the non-telephone households
with personal visit interviews or mailed questionnaires. (Note: a frame is a list
from which to select a sample.) A dual frame consists of two sample frames that
overlap in such a way to remove the coverage bias of the telephone frame and maximize
the representativeness of the target population. For more information on dual frames
refer to Hartley (1962), Lund (1968), Casady and Sirken (1980), Biemer (1983),
Lepkowski and Groves (1986), and McCarthy and Bateman (1988).

Hartley (1962) initially considered the need to combine frames and developed
formulas to optimally allocate sample sizes to the separate frames based upon cost,
variance, and bias estimates. Since that time his work has been carried on by other
researchers (Casady and Sirken, 1980; Biemer, 1983; Lepkowski and Groves, 1986). This
section of the paper will present a simple approach to optimizing the design of a
dual frame survey.

It should be noted here that only Study B considered dual frame sample designs.
Study A did not use a dual frame approach, it only used CATI as a means of collecting
data for those interviews where the current data collection methodology was not effective. In addition, Study A did not optimally allocate its sample into the CATI methodology.

2.1 General Methodology

This section of the paper describes a general methodology for determining the
optimal allocation of sample units among dual frames. In addition, this methodology
also allows one to conduct a post optimality analysis in order to study how various
sample design and cost parameters affect the optimization of the dual frame sample
allocation.

In particular, a set of models which relate survey costs with statistical precision/accuracy, as well as other relevant constraints, are used. These models are used to create a mathematical program (optimization problem) such that: 1) the cost of conducting the survey is minimized subject to a prescribed level of statistical precision/accuracy, or 2) the statistical precision/accuracy is maximized subject to an expected fixed cost for conducting the survey. Since the objective of Study B was to see if using CATI as a major means of data collection could save the Bureau money and at the same time generate estimates having the same level of precision that the current data collection methodology produced, it was decided to use approach 1 mentioned above.

A mathematical program is an optimization problem in which the objective and its constraints are given as mathematical functions and functional relationships. In general, they have the form

$$
\begin{array}{ll}
\text{optimize:} & f(x) \quad\quad \text{where optimize is maximize or minimize} \\
\text{subject to:} & \left.
\begin{array}{l}
g_1(x) \\
g_2(x) \\
\dots \\
g_m(x)
\end{array}
\right\}
\begin{array}{c}
\le \\
= \\
\dots \\
\ge
\end{array}
\left\{
\begin{array}{l}
b_1 \\
b_2 \\
\dots \\
b_m
\end{array}
\right.
\end{array}
$$

with $x \ge 0$.

Each of the m constraints involves one of the three signs $\le$, $=$, $\ge$. In some cases, the additional restriction that x is integral is added. If $f(x)$ and each $g_i(x)$ (i= 1,2,...,m) are linear, then the mathematical program is linear. Any other mathematical program is considered nonlinear. The mathematical programs that are used in the designing of dual frame surveys are nonlinear and usually have the restriction $x \ge 0$ and integral.

For those readers seeking a review of the theory of mathematical programming (formulation and solution), they should refer to Himmelblau (1972), Phillips, Ravindran and Solberg (1976), and Arthanari and Dodge (1981). Those interested in how dual frame cost models are constructed should refer to Hartley (1962), Lund (1968), Casady, Snowden and Sirken (1981), Biemer (1983), Lepkowski and Groves (1986), McCarthy (1988 B), and McCarthy and Bateman (1988). All of the previously mentioned authors can also provide examples of dual frame statistical precision/accuracy models.

Mathematical programming has three major benefits for studying dual frame designs: 1) complex (both linear and nonlinear) cost models can be used; 2) the complex and sophisticated statistical precision/accuracy models associated with dual frame designs can be efficiently dealt with; and 3) post optimality analysis (sensitivity analysis) can be conducted to investigate how various sample design and cost parameters affect the optimization of the dual frame sample allocation. An additional benefit is that there are software packages available for mathematical programming that all but eliminate the necessity to write customized computer programs. One such package is GINO (General Interactive Optimizer) produced by LINDO Systems, Inc.

2.2 Methodology Used for Study B

As mentioned earlier, the mathematical program that was used for Study B had the following form:

> minimize: The overall total cost of conducting a dual frame survey
>
> subject to: The fixed level of precision desired, with all variables non-negative and integral.

It should be noted that other constraints such as time available to conduct the survey, staffing requirements, etc. were built into Model I and ultimately the effects of these constraints were implicitly contained in the coefficients of the cost model that was used in the objective function of the above mathematical program.

The variance model is an abbreviated version of one developed by Casady, Snowden and Sirken (1981). Reasonable assumptions were made that greatly simplify this formula. This model assumes that we have a self weighting sample of m_1 clusters of households from an area household sample survey frame and an independent simple random sample of m_2 clusters of telephone households from a telephone number frame.

The variance model is developed for estimating a characteristic possessed by ten percent of the population. It is assumed that the two frames are a telephone frame and an area sample frame. Since the variance constraint is usually specified in relative terms, the following formula is for the rel-variance of the estimate.

$$\text{RELVAR } (r) \cong (1/r^2)(((p_1 \sigma_1^2 \delta_{11})/(m_1 \overline{N}_1)) + (((1-p_1)^2 \delta_{12} \delta_2 \sigma_2^2)/(m_1 (1-p_1)\overline{N}_1 + m_2 \overline{N}_2 \delta_{12})))$$

The cost model is of the form: $C = C_1 m_1 + C_2 m_2$

The values for C_1 and C_2 were generated by Model I, mentioned in Section 1.1 . The above parameters are defined thusly:

$\sigma_1^2 = r_1(1-r_1)$ $\sigma_2^2 = r_2(1-r_2)$

   r = the proportion of the population having the characteristic of interest

   r_1 = the proportion of the population in the household frame having the characteristic of interest

   r_2 = the proportion of the population in the telephone frame having the characteristic of interest

   p_1 = the proportion of non-telephone persons in the population

   $\overline{N}_1$ = the average number of persons per cluster from the household survey

   $\overline{N}_2$ = the average number of persons per household from the telephone survey

   m_1 = the number of clusters of personal interviews in the area sample household frame

m_2 = the number of telephone interview households from the telephone frame

δ_{11} = the design effect for the proportion having the desired characteristic in non-telephone population from the household frame

δ_{12} = the design effect for the proportion having the desired characteristic in the telephone population from the household frame

δ_2 = the design effect for the proportion having the desired characteristic in the telephone population from the telephone frame

C_1 = the cost of having a cluster of personal interview households from the household frame in the sample

C_2 = the cost of having a telephone interview in the sample from the telephone frame.

As with the cost models, it was felt that sensitivity analyses should be conducted to get a sense of what the overall total cost might be under different sets of assumptions. In particular, all of the parameters of the variance model were varied to see what effect the variations had on the overall total cost of conducting surveys and census sample surveys with the dual frame design mentioned earlier in this section.

The optimal allocation was based on the solution values that were generated for m_1 and m_2. Thus, from the mathematical program, one was able to determine if the dual frame design with CATI was cheaper than the current data collection methodology and also what the optimal allocation of sample was between the telephone and area/household frames which would ensure the minimization of cost and the achievement of the prespecified level of precision (variance) desired.

3. The Results of the Analyses

The feasibility testing seems to indicate that the dual frame design (Study B) generates the best results. Not only are the advantages of CATI maximized with the dual frame design, but the overall total cost, in comparison with the current data collection methodology, is lower. Under the worst case scenario (generated during the sensitivity analyses by using the worst case assumptions), the overall total cost of the dual frame design is at most the same as the overall total cost generated by the current data collection methodology (Herriot, Bateman and McCarthy, 1988). It should be noted that the results of Study A indicated that even when a dual frame design is not utilized and the sample is not optimally allocated into the CATI methodology, the overall total cost is at least the same as the overall total cost generated by the current data collection methodology (McCarthy, 1988 A). For example, Study A showed that the unit cost for the CATI methodology was $30.47 compared to $29.22 for the current data collection methodology. The NCS cost results have been validated by benchmarking the model results to actual Census Bureau budget reports. (NCS is currently experimenting with the CATI methodology mentioned in Study A.)

The results of Study B have not been validated. The reason for this is due to the fact that there is no current experimental design being employed by the Census Bureau to determine the actual costs associated with a dual frame approach (as mentioned in Study B). The costs associated with the current data collection methodology of the census sample are well established. Therefore only theorectical findings can be benchmarked to the current data collection methodology. However, Biemer (1983), as well as others, has shown that the costs associated with dual frames (as employed in Study B) are less than those associated with the current data collection methodology. Herriot, Bateman and McCarthy (1988) are currently designing an experiment for Study B. This experiment will allow for the actual determination of costs associated with the dual frame approach. Once sufficient cost information has been collected, as well as relevant operational and support data, then the author will be able to benchmark the cost model of Study B and then do a comparative analysis of costs (between the CATI methodology and the current methodology).

In summary, the U.S. Bureau of the Census is using CATI in the sense of the design mentioned in Study A. Two current demographic surveys are actively involved with the CATI methodology, the Current Population Survey (CPS) and the National Crime Survey (NCS). Several new approaches of collecting data with dual frame sample designs are now being considered by Herriot, Bateman and McCarthy (1988). Both Study A and Study B have demonstrated that CATI is a feasible data collection methodology.

Attachment 1. A Partial Listing of the Cost Categories/Elements That Were Used.

```
    DIRECT COSTS
        interviewing
        reinterviewing
        initial observation of interviewers
        systematic and special needs observations of interviewers
        initial training of staff
        home training of staff (self-study)
        refresher training of staff
        office work
        total salaries (based on hourly wages)
    APPLICATIONS & OVERHEADS
        personal benefits
            leave
            employee benefits
            unemployment
            use of equipment & supplies
```

other direct costs

    questionnaire development, printing

    editing

    communications (for the telephone facility which conducts CATI)

    travel (for the personal visit interviews and observation of interviewers)

    data keying

    postage

    programming/data tape generation

    development of training materials

    sample design and selection

    analysis of data

    publication of results

other applied costs

    specific overheads unique to the U.S. Bureau of the Census

Attachment 2. An Example of the Corresponding Cost Formulae Used.

INTERVIEWERS

Number   ((avg. No. of CATI cases)*(payroll min. per case))/((300 min)*(7 days))

New Interviewers   (No. of interviewers)*(monthly turnover rate)

I1 Salaries   (rate per hr.*payroll min. per case/60 min.)*(avg. No. of CATI cases)

I2 Night Dif. (I1 salaries)*(workload affected by night dif)*(night dif. rate)

I3 Quality Assurance (No. of interviewers)*(rate per hr.)*(time allocated to QA)

I4 Initial Training 25 hr,*(starting interviewer rate per hr)*(No. of new
                   interviewers)

I5 Refresher Training 7 hr*(3 times per yr)*(interviewer rate per hr)*(No. of
                interviewers)/12 months

I6 Self Study   0.25 hr *(interviewer rate per hr)*(No. of interviewers)

TOTAL INTERVIEWER SALARIES (I1 + I2 + I3 + I4 + I5 + I6)

Etc.

    Note: The format above is indicative of how the formulas were written using Lotus 1-2-3 and Symphony.

References

Arthanari,T.S. and Dodge,Y. (1981). Mathematical Programming in Statistics. John Wiley & Sons, NY.

Baker,G.L.,Clark,W.A., Frund,J.J. and Wandell,R.(1987). Production Planning and Cost Analysis on a Microcomputer. Interfaces,17,4, July-August, pp 53-60.

Biemer,P.(1983). Optimal Dual Frame Designs: Results of a Simulation Study. ASA Proceedings of Survey Research Methods, pp 630-635.

Casady,R.J. and Sirkin,M.G. (1980). A Multiplicity Estimator for Multiple Frame Sampling, Proceeding of the American Statistical Association, Social Statistics Section, pp 601-605.

Casady,R.J., Snowden, C.B. and Sirkin,M.G. (1981). A Study of Dual Frame Estimators for the National Health Interview Survey, Proceedings of the American Statistical Association, Section on Survey Research Methods.

Fisher,G.H. (1970). Some Comments on Conceptual Frameworks for Comparing Alternatives, Rand Corporation Paper, P-4506, Santa Monica, CA.

GINO (General Interactive Optimizer), developed by LINDO Systems,Inc., Chicago, IL.

Groves,R.M. (1983). Implications of CATI: Costs, Errors, and Organization of Telephone Survey Research, Sociological Methods and Research, 12, 2, pp 199-215.

Groves,R.M. and Mathiowetz, N.A. (1984). Computer Assisted Telephone Interviewing: Effects on Interviewers and Respondents, Public Opinion Quarterly,48, pp 356-369.

Hartley,H.O. (1962). Multiple Frame Surveys, Proceedings of the American Statistical Association, Section on Social Statistics, pp 203-206.

Herriot,R., Bateman,D. and McCarthy,W.F. (1988). ISAS- Integrated System of Area Statistics: A New Approach for Meeting the Nation's Needs for Sub-National Data,Internal Census Bureau Document.

Himmelblau,D.M. (1972). Applied Nonlinear Programming, McGraw-Hill,NY.

Lepkowski,J.M. and Groves,R.M. (1986). A Mean Squared Error Model for Dual Frame, Mixed-Mode Survey Design, Journal of the American Statistical Association, 81(396), pp 930-937.

Lund,R.E. (1986). Estimators in Multiple Frame Surveys, Proceedings of the American Statistical Association, Social Science Section.

Massey,H.G., Novick,D. and Peterson,R.E. (1972). Cost Measurement: Tools and Methodology for Cost Effectiveness Analysis, Rand Corporation, Paper P-4762, Santa Monica, CA.

McCarthy,W.F.(1988 A). NCS/CATI Cost Analysis: CATI Research Report No. NCS-1, Final Report, unpublished internal Census Bureau Document.

McCarthy,W.F. (1988 B). OR/MS Applications in Computer Assisted Telephone Interviewing (CATI) Survey Research. Part 1: Cost Modeling, The Institute of Management Sciences and Operations Research Society of America Joint National Meeting, April, Washington,DC.

McCarthy,W.F. and Bateman,D. (1988). OR/MS Applications in Computer Assisted Telephone Interviewing (CATI) Survey Research. Part 2: Optimal Allocation of Sample Sizes for Mixed Mode, Dual Frame Survey Designs, The Institute of Management Sciences and Operations Research Society of America Joint National Meeting, April, Washington, DC.

McCullough,J.D. (1965). Cost-Effectiveness: Estimating Systems Costs, Rand Corporation, Paper P-3229, Santa Monica,CA.

Nicholls,W.L.(1978). Experiences with CATI in a Large-Scale Survey,Proceedings of the American Statistical Association, Section on Survey Research Methods.

Nicholls,W.L. (1983). CATI Research and Development at the Census Bureau, Sociological Methods and Research, 12,2, pp 191-197.

Nicholls,W.L. and Groves,R. (1986). The Status of Computer Assisted Telephone Interviewing, Computer Science and Statistics: 1986 Proceedings of the 18th Symposium on the Interface, pp130-137.

Phillips.D.T., Ravindran,A. and Solberg,J.J. (1976). Operations Research: Principles and Practices, Wiley & Sons, NY.

Quade,E.S. (1966). Systems Analysis Techniques for Planning- Programming- Budgeting, Rand Corporation, Paper P-3322, Santa Monica, CA.

Thornberry,O.T. and Massey,J.T. (1978). Correcting the Undercoverage Bias in Random Digit Dialed National Health Surveys, Proceedings of the American Statistical Association, Section on Survey Research, pp 224-229.

TWO QUADRATIC PROGRAMMING ACQUISITION MODELS WITH RECIPROCAL SERVICES

Chin-Wei Yang, Associate Professor
Department of Economics
Clarion University of Pennsylvania
Clarion, Pennsylvania 16214

James Bray McNamara, CPA, Professor
Department of Accountancy
Clarion University of Pennsylvania
Clarion, Pennsylvania 16214

INTRODUCTION

The use of the cost allocation and external acquisition models has centered on the linear programming cost allocation (LPCA) models (Baker and Taylor, 1974; Manes, Park and Jensen, 1982; Chen, 1983; Yang and Pineno, 1984A) and the simultaneous equation approach (Ijiri, 1968; Livingstone, 1969; Kaplan, 1973; Capettini and Salamon, 1977; Yang, 1988). The LP approaches, while being extremely operationally efficient (the number of iterations needed in the simplex method can be found in Dantzig (1980)), have a property of being insensitive to exogenous shock administered to the model. This property and other characteristics of LPCA are discussed in the next section. The difficulty associated with the simultaneous equation approach lies in the fact that the solution may not be positive (Yang, 1988) and hence may not have a reasonable interpretation.

The quadratic programming cost allocation (QPCA) models are presented to incorporate general economic phenomena in applying cost allocation and external acquisition models. The convex QPCA model is employed to account for (a) the so-called "law of diminishing marginal returns" in the short run or (b) decreasing returns to scale due to managerial inefficiency in a complex organization. In addition, the concave QPCA model is used to explain either economies of scale or purchasing discounts that are common in business practice. These are important economic or business phenomena in cost allocation models. The results of the quadratic versions are evaluated under the same constraints used in the linear version.

THE LINEAR PROGRAMMING COST ALLOCATION MODEL REVISITED

Baker and Taylor (1979) proposed the following LPCA model.

$$\text{Minimize } TC = \sum_{i \in I} f_i\, x_i + \sum_{i \in I} g_i\, v_i \qquad (1)$$
$$x_i, v_i$$

subject to

$$x_i - \sum_{j \neq i} a_{ij} x_j + v_i = b_i \text{ for every } i\epsilon I \qquad (2)$$

$$x_i \geq 0, \text{ and } v_i \geq 0 \qquad (3)$$

where

x_i = the number of outputs from service department i

v_i = quantity of service i to be purchased externally

I = integer index set (1, 2, 3, ...n) representing n service departments

b_i = the number of output units from service department i directly required for the total output production

a_{ij} = the amount of output units i required to produce one unit of output from department j

f_i = average cost of production of x_i

g_i = average cost of purchasing of v_i

Equations (1), (2), and (3) can be written more compactly as:

Minimize $F'X + G'V$ (4)

$\quad$ X,V

subject to $(I - A) X + V = B$ (5)

$\quad$ $X \geq 0$, and $V \geq 0$ (6)

where $F' = (f_i \ldots f_n)$, $G' = (g_i \ldots g_n)$, $X' = (x_i \ldots x_n)$,

$\quad$ $V' = (v_i \ldots v_n)$, $B' = (b_i \ldots b_n)$

A is an n x n input-output matrix. The upper-case letters denote matrix or vector and the primes denote conventional transpose.

As a basis for comparing the models, the numerical example presented by Baker and Taylor is reproduced here for sensitivity analysis.

$$\text{Minimize TC} = (4, 3, 2, 1, 5.25, 4.22, 3.14, 1.8) \begin{pmatrix} x_1 \\ x_2 \\ x_3 \\ x_4 \\ v_1 \\ v_2 \\ v_3 \\ v_4 \end{pmatrix} \qquad (7)$$

subject to

$$\begin{bmatrix} 1 - 0.12 - 0.05 - 0.08 + 1 \\ - 0.24 + 1 \quad - 0.10 - 0.06 \quad + 1 \\ - 0.15 - 0.10 + 1 \quad - 0.04 \quad + 1 \\ - 0.05 - 0.15 - 0.25 + 1 \quad\quad + 1 \end{bmatrix} \begin{bmatrix} x_1 \\ x_2 \\ x_3 \\ x_4 \\ v_1 \\ v_2 \\ v_3 \\ v_4 \end{bmatrix} = \begin{bmatrix} 21000 \\ 13000 \\ 21000 \\ 24000 \end{bmatrix} \quad (8)$$

$$x_i \geq 0, \ v_i \geq 0 \text{ for } i \varepsilon I \quad\quad\quad (9)$$

The optimum solution is shown in Table 1 (y_i is a dual variable).

Basically, four characteristics distinguish the LPCA model from the convex QPCA model. First, dual variables remain totally unchanged (see Table 1) as one varies b_4 either from 24,000 to 95,000 (a 296% increase) or from 24,000 to 500 (a 98% decrease). Because dual variables (or imputed marginal costs) provide valuable information to the decision maker in a model of this type, their constancy over a range may not provide adequate information.

Second, as the average cost of x_3 is decreased by 50% the optimum x's remain unchanged (see Table 1). Again, optimum numbers of outputs do not respond to the 50% decrease in average cost. This property is clearly unrealistic to a rational decision maker.

Third, it is a well-known theorem (Gass, 1985, p. 70 and p. 322) in linear programming that the number of positive-valued variables cannot exceed the number of constraints, i.e., nondegenerate basic feasible solution. As shown in the numerical example, we have exactly four positive variables in the model. This property may very well limit the decision maker's choices in a short run make-buy model of this type. As shown in Table 1, the Baker-Taylor model allows internal productions of x_2, x_3, and x_4 and one external acquisition v_1 from the outside market. Though such an outcome may be realistic to some organizations, it excludes the possibility of make and buy simultaneously, i.e., it precludes the possibility in the Baker-Taylor example of producing and purchasing output x_1 at the same time.

TABLE 1

Sensitivity Results of the LPCA Model

Source of Sensitivity

Optimum Solution	LPCA Model Without $\Delta = 0$	$\Delta g_1 = -1$	$\Delta f_3 = -1$	$\Delta b_4 = 71000$	$\Delta b_4 = -23500$
Total Cost	273975	247080	249934	401640	231719
x_1	0	0	0	0	0
x_2	17361	17361	17361	22051	15808.6
x_3	24041	24041	24041	27412	22925
x_4	32614	32614	32614	105160	8602.5
v_1	26894	26894	26894	33430	24731.5
v_2	0	0	0	0	0
v_3	0	0	0	0	0
v_4	0	0	0	0	0
y_1	5.25	4.25	5.25	5.25	5.25
y_2	4.213	4.07	4.104	4.213	4.213
y_3	3.133	3.05	2.111	3.133	3.133
y_4	1.798	1.71	1.751	1.798	1.798

*y's are dual prices

Finally, a constant average cost assumption in the Baker-Taylor model is only a special case of a typical U-shaped average cost curve. In the short run, the shape of the average cost curve is dominated by the "law of diminishing marginal returns." Similarly, the average purchasing cost may be increasing because of the limited availability of resources such as specialized labor and material. In addition, the average cost may be rising in the long run because of managerial inefficiency, especially in a large and complex organization.

In the next section we formulate a convex quadratic programming cost allocation model to overcome the limitations of the LPCA model.

CONVEX QUADRATIC COST ALLOCATION MODELS

Assuming linearly increasing average cost or diminishing marginal returns and purchasing functions of $AC_i = c_i + d_i x_i$ and $P_i = l_i + k_i v_i$ for $i \varepsilon I$, we can formulate a standard convex quadratic programming cost allocation model.

$$\text{Minimize } TC = C' X + X' D X + L' V + V' K V \tag{10}$$

$$= \Sigma_i c_i x_i + \Sigma_i d_i x_i^2 + \Sigma_i l_i v_i + \Sigma_i k_i v_i^2$$

$$X \varepsilon R_+^n$$

$$V \varepsilon R_+^n$$

subject to $(I - A) X + V = B \tag{11}$

where $C \varepsilon R^n$, $D \varepsilon R^{nxn}$, $L \varepsilon R^n$, $K \varepsilon R^{nxn}$

$C' \quad = (c_1 \ldots c_n)$, $L' = (l_1 \ldots l_n)$

$D \quad$ = positive diagonal matrix with d_i's > 0

$K \quad$ = positive diagonal matrix with k_i's > 0

$R_+^n \quad$ = nonnegative orthant of the Euclidean n - space R^n

R^{nxn} = the class of real $n \times n$ matrices.

Note that the constraint set (11) is equivalent to (2) because D and K are obviously positively definite (positive diagonal elements) and the objective function (10) is strictly convex. With the assumption of non-empty linear constraints (11), this convex quadratic programming cost allocation model (VXQPCA) has unique global minima (Luenberger, 1973). (The LPCA model may not have a unique solution.) Hence, the optimality conditions for the VXQPCA model can be shown as:

$$\frac{\partial L}{\partial x_i} = c_i + 2d_i x_i^* - \lambda_i^* + \sum_{\substack{k \neq i \\ k=1}}^{n} \lambda_k^* a_{ki} = 0 \tag{12}$$

$$\frac{\partial L}{\partial v_i} = l_i + 2k_i v_i^* - \lambda_i^* = 0 \tag{13}$$

$$\frac{\partial L}{\partial \lambda_i} = x_i - \sum_{j \neq i} a_{ij} x_j + v_i = b_i \tag{14}$$

where $L = TC + \lambda (B - (I - A) X - V)$ is the Lagrangian equation for this VXQPCA model.

λ is a row vector of r Lagrangian multipliers.

To preserve the non-negativity of the Lagrangian multipliers ($\lambda_i \geq 0$), we enhance the flexibility by adding inequality constraints for (11). The optimality conditions then can be easily generalized to be:

$$\frac{\partial L}{\partial x_i} \geq 0 \text{ and } \frac{\partial L}{\partial x_i} x_i^* = 0 \tag{15}$$

$$\frac{\partial L}{\partial v_i} \geq 0 \text{ and } \frac{\partial L}{\partial v_i} v_i^* = 0 \text{ for all } i \varepsilon I \tag{16}$$

$$\frac{\partial L}{\partial \lambda_i} \leq 0 \text{ and } \frac{\partial L}{\partial \lambda_i} \lambda_i^* = 0 \tag{17}$$

Condition (15) implies that if $x_i^* > 0$, equality relation (12) must hold, i.e., the imputed value λ_i^* (due to a small change in b_i) or the marginal capacity cost of department i equals the sum of direct marginal production cost ($c_i + 2d_i x_i$) and weighted marginal capacity costs in other departments ($k \neq i$) allocated to department i (the weights are the input-output technical coefficients a_{ki}). Condition (16) implies that for $v_i > 0$, the imputed value λ_i^* must equal the marginal purchasing cost ($l_i + 2k_i v_i$). Condition (14) is the constraint itself and condition (17) ensures that for any $\lambda_i^* > 0$, the constraints of the model must be active.

SENSITIVITY ANALYSES OF THE CONVEX QUADRATIC COST ALLOCATION MODELS

The mathematical sensitivity analysis of the standard quadratic allocation model is given by Irwin and Yang (1982). To further evaluate the performance of the VXQPCA model, we assign the following problem parameters with constraints identical to those used in the LPCA model.

$$C' = (2.3, 1.8, 2.1, 1.5) \quad L' = (2.35, 3.12, 2.27, 1.95)$$

$$D = \begin{bmatrix} 0.005 & & & 0 \\ & 0.003 & & \\ & & 0.006 & \\ 0 & & & 0.002 \end{bmatrix} \quad K = \begin{bmatrix} 0.004 & & & 0 \\ & 0.007 & & \\ & & 0.009 & \\ 0 & & & 0.001 \end{bmatrix}$$

The optimal solution to the VXQPCA model is presented in Table 2. First, the number of positive-valued variables is not limited by the number of constraints as in the LPCA model. In this simulation, we have eight positive decision variables in the solution set. Note that the number of positive decision variables in VXQPCA models need not be eight. Second, the optimal x_i's and v_i's are sensitive to changes in any cost parameter l_i, c_i, d_i, or k_i, in contrast to the linear program version. Similarly, the dual variables (λ_i's) respond to even a small change in the output requirement b_1. It is evident that the VXQPCA model has some degree of flexibility in comparison with the linear version.

To incorporate various business and economic situations into the model, we relax some assumptions on the forms of the objective function. First, we make average purchasing cost constant and retain the convexity on the average cost of production. The new convex (not strictly convex) quadratic programming cost allocation model (VXQPCA1) has the following formulation.

TABLE 2

Sensitivity Analysis of the VXQPCA Model

	Source of Sensitivity				
Optimum Solution	VXZPCA Model With No Shocks $\Delta = 0$	$\Delta l_1 = 0.1$	$\Delta l_1 = -0.1$	$\Delta b_1 = 100$	$\Delta b_1 = -100$
Total Cost	64325	64489	64159	72668	62794
x_1	675.03	680.37	669.7	888.44	632.35
x_2	954.33	954.81	953.85	973.56	950.48
x_3	1274.72	1275.06	1274.39	1288.22	1272.03
x_4	567.62	566.83	568.42	535.95	573.96
v_1	1648.63	1643.31	1653.96	1935.67	1591.23
v_2	669.21	670.00	668.42	700.64	662.92
v_3	1044.67	1045.15	1044.19	1063.84	1040.83
v_4	2327.96	2329.17	2326.74	2376.56	2318.24
y_1	15.539	15.597	15.482	17.835	15.08
y_2	12.489	12.5	12.478	12.929	12.401
y_3	21.074	21.083	21.065	21.419	21.005
y_4	6.606	6.608	6.604	6.703	6.587

$$\text{Minimize } C' X + X' DX + G' V \qquad (18)$$
$$X \ V$$

$$\text{subject to } (I - A) X + V = B \qquad (19)$$

$$X \geq 0, \ V \geq 0 \qquad (20)$$

where $C \epsilon R^n$, $D \epsilon R^n$, $A \epsilon R^{nxn}$, $V \epsilon R^n$, $B \epsilon R^n$, $G \epsilon R^n$, and $X \epsilon R^n$ are as defined in the preceding problems.

The problem parameters C, D, G, A, and B are given in the preceding linear and convex models. The sensitivity results of this convex quadratic programming cost allocation model with constant average purchasing cost functions (VXQPCA1) are reported in Table 3.

It is interesting to see from Table 3 that most of the primal decision variables are sensitive to the cost parameter c_1. However, the sensitivity is not as strong as that in the VXQPCA model because x_2 remains stable. As in the LPCA model, sensitivity of the dual variables is lacking. Furthermore, the number of positive-valued decision variables (6) is not limited by the number of constraints (4), but is less than the number of positive-valued variables (8) of the VXQPCA model.

A CONCAVE QUADRATIC ALLOCATION MODEL

In the long run, a firm must make the best choice in the make or buy decision. In many cases, the average cost function is dominated by the economies of scale in the long run, and the average purchasing function is heavily influenced by a common business practice--purchasing discounts. Within this framework, the cost allocation model can be formulated as:

$$\text{Minimize } W'X + X'ZX + S'V + V'TV \qquad (21)$$
$$\text{X} \quad \text{V}$$

subject to (4) and (5)

where $W \epsilon R^n$, $S \epsilon R^n$, $Z \epsilon R^{n \times n}$ and $T \epsilon R^{n \times n}$

are column vectors and diagonal matrices (with each $z_i < 0$ and $t_i < 0$ for all $i \epsilon I$) denoting intercepts and slopes of the linearly decreasing average cost functions, i.e., $AC_i = w_i - z_i x_i$ and $g_i = s_i - t_i v_i$. To evaluate the properties this concave quadratic programming cost alloca- tion (VAQPCA) model, we assume the following parameters.

$W' = (185, 176, 290, 357)$

$S' = (390, 395, 415, 435)$

$$Z = \begin{bmatrix} -0.03 & & & 0 \\ & -0.01 & & \\ & & -0.05 & \\ 0 & & & -0.04 \end{bmatrix}$$

$$T = \begin{bmatrix} -0.009 & & & 0 \\ & -0.001 & & \\ & & -0.008 & \\ 0 & & & -0.006 \end{bmatrix}$$

TABLE 3

Sensitivity Results of the VXQPCA1 Model

	Source of Sensitivity				
Optimum Solution	VXQPCA1 Model $\Delta = 0$	$\Delta c_1 = +1$	$\Delta c_1 = -1$	$\Delta b_1 = 100$	$\Delta b_1 = -100$
Total Cost	27209	27222	27195	27734	26684
x_1	137.62	127.62	147.62	137.62	137.62
x_2	201.00	201.00	201.00	201.00	201.00
x_3	0	0	0	0	0
x_4	0	0	0	0	0
v_1	1986.5	1996.50	1976.50	2086.5	1886.50
v_2	1132.03	1129.63	1134.43	1132.03	1132.03
v_3	2140.74	2139.24	2142.24	2140.74	2140.74
v_4	2437.03	2436.53	2437.53	2437.03	2437.03
y_1	5.25	5.25	5.25	5.25	5.25
y_2	4.22	4.22	4.22	4.22	4.22
y_3	3.14	3.14	3.14	3.14	3.14
y_4	1.80	1.80	1.80	1.80	1.80

Again, identical constraints on LPCA, VXQPCA, and VXQPCA1 are imposed here and the optimal solutions are reported in Table 4.

As is the case in the LPCA model, the optimal x_i's and v_i's are not sensitive to the changes in the cost parameter (s_3). However, the optimal x_i's, v_i's and y_i's in the VAQPCA model respond to the change in b_1. This is similar to the VXQPCA model. The number of positive-valued x_i's and v_i's is limited by the number of constraints as in the LPCA model. This result is not surprising because in the long run a business firm must make most efficient use of the available resources, i.e., it must either manufacture the good or service or purchase it externally, whichever is more cost-saving. These properties can also be seen in the case of the production process. With a fixed linear budget line and a concave cost function (shapes like a circle in the first quadrant), there is a tendency for the

TABLE 4

Sensitivity Results of the VAQPCA Model

Optimum Solutions	VAQPCA Model $\Delta = 0$	Source of Sensitivity			
		$\Delta s_3 = 5$ (or 1.2% change in s_3)	$\Delta s_3 = 20$ (or 4.8% change in s_3)	$\Delta b_1 = 100$	$\Delta b_1 = -100$
Total Cost	2766812	2779983	2819496	2784849	2748121
x_1	2322.9	2322.9	2322.9	2425.86	2219.93
x_2	1857.5	1857.5	1857.5	1882.21	1832.78
x_3	0	0	0	0	0
x_4	0	0	0	0	0
v_1	0	0	0	0	0
v_2	0	0	0	0	0
v_3	2634.18	2634.18	2634.18	2652.10	2616.27
v_4	2794.77	2794.77	2794.77	2803.62	2785.91
y_1	183.64	184.54	187.22	177.10	190.19
y_2	258.39	259.00	260.82	257.07	259.72
y_3	372.85	377.85	392.85	372.57	373.14
y_4	401.46	401.46	401.46	401.36	401.57

optimum solution to occur at the corner, i.e., the number of positive-valued variables (one) equals the number of constraints (one). In this sense, the concave quadratic cost allocation model is preferred to other types of models with either a linear or convex objective function.

CRITICAL EVALUATIONS OF THE MATHEMATICAL PROGRAMMING COST ALLOCATION MODELS: A CONCLUDING REMARK

Four mathematical programming models with identical constraints are evaluated. The LPCA model has rather limited positive x_i's and v_i's in the optimal basic solution set in terms of a nondegenerate basic feasible solution in linear programming. Likewise, the VAQPCA model offers very limited choices because a firm must operate in the most efficient way to survive in the long run. On the other hand, the number of positive-valued variables in the VXQPCA and VXQPCA1 model is not limited by the number of constraints. This property allows the firm to make and buy, especially in the short run to minimize risk (price increases).

Sensitivity of optimal x_i's and v_i's is clearly lacking in both the LPCA and VAQPCA models as the cost parameters are varied. In contrast, the optimal x_i's and v_i's respond to changes in cost parameters in both convex quadratic formulations, especially in the VXQPCA model. This property of sensitivity enables cost accounting managers to react to cost or price changes.

Furthermore, the dual variables (imputed marginal costs) are not responsive to the changes in the output requirement (b_i) in the LPCA and VXQPCA1 models. The implication is that the marginal costs generated from the two models are step functions or piecewise constant. In contrast, the sensitivity of the dual variables is obvious in both the VXQPCA and VAQPCA models. A variable marginal cost function can be more reasonable than a constant one in real accounting/business practice.

It should be pointed out that the original LPCA model is only a special case of the VXQPCA model. As the average purchasing price is assumed constant, the VXQPCA is reduced to the VXQPCA1 model. If one further assumes the constancy on the average cost functions of production, the convex quadratic programming model (VXQPCA1) is reduced to the linear programming model (LPCA). In the long run, however, a decision maker must consider the economies of scale and purchase discounts. Hence, a concave quadratic model (VAQPCA) is likely to be preferable. The VAQPCA model, like the LPCA model, offers rather limited choices and sensitivity in some cases, but its dual variables are sensitive to shocks as in the convex case. In the very short run when average costs of purchasing and production fail to adjust to the market (or f_i and g_i are constant), linear programming acquisition model may be employed. In the short run when the production process is dominated by the law of diminishing returns and competitive bidding drives up the average purchase cost, one may prefer the convex quadratic acquisition model. In the long run, the production process is normally dominated by economies of scale and average purchasing costs may be influenced by various quantity discounts. Under these circumstances, a concave quadratic acquisition model may be appropriate. However, the advantages of the two quadratic models may be offset by the cost of data collection in estimating the average cost of production and purchasing. The final choice of the model cannot be made without considering the accuracy of the models, cost of data collection, and time frame.

REFERENCES

Baker, K. R. and R. E. Taylor, "A Linear Programming Framework for Cost Allocation and External Acquisition When Reciprocal Services Exist," The Accounting Review, (October, 1979), pp. 784-790.

Capettini, R. and G. L. Salamon, "Internal Versus External Acquisition of Services When Reciprocal Services Exist," The Accounting Review, (July, 1977), pp. 690-698.

Chen, Joyce T., "Cost Allocation and External Acquisition of Services When Self-Services Exist," The Accounting Review, (July, 1983), pp. 600-605.

Culter, L. and D. S. Pass, A Computer Program for Quadratic Mathematical Models Involving Linear Constraints, Rand Report, R-516-PR, (June, 1971).

Danzig, G. B., "Expected Number of Steps of the Simplex Method for a Linear Program with a Convexity Constraint," Technical Report SOL 80-3, Stanford University (1980).

Gass, S. I., Linear Programming: Methods and Applications, 5th edition, New York: McGraw-Hill Book Company, 1985.

Ijiri, Y., "An Application of Input-Output Analysis to Some Problems in Cost Accounting," Management Accounting (April, 1968), pp. 49-61.

Irwin, C. L. and C. W. Yang, "Iteration and Sensitivity for a Spatial Equilibrium Problem With Linear Supply and Demand Functions," Operations Research, Vol. 30, No. 2, (March-April, 1982), pp. 319-335.

Kaplan, R. S., "Variable and Self-Service Costs in Reciprocal Allocation Models," The Accounting Review (October, 1973), pp. 738-748.

Livingstone, J. L., "Input-Output Analysis for Cost Accounting, Planning and Control," The Accounting Review (January, 1969), pp. 48-64.

Luenberger, D. G., Introduction to Linear and Nonlinear Programming, Addison-Wesley Publishing Company, Inc., (Reading, MA), 1973.

Manes, R. P., S. H. Park and R. Jensen, "Relevant Cost of Intermediate Goods and Services," Accounting Review (July, 1982), pp. 594-606.

Yang, C. W. and C. Pineno, "A Nonlinear Programming Model for External Acquisition With Reciprocal Services," Northeast AIDS Proceedings: The Award-Winning Theoretical Paper (1984), pp. 1-2.

Yang, C. W., "Theory of Nonnegative Matrix and the Simultaneous Equation Approach in the Cost Allocation Model," (Working Paper, 1988).

VII. Operations and Support Cost

Analyzing the Economic Impacts of a Military Mobilization

Robert E. Chapman, * Carl M. Harris † and Saul I. Gass ‡

Abstract

A military mobilization is a complex series of events, which if modeled adequately, can specify how a national economy makes the transition from a peace-time to a war-time footing. Problems in modeling such situations have highlighted the importance of evaluating large-scale, policy-oriented models prior to their use by decision makers. The current study outlines a generic procedure for conducting such an evaluation. Specifically, macro- economic modeling and a structured sensitivity analysis can be combined to measure and evaluate the economic impacts of a military mobilization.

*National Institute of Standards and Technology, Gaithersburg, MD 20899
†George Mason University, Fairfax, VA 22030
‡University of Maryland, College Park, MD 20742

1 Introduction

Modern military systems are by definition complex and large-scale. The ability of analysts to produce accurate and realistic cost estimates has thus become a most challenging task. Such estimates often rely on results derived from mathematical and econometric models that are used in analyzing system design characteristics and alternatives. Often, the models themselves are of questionable validity and are jerry-built to meet the demands of the analysis at hand. In turn, the models are dependent on databases that are gathered and maintained by diverse organizations, with each data base having a *raison d'etre* that may or may not be relevant to the studies to which it is applied. It should then be clear that the acceptance of model outputs as inputs to the decision-making process without investigating the validity of their generation is a luxury that the community of cost analysts can no longer afford.

Over the past 15 years a body of research has been developed that addresses the concerns of model users who, upon being presented with the results of a computer-based model analysis, must decide whether the results are accurate enough or appropriate for the problem under review. This research – termed model evaluation – has contributed greatly to our ability to understand better the role of modeling in policy-oriented decision making. Cost analysts need to be aware of this research. Extracting and applying the appropriate elements of this research to cost analysis studies will increase the acceptability and understanding of the studies and their results.

This paper presents the results of an evaluation of the Dynamic General Equilibrium Model (DGEM) [1]. The intent is that the reader should be able to obtain an appropriate sense of the value of such an evaluation for other models. The theme of our evaluation methodology is that evaluation is an integral part of the building and use of any large-scale, policy-oriented model [2]. This philosophy also applies to cost analyses considered to be complex and critical. In what follows, we describe elements of model evaluation, present the DGEM analysis framework, and then how the evaluation framework was applied to DGEM, with special emphasis placed on how the use of a structured sensitivity analysis facilitates such an evaluation. Although model evaluation may take on a variety of forms and levels of complexity, any evaluation procedure has at least the following essential phases:

1. Obtain a clear and comprehensive statement of user requirements and objectives pertaining to the application of the model;

2. Generate appropriate information about the model design and performance pertaining to user requirements; and

3. Evaluate model attributes and properties according to predetermined criteria of performance required by the user.

These phases are characterized by the following activities:

- Determine user requirements and objectives.

- Based on user requirements, develop questions to be answered about model performance and identify problems to be resolved or analyses to be performed.

- Ascertain from the questions any problems for which specialized techniques are to be used to generate information needed about model design or performance relevant to the intended application of the model by the user.

- Perform the necessary tasks to generate the needed information for the evaluation.

- Establish criteria for the model evaluation.

- Conduct a formal evaluation to judge the integrity of the model relative to its intended use.

These activities emphasize the importance of a thorough and comprehensive statement of user requirements to the process and to the success or failure of the evaluation.

2   The Dynamic General Equilibrium Model

The Dynamic General Equilibrium Model (DGEM) is an annual model for analyzing the structure and growth of the U.S. economy. DGEM incorporates a methodology for contingency planning so that quantitative analyses of the impact of economic policies and disruptions of the U.S. economy may be conducted. DGEM provides for detailed analyses of supply and demand factors through the year 2000. DGEM is well suited for determining sector-specific demands and supplies, and for relating these developments to other sectors of the economy. DGEM is an expanded version of the Long Term Interindustry Transactions Model [3], also known as the Hudson-Jorgenson Model [4]. The model was designed to deal with three major types of emergency situations: (1) energy-economic interactions associated with supply interruptions or strategic policies; (2) the economic impacts of a loss of resources due to an enemy attack on the United States with particular emphasis on which policies could stimulate recovery; and (3) the economic impacts of demand surges and resource constraints typical during a military mobilization.

DGEM was selected for evaluation primarily for its unique approach to modeling emergency situations. The availability of documentation is also a major factor, since documentation is the principal means through which performance against user requirements can be measured.

From a review of the documentation, it became clear that much care went into the design, development and testing of the model. Furthermore, the model's documentation is sufficient for an analyst to: (a) set it up on their host system; (b) execute a "base-case" simulation; (c) interpret the results of the "base-case" simulation; and (d) create, run, and interpret user-specified simulations.

Several documentation reports which were essential to the model evaluation process were concerned with: (a) comparisons of the DGEM predictions against realized values up through 1974 [5]; (b) results from a series of tests on the convergence properties of the model for extreme changes in certain key variables [6]; (c) explicit instructions for applying the model to a wide variety of emergency situations [7]; (d) descriptions of key variables, comparisons of how the model performed outside the estimation period, and details of the "base-case" simulation through the year 2000 [8]; and (e) a mathematical description of the model [9].

The approach used in DGEM is based on the application of econometric modeling to input-output analysis. Where input-output analysis assumes fixed input-output coefficients at any point in time, DGEM provides for flexible input-output coefficients induced by price variations in primary inputs which are associated with economic policies or anticipated contingencies.

The complete model consists of an inter-industry model incorporating the flexible input-output methodology and a macroeconometric model that integrates demand and supply conditions for consumption, investment, capital, and labor.

The macroeconometric model divides economic activity into two types of goods – consumption and investment goods – and two types of services – capital and labor. A production function relates the output of consumption and investment goods to the inputs of capital and labor services, for a given level of technical efficiency.

The inter-industry model determines inter-industry transactions for 36 domestic sectors, the demand for primary inputs, the allocation of the Gross National Product (GNP) as final demand among the sectors, and the total sector outputs. The technology of each producing sector is represented by a price possibility frontier that determines the supply price of output as a function of the prices of primary and intermediate inputs and the level of technical efficiency.

Each of the 36 sectors in the domestic economy is represented by a submodel of producer behavior. These submodels are based on the translog price possibility frontier. This frontier is a function relating the price of output charged by a sector to the prices that the sector pays for its inputs. The output price represents the least price that will cover input costs, including a normal return on capital. Also, technical change is included in the price frontiers.

The household sector is also explicitly analyzed, not only in terms of its demand for the output of the producing sectors, but also in terms of the supply of labor and the volume of saving. Part of the model is organized within an inter-industry transactions framework. This permits balance and consistency between input and output patterns to be achieved over all intermediate and final goods markets. Another part of the model covers the supply of primary inputs, in particular, of capital and labor, the demand for these inputs, and the adjustment of activity patterns so that the input markets are in balance. The model also covers the growth of the economy over time. Explicit attention is given to savings and investment mechanisms and to expansions of productive capacities through increases in capital and labor input and improvements in technical efficiencies.

The analytical framework in DGEM incorporates several key factors. The consistency of the framework ensures that the quantity and the value of flows in each market in the economy are simultaneously in balance. Both price and quantity aspects of economic activity are explicitly included in the model. Behavior by producers and consumers is considered in both price and quantity terms. For producers, the formation of output prices is considered, as well as the selection of those input patterns that are appropriate in the face of these prevailing input and output prices (i.e., the determination of the input-output coefficients for each producer as a function of technological information and of prevailing prices). Household behavior is modeled to simulate consumer response to market forces as consumption and labor decisions are made by the household in an attempt to maximize satisfaction. This generates consumption expenditure and labor supply functions that depend on prices, wealth, time, and preference parameters.

The flow of inputs to and outputs from production is handled within an inter-industry transaction framework. In this framework, the transactions are organized in a matrix with each column representing inputs to an industry and with each row representing sales or output from an industry. Each row corresponds to supply from a sector; each column represents purchases by a sector. There are 36 producing sectors. There are three further sources of supply: (1) capital services; (2) labor services; and (3) imports. Also, there are four more purchasing sectors. These final demand activities are: (1) personal consumption; (2) investment; (3) government purchases; and (4) exports.

The DGEM database contains the "base-case" values for all endogenous variables, exogenous variables, and coefficients. The post-1982 values in the database are projections, based on data available in 1983. The projections include: (1) trends in real economic growth and inflation; (2) the business cycle; (3) aggregate sources of growth; (4) trends in final demand; (5) energy use; and (6) industry developments.

To summarize, DGEM is comprised of several components.

1. Submodels of producer behavior – one for each of the 36 domestic producing sectors.

2. A model of consumer behavior.

3. Balance equations covering physical flows through the inter-industry system equating demand and supply quantities of each good or service transacted.

4. Market balance equations equating value of expenditure and receipts for each good or service transacted.

5. Financial identities aggregating value flows into aggregate income, financial and economic accounts.

6. Government and rest of the world accounts.

3 The Mobilization Scenario

The mobilization scenario analyzed with DGEM is patterned after an unclassified scenario approved by F.C. Ikle, the DoD Under Secretary for Policy. The scenario poses a conventional war of three years duration in Europe, the Persian Gulf, and Korea. For purposes of the current study, a one year warning period is assumed. The scenario allows the analyst to evaluate how changes in combinations of numerical values for key variables that describe wars of greater or lesser intensity will affect the U.S. industrial infrastructure.

A military mobilization is an ideal means for evaluating a model designed to deal with emergency management situations. For example, macroeconomic models, such as DGEM, provide the kind of information needed to understand how the national economy makes the transition from a peacetime to a war-time footing. Several factors which are critical in analyzing the transition, or in designing contingency plans to ease potential bottlenecks, are the following: (a) the increasing importance of international trade; (b) the business cycle concept; (c) the changing composition of the Gross National Product (GNP); (d) the concepts of investment, capital services, depreciation, and emergency capacity; (e) both supply (e.g., capital and labor services available) and demand (e.g., military requirements) concepts; (f) an explicit treatment of fiscal policy; and (g) dynamic characteristics whereby production and consumption decisions in one period affect the economy in future periods.

Items (a) through (g) are at the heart of most mobilization modeling problems. Consequently, it is essential that the model provide a means through which the analyst can address each item both individually and in combination. Only in this manner can the importance of individual items to the overall problem be measured. For example, a model which does not incorporate the business cycle may be unable to measure the impact on wages and prices due to a mobilization which begins in a recession versus one which begins during a period of full employment. Similarly, defense expenditures are going to exert a different impact on certain sectors of the national economy than are other government expenditures. Finally, the model should provide sufficient sectoral detail to identify areas where in-depth studies may be worthwhile.

The previous discussion serves to highlight several important distinctions between input-output models and general equilibrium models such as DGEM. First, an input-output model requires a vector of final demands to produce estimates of the requirements being placed on an industry. How the vector of final demands is produced may call into question the validity of the estimated values for inter-industry transactions. DGEM avoids this problem by providing a consistent framework for integrating final demand and interindustry transactions.

A related issue concerns how final demand is disaggregated. Disaggregating GNP and its components among industries is usually accomplished via bridge tables. If the bridge tables are based on "business as usual" data, they may not reflect the changes in the structure of the economy caused by a mobilization.

Finally, input-output models assume that no input substitution among industries can take place. DGEM's system of flexible input-output coefficients, induced by price variations in primary inputs, allows input substitution among industries to take place. Unfortunately, this "flexibility" exacts a price. DGEM assumes all inputs – including durable plant and equipment, land, and working capital – are adjustable among industries. Consequently, there is no notion of industry-specific capital. This has as an implication that production estimates from DGEM may be somewhat optimistic.

The analysis of the mobilization scenario was carried out in two stages. In the first stage, a *mobilization baseline* was constructed which documented the departures for key variables from the base-case values (i.e., those contained in the database) due to the mobilization. The results from the first stage of the analysis provided information on gross-level changes in the National

Income and Product Accounts (NIPA) components, as well as measures of the economic impacts of mobilization on a sector-by-sector basis.

In the second stage, six variables were varied in combination according to an experimental design. The six variables which were the subject of the *structured sensitivity analysis* and their names, as they appear in the tables which follow, are:

1. Federal defense purchases, GZ(1);

2. Federal nondefense purchases, GZ(2);

3. The Federal deficit, DG;

4. The efficiency with which capital is employed, AKD;

5. The rate of depreciation of capital, U; and

6. The effective supply of labor services, LB.

The structured sensitivity analysis was based on Monte Carlo techniques. The objective was to evaluate how uncertainty in the values of the six input variables translated into changes in the level and composition of the NIPA components, energy consumption, and the 36 producing sectors.

The period of the mobilization follows that of the unclassified DoD scenario and is assumed to be 1983 through 1986. The first year represents a period of buildup prior to the onset of hostilities. For each year of the mobilization, values for key economic variables were specified. Once the mobilization baseline had been established, a structured sensitivity analysis was performed. The values of the six variables which were the subject of the structured sensitivity analysis, their base-case values, and their mobilization values are compared at the end of this section. The specification of the military mobilization scenario is as follows.

Government purchases

Defense purchases are central to any mobilization effort. Through DGEM it is possible to control both the level and composition of defense purchases. However, for the case at hand, only the level is increased so that all defense purchases are increased in the same proportion. Defense purchases are increased by 50 percent in 1983, prior to the onset of hostilities, 80 percent in 1984, 120 percent in 1985, and by 150 percent in 1986. These increases are relative to the base case, or the economic conditions in the absence of mobilization. Since most Federal agencies will assume new responsibilities during a mobilization, federal nondefense purchases are increased by 25 percent in the first year and by 50 percent for the three following years.

Labor services

During the mobilization, many additional people will be recruited or conscripted into the armed forces. This is taken into account through the increase in defense purchases. However, mobilization measures will also be applied to the civilian population and the civilian labor force. Additional people – some of whom are less skilled than those they replace – are assumed to join the labor force. To reflect this, the labor force participation rate is increased by 4 percent in every year. Workers are also assumed to work longer hours through overtime or just through an extension of the standard workweek. Average hours per week are raised by 13 percent. Since these changes are likely to affect adversely labor efficiency, the average efficiency of each hour of labor is reduced by 7 percent. These combined factors produce a 9 percent net increase in the effective supply of labor services.

Capital services

A forced increase in capital use is assumed. This corresponds to the more intensive use of existing capital, as plant and equipment are used more hours per week, and the inclusion of emergency capacity. The overall increase in the efficiency with which capital is employed is taken to be 5 percent. This figure is a very conservative estimate of the potential for increasing the efficiency of the capital stock, since estimates of emergency capacity which can be brought on line within one year frequently exceed peacetime capacity levels by 25 percent. However, even this modest increase is likely to accelerate the wear and tear on capital. Accordingly, the rate of depreciation of capital is increased by 10 percent.

Foreign trade

It is assumed that all imports will be threatened. An-across-the-board reduction of 20 percent in imports is planned. Also, in order to ensure that mobilization requirements, including those of our allies, are satisfied first, an across-the-board reduction of 50 percent in exports is planned.

Fiscal policy

The major emphasis here is the federal deficit, since government purchases have already been addressed. The government deficit is allowed to exceed the base-case level by no more than a fixed percentage. Tax rates are increased in order to secure the additional revenue that is required to maintain the targeted budget deficit in the face of higher federal spending. This means that the increase in government expenditure is paid for in part by an increase in taxes and in part by increased deficits. This mixed strategy was designed to strike a balance between increased investment and inflationary pressures. For example, if the mobilization were financed by taxes, it would not necessarily come at the expense of investment, since the government is not claiming an additional share of the capital market in order to finance defense purchases, but would come primarily from consumption, since it is households and consumers who carry the main burden of taxes. If, in contrast, the mobilization were deficit financed, then the government would be claiming a larger share of investible funds so investment rather than consumption would likely carry a greater burden of the mobilization (i.e., private investment is crowded out). For the case at hand, the federal deficit is allowed to increase (over the base-case values) by 50 percent in 1983 and by 80 percent in 1984 through 1986.

Structured sensitivity analysis

Because the values of many key variables in the mobilization scenario are not known with certainty, it is advisable to select a few variables whose impact is likely to be substantial, and subject them to a structured sensitivity analysis. Variations in the values of these *input variables* translate into variations in the values of the *output or endogenous variables* in such a manner that the economic impacts of *shocks* to the system can be measured quantitatively.

The approach selected for this study makes use of recent work by Harris [10], [11] and by McKay, Conover, and Beckman [12]. Their work is based on the method of model sampling. The method of model sampling is a procedure for sampling from a set stochastic variables to determine, through multiple trials, the nature and effects of an output probability distribution. The method of model sampling, or distribution sampling as it is also called, has a long history of use by statisticians to derive distributions empirically that are difficult or impossible to derive by other means. It permits the effects of uncertainty to be rigorously analyzed.

Since repeated DGEM simulations are costly, a type of stratified sampling procedure, known as the *Latin hypercube sampling scheme* is employed. The procedure, as its name implies, is patterned after the classical *Latin square*. Latin squares consist of a set of permutations such that a given character or value appears only once in each row and each column. A Latin hypercube is similar to a Latin square with the important exception that it contains more rows than columns. For example, if each column is thought of as a variable and each row as a simulation number, then entries in the *cells* contain the values of a set of equally spaced percentiles from the parent *cumulative distribution function (CDF)* of the variable of interest. For the case at hand, with six variables of interest and ten simulations, the entries in the cells are the $5^{th}, 15^{th}, \cdots, 95^{th}$ percentiles of the parent CDF.

In reality, the exact nature of the parent CDF (e.g., measures of central tendency and dispersion) is unknown. Estimates of the parameters (e.g., mean and variance) of the CDF can be made and uncertainty can be reduced by investigation and research. However, uncertainty can never be eliminated completely because new sources of uncertainty are arising all the time. The true specification of the CDF can only be known when the mobilization is actually underway.

So that the flexibility of the procedure could be illustrated without undue attention on the characterization of the CDF, it was decided to focus on the triangular distribution. The triangular distribution was chosen because it may be specified by three values, low, median, and high, which correspond to the $0^{th}, 50^{th}$ and 100th percentiles.

Individual values within each of the six triangular distributions were chosen according to the Latin hypercube sampling scheme (i.e., the percentiles recorded in the cells). These values were then recorded in a runstream file. Each of the runstream files were then executed and the results of the simulation were stored on-line for further analysis.

Tabular summary

The data which were the focus of the structured sensitivity analysis are summarized in Tables 1, 2 and 3. Table 1 records the base-case values of the six variables (i.e., as they appear in the DGEM database). Table 2 records the values of the same six variables for the mobilization. These mobilization values are also the median values used in fitting triangular distributions to each variable. The minimum and maximum values for each of the six variables are recorded in Table 3. The information in Tables 2 and 3 served to define the CDF for each variable. Values were then selected from each CDF according to the Latin hypercube sampling scheme.

4 Impacts of the Mobilization Scenario

4.1 Analysis of the Mobilization

The volume of economic output increases as a result of mobilization. Demand increases due to higher government purchases. The effective volume of available resources also rises as a result of the increase in capital and labor services. Demand pulls production higher while resources and capacity permit an accompanying increase in production.

Total production

Real GNP figures for 1983 are estimated to be:

1. Base case real GNP $3277.7 ($10^9$)

2. Real GNP with mobilization $3634.4

3. Increase in real GNP $356.7; and

4. Percentage increase in real GNP 10.9.

The higher level of real GNP is continued from 1984 through 1986 where the relative increases are 11.5, 11.3, and 10.8 percent.

Thus, the mobilization stimulates economic activity. Production responds; the entire level of economic activity is increased. Real GNP increases by an average of 11.1 percent compared to the base-case economic situation.

Use of output

This gain in production is used in the form of higher levels of final demand. Clearly, government purchases will increase substantially, since the rise in defense spending is the initiating factor in all these adjustments. The average increases in final demand during the period of mobilization are:

1. Personal consumption expenditures, 6.2%

2. Gross private domestic investment, 13.1%

3. Government purchases, 38.0%

4. Exports, -50.0%

5. Imports, -20.0%

Consumption and investment rise slightly, while government purchases rise most of all. Thus, the gains from the shift to mobilization do not accrue to businesses, per se, although businesses in certain sectors may benefit substantially. Instead, the gains go to the government. Mobilization generates a shift in economic structure away from business, investment, and consumption, and towards government activity.

Economic growth

The initial effect of the mobilization is to increase economic activity. Real GNP in 1983 is some 10.9 percent higher than in the base case. Yet mobilization does not increase economic growth. Although the growth in real GNP from 1983 is accelerated, this is only a one-time jump to a higher level of economic activity. Once production is at this new, higher level, growth rates revert to their former pattern. Thus, mobilization generates a single shift to more production, as both final demand and available resources are boosted. Mobilization does not generate a continuing gain in achievable rates of economic growth.

This is important, for it means that the early gains under mobilization will not be repeated. A higher level of production is sustainable, at least for some time, but large continuing gains are not realistic.

Prices

The mobilization does affect price levels. Inflation accelerates (i.e., the rate of increase in the general level of prices rises). The GNP price deflator shows an acceleration, *over the GNP price deflator for the base case*, of 2.3 percent in 1983, 4.5 percent in 1984, 9.7 percent in 1985, and 13.8 percent in 1986. The estimated inflationary impact is not immediate. It is not until the third year of the mobilization that the inflationary effects become striking.

Industry effects

Different industries are affected to different degrees by the mobilization. These impacts reflect several forces: the rise in defense purchases; and a change in input patterns accompanying any restructuring in relative prices.

On the average, overall production rises by 10.1 percent compared to the base-case conditions. The percentage change in individual industries ranges from a decline of 11.5 percent for metal mining to a rise of 32.1 percent for transportation equipment and ordnance.

Several industries have increases in output volumes. These involve crude petroleum and gas, petroleum refining, gas utilities, electric utilities, construction, services, and, with the largest gain, transportation equipment, and ordnance. Some of these are expected because they are the materials directly purchased for defense purposes. Others, however, reflect the indirect effects as requirements work their way through the industrial system. For example, transportation equipment and ordnance and petroleum are directly related to defense purchases, whereas most of the remaining industries are indirectly related.

In contrast, some industries are estimated to experience a reduction in volume. Even though overall economic activity is higher, these industries are less needed than in the base case.

Information on specific industries can be used in several ways. As a projection, it estimates what would happen under mobilization conditions. As a prescription, it indicates which industries are most important to the mobilization effort. Industries with a greater-than-average increase in output are of greater-than-average importance. Some of these are obvious, given their direct role in defense purchases. Others, however, are less obvious, and the ability to reveal such industries is an important benefit from an analysis such as this. By indicating the relative importance of each industry, this analysis can help mobilization planners determine how a policy, if implemented, would affect the allocation of resources. We note that the essence of such allocations is to differentiate higher from lower priority claimants on available resources.

A related application of this analysis involves the identification of bottlenecks. The increases in industry outputs are the increases required to sustain the mobilization. These increases might be compared with the expansion capability of an industry based on detailed knowledge of the industry and of constraints specific to the industry. If the required expansion exceeds the maximum likely expansion, or surge capacity, then the analyst has identified a potential bottleneck. Contingency plans can then be developed to ease such bottlenecks in the event of a mobilization.

4.2   Results of the Structured Sensitivity Analysis

The structured sensitivity analysis focuses on how perturbations about the mobilization values of the six key input variables given in Table 2 translate into changes in three major output variables. These output variables are:

1. Real Gross National Product;

2. Real Gross Private Domestic Investment; and

3. Real Private Domestic Capital Services.

The first two are NIPA variables; they are referred to in the text, tables, and figures which follow as real GNP and real investment, respectively. The third variable registers the joint effects of variations in the efficiency with which capital is employed, AKD, and capital accumulation over the mobilization period. It is important to note that capital accumulation incorporates the effects of investment and another key input variable in Table 2, U, the rate of depreciation of capital. For each year in the mobilization, capital services are equal to the product of AKD and the total real private domestic capital stock at the beginning of the year.

These three variables were chosen because they provide a convenient summary of how the economy makes the transition from the "business as usual" base-case simulation to a war-time footing. We note that those industries with greater-than-average increases in output in the mobilization baseline tended to have greater-than-average increases in output in the structured sensitivity analysis. The structured sensitivity analysis therefore provides a basis for prioritizing industries; it also shows where detailed studies are needed (e.g., expansion capacity, labor avilability by skill type, and input vulnerability).

The results obtained from the structured sensitivity analysis on each of the three major output variables are described through reference to a series of tables and figures. These tables and figures summarize three basic types of information for each variable:

1. The equilibrium levels experienced as a result of mobilization;

2. The percentage change (increase or decrease) over the base-case simulation as a result of mobilization; and

3. The annual percentage change in the equilibrium levels during the period of the mobilization.

These three types of information are hereafter referred to as mobilization values, base-case deviations, and annual rates of change, respectively. Figures 2 and 4 make use of a graphical analysis technique known as the box plot. Box plots provide a convenient means for summarizing graphically an entire data set. Box plots are essentially a graphical analysis of variance. One advantage of box plots for the structured sensitivity analysis is that they permit multiple years worth of data to be compared in a single diagram. The box plot consists of a box with its "hinges" drawn at the 25th and 75th percentiles, respectively. The width of the box is proportional to the number of observations. The median (i.e., the 50th percentile) is marked within the

box. The extreme values are marked and connected to the hinges of the box
with "whiskers."

The box plot thus graphically summarizes both the central tendency of
the data as well as its dispersion. Non-overlapping boxes on the same plot
are a strong indication that the two sets of data are significantly different.
All box plots presented in this section were generated through application of
the statistical analysis package DATAPLOT [13].

Growth in total production

As was shown earlier, the output of the economy increases during the mobilization. Figure 1 provides a graphical summary of the economic impacts
of mobilization for three sets of values for real GNP between 1982 and 1986.
The first year, 1982, is prior to the mobilization period and is included as a
reference point. The first set of values is for the base-case simulation; these
values are traced out by a solid line. These values provide a basis for comparing the output of the peace-time economy to outputs anticipated during
the mobilization. The second set of values is for the mobilization baseline;
these values are traced out by a dotted line. The third set of values is for
the mobilization maxima (i.e., the set of highest values for each year across
all simulations); these values are traced out with triangles and dashed lines.
Through reference to Figure 1, it can be seen that real GNP increased from
just under $3200 billion in 1982 to nearly $4100 billion in 1986. The figure documents the rapid increases in real GNP in 1983 and 1984. In 1985
and 1986, the economy gives indications of a return to its long-run growth
trend, since the traces associated with the mobilization parallel that of the
base-case simulation. The figure also shows that mobilization has resulted
in a net increase of approximately $400 billion in the level of real GNP over
the base-case simulation for 1984 through 1986. Figure 2 is a sequence of
box plots showing the range of the mobilization values for real GNP. The
figure demonstrates that significant increases in the output of the economy
are experienced in each year of the mobilization. A tabular summary of the
data in Figure 2 is given in Table 4. From Part A Table 4, it can be seen that
the range (i.e., the difference between the maximum and minimum values)
increases from approximately $55 billion in 1983 to nearly $80 billion in 1986.
Although the standard deviation of the simulated values increases each year,

it averages about 0.5 percent of the mean. Consequently, the increases in real GNP noted earlier are statistically significant. Part B of Table 4 documents the magnitude of the change in the output of the economy due to mobilization. Part B of Table 4 indicates that the war-time economy averages an increase of approximately 11 percent over the base-case simulation. Note that the base-case deviations reach a peak in 1984 and then decline slightly through 1986. This observation is consistent with the statement made earlier that the economy returned to its long-run growth trend once the initial shocks of the mobilization worked their way through the model. The data in Part B of Table 4 shows the significance of the initial surges, followed by the resumption of a trend. Part C of Table 4 illustrates how the output of the economy has grown over the mobilization period. The initial surge in government purchases produces a rapid increase in output. Reference to the table shows that the annual rate of change in real GNP is nearly 15 percent in 1983. The annual rate of change for 1983 is computed using the 1982 value of the base-case simulation. Consequently, the annual rate of change of nearly 15 percent incorporates an underlying growth trend plus a deviation from the base-case simulation. It is for this reason that the annual rate of change for 1983 exceeds the base-case deviation for 1983. In 1984, the annual rate of change has slowed to approximately 7.5 percent. By 1985, real GNP has returned to its long-term growth rate. The data in the table show how the initial surge produces both a high rate of change and a high variability in that rate. By 1984, although the rate of change is still high, the variability has been reduced substantially. The variability in the growth rate then hovers around 0.1 percent through 1986. These observations lend support to the claim made earlier that mobilization produces a one-time jump to a higher level of economic activity rather than a continuing gain in achievable rates of economic growth.

Real Investment

The mobilization values of real investment follow a cyclical rather than a secular trend. These values plotted in Figure 3 reflect the underlying business cycle. Investment increases sharply in 1983 and 1984, turns down in 1985, and experiences a rate of increase approximately equal to that of the base-case simulation in 1986. The box plots of the mobilization values of real investment in Figure 4 indicate that all changes, both increases and decreases, are ikely to be highly significant. These observations are borne out through reference to Part A of Table 5. The early gains in investment due to mobilization are narrowing by 1985. Reference to Part B of Table 5 suggests that real investment in the post mobilization years may exceed the base-case levels by some positive amount. Part C of Table 5 illustrates the importance of the business cycle. Due to the combined effects of the accelerator principle (i.e., net investment is a function of the rate of change in final output rather than of the absolute level of output) and the potential for crowding out due to deficit financing, the rate of change in real investment is quite volatile. After increasing by almost 41 percent in 1983, the rate of change in real investment drops to slightly under 21 percent in 1984; it then turns sharply negative to -8 percent in 1985. Investment spending then increases in 1986, although the level is still less than at its peak in 1984.

Capital Services

The wide swings in investment experienced during the mobilization lead one to conjecture about their impact on capital services. Recall that capital services are a function of the level of the capital stock at the beginning of each year and the "efficiency" with which that stock can be utilized. Figure 5 illustrates that, even though investment is quite volatile, capital services increase steadily. By 1985, capital services appear to be changing according to the same long-term trend that underlies the base-case simulation. The pattern of tapering off shown in Figure 5 is rather pronounced. In particular, after significant increases in capital services experienced between 1983 and 1985, the change is quite modest in 1986. Reference to Part A of Table 6 demonstrates the degree of overlap for capital services in 1985 and 1986. From Figure 5, it is clear that capital services exceed those under the base-case simulation. It is now important to determine if these increases are significant. Reference to Part B of Table 6 indicates that except for 1983, the mobilization level of capital services is significantly higher than in the base-case simulation. Thus investment volatility in the war-time economy and increased shifts, which produce increased wear and tear on the entire stock, is not sufficent to reduce the "productive flow" of services from the capital stock. Since capital services are based on the quantity of capital stock available at the beginning of the year, the largest annual rate of change is experienced in 1984. Recall that the largest rate of change for investment was in 1983. Consequently, capital put in place through investment in 1983 is included in the quantity of capital stock available at the beginning of 1984. The rate of change in capital services then drops markedly due in part to investment volatility and the high rates of depreciation included to reflect wear and tear on the capital stock. Part C of Table 6 provides a tabular summary of the data.

5 Summary and Concluding Remarks

Large-scale models should be subjected to a critical examination prior to their use by cost analysts. To the maximum extent possible, models should also be subjected to an independent evaluation. To this end, the current paper has outlined a generic procedure for conducting such an evaluation.

Selected results from a critical evaluation of the Dynamic General Equilibrium Model (DGEM) are presented which illustrate how such an evaluation may be carried out in practice. The critical role of documentation is stressed, since it is the principal means through which performance against user requirements can be measured.

The analysis of the U. S. economy during a military mobilization is used to illustrate a generic evaluation procedure. This approach was taken for two reasons. First, a mobilization represents a major perturbation about the "business as usual" base-case simulation. Consequently, any weaknesses of the model (e.g., instabilities, implausible results, etc.) will be revealed by such a perturbation. Second, a mobilization requires an explicit treatment of the joint interactions of several factors (e.g., international trade, the business cycle, available capacity, investment, etc.). The evaluation of DGEM was a two-stage process. In the first, a mobilization baseline was constructed which made explicit the perturbations about the business as usual values in the DGEM database. The mobilization baseline also provided a point of reference for how the joint interactions of these perturbations affected the path of the national economy. In the second, six key variables were varied in combination subject to an experimental design. This enabled us to explore in detail certain patterns which were uncovered in the mobilization baseline.

For the case at hand, DGEM was found to produce solutions which were both realistic and internally consistent from an economic perspective. This is especially important in light of the results of the structured sensitivity analysis because one can see how techniques used in a model evaluation can be applied to major studies with policy implications.

We wish to thank Drs. E. A. Hudson and R. J. Goettle of Dale Jorgenson and Associates and R. R. Wilson of the Federal Emergency Management Agency for their many insights on DGEM. This research was partially supported by the Federal Emergency Management Agency.

Table 1:   Base-Case Values

| Variable | Values by year | | | |
name	1983	1984	1985	1986
GZ(1)	207.3	220.3	235.7	233.2
GZ(2)	68.3	72.3	86.9	67.6
AKD	0.146	0.159	0.160	0.156
U	0.062	0.062	0.062	0.062
LB	1037.7	1058.3	1050.9	1068.9
DG	174.0	167.3	211.9	192.5

Table 2:   Mobilization Values

| Variable | Values by year | | | |
name	1983	1984	1985	1986
GZ(1)	311.0	396.5	518.5	583.0
GZ(2)	85.4	108.5	130.4	101.4
AKD	0.154	0.167	0.168	0.164
U	0.068	0.068	0.068	0.068
LB	1131.1	1153.6	1145.5	1165.1
DG	261.1	301.1	381.5	346.5

Table 3:   Extreme Values Used in the Structured Sensitivity Analysis

Variable name	Setting	Values by year			
		1983	1984	1985	1986
GZ(1)	MIN	290.2	374.5	471.4	513.0
	MAX	331.7	418.6	565.7	653.0
GZ(2)	MIN	82.0	101.2	121.7	94.6
	MAX	88.8	115.7	139.0	108.2
AKD	MIN	0.150	0.164	0.165	0.161
	MAX	0.156	0.170	0.171	0.167
U	MIN	0.065	0.065	0.065	0.065
	MAX	0.071	0.071	0.071	0.071
LB	MIN	1110.3	1132.4	1124.5	1143.7
	MAX	1151.8	1174.7	1166.5	1186.5
DG	MIN	226.2	284.4	339.0	308.0
	MAX	295.8	317.9	423.8	385.0

Table 4: Summary Statistics for Real GNP

Part A: Mobilization Values

Year	Mean	Minimum	Maximum	Std. Dev.
1983	3629.6	3606.4	3659.7	15.97
1984	3893.5	3862.4	3932.0	19.58
1985	3970.9	3936.7	4010.0	20.96
1986	4069.1	4035.0	4113.1	23.44

Part B: Base-Case Deviations

Year	Mean	Minimum	Maximum	Std. Dev.
1983	10.74	10.03	11.66	0.487
1984	11.50	10.61	12.60	0.561
1985	11.23	10.27	12.32	0.587
1986	10.77	9.84	11.97	0.638

Part C: Annual Rates of Change

Year	Mean	Minimum	Maximum	Std. Dev.
1983	14.64	13.91	15.60	0.505
1984	7.27	7.10	7.44	0.107
1985	1.99	1.90	2.13	0.078
1986	2.47	2.25	2.61	0.100

Table 5:   Summary Statistics for Real Investment

Part A: Mobilization Values

Year	Mean	Minimum	Maximum	Std. Dev.
1983	629.8	617.6	645.1	7.62
1984	761.4	753.4	775.0	5.91
1985	700.1	687.1	720.1	9.83
1986	739.1	725.3	759.9	11.95

Part B: Base-Case Deviations

Year	Mean	Minimum	Maximum	Std. Dev.
1983	25.12	22.68	28.15	1.515
1984	15.14	13.92	17.20	0.894
1985	7.87	5.88	10.95	1.514
1986	6.75	4.75	9.74	1.726

Part C: Annual Rates of Change

Year	Mean	Minimum	1—c—Maximum	Std. Dev.
1983	40.81	38.07	44.23	1.705
1984	20.90	20.02	22.13	0.740
1985	-8.06	-8.79	-7.09	0.629
1986	5.58	4.67	6.39	0.489

Table 6: Summary Statistics for Capital Services

Part A: Mobilization Values

Year	Mean	Mininum	Maximum	Std. Dev.
1983	651.9	642.3	659.3	5.41
1984	737.0	727.2	746.9	5.64
1985	777.4	766.1	788.1	6.47
1986	785.4	770.3	797.6	8.09

Part B: Base-Case Deviations

Year	Mean	Minimum	Maximum	Std. Dev.
1983	0.95	-0.54	2.09	0.838
1984	2.93	1.56	4.31	0.788
1985	4.39	2.87	5.83	0.869
1986	4.41	2.39	6.03	0.108

Part C: Annual Rates of Change

Year	Mean	Minimum	Maximum	Std. Dev
1983	9.79	8.16	11.03	0.911
1984	13.05	12.49	13.51	0.389
1985	5.48	5.17	5.93	0.191
1986	1.04	0.24	1.33	1.344

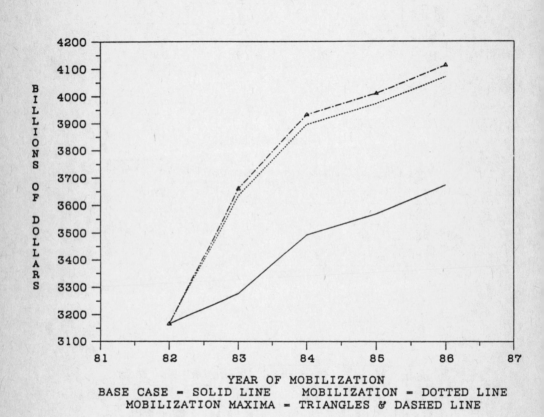

Figure 1. Values of Real GNP for the Base-Case Simulation, the Mobilization Baseline, and the Mobilization Maxima.

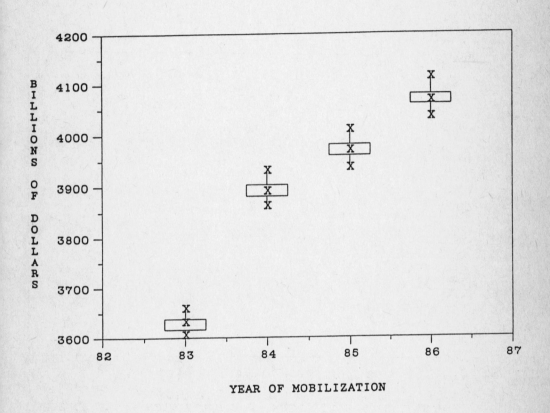

Figure 2. Box Plots of Mobilization Values for Real GNP.

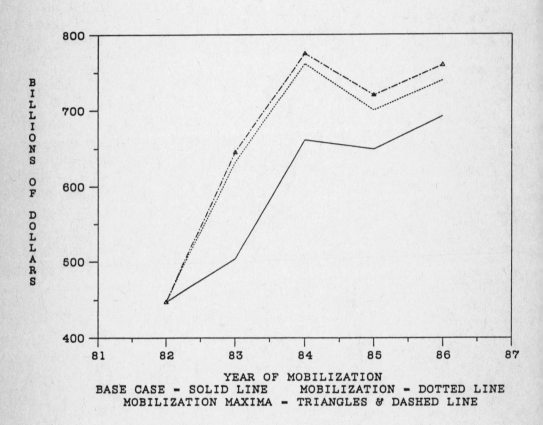

Figure 3. Values of Real Investment for the Base-Case Simulation, the
Mobilization Baseline, and the Mobilization Maxima

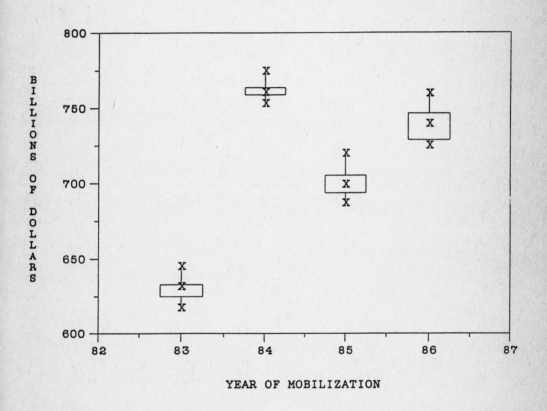

Figure 4. Box Plots of Mobilization Values for Real Investment

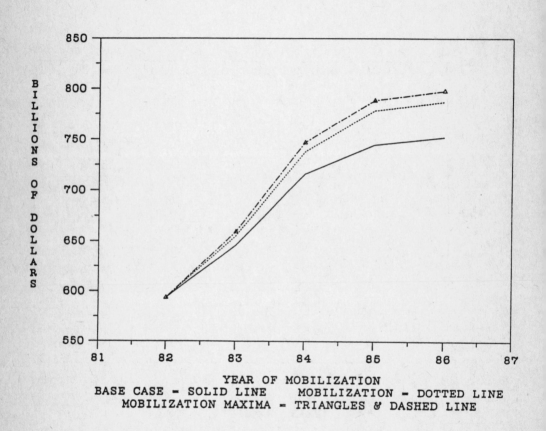

Figure 5. Values of Capital Services for the Base-Case Simulation, the Mobilization Baseline, and the Mobilization Maxima

References

[1] Chapman, R. E., Gass, S. I., Filliben, J. J., and Harris, C. M., *Guidelines for Evaluating Emergency Management Models and Databases: A Suggested Approach*, Gaithersburg, MD: National Institute of Standards and Technology, NISTIR 88-3826, 1989.

[2] Gass, S. I., "Decision-Aiding Models, Validation, Assessment, and Related Issues for Policy Analysis," *Operations Research*, **Vol. 31**, 1983, pp. 603-631.

[3] Hudson, E. A., and Jorgenson, D. W., *The Long Term Interindustry Transactions Model: A Simulation Model for Energy and Economic Analysis*, Washington, DC: Federal Preparedness Agency, 1979.

[4] Hudson, E. A., and Jorgenson, D. W., "U. S. Energy Policy and Economic Growth, 1975-2000," *The Bell Journal of Economics and Management Science*, **Vol. 5**, Autumn 1974, pp. 461-514.

[5] *Simulations of the 36 DGEM Over the Historical Period*, Lexington, MA: Data Resources, Inc., 1980.

[6] *Test and Sensitivity Simulations of the 36 Sector Dynamic General Equilibrium Model*, Lexington, MA: Data Resources, Inc., 1980.

[7] Goettle, R. J., and Hudson, E. A., *User's Guide to the 36 DGEM Simulation Model*, Cambridge, MA: Dale Jorgenson and Associates, 1984.

[8] Goettle, R. J., and Hudson, E. A., *Final Report on the Dynamic General Equilibrium Model*, Cambridge, MA: Dale Jorgenson and Associates, 1984.

[9] Goettle, R. J., and Hudson, E. A., *36 DGEM: The Dynamic General Equilibrium Simulation Model*, Cambridge, MA: Dale Jorgenson and Associates, 1984.

[10] Harris, C. M., *Issues in Sensitivity and Statistical Analysis of Large-Scale, Computer-Based Models*, Gaithersburg, MD: National Bureau of Standards, NBS GCR 84-466, 1984.

[11] Harris, C. M., *Computer Generation of Latin Hypercube Sampling Plans*, Gaithersburg, MD: National Bureau of Standards, NBS GCR 84-476, 1984.

[12] McKay, M. D., Conover, W. J., and Beckman, R. J., "A Comparison of Three Methods for Selecting Values of Input Variables in the Analysis of Output from a Computer Code," *Technometrics*, **Vol. 21**, 1979, pp. 239-245.

[13] Filliben, J. J., *DATAPLOT – Introduction and Overview*, Gaithersburg, MD: National Bureau of Standards, Special Publication 667, 1984.

THE VALUE OF WEAPON SYSTEM RELIABILITY IN A COMBAT ENVIRONMENT: COSTS AND PERFORMANCE

Karen W. Tyson, Stanley A. Horowitz,
and D. Graham McBryde
Institute for Defense Analyses
1801 N. Beauregard Street
Alexandria, Virginia 22311

Peter Evanovich
Center for Naval Analyses
4401 Ford Avenue
Alexandria, Virginia 22302

INTRODUCTION

This paper reports on the development of a methodology for assessing the cost and performance trade-offs between equipment reliability and logistic support under combat conditions. In other words, does reliability make a difference and, if so, how much?

Improvements in the reliability of equipment have two important payoffs, in theory:

- Cost is lower. A given peacetime or wartime flying program could be completed at a lower cost for spare parts, manpower, support equipment, etc.

- Performance is higher. For a given set of support conditions, more missions can be flown. This would be particularly true in the case of non-standard logistic support.

The role of support cost analysis should be to examine the cost of alternative ways of achieving specified levels of combat effectiveness. Thus, there is a need for tools that allow evaluation of the value of improved reliability in a wartime context. As with other aspects of system design, desired reliability should be determined through explicit consideration of the environment in which the system is meant to be used. This implies not only using methods designed to reflect the combat environment as closely as possible, but also applying the methods to data developed in as combat-like a setting as possible. However, empirical support cost and failure rate data typically is based on peacetime operations.

These methods must be used to assess the reliability of systems for which reliability can still be changed. Thus, it is our goal to develop a method for evaluating these issues which can also be used for prospective systems.

A three-step procedure was undertaken to fulfill these objectives:

- Develop or adapt a model that can relate the reliability and cost of the components of a weapon system to the performance of the system in a combat environment and to the cost of achieving that level of performance.

- Demonstrate the methodology with an existing system. The F-15 was chosen for this purpose.

The authors are grateful for the sponsorship of the Weapon Support Improvement Group, Office of the Assistant Secretary of Defense (Production and Logistics). Mei-Ling Eng, Joseph Presta, and Dianne St. Jean provided programming assistance.

- Develop techniques to allow analysis of the value of alternative levels of reliability for weapon systems that are in an early stage of the acquisition process. In future work, we will apply these techniques to a prospective system.

Model Selection

Since many models have already been developed that can link reliability to the sortie generation capability of a squadron of aircraft, it was not necessary for us to develop our own model. Two kinds of simulation models were considered, Monte Carlo models such as LCOM, SPECTRUM and CASEE, and analytic simulators such as Dyna-METRIC, ACIM and MIME.[1]

We chose among these on the basis of their ease of use and on the basis of their ability to adequately capture four critical aspects of wartime operations. These were:

- ability to accommodate a varying sortie rate over the period of the conflict.

- ability to simulate an austere operating environment, one in which only limited repairs can be accomplished for at least part of the period being studied.

- ability to simulate vulnerable logistic support, the situation in which the delivery of additional spare parts is interrupted.

- ability to capture the effects of battle damage.

The first three of these characteristics of wartime operations are important to examine because analysis that includes them is likely to point out the value of reliability. If particularly challenging sortie rates are to be accomplished at critical junctures in the war, and if repairs are inhibited by the lack of equipment or spare parts, reductions in the number of aircraft that become inoperative due to parts failures could make an important difference in mission accomplishment.

Battle damage, however, could cut the other way. If most inoperative aircraft are not mission capable because they have been damaged by enemy fire, improved reliability is unlikely to make as much difference. Most of the down aircraft will still be down, even if they are more reliable.

A fair analysis of the net value of improved reliability in a battlefield context requires that all these considerations be examined.

Other aspects of combat operations were not considered in our analysis of sortie generation capability. These include the availability of personnel to perform repair work and the impact of airfield damage. We plan ultimately to include estimates of the cost of personnel under different reliability assumptions in our analysis, but spare parts and repair capability are the only resources we have treated as determining the availability of aircraft. They seem the most intertwined with the reliability of equipment.

Dyna-METRIC was chosen as our analytic tool. Its workings will be discussed in more detail in the next section.

---

[1] LCOM and Dyna-METRIC were developed by Rand; SPECTRUM, by the Naval Air Development Center; CASEE, by Information Spectrum Incorporated; ACIM, by CACI; and MIME, by the Center for Naval Analyses.

Demonstrating the Methodology With an Existing System

Our purpose was to show that a methodology based on the use of Dyna-METRIC could be used to assess the value of higher reliability under wartime conditions. Toward this end the following sequence of steps was carried out:

- Data reflecting the reliability and cost of the components of the F-15 were gathered and the capability to use Dyna-METRIC to analyze these data was developed.

- A wartime flying scenario was obtained.

- Dyna-METRIC was used to generate war reserve spares kits (WRSK kits) for a deployed F-15 squadron. Kits were developed for three levels of reliability – the observed level, a level reflecting failure rates 50% of the historical level (a doubling of reliability), and a level reflecting failure rates 150% of the historical level. In developing WRSK kits, Dyna-METRIC focuses on buying parts that achieve specified levels of aircraft availability under a specified scenario as cheaply as possible.

- The impact of reliability on the cost of WRSK kits was calculated. These costs can be expected to be accurate, since this same methodology is used by the Air Force to develop spares packages.

- For all three levels of reliability, baseline sortie generation profiles were developed for thirty days of simulated operations under standard assumptions about logistic support (resupply times and maintenance capability). These profiles were compared with the levels of sortie generation called for by the scenario. Following Air Force practice, in the baseline case simple repairs were allowed to begin on the fifth day of operations, and more complex repairs were delayed to the thirtieth day (and thus did not affect our calculations). Standard Air Force assumptions for the resupply times for individual parts were used. No battle damage or attrition was assumed. All of our analyses (both the baseline and excursions from it) permitted cannibalization and incorporated a delay for the performance of corrective maintenance.

- The heart of our analysis involved modifying the baseline assumptions in ways that incorporated more of the characteristics of combat and developing sortie generation curves that reflected the new assumptions. The onset of simple repairs (remove and replace) was delayed. A one-percent attrition rate was incorporated, and a level of battle damage reflecting Vietnam experience was introduced into the analysis. These departures from the baseline were examined both singly and together for all three levels of reliability.

- The sortie profiles developed under the more combat-like assumptions were compared with those developed under the baseline. Inferences about whether reliability is likely to be more important in a combat environment than in a more benign environment could now be drawn.

Analyzing Reliability Early in the Acquisition Process

It would be useful to learn more about the value of improved reliability for existing weapon systems. This knowledge could help guide actions concerning reliability improvement programs. But it would be even more useful to learn about the value of reliability for systems still in an early stage of the design process. That is where improvements can be made most cheaply and with the least disruption. The analytic procedure that was outlined above must be modified to permit analysis of systems that do not yet have firm designs or detailed data on the cost and failure rates of their components.

To develop and test such modifications, we will analyze the F-15 as if it were a system in an early stage of development. This involves pretending that we only have the kind of aggregate information on the reliability of the F-15 and the cost of its components that is typically available at such a stage. In addition to the average failure rate and cost of the components of the system, we are assuming the availability of specific information on a small number of critical parts. We are attempting to develop a set of disaggregation rules that (when applied to the aggregated F-15 data) would yield a good approximation of the results we got using actual disaggregated data for the F-15. This exercise in simulating disaggregate data with aggregate data involves making alternative assumptions about the relationship between the cost and the failure rate of components.

MODEL AND DATA

The Dyna-METRIC Model

Dyna-METRIC (Dynamic Multi-Echelon Technique for Recoverable Item Control) is a model which is used to (1) develop inventory requirements to meet specified levels of supply readiness (at minimal cost) and (2) evaluate the readiness and sortie generation capability of aircraft in terms of logistic support (supply and maintenance) and operational considerations (flight scenarios, attrition rates, etc.).

Dyna-METRIC was selected for use in this study because:

- It is capable of assessing the following factors of readiness and sortie generation capability in an integrated fashion:
  - Reliability of aircraft components
  - Dynamic (fluctuating) flight hour programs
  - Dynamic logistic support availability (e.g. resupply cut-off and delayed intermediate-level maintenance support)
  - Aircraft attrition

- It is flexible in terms of data requirements. This makes it suitable for use during the entire acquisition process. It is capable of assessing baseline reliability and maintainability, aircraft configurations and generic logistics support, and force deployment strategies. As improved data on aircraft configuration, component reliability, not/component cost, maintainability and logistic support structures become available, data bases can be easily modified for use in the model. Thus, while data quality improves, the evaluation technique remains constant. This improves the accuracy of model estimates of, say readiness, and maintains consistency so that changes in results can always be related to data rather than the peculiarities of models.

- It has become accepted by a large section of the Air Force community as a tool for evaluating logistic support in terms of performance.

- It is used by AFLC to determine inventory requirements (for example, War Reserve Spares Kits) to meet readiness objectives.

- It is relatively easy to use. Data elements are transparent to decision makers, and model execution is relatively inexpensive and timely.

Limitations of the Model

Dyna-METRIC, like any model of this type, provides assessments of performance on the basis of assumptions made about the *general* operations of supply, maintenance, and sortie generation built into the model and the relevant *data* fed into the model. However, models have some limitations. They cannot, for example, take into account the ingenuity of supply and maintenance officers, all of the unobserved or unexpected conditions resulting from wartime operations, or the perturbations in failure rates and repair times (from expected values) that can result during any operation. In general, Dyna-METRIC does not model every nuance of aviation support and operations. Nevertheless, it does model aircraft operations and supply and maintenance with sufficient accuracy and detail to allow managers to make effective decisions about support and design requirements for aircraft. The following discussion describes the basic characteristics of Dyna-METRIC and how the model was used in this study to evaluate alternative aircraft reliability levels and support concepts. This discussion centers on the use of the model in this study. Additional features were developed by the study team for this analysis. The reader is referred to Isaacson, et al., (1985) for a more complete description of the model.

Data Required To Use Dyna-METRIC

Dyna-METRIC attempts to estimate the impact of logistic support on a planned operating scenario. In this analysis, we analyzed operations at one base and for one Type-Model-Series (TMS) aircraft. Assuming a specified level of rear-echelon support, Dyna-METRIC is capable of simultaneously analyzing multiple site operations in a multi-echelon support network. As input to the model, the user must supply the following to define the planned platform operating scenario:

- Force levels (number of aircraft)
- Flying hour program
  - Number of sorties per day
    - Peacetime rate
    - Number per day for each day of wartime portion of the scenario
  - Flight hours per sortie
- Attrition rates (Separate rates can be specified for each day of the wartime portion of the scenario.)

To analyze operations in terms of logistic support each aircraft must be described in terms of its components (Line Replaceable Assemblies (LRUs)) and if possible the lower identured components of the LRUs (Shop Replaceable Units (SRUs) and sub SRUs). Analysis conducted in this study focused on

LRUs. The following LRU factors are used by the model in analyzing the effectiveness of a logistic support system:[2]

- Aircraft configuration (a complete list of LRUs on the aircraft)
- Removal rate for each component (per flight hour or per sortie)
- Quantity per aircraft for each LRU
- Level of repair for each component (i.e. an indicator to describe if component can be repaired on site or must be repaired at higher echelons of support (for example, depots)
- Not Repairable This Site (NRTS) rate for each LRU. This is the percentage of removals that must be condemned or sent to higher repair echelons because, for example, the site is not given complete repair capability.
- Turn Around Time[3] (TAT) for each LRU. This is the time it takes maintenance to return a failed part to a ready-for-issue state and should not be confused with the time it takes to remove a failed part from an aircraft and replace it with a working part.
- Resupply time for each LRU. This is the time it takes rear-echelon support to meet requirements for parts that fail and cannot be repaired on site.

In addition to these factors, which Dyna-METRIC has been programmed to treat, we have adjusted the model to analyze the effects of battle damage. Since Dyna-METRIC has no specially designed feature to analyze battle damage, the model had to be adapted for this purpose, as discussed below. To take advantage of this option, the user must supply the following battle damage operating scenario specification:

- Battle damage rate as the number of battle damage incidents per sortie.[4]

Adaptation of the Model for Maintenance Delay and Battle Damage

An important factor not programmed into Dyna-METRIC is organizational maintenance. In particular, the model was not specifically designed to consider aircraft repair delays caused by maintenance on aircraft. It does consider repair delay caused by supply support, but this disregards the time it takes to remove and replace a part when a replacement spare part is available. Therefore, IDA has developed a technique so that the model incorporates organizational maintenance into the model. To do this, the following must be specified:

- Mean Time to Repair for each LRU. This is the time it takes organizational maintenance to remove a failed part, acquire a replacement from supply (assuming a replacement is in stock) and install the ready-for-issue part on the aircraft.

The modifications of Dyna-METRIC by IDA to include battle, damage and organizational level repair time analyses are done through Dyna-METRIC's modeling of LRUs.

---

2 If lower indentured parts are analyzed, similar factors must be supplied for these SRUs and sub SRUs.
3 When analyzing rear-echelon support, these factors must be supplied for repair done at these sites.
4 Current IDA programming of this feature assumes battle damage rates are constant during the wartime scenario, but with additional computer time and analyst intervention the model can evaluate variations in the battle damage rate.

Aircraft downtime due to organizational-level repair is modeled by constructing a "pseudo LRU" for each LRU in the data base. Each pseudo-LRU has the same failure rate and quantity per aircraft as its associated LRU. However, the NRTS rate for the pseudo-LRU is always 0, and its TAT is taken to be a specified associated LRU's Mean Time to Repair (MTTR). The objective is to have the model fail a pseudo-LRU whenever its corresponding LRU fails. By assuming the pseudo LRU stock level to be zero, Dyna-METRIC delays repair of the LRU on the aircraft (through the pseudo-LRU) by MTTR. Delays in repair due to supply (Awaiting Parts Time) are modeled explicitly by Dyna-METRIC using data supplied for the LRU.[5]

Delays in aircraft repair due to battle damage are modeled in a similar manner. Currently, functional areas of the aircraft are designated as "battle damage" LRUs. Failure rates (battle damage rates) are specified for each area. A mean time to repair is specified and used with battle damage LRUs to have the model simulate repair and associated down time due to battle damage repair.[6]

Logistic Support Variations

An operational scenario is also specified for logistic support. In particular, the following input variables specify this scenario:

- Times and durations of cut-offs in resupply
- Delays in establishing repair capability for components.

Although resupply delays are applied to all demands for replenishment of components from rear-echelon support, maintenance capability delays can be specified for each LRU (and SRU if appropriate). This is important since developing total repair capability at advanced bases is incremental over time. Moreover, it permits battle damage repair and organizational-level repair analysis via the techniques described above.

What Dyna-METRIC Does

When supplied with LRU inventory levels, Dyna-METRIC simulates[7] flight operations and resulting supply and maintenance responses. Unavailability of repair parts is recognized by the model as causing "holes" in aircraft (i.e., down aircraft). The Dyna-METRIC provision to allow component cannibalization is used for all LRUs. (Holes are consolidated). Cannibalization is not allowed for organizational-level maintenance parts (pseudo-LRUs) and battle damage parts, since the requirements for repairs on an aircraft cannot be transferred from one aircraft to another.

---

5   Because the model assumes parts fail independently, this technique only approximates delays due to organizational maintenance, since it does not really guarantee that MTTR is added in total to awaiting parts time in the removal and replacement of a failed LRU.

6   Plans have been made to analyze battle damage by component. This requires tbat LRU failure rates MTTRs, TATs and NRTS rate be adjusted to reflect battle damage. Development of such factors is currently underway, but estimates are not available at this time.

7   Dyna-METRIC is not a Monte-Carlo simulation (like, for example, the Logistic Composite Model – LCOM), but an analytic simulator.

Dyna-METRIC can then estimate the percentage of aircraft available at any point in the scenario. Using this information with the specified maximum number of sorties per aircraft per day, the model estimates the number of planned sorties that can be accomplished at each point in the scenario.

The above discussion centers on how and in what context Dyna-METRIC can be used to evaluate logistic support in meeting a planned scenario. Note that inventory level specifications must be made for each aircraft component in this analysis.

For this study, Dyna-METRIC was also used to determine inventory requirements. Dyna-METRIC has an optimization routine that uses its evaluation methodology to select an inventory that will meet a (supply) readiness objective at minimal inventory cost. In particular, it meets a specified not-mission-capable rate due to supply at minimal cost. Any inventory developed by Dyna-METRIC for use in this study was constructed using the same parameters that would typically be used by AFLC in inventory requirements development.

Data

In this section the F-15C data used to illustrate the use of Dyna-METRIC in analyzing aircraft reliability are described. They are presented in terms of the Dyna-METRIC input variables listed in the previous section.

Operating Scenario

All analysis presented in this paper is centered on supporting 24 forward-deployed F-15 aircraft during a 30-day wartime scenario with a flying schedule as in Table 1.

Table 1. Wartime Flying Scenario Used in the Analysis

Day of Scenario	Planned Sorties Per a/c Per Day	Flight Hours Per Sortie	Total Planned Flight Hours Per Day
1-3	3.13	2	150.2
4-6	3.09	2	148.3
7-19	1.00	2	48.0
20-30	.98	2	47.0

Attrition rates (when used) were assumed to be 2 per 100 sorties for days 1-6 of the scenario and 1 per 100 sorties for day 7-30.

Battle damage rates (when used) were assumed, throughout the scenario, to be 10 per 100 sorties.[8]

Recall that in this analysis battle damage was modeled from a maintenance delay point of view, and the impact of the unavailability of repair material was not modeled. In particular, battle damage repair was modeled for eight areas of the aircraft. (See Table 2.) Two types of battle damage were considered: damage from small arms fire and damage from high explosives. The probabilities of battle damage in each functional area (given a battle damage incident) assuming small arms or high explosive damage are given in Table 2. All figures were based on combat damage on USAF fighter aircraft involved in the Southeast Asia conflict as reported in Dubek (1984).

Mean repair times for individual battle damage repair were also taken from data in [1]. They are shown in Table 3.

In the analysis, the data in Tables 2 and 3 were used to describe requirements based on the assumed number of battle damage incidents (10 per 100 sorties) and an assumed split between small arms and high explosive battle damage. For the analysis presented later, we assumed a 50-50 split, but the model can easily examine any desired split of battle damage between small arms and high explosive threats.

**Table 2. Probability of Battle Damage,
by Type of Threat and Functional Area**

F-15 Functional Area	Probability of Battle Damage (BD) Given:	
	Small Arms BD	High Explosive BD
Structure	.933	.927
Flight Controls	.126	.182
Propulsion	.163	.225
Fuel	.153	.309
Power	.047	.309
Avionics	.140	.091
Crew Station	.042	.073
Armament	.032	.055

Logistic Support Scenario

Although the operating scenario was kept constant in all of the analyses presented in this study, the logistic support scenario described below was used as a baseline. As reported later, elements like re-supply times and intermediate level maintenance capability were varied to test the sensitivity of results to these logistic parameters.

---

8   Although, for the purposes of this analysis, battle damage rates were assumed constant over the scenario Dyna-METRIC can analyze dynamic battle damage rates. However, user intervention at appropriate points in the simulated scenario and additional computer time are required.

Table 3. Mean Battle Damage Repair Times, by Type of Threat and Functional Area

F-15 Functional Area	Mean BD Repair Times (hours) Assuming:	
	Small Arms (BD	High Explosive BD
Structure	8.4	21.3
Flight Controls	30.6	27.7
Propulsion	17.8	157.3
Fuel	5.0	5.0
Power	35.0	652.2
Crew Station	20.0	51.9
Armament	5.0	5.0

The baseline parameters for logistic elements were:

• No re-supply from rear-echelon support points during the 30-day scenario. Spare part inventories were designed to support 30 days of operations and were assumed to be on hand at the beginning of the scenario.

• Intermediate-level component repair capability varied by aircraft component

   – Repair of Remove, Repair and Replace (RRR) F-15 components (as designated by AFLC) could begin any time after day 4 of the scenario.

   – Repair of Remove and Repair (RR) F-15 components (as designated by AFLC) could not be accomplished at all during the first 30 days.

Component repair capability varies because of requirements for support equipment and personnel. The designation of RR and RRR components is made on the basis of failure rates, mission criticality and the amount of equipment needed to perform repair. The capability to perform organizational-level maintenance and to do battle damage repair was assumed to commence on day 1 of the scenario. Time to repair failed components at the organizational level (assuming repair parts are available), that is, MTTR, was taken to be 2 hours for each LRU.

Component Reliability and Maintainability (R&M) Data

Baseline R&M data specifying LRU's of the F-15, LRU failure and NRTS rates and LRU intermediate level maintenance repair times (TATs) were developed for PACAF (Pacific Air Force) WRSK kit components. In particular, results of the analyses are based on the 387 LRUs of this database as established by AFLC for spares requirements determination.

Analyses of alternative aircraft reliability levels were carried out by scaling failure rate parameters of the R&M data base. For example, to analyze the impact of a doubling of reliability, the failure rate of each LRU in the database was multiplied by .5.

Finally, note that any evaluation of F-15 performance required a specification of the WRSKs. These were developed using the appropriate parameters via the Dyna-METRIC inventory selection routine.

The analysis of the sortie generation capability of aircraft with double the baseline level of reliability was based on a WRSK kit developed on the basis of this higher reliability. This mirrors current AFLC practice.

THE IMPACT OF RELIABILITY ON COST AND PERFORMANCE

In this section, we report on results of computer runs using F-15 data and the Dyna-METRIC model to demonstrate the impact of changes in the reliability of the system on cost of spares and sortie generation. As discussed in the previous section, we made the following baseline assumptions:

- Sortie program with surge in first six days (See Table 4 for details)

- RRR repair beginning on day 5, no RR repair during the scenario

Our process of analysis was:

- Buy spares to achieve this baseline scenario, at three levels of reliability.

- Analyze the cost of these spares.

- Vary the assumptions about attrition, battle damage, and other characteristics. In each case, begin with sufficient spares to achieve the flying program, under baseline conditions, at each level of reliability. Determine how well the squadron does with these spares packages in each excursion.

- Evaluate the percentage of sorties achieved and the total sorties achieved in each excursion.

In each case, as will be shown, increased reliability allows the squadron to achieve more sorties. This is always the case during the initial surge period, a crucial time of the conflict, and usually true even during the last 24 days of the scenario, when we are requiring only one sortie per aircraft per day. Diminished reliability decreases the percentage of the flying program achieved.

In addition, we did some preliminary work on how such evaluations might be performed on systems with incomplete data. We analyze the F-15 as if it were a system in the early stages of development. This involves using aggregated F-15 data to see whether we can obtain a good approximation of the results obtained from actual data.

Assessing the Cost of Sparing Under Different Reliability Levels

The first step in the analysis was to determine the spare parts packages required to achieve the flying program under the baseline assumptions and the three reliability levels. As we would expect, the costs of the spare parts packages are substantially different under the three different reliability assumptions:

Level of Reliability	Cost (thousands)
Normal (AFLC Failure Rates)	$78,791
High (.5 Times Normal Failure Rate)	32,389
Low (1.5 Times Normal Failure Rate)	107,133

These results show that one of the ways that reliability helps is in terms of cost to achieve a given flying program under given conditions. It is also important to note that this cost advantage continues throughout the analysis below. That is, we have **not** tried to run each variation with equal spare parts packages regardless of failure rates. Rather, we start off with spares packages that allow the flying program to be achieved under baseline conditions. This reflects Air Force practice.

Assessing the Impact of Reliability on Sortie Generation Capability Under Differing Conditions

Figure 1 shows the sortie program for the analysis – a 30-day scenario with a surge in the first six days. We evaluated the ability of the squadron to fly the sortie program under the following sets of conditions:

- Organizational-level **maintenance delay** of two hours for each failure, an approximation of the time required to diagnose the problem, find the part, and fix the problem

- **Attrition** of two percent per sortie during the surge and one percent thereafter, along with maintenance delay

- **Battle damage** of ten percent per sortie, along with maintenance delay. This section represents a preliminary look at battle damage. As a starting point, we assumed a ten-percent battle damage rate per sortie throughout the scenario. (Planning factors indicate that battle damage generally runs four to five times higher than attrition.) Since we assumed this rate throughout the scenario, it is a severe test of our concern that battle damage may "snow" the value of reliability. This analysis also included a two-hour maintenance delay.

- **Battle damage, attrition, and maintenance delay** taken together

- **Delayed repair**, no RRR repair capability until day 10 (vs. day 5 in the baseline), combined with **attrition, battle damage, and maintenance delay.**

Figures 1, 2, and 3 and Table 4 summarize the results. The figures show the percent of planned sorties achieved on each day, at each level of reliability. The table shows the cumulative number of sorties achieved by day 7 and by day 30.

Organizational-level **maintenance delay** has an effect on sortie generation during the initial six-day surge, as seen in Figure 2. While we still achieve almost all sorties in the high-reliability case, we achieve fewer than two-thirds of the sorties during the surge in the normal-reliability case and about 42 percent of the sorties in the low-reliability case. After the first six days, all sorties are achieved in all cases.

Thus, the level of reliability makes a difference in the ability of the squadron to fly when the model is adjusted to reflect reasonable repair times each time a part fails. We do not even have to introduce combat-like conditions to show that reliability has more of a payoff than is identified in the Air Force's provisioning analysis, which incorporates no repair time.

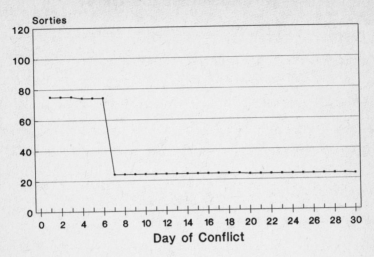

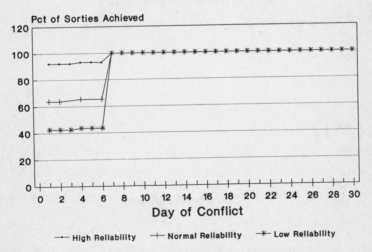

Figure 1.   F-15C Sortie Program and Percent of Sorties Achieved in the Maintenance Delay Case

Attrition
with Maintenance Delay

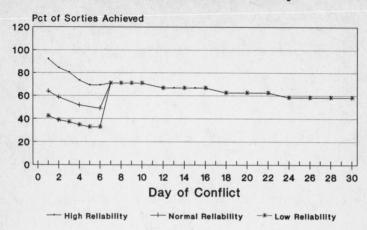

Battle Damage
with Maintenance Delay

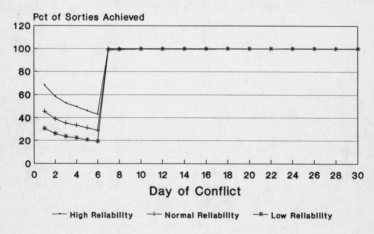

Figure 2. Percent of Sorties Achieved in Attrition and Battle Damage Case

Battle Damage and Attrition
with Maintenance Delay

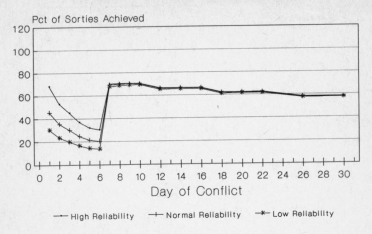

Delayed Repair, Attr., and BD
with Maintenance Delay

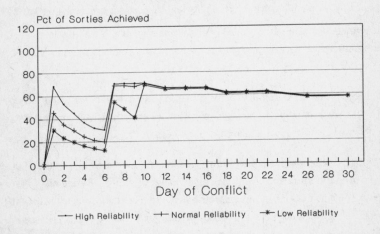

Figure 3. Percent of Sorties Achieved in Battle Damage/Attrition and Delayed Repair Cases

Table 4. Sorties Flown Under Different Conditions and Varying Levels of Reliability

	First 7 Days	Entire 30 Days
Baseline		
High	471.8	1,018.2
Normal	471.8	1,018.2
Low	470.5	1,017.0
Maintenance Delay		
High	438.8	985.3
Normal	313.3	859.8
Low	216.8	763.2
Attrition		
High	366.8	713.8
Normal	261.8	608.8
Low	180.2	527.2
Battle Damage		
High	261.8	808.2
Normal	182.6	728.7
Low	129.4	673.9
Attrition and Battle Damage		
High	215.5	562.5
Normal	149.2	494.4
Low	104.5	445.8
RRR Day 10		
High	215.4	562.4
Normal	148.9	493.3
Low	100.3	429.6

Adding **attrition** to the maintenance delay excursion has a dramatic effect on sortie generation during the initial six-day surge. During the surge, the percent of sorties achieved falls to 49 by the end of day 6 in the normal-reliability case, 69 percent in the high-reliability case, and 33 percent in the low-reliability case. There are no differences by reliability level in performance during the last 24 days.

Battle damage substantially degraded mission capability at all reliability levels, but the reliability level still made a difference in sortie generation capability during the surge period. After the surge, there were essentially no differences by reliability level.

The hypothesis that the existence of battle damage makes reliability less important does not seem to be borne out for the levels of battle damage and reliability we examined. Having aircraft that suffer battle damage makes it more important to have the other aircraft failure-free.

Combining **battle damage, attrition, and maintenance delay** resulted in considerable deterioration in overall performance from the cases examined above. By the end of day six, only 20 percent of sorties could be flown in the normal-reliability case. Reliability made a major difference during the surge period. On day six, 30 percent of sorties were flown in the high-reliability case and 14 percent in the low-reliability case. If the squadron made it past the surge, however, reliability made less of a difference in sortie generation. Still, the difference between high reliability and normal reliability is more than 50 sorties over the 30-day period.

Delayed repair (RRR on day 10) made only a relatively small difference compared to RRR on day 5, within reliability levels.

Assessing the Case of Incomplete Data – A Preliminary Look

As a first step in using the model to analyze reliability in new systems, we are beginning to analyze the F-15 as if it were a system in the early stages of development. If we can obtain a reasonable approximation of results from actual data, this would be an indication that the method could be used for new systems.

We took the actual F-15 data and aggregated it to a level similar to that which might be available for a new system. Using a method described in Ince and Evanovich (1986), we divided the F-15 LRUs into an 8-by-8 matrix based on the distribution of cost and failure rate. LRUs with low costs and low failure rates appeared in the top right of the matrix; LRUs with high costs and high failure rates appeared in the bottom left of the matrix. Then, we assigned LRUs in each of the 64 cells the mean cost and failure rate in the cell. Quantity per aircraft was always assumed to be one. Thus, we had a "false" data set of 387 LRUs with assigned costs and failure rates. We refer to this as the general knowledge scenario. We tested another false data set, referred to as the 14-LRU scenario, in which we assumed that we knew the actual data for the 14 LRUs with the highest costs and failure rates, while the rest of the LRUs had assigned data as before.

Table 5 presents preliminary results of the first tests of the method. Rankings of costs by reliability level were the same in all cases – the low-reliability case had the highest costs and the high-reliability case the lowest. However, magnitudes were different. In the normal reliability case, knowledge of only 14 LRUs led to cost estimates 11.5 percent higher. General knowledge of the cost distribution led to cost estimates 27 percent higher. The spread between high and low reliability also showed some differences in cases of incomplete knowledge.

Our analysis in this area is only beginning. In the future, we will analyze the impact of incomplete data knowledge on sortie generation and mission capable rates.

Table 5. Costs of Spare Parts Packages With Incomplete Data, by Reliability Level

| | Level of Data Knowledge | | |
Reliability Level	Complete	14 LRUs	General
		Costs	
High	32,389	43,198	50,911
Normal	78,791	87,883	100,070
Low	107,133	129,403	145,859
		Ratio to Complete Knowledge	
High	1	1.334	1.572
Normal	1	1.115	1.270
Low	1	1.208	1.361
		Ratio to Normal Reliability	
High	0.411	0.492	0.509
Normal	1	1	1
Low	1.360	1.472	1.458

IMPLICATIONS

Initial Conclusions

These results indicate that:

- The method we have chosen for assessing the value of reliability produces credible results for an existing system.

- The methods of incorporating maintenance delay and battle damage repair into Dyna-METRIC also seem to produce credible results for an existing system.

- Even with a relatively high assumed rate of battle damage, greater reliability does have a positive value in the surge portion of the scenario.

- As long as WRSK kits are bought using a methodology that does not account for the time needed to replace parts, higher reliability makes a big difference in being able to meet early surge flying requirements. This is true whether the logistic system is stressed by attrition, battle damage, and lack of repair capability or not.

- When circumstances are particularly trying, higher reliability allows significatly more sorties to be flown even after the surge portion of the scenario has passed. To this extent, reliability seems more important under combat-like conditions than in more benign circumstances.

Refining the Method To Include Battle Damage

As mentioned above, the method used to evaluate battle damage seems to produce credible results. However, improved estimates are needed.

The estimates of time to repair and the distribution of damage by system used in the current analysis are not F-15 specific but were based on data from the Vietnam war. The F-4 is the most prevalent aircraft in the data. The battle damage rate per sortie is based on commonly used planning factors that suggest that battle damage occurs at four or five times the rate of attrition. Better data inputs would yield better estimates.

Assessing New Systems

The preliminary results of this analysis suggest that it is possible to use sketchy data to assess the value of reliability in new systems. These methods do not provide exact magnitudes but appear to be useful for sensitivity analyses.

However, the unique architecture of the ATF presents some problems for analysis, such as redundancy and the flying program. We will strive to integrate as much data as can be obtained on the new system.

Future Plans

It is to be emphasized that the conclusions of this paper are preliminary. We have demonstrated the practicality of this method of assessing the value of reliability in a combat-like environment. However, we have not come anywhere near exhausting its potential.

In the future, we will strive to develop estimates of the value of reliability for the next-generation tactical fighter. The quality of these estimates will, of course, depend on the quality of the data inputs we are able to obtain from the Air Force.

Another area of potential future work is to identify the impact on combat sorties of changing the reliability of particular parts. This could be useful in analyzing the value of component improvement programs.

GLOSSARY

BLSS   base-level self-sufficiency spares.

Cannibalization   the practice of transferring a serviceable component from one aircraft to repair another. The aircraft must already be unserviceable because of another component failure, and the needed serviceable component cannot be obtained from local supplies.

CIRF   Centralized Intermediate Repair Facility.

Component impact   an approximation of the expected number of aircraft rendered NFMC by shortages of a particular LRU, computed by dividing the LRU's expected number of backorders by its QPA.

Condemnation   a decision or status indicating a component or subcomponent is irreparably damaged.

Dyna-METRIC   Dynamic Multi-Echelon Technique for Recoverable Item Control.

FMC   fully mission capable; an aircraft status indicating that the weapon system can accomplish any of its wartime missions.

LRU   line replaceable unit; a component typically removed from the aircraft at the flight line, rather than in a back shop.

MTTR   mean time to repair; the time it takes to remove a failed part, acquire a replacement from supply, and install the part on the aircraft.

NFMC	not fully mission capable; an aircraft status indicating that the weapon system's ability to accomplish at least one wartime mission has been degraded.
NRTS	not repairable this station; a decision or status indicating that a component cannot be repaired at a specified facility.
Pipeline	a network of repair and transportation processes through which repairable and serviceable parts flow as they are removed from their higher assemblies, repaired, and requisitioned from other points of supply.
Pipeline segment	a single process in the pipeline characterized by part arrivals over time, a delay time, and part departures over time.
PMC	partially mission capable; an aircraft status indicating that the weapon system can perform at least one wartime mission, though perhaps in a degraded mode.
QPA	quantity per aircraft; the number of a particular component or subcomponent physically mounted on an aircraft. Not the same as quantity per application (except for LRUs).
SRU	shop replaceable unit; a subcomponent of an LRU, typically removed from the LRU in the shop.
SubSRU	a subcomponent of an SRU, including bits and pieces that are often consumed during repair of the SRU. A subSRU may be repairable itself.
TAT	Turn Around Time, the time it takes maintenance to return a failed part to a ready-for-issue state.
WRSK	War Reserve Spares Kits.

BIBLIOGRAPHY

Dubek, First Lt. Robert D., Insights in Aircraft Battle Damage Repair through Combat Data, AFWAL-T09 85-288 FIEA, July 1984.

Ince, John F., and Peter Evanovich, Timely Analysis of the Readiness of New Systems, Report No. CRM 86-119, Center for Naval Analyses, June 1986.

Isaacson, K., P. Boren, C. Tsai, and R. Pyles, Dyna-METRIC Version 4: Modeling Worldwide Logistic Support of Aircraft Components, Report No. R-3389-AF, The RAND Corporation, May 1985.

U.S. Air Force Logistics Command, Coronet Warrior Exercise, Briefing presented at LOGCAS-88, Logistics Capability Assessment Symposium, Colorado Springs, April 1988.

THE USE OF THE ARMY COLLEGE FUND: IMPLICATIONS FOR PROGRAM COST EFFECTIVENESS

Edward J. Schmitz, Charles Dale, and Alan F. Drisko
U.S. Army Research Institute
5001 Eisenhower Avenue
Alexandria, VA   22333-5600

1. Introduction

In FY82 the U.S. Army introduced the Army College Fund (ACF) to promote the recruiting of highly capable young men and women into critical skills. Eligible individuals are given supplemental benefits of up to $14,400 above the basic military benefits if they qualify. Over 300,000 recruits have enlisted under the ACF Program since its inception.

This paper produces the first empirical estimates of the cost of the Army College Fund Program. The benefit usage of participants is projected and discounted to the enlistment point so that comparisons can be made with other recruiting resources.

Our results find that only about one quarter of the benefits available to recruits would ever be used, because significant numbers of individuals attrit from the program at various stages after enlistment.

By combining the cost analysis with projections of the program's enlistment effects it is possible to estimate the program's cost-effectiveness. We find that the Army College Fund is likely to be a cost-effective enlistment incentive. In fact, we project that the ACF Program's average cost per additional enlistment will be about half that of enlistment bonuses.

2. Background

Educational benefits have long been a part of the military compensation system. The GI Bill provided all military personnel with substantial educational benefits to compensate for the interruption of careers and provide an adjustment mechanism to aid their return to the civilian labor market. In 1977 the GI Bill was replaced by the Veterans' Educational Assistance Program (VEAP). VEAP differed from the GI Bill in that benefits were substantially reduced and soldiers were required to contribute to participate. The soldier's contribution was matched two for one, up to a maximum contribution of $2,700, for a total benefit of $8,100.

The development of educational benefits as an enlistment program began in 1979 with the test of the supplemental educational benefits, also called "kickers". The kickers differed from all previous educational benefits in that they were only offered to high quality recruits (high school graduates who score above the median on the enlistment test) enlisting in specific hard-to-fill jobs. One of the test programs was implemented in FY82 as the Army College Fund (ACF). Presently, the kickers offered range from $8,000 to $14,400, depending on the enlistment term.

Benefits are earned by satisfactory military service. A recruit must serve a minimum of 20 months to be eligible for any benefits; after that benefits are earned in proportion to the amount of the enlistment term served. An individual has up to ten years after completing military service to use the benefits.

3. Development Of A Cost Model

While it will take many years for the ACF participants to use their benefits, the Army must allocate dollars for the program at the time of enlistment. The Department of Defense has established rates based on the assumption of an arbitrary program usage factor.

We make the first empirical estimates of the kinds of factors necessary to produce an accrual cost model. This requires the estimation of both the amount of benefits used and the timing of when benefits will be used, as both affect the present value.

The first task in estimating costs is to project the number of users of the program. We forecast two user populations:

o Those individuals who serve one term, then separate.
o Those who reenlist, stay until a later date, and then become users.

An individual must successfully accomplish four steps to become a benefit user:

1. contribute
2. perform military service
3. separate from the military
4. attend school

Once a recruit has enlisted he or she must contribute to maintain eligibility for the additional ACF entitlement. If the recruit fails to contribute to the VEAP then eligibility for both ACF and VEAP is lost.

The second step required to obtain eligibility for the ACF is the performance of acceptable military service. The recruit who contributes must serve honorably at least 20 months for a two year enlistment, and 30 months for a three or four year ACF contract.

The third step required to become a benefit user is to leave the Army. While soldiers can theoretically use benefits while still in the Army, very few choose to do so. Opportunities to pursue college while on active duty are limited, and other in service tuition assistance is available.

The final step in becoming a benefit user is to attend school and apply for benefits through the Veterans' Administration.

Once the population of Army College Fund users has been projected
it is necessary to estimate the amount of benefits the average user will
actually spend. While an individual may have up to $14,400 in ACF
benefits available to him or her, two conditions determine the actual
amount used:

    (1) The size of the kicker earned.
    (2) The percentage of the available kicker used.

Kickers are earned in proportion to months served. In addition to
requiring at least 20 months of honorable service, the full kicker is
earned only if the soldier serves the full enlistment term. If the
recruit serves only 36 months of a 48 month enlistment, only 36/48 or 75
percent of the four year kicker, or $10,800, would be earned.

The proportion of available benefits that are actually awarded to
an ACF participant is determined by the length of time he or she attends
school. An individual's benefits are allocated over 36 months of full
time school attendance. The full benefit would not be used if the
individual attended school less than 36 months or did not attend full
time.

Benefits are earned in nominal terms, which means they are not
adjusted for inflation. Hence, the Defense Department discounts program
costs by an appropriate interest rate for the time between accession and
benefit usage. This length of time can be broken down into three
periods:

    (1) The time between accession and separation from the military.
    (2) The time between separation and the start of benefit usage.
    (3) The time between the start of benefit usage and the midpoint
        of benefit usage.

Once the usage of benefits and the time between accession and the
midpoint of benefit usage has been estimated, these factors can be
combined according to a present value formula. The Defense Department
sets an appropriate interest rate to estimate the amount of money to be
set aside for each ACF accession so that sufficient funds would be

available to pay for their future use of the program. In the next
section we make estimates of each of these factors for the ACF
population so that such calculations can be made.

4. Results

We merged data from the Defense Manpower Data Center, U.S. Army
Finance and Accounting Center, and Veterans' Administration. This data
file gives a complete picture of what has happened to Army College Fund
enlistments from the first test of the program in FY81 through any
benefit usage that has occurred with the Veterans' Administration
through July 1986. Thus, the behavior of ACF recruits with respect to
attrition, separation, and benefit usage for up to nearly three years
beyond separation can be analyzed.

Estimates of the ACF program costs are made for two populations:

o Individuals who serve one enlistment
o Individuals who reenlist

The greatest usage of the program would be expected to occur from
those who serve only one enlistment term, and the most accurate data is
available for this population. However, individuals who have reenlisted
will retain their entitlement for ten years until after they complete
military service.

The first factor to examine is the proportion of ACF recruits who
make contributions to VEAP. Finance records identify those individuals
who enlisted for the ACF and make contributions, a prerequisite to
receiving benefits. Not all recruits eligible for the program choose to
make contributions. They may decide not to attend college, or they may
separate prior to having an account established for them with the U.S.
Army Finance and Accounting Center.

The percentage of accessions by enlistment term who made
contributions are:

```
2 year    91.6 percent
3 year    88.5 percent
4 year    82.4 percent
```

The next factor in the ACF benefit usage computation is the probability of performing honorable service for 20 months or more for two year enlistees, or 30 months or more for three and four year recruits. We examined the probability of this occurring for the FY82 ACF population. The rates by enlistment term were:

```
2 year    88.4 percent
3 year    74.7 percent
4 year    67.0 percent
```

In order to use the benefits, the individual separates from the Army. The population that made contributions and performed the required service was analyzed to determine their probability of separating from the Army. The separation rates by enlistment term were:

```
2 year    83.1 percent
3 year    70.1 percent
4 year    69.5 percent
```

The next critical task is estimating the probability that an individual who has separated from the Army will draw upon his or her military educational benefits. Historically, the user rates for those individuals who have contributed, served, and separated were observed as of five years after enlistment:

```
2 year    64.0  percent
3 year    46.9  percent
4 year    14.0  percent
```

These individuals have several more years within which to begin benefit usage. However, previous research on college attendance (Manski and Wise 1983) and the historical experience of the Veterans Administration (1981) finds that most individuals who plan to use the benefits will begin to do so within a few years of separating from the service. The opportunity costs of attending college increase as one gains work experience. Also, since the benefits are in nominal dollars, it is advantageous to use them as soon as possible.

Figure 1 illustrates the percent of eligible users who had enlisted for two year terms and who had begun using benefits since their date of separation. The FY82 cohort data file was sorted in ascending order of time from separation to first use. The longest time from separation date to first usage was 2.8 years. A sharp dropoff in new users was observed about one year after separation.

Exponential smoothing was used to project the cumulative number of users that can be expected. (See Nelson 1973, Little and Sall 1984.) This technique was appropriate here because there was enough data past the inflection point near one year to project this trend. Similar extrapolations were performed for three and four year enlistees. The projected total number of users by enlistment term is:

    2 year   73.8 percent
    3 year   64.5 percent
    4 year   44.8 percent

The final factors in the benefit usage computation are the utilization factors, or the proportions of the kickers that are used. The first of these is the proportion of the maximum kicker earned. Those soldiers who begin contributions, serve the required time, and separate had served enough time on active duty to earn the following percentage of the maximum kickers:

    2 year   97.9 percent
    3 year   98.6 percent
    4 year   93.7 percent

The second utilization factor is the percent of available kicker that would be spent by each user. Through August 1986 the FY82 ACF users had spent the following proportions by enlistment term:

2 year   56.7 percent
3 year   39.0 percent
4 year   14.1 percent

The same exponential smoothing technique described previously was used to project the number of users. The estimates of available kicker utilization by enlistment term were:

2 year   90.3 percent
3 year   56.4 percent
4 year   56.4 percent

The same projected rate was used for both three and four year enlistments because four year enlistments had not had sufficient time from their separation date to exhibit more than minimal benefit usage. Thus, the 56.4 percent utilization of kickers is likely to be conservative, since the four year recruits will be older and more likely to be married, two factors which have been associated with lower benefit usage (Schmitz 1988).

Because the proportion of benefits used was derived separately from utilization trends of existing users, it is likely to overestimate actual usage. This approach implicitly assumes that individuals beginning to use their benefits after we have observed them will use the same proportion of benefits as those who we have already observed. Vietnam era GI Bill users who delayed using their benefits used a lower proportion of their benefits (Veterans' Administration, 1981).

Individuals who reenlist may eventually become benefit users at a later date. However, most reenlistees can be expected to stay until retirement. Veterans' Administration (1981) data on the proportion of users who separate at age 31 or older indicates 50.5 percent of such individuals use any benefits. As a simplifying assumption, we estimate that these individuals utilize 100 percent of their benefits.

To compute the time between enlistment and completion of benefit use assume each recruit serves exactly the enlistment term and that all benefits are used over the first three years of college. Thus, the

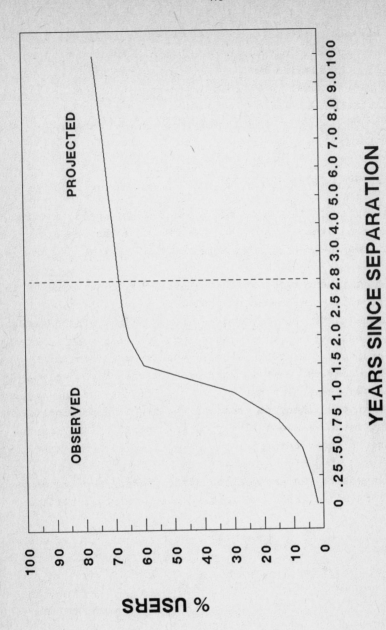

Figure 1. Users of ACF benefits: 2-year enlistees, FY82 cohort.

midpoint of benefit utilization is 1.5 years after the start of benefit usage. The average time between separation and the start of benefit usage appears to be similar for all groups. A factor of 1.5 years is used in each case. Thus, the time between accession and the midpoint of usage by enlistment term is:

        2-year term: 5 years
        3-year term: 6 years
        4-year term: 7 years

For reenlistees, all are expected to serve 20 years, retire, and start school immediately. Thus, the average time between accession and usage for all reenlistments is 21.5 years.

Once the different rates were estimated they were combined to project the benefit usage of each population. Table 1 shows the percentage of benefits used by single term soldiers. The greatest proportion of benefits would be used by the two year term soldiers, while three and four year term soldiers would use a considerably smaller share of their benefits. All factors are associated with higher benefit usage for the two year enlistments. They contribute at the highest percentage, are most likely to complete the required service, separate at the highest rate, are most likely to use benefits, and use the greatest share of their benefits.

Table 2 projects the share of benefits used by reenlistees. Three year term soldiers are projected to have the highest reenlistment usage.

TABLE 1

College Fund Usage Factors For Single Term Soldiers

	2 Year	3 Year	4 Year	Average
Served 20/30 Months	88.4%	74.7%	67.0%	76.7%
Separated	83.1%	70.1%	69.5%	74.2%
Cumulative Percent	73.5%	52.4%	46.6%	57.5%
Used Benefits	73.8%	64.5%	44.8%	61.0%
Cumulative Percent	54.2%	33.8%	20.9%	36.3%
Percent of Maximum Kicker Earned	97.9%	98.6%	93.7%	96.7%
Cumulative Percent	53.1%	33.3%	19.6%	35.3%
Percent Kicker Used	90.3%	56.4%	56.4%	67.7%
Cumulative Percent	47.9%	18.8%	11.0%	25.9%
Total Usage	47.9%	18.8%	11.0%	25.9%

TABLE 2

College Fund Usage Factors For Reenlistees

	2 Year Rate	3 Year Rate	4 Year Rate	Average
Served 20/30 Months	88.4%	74.7%	67.0%	76.7%
Reenlisted	16.9%	29.9%	30.5%	25.8%
Cumulative Percent	14.9%	22.3%	20.4%	19.2%
Used Benefits	50.5%	50.5%	50.5%	50.5%
Cumulative Percent	7.5%	11.3%	10.3%	9.7%
Percent of Maximum Kicker Earned	100.0%	100.0%	100.0%	100.0%
Cumulative Percent	7.5%	11.3%	10.3%	9.7%
Percent Kicker Used	100.0%	100.0%	100.0%	100.0%
Cumulative Percent	7.5%	11.3%	10.3%	9.7%
Total Usage	7.5%	11.3%	10.3%	9.7%

Once usage and time to usage have been estimated projections of the present value cost of each kicker can be made. The DoD actuary uses the following formula:

Present Value = Kicker * Usage Factor/$(1.085)^N$.

The factor N has three components estimated by the DoD Actuary (1985). N is the sum of the numbers of years of obligation, the average number of years until the member separates after serving his initial obligation, and the number of years to the midpoint of the payment stream.

Table 3 combines the usage rates with the time factors, interest rate (8.5 percent), and kicker amounts to project the expected costs of kickers by one term soldiers and reenlistees. The 2 + 2 year amount refers to a special program for two-year enlistees who already had 60 semester hours (2 academic years) of college. As expected, most of the costs would be generated by single term soldiers. The total costs of each of the four types of kickers are:

	NOMINAL KICKER	ACTUARY	ARI
2 year	$ 8,000	$2,772	$2,652
3 year	12,000	3,528	1,618
4 year	14,400	3,600	1,152

The enlistment and cost analyses that have been performed permit some assessment of the cost-effectiveness of the ACF as an enlistment incentive. By combining our cost estimates with enlistment effects of the ACF estimated by the RAND Corporation (Fernandez 1982) one can estimate the relative efficiency of the program as to its effect on high quality manpower.

TABLE 3

Actuarial Costs of Kickers

Kicker Type	Nominal Kicker	Usage	Time In Service (Years)	Time Fr ETS To School (Years)	Time In School (Years)	Total Elapsed Time (Years)	Present Value
			Single Term Soldiers				
2 Year	$ 8,000	47.9%	2	1.5	1.5	5	$2,548
2+2 Year	$12,000	47.9%	2	1.5	1.5	5	$3,823
3 Year	$12,000	18.8%	3	1.5	1.5	6	$1,383
4 Year	$14,400	11.0%	4	1.5	1.5	7	$ 895
			Reenlistees				
2 Year	$ 8,000	7.5%	20	0	1.5	21.5	$ 104
2+2 Year	$12,000	7.5%	20	0	1.5	21.5	$ 156
3 Year	$12,000	11.3%	20	0	1.5	21.5	$ 235
4 Year	$14,400	10.3%	20	0	1.5	21.5	$ 257
			Total Costs				
2 Year	$ 8,000						$2,652
2+2 Year	$12,000						$3,979
3 Year	$12,000						$1,618
4 Year	$14,400						$1,152

Fernandez estimated that the ACF increased high quality enlistments by 9.1 percent over its predecessor program, called Super VEAP. In FY82 this would have amounted to just over 5,000 additional high quality recruits. The full introduction of the ACF is projected to cost about 38 million dollars more than Super VEAP. Thus, the ACF costs about $7,600 per additional high quality recruit.

The ACF Program compares favorably with alternative market expansion mechanisms available to the Army. RAND also estimated the marginal cost of enlistment bonuses to be about $16,000 per additional high quality recruit (Polich et al. 1986). Only recruiters, which were estimated to produce additional enlistments at a cost of about $6,000, have been found to have a more cost-effective market expansion effect.

5. Discussion

Our results provide three important findings:

1. Overall Army College Fund usage will be considerably below what is presently assumed in the actuarial calculations.

2. Army College Fund usage will vary considerably by enlistment term, with usage declining as enlistment term increases.

3. The Army College Fund is more cost-effective than bonuses for enlisting high quality recruits.

The Department of Defense Actuary sets costs to the Army based on an arbitrarily assumed usage factor of 50 percent. The fact that the usage would be likely to be much lower than assumed could not be known until enough relevant history of usage from a similar program had been gathered. However, once the usage rate is decomposed into a number of different factors it becomes apparent that usage will be substantially under 50 percent of the kickers. Our result of an average usage rate of 25.9% (Table 1) is closer to the approximately 30% usage estimates made by the Veterans' Administration and the Congressional Budget Office (CBO, 1985) prior to the start of the program. Contribution, attrition, and reenlistment eliminate well over half the population from immediate use.

We also estimate usage and costs will vary considerably by enlistment term. The present rates indicate that the proportional costs would be lower for longer term soldiers due to higher reenlistment rates. We estimate the usage to be much lower for three and four year enlistments due to a number of factors. Three and four year soldiers will be much less likely to qualify for benefits, based upon historical contribution and attrition results. They also appear to be less likely to attend school and use a smaller portion of their kickers, even when we control for the shorter time they have had to use benefits. This can be explained by the fact they are much older when they leave the service, and much more likely to be married, two factors which have been shown to be associated with reduced college attendance. Also, those most motivated to attend college appear to be attracted to the two year program.

Traditionally, analysts have believed that pay was the most efficient mechanism for increasing the supply of labor to the Army. Organizations, such as the Congressional Budget Office (1986) have assumed that recruits would prefer money now (bonuses) over deferred benefits, such as the ACF. Our analysis shows that educational assistance may be less expensive than bonuses for acquiring manpower. Of course, further work needs to be done on the cost-effectiveness of both bonuses and educational benefits, since it is likely that these two incentives will have very different retention effects.

The estimates of ACF program cost can be improved substantially in the future as a longer history of participation and usage is observed. We believe the approach presented here can serve as the basis for adjusting future cost projections. Given our analysis of the factors that could affect ACF costs and our analysis of historical data, we believe that our projections are reasonable and conservative estimates of eventuual ACF costs.

6. References

Congressional Budget Office, _Budgetary Costs Of Military Educational Benefits_, (1985).

Congressional Budget Office, _Quality Soldiers: Costs of Manning the Active Army_, (1986).

Department of Defense Actuary, "Derivation of Discount Factors for the Army College Fund," mimeographed, (1985).

Fernandez, R., _Enlistment Effects and Policy Implications Of The Educational Assistance Test Program_ (R-2935-MIL). Santa Monica, CA: Rand Corporation, (1982).

Little, M., and J. Sall, _SAS/ETS User's Guide_. Cary, NC: SAS Institute, Inc., (1984).

Manski, C. and D. Wise, _College Choice In America_. Cambridge, MA: Harvard University Press, (1983).

Nelson, C., _Applied Time Series Analysis For Managerial Forecasting_. San Francisco, CA: Holden Day, Inc., (1973).

Polich, J. M., J. N. Dertouzos, and S. J. Press, _The Enlistment Bonus Experiment_, (R-3353-FMP). Santa Monica, CA: The RAND Corporation, (1986).

Schmitz, E., _Military Service and College Attendance: An Evaluation of the Educational Assistance Test Program_. Paper presented at joint national meeting of the Operations Research Society of America/The Institute of Management Sciences, Denver, CO, (1988).

Veterans' Administration, _Final Report On The Utilization Of Educational Entitlement By Veterans Of The Post-Korean Conflict and Vietnam Era_. Washington, D.C.: U. S. Government Printing Office, (1981).

Vol. 292: I. Tchijov, L. Tomaszewicz (Eds.), Input-Output Modeling. Proceedings, 1985. VI, 195 pages. 1987.

Vol. 293: D. Batten, J. Casti, B. Johansson (Eds.), Economic Evolution and Structural Adjustment. Proceedings, 1985. VI, 382 pages. 1987.

Vol. 294: J. Jahn, W. Krabs (Eds.), Recent Advances and Historical Development of Vector Optimization. VII, 405 pages. 1987.

Vol. 295: H. Meister, The Purification Problem for Constrained Games with Incomplete Information. X, 127 pages. 1987.

Vol. 296: A. Börsch-Supan, Econometric Analysis of Discrete Choice. VIII, 211 pages. 1987.

Vol. 297: V. Fedorov, H. Läuter (Eds.), Model-Oriented Data Analysis. Proceedings, 1987. VI, 239 pages. 1988.

Vol. 298: S.H. Chew, Q. Zheng, Integral Global Optimization. VII, 179 pages. 1988.

Vol. 299: K. Marti, Descent Directions and Efficient Solutions in Discretely Distributed Stochastic Programs. XIV, 178 pages. 1988.

Vol. 300: U. Derigs, Programming in Networks and Graphs. XI, 315 pages. 1988.

Vol. 301: J. Kacprzyk, M. Roubens (Eds.), Non-Conventional Preference Relations in Decision Making. VII, 155 pages. 1988.

Vol. 302: H.A. Eiselt, G. Pederzoli (Eds.), Advances in Optimization and Control. Proceedings, 1986. VIII, 372 pages. 1988.

Vol. 303: F.X. Diebold, Empirical Modeling of Exchange Rate Dynamics. VII, 143 pages. 1988.

Vol. 304: A. Kurzhanski, K. Neumann, D. Pallaschke (Eds.), Optimization, Parallel Processing and Applications. Proceedings, 1987. VI, 292 pages. 1988.

Vol. 305: G.-J.C.Th. van Schijndel, Dynamic Firm and Investor Behaviour under Progressive Personal Taxation. X, 215 pages. 1988.

Vol. 306: Ch. Klein, A Static Microeconomic Model of Pure Competition. VIII, 139 pages. 1988.

Vol. 307: T.K. Dijkstra (Ed.), On Model Uncertainty and its Statistical Implications. VII, 138 pages. 1988.

Vol. 308: J.R. Daduna, A. Wren (Eds.), Computer-Aided Transit Scheduling. VIII, 339 pages. 1988.

Vol. 309: G. Ricci, K. Velupillai (Eds.), Growth Cycles and Multisectoral Economics: the Goodwin Tradition. III, 126 pages. 1988.

Vol. 310: J. Kacprzyk, M. Fedrizzi (Eds.), Combining Fuzzy Imprecision with Probabilistic Uncertainty in Decision Making. IX, 399 pages. 1988.

Vol. 311: R. Färe, Fundamentals of Production Theory. IX, 163 pages. 1988.

Vol. 312: J. Krishnakumar, Estimation of Simultaneous Equation Models with Error Components Structure. X, 357 pages. 1988.

Vol. 313: W. Jammernegg, Sequential Binary Investment Decisions. VI, 156 pages. 1988.

Vol. 314: R. Tietz, W. Albers, R. Selten (Eds.), Bounded Rational Behavior in Experimental Games and Markets. VI, 368 pages. 1988.

Vol. 315: I. Orishimo, G.J.D. Hewings, P. Nijkamp (Eds.), Information Technology: Social and Spatial Perspectives. Proceedings, 1986. VI, 268 pages. 1988.

Vol. 316: R.L. Basmann, D.J. Slottje, K. Hayes, J.D. Johnson, D.J. Molina, The Generalized Fechner-Thurstone Direct Utility Function and Some of its Uses. VIII, 159 pages. 1988.

Vol. 317: L. Bianco, A. La Bella (Eds.), Freight Transport Planning and Logistics. Proceedings, 1987. X, 568 pages. 1988.

Vol. 318: T. Doup, Simplicial Algorithms on the Simplotope. VIII, 262 pages. 1988.

Vol. 319: D.T. Luc, Theory of Vector Optimization. VIII, 173 pages. 1989.

Vol. 320: D. van der Wijst, Financial Structure in Small Business. VII, 181 pages. 1989.

Vol. 321: M. Di Matteo, R.M. Goodwin, A. Vercelli (Eds.), Technological and Social Factors in Long Term Fluctuations. Proceedings. IX, 442 pages. 1989.

Vol. 322: T. Kollintzas (Ed.), The Rational Expectations Equilibrium Inventory Model. XI, 269 pages. 1989.

Vol. 323: M.B.M. de Koster, Capacity Oriented Analysis and Design of Production Systems. XII, 245 pages. 1989.

Vol. 324: I.M. Bomze, B.M. Pötscher, Game Theoretical Foundations of Evolutionary Stability. VI, 145 pages. 1989.

Vol. 325: P. Ferri, E. Greenberg, The Labor Market and Business Cycle Theories. X, 183 pages. 1989.

Vol. 326: Ch. Sauer, Alternative Theories of Output, Unemployment, and Inflation in Germany: 1960–1985. XIII, 206 pages. 1989.

Vol. 327: M. Tawada, Production Structure and International Trade. V, 132 pages. 1989.

Vol. 328: W. Güth, B. Kalkofen, Unique Solutions for Strategic Games. VII, 200 pages. 1989.

Vol. 329: G. Tillmann, Equity, Incentives, and Taxation. VI, 132 pages. 1989.

Vol. 330: P.M. Kort, Optimal Dynamic Investment Policies of a Value Maximizing Firm. VII, 185 pages. 1989.

Vol. 331: A. Lewandowski, A.P. Wierzbicki (Eds.), Aspiration Based Decision Support Systems. X, 400 pages. 1989.

Vol. 332: T.R. Gulledge, Jr., L.A. Litteral (Eds.), Cost Analysis Applications of Economics and Operations Research. Proceedings. VII, 422 pages. 1989.